Understanding the Role of Religion in Building up Sustainable Existence

Understanding the Role of Religion in Building up Sustainable Existence

Issues and Challenges

Selvam Robertson

Christian World Imprints

First Published in 2021 by

Christian World Imprints
Christian Publishing & Books from India
C-3, Wazirpur Industrial Area
Delhi-110052
cwidelhi2017@gmail.com
www.ChristianWorldImprints.com
Phone: +91 11 41526079

ISBN: 978-93-5148-506-3

Printed in India.

Contents

Acknowledgement

Ever since I entered teaching ministry after completing my doctoral studies, I had the privilege of being invited to present papers on different occasions. Most of my papers were published in different journals or became part of some edited works. It was my long cherished desire that all my papers should be presented together in a single book form. In order to do this, most importantly, I appeal to the journal and book publishers who published my articles to accept my consideration and relax copyright issues if there is any. My wish has come true only because of Rev. Arun Kumar Wesley who was kind enough to edit the entire work. Hearty thanks to Ms. Esthaleena Margaret who took the initiative to speak on behalf of me to Rev. Arun Kumar Wesley and of course she has been rendering yeoman service for quite long time since I came to know her during my methodology seminar for doctoral studies in 1996.

I am also grateful to Christian World Imprints for coming forward to publish the work.

Last but not the least is my wife S. R. Selin Rani and son Ayush Robertson who deserve special appreciation for enduring with my vocation of theological education.

Bethel Bible College, Guntur, Andhra Pradesh, India cannot be left unacknowledged as I have been associated with it for almost more than one and a half decades.

Preface

As a student of religion, I am constantly engaged with different levels of students to inculcate in them the need for the study of religion with all its implications for life, since the inception of my theological education. The need for clarity on different methods and the tools used in different methods of research for the systematic study of religion among emerging Indian scholars is the compelling spirit behind my endeavors. This has, thus far, taken me through the serious academic and to some extent practical, engagement in exploring the possibilities of understanding religion in relation to other religions including my own. It was never a smooth sailing – I was dogged by controversies, differing viewpoints and even failures. Another dimension that unfolded in the process of study and relation is the interrelatedness of religion and politics and the fear that religion, with all its integrative and disintegrative nature may succumb to serve overwhelmingly political ends. The fact however, remains that these developments have neither incited a decline in the interest on the life and work of Jesus Christ nor drastically drew away from my faith life. This work is a testimony to that stand.

Introduction

1. In this chapter, I make an overview of the purposes/objectives of the study of religions in theological institutions and then try to assess whether these are satisfactorily addressed in the new curriculum of the Senate -2010.
2. This chapter explores the various factors and persons that were responsible for the establishment of the department of *Science of Religion* with special reference to the contributions of Max Muller who was called the Father of Comparative Religion. The first part of the paper focuses on the factors surrounding religions and the second part considers the early founders. And the third part concentrates on the contributions of Max Muller.
3. This chapter is an attempt to evaluate the origin and development of the scientific study of religion and to highlight the common issues in studying religion and their implications for the Indian context, in four parts. The first part is an exploration into the various factors, which were responsible for the emergence of the science of religion, with special reference to the contributions of Max Muller. The second part is an evaluation of the major methods used for the scientific study of religion. The third part examines the main issues emerging from different methods. And the fourth part is an attempt to examine the possibilities for an appropriate Indian approach to the study of religion.
4. The hyphenated title of the chapter implicitly suggests that the gap between different disciplines, particularly religion and theology can be filled in or at least reduced to a minimum if researches can be pursued keeping in mind the necessity of dialogical existence. The multidisciplinary setting of our seminar, without ignoring our own disciplines, obviously calls for researches leading to this end. I am also compelled to think that the realms of spirited research are still very vast and inspiring. As a student of religion, I have started this exercise beginning from the openness created by the science of religion. Sufficient amount of concentration is dedicated to the possibilities of explaining the interconnectedness between religion and theology with

specific focus to inspire or provoke serious research. Final discussion revolves around the dialogical approach.

5. This chapter is an attempt to draw insights from the larger arena of scientific study of religions, glimpses from missiology and sketchy significance from the values of secular principles in India; and to evolve relevant models from Jesus to serve God dynamically in the Indian texture towards a sustainable existence based on the struggles of life. The basic assumption is that the struggles of life can be a starting point for different faith-traditions to meaningfully contribute to a sustainable life. This is not a random thought but the logical conclusion emerging from the analysis of faith-traditions as applied in this paper.
6. Plurality of religion is as old as human history but what is new now is religious pluralism. It is the recognition of the real existence of different religions and their history and to sincerely attempt to live together. This process has necessitated the planning and programs of dialogue. Dialogue is not only between different faith traditions but also with ideologies both political or any for that matter. In the first place there are many factors that have contributed to the development of "dialogue," particularly interreligious. Secondly there were genuine attempts whether relevant or otherwise in today's context, by both Catholic and Protestant churches and individual thinkers / theologians which have moved the discussion on dialogue much forward. In the third place, these initial attempts have contributed to some of the major developments in the contemporary debates on dialogue among religions and ideologies. In the fourth place, the paradigm of dialogue is often attacked as the Christian attempt to continue mission, particularly in the Indian context. And finally it is useful to present a "life sustaining" paradigm to continue practicing dialogue in a multi-faith and ideologies context.
7. Human beings never lived without practicing one or another form of religion. They always attempted to comprehend the ultimate mystery in manifold forms, as their intellect and cultural context permitted. Thus, plurality of religion is as old as human history. Our time has witnessed a shift from plurality of religions to religious pluralism. That is, religious pluralism has become a significant subject matter concerned with all religions. It is not just accepting the diversity of religions but venturing to fuse a cooperative relationship among religions in order to actualize the real purpose, of religions-protecting and enhancing life. It is not uniformity but unity without losing individuality. This paradoxical context of our time devolves Christianity to formulate theology of religions relevant to pluralistic contexts in the light of the life and work of Jesus Christ who was committed to the ultimate mystery on the one hand and life sustaining on the other. Hence, exploring the possibilities for a life sustaining pluralist perspective is the immediate task of

any contemporary and relevant Christian theology of religions. It is necessary because the global and religious context and new sciences have brought different peoples, cultures, and religions much closer than ever before. People are face to face with traditions once foreign and alien to them. The specific Indian context, particularly the neo-Hindu assertion reveals that each religion needs to be left unintervened because each is complete and sufficient enough for the votaries to attain the purpose of religion. And no religion or religious person has anything significant, which the other religions or religious persons do not posses. The ever increasing misuse of religions for extremist purposes and political gains and the large scale human made disasters, which threaten the existence of life on the planet earth require that religions should be united without damaging the differences for the sake of life itself. This is possible only in a life sustaining pluralistic perspective. It is the enabling of different religions to address the issues, which challenge and threaten life as a whole.

8. The simple thesis of this chapter is that religion and politics were never purely or completely separated in India, in spite of the contributions of modernity and hence it is necessary to strive hard to separate them as secularism seems to be more viable in a pluralistic context. While working towards this direction, it may also be asked how best positive religious insights can guide political wisdom. To derive at this point, I shall attempt a sketchy and graphic historical development of the process of secularization leading to the formulation of secularism and secular state. While attempting to do so, I shall also highlight the never-ceasing influence of religion on politics and how politicization of religion takes place. To prove the thesis I shall analyze the role of the Congress party, the emergence of Muslim League and religious interest organizations leading to the formation of BJP. Considerable space shall be devoted for the patterns in which BJP attempts to subscribe to communal politics. Before concluding the analysis the areas and issues that need to be considered and addressed can be underlined.

9. This chapter attempts to suggest that freedom of religion is a constitutional privilege of all the citizens of India besides it being one of the basic human rights and the flawless practice of freedom of religion is an imperative to any peace initiative. The discussion will start considering the constitutional and human rights basis for freedom of religion, which is essential to peace initiatives and explain the possible role that religion can play in peace building. Before doing so a glimpse at a few relevant constituents of freedom of religion and peace are graphically highlighted. Freedom of religion implies one's freedom to freely choose or abandon his or her choice of religion subject to the constitutional and legal provisions of her/his State. Any discussion on the freedom of religion in India is grounded on the premise that every individual has the freedom to convert to any religion but no one has the right to convert others. What is asked in this discussion is freedom of religion which leads

to peace and harmonious living and not freedom to convert others. Among the many meanings of the word peace, the following are worth remembering from the point of this paper. Peace is the state prevailing during the absence of hostilities; a treaty or an agreement to end hostilities; harmonious relations or a state of mutual harmony between people or groups; the normal freedom from civil commotion and violence of a community or cessation of or freedom from any strife or dissension; the general security of public places or public security and order. Peace also represents a larger concept wherein there are healthy or newly-healed interpersonal or international relationships, safety in matters of social or economic welfare, the acknowledgment of equality and fairness in political relationships and, in world matters. Reflection on the nature of peace is also bound up with considerations of potential causes for its absence: insecurity, social injustice, economic inequality, political and religious radicalism, and acute nationalism.

10. Stranger is a person whom we do not know, a person who is in a place that he/she has not been in before, an unfamiliar person, foreigner, alien, outsider, visitor, guest and a new arrival. The unique condition of us is that there is an ongoing attempt to make us strangers in our own country. It is also alarming that people migrate because of religious persecution. Religion is supposed to unite but it 'brews' strangers and often excludes them and that is our concern. This paper is a modest attempt to highlight the process of 'brewing strangers' that are attempted at various levels and to appeal for vigilance and involvement to counter them in our context.

11. As I embark on to discuss the theological contributions of Aleaz, let me start with his insights to the religions department, particularly highlighting his definition of religion, preferential method to study religions, theology of religions underlying pluralism, pluralistic inclusivism, relational convergence of religions and the connection between religion and culture. Following his contributions to the religious studies, I shall focus on his contributions to Indian philosophy by underlining his consideration of *pramanas,* Advaita, Christian Response to Indian philosophy and Indian Christian Philosophy. Next in the order is his interpretation of theology, mainly focused on Indian Christian theology, Eastern Christian thought and Dalit theology. His proposal for an Indian spirituality is no less a significant contribution. Aleaz's bent of knowledge and commitment can further be drawn from his important constructs like Jesus, Gospel and proclamation & mission.

12. This chapter is an attempt to explain Hindutva as propagated and practiced by RSS ideologues and its challenges for Christian witness in India, as BJP the political arm of RSS is at the centre with absolute majority. In the first place, I have graphically described the various attempts that are underway to communalize the nation and its various instruments against religious

minorities particularly, Christians, without excluding the Muslims. And in the second place some issues are highlighted, without causing panic, to reflect upon.

13. This chapter is an attempt to graphically highlight a few challenges that affect religious harmony in India and to suggest seemingly possible space to youth to engage themselves working towards religious harmony. In the process I have sketchily mentioned some salient characteristics of youth and why Christian youth should involve in bringing about religious harmony.
14. This chapter attempts to recollect insights from the various Supreme Court interpretations of Article 25 of the Indian Constitution and to understand freedom of religion to bear diligent Christian witness. A detailed study of each case is an interesting research, but owing to our purpose I restricted myself to the verdict of cases as interpreted by eminent jurists. Anyone interested in detail may use the foot notes to trace the cases.
15. This chapter is an attempt to study 'a belligerent ideological narrative' that challenges to obliterate the thus-far prevalent constructs in various realms and to prepare ourselves for improving the capabilities of the deprived sections through a sustainable interpretation of the word of God in the background of 500th year of the dawning of the Reformation. The word ideology, in essence, has an aggressive nature and political underpinning that are occasionally explicit and more often implicit in some of its narratives. The narratives are ideological goals that wish to replace broader perspectives. The expression 'Sustainable capability enhancement' is used to highlight the dynamic role of 'interpreting scripture' to derive substantial resources to empower people who are otherwise disadvantaged of basic facilities and privileges to improve themselves. It is also to reflect that any interpretation of scripture should preserve its classic nature. While allowing critical musings, it should do justice to all the previous interpretations and explore relevant contextual interpretations to allow the inherent potency of the word of God to enhance the capabilities of the ones who are in need. More aptly and precisely, 'sustainable' refers to the principle of interpretation or hermeneutics and 'capability enhancement' to mission, implying that both interpretation and mission should be 'sustainable.' It is not unusual to be aggressive for any ideology that enjoys 'state patronage' as the church might have been in the pre-reformation era. What is striking in the present context is that we are amidst the new narrative and we are reforming ourselves to continue in sustainable capability enhancement.
16. This chapter attempts to explain Hidutva nationalism and tentatively thinks along the possibilities of Christian identity and witness in this context. As Hindutva nationalism is an identity politics and our concern is Christian identity and witness, I shall start with a cursory discussion on identity and

move on. In the second place, I will discuss the development of secular nationalism and the growth of Hindutva nationalism which is a derivative of Hindu nationalism. Finally I will try to sneak through Christian identity and witness before conclusion.

17. I always distill appreciable Hindu constructs as a part of my commitment to interreligious relations. It continued in my article (subsequently part of a book) on 'Hindu Spirituality' wherein I profusely appreciated certain Hindu values. My doctoral research was to draw insights for theology of religions from the *bhakti* tradition of Vaishnava Alvars. However the communal violence that consumes so many lives, constant anti-minority polemic and the murderous lynching that honored animals more than human beings and brutally killed many poor, weak, aged, vulnerable people who eked a living on animals, changed my perceptions. Added to these are my reading on Dr. Ambedkar, Manu Smriti and Bhagavad Gita and my own analysis of 'Christian identity and witness in India in the context of Hindutva politics.' However, with due respect to my topic I shall attempt, in the first place, a graphic overview of some of the Hindu concepts, of course not complete, on which equality, although difficult, is claimed in Hinduism. I shall also, in the second place, highlight the inequality or hierarchy prevalent in Hinduism. This of course is an outsider's understanding of Hinduism and hence subject to the necessary limitations.
18. Protests against superstitious beliefs and practices associated with religion and the caste system is exceedingly old in India. The indigenous, ascetic and pre-Aryan religious movement called the *Sramanas* was the first to oppose priestly rituals, superstitions and caste system. Its two offshoots, Jainism and Buddhism laid great emphasis on reason and disapproved irrational practices and inequalities in the society. The materialist *carvaka* system insisted that there is no necessity for faith in religion, rites, priests and Vedas. The Upanishads are the earnest quests for truth beyond externals of religions. The Bhakthi movement in Hinduism, to some extent, disfavored mechanical rites and caste system. *Siddhars* in the South and *Sants* in the North India advocated simple life and negated ritualism. Ramalinga Swami, in Tamil Nadu condemned caste and superstitious beliefs. Sikkism was still another attempt in this direction. With the influence of the British, people like Ram Mohan Roy, Keshub Chander Sen and Ranade initiated many social reforms. Mahatma Jotirao Phooley and Ambedkar radically criticized priestly exploitations. It was in this context that Periyar E. V. Ramasami is significant. He was of the opinion that, all the inequalities and oppressions found in the society were created by priestly/Bramanic religion. Rather than opting for a new religion, Periyar thought, religions should be rationally evaluated from the perspective of human life. Any religion or religious practice that obstructs

human dignity should be abandoned. He stood for self-respect (individual freedom and dignity).

19. Although the traits of prophet, priest, preceptor or a reformer can be discerned from the life of William Carey, I do not know whether he was one among them in the strict sense but am sure, like them, he too was 'at the Lord's disposal.' The following description illustrates his life so that we may learn a few characteristics of people who are at the Lord's disposal. It is also fitting that the Serampore College (established by William Carey) celebrated this year (2018) its bicentenary and the centenary of the Senate of Serampore College.

1

Religions and Theological Education
An Evaluation of the Religion Cluster of the New BD Curiculam-2010 of the Senate of Serampore College (University)

Introduction

In this paper I shall make an overview of purposes/objectives of the study of religions in theological institutions and then try to assess whether these are satisfactorily addressed in the new curriculum of the Senate - 2010.

Pedagogy is the study of being a teacher or the process of teaching. The term generally refers to strategies of instruction, or a style of instruction. Pedagogy is also occasionally referred to as the correct use of instructive strategies.[1]

While dealing with instructive strategies or instructive theory pertaining to teaching religions in theological institutions it is appropriate to remember some limitations too. Eric J. Lot warns, "any one attempting a scholarly investigation of a religious tradition must first recognize the complexity of religion, no matter how simple it may seem to those who participate in its life."[2] Added to this is the following advice of Raimon Panikkar that, "Truth although one is multifaceted and we can only have a glimpse of some of the aspects of the truth…We are

1 For example, Paulo Freire referred to his method of teaching adult humans as "critical pedagogy." In correlation with those instructive strategies the instructor's own philosophical beliefs of instruction are harbored and governed by the pupil's background knowledge and experience, situation, and environment, as well as learning goals set by the student and teacher.

2 Eric J. Lott, "Approaching Religious Tradition," in *Religious Traditions of India,* edited by P. S. Daniel, David C. Scott and G. R. Singh (New Delhi: ISPCK, 2002), p. 1.

conditioned by our perspectives, attitudes and culture; and what is needed is that we accept these limitations and cooperate with others in the search for Reality."[3] Considering these limitations it is proper to graphically highlight the necessities of learning other religions in our theological education.

1. Necessity to Study Religions

According to Ninian Smart, "understanding the world's religions and ideologies is important in three ways. First, they are a vital ingredient in the varied story of humankind's various experiments in living....Second, and of more immediate importance, is the fact that in order to grasp the meanings and values of the plural cultures of today's world, we need to know something of the worldviews which underlie them....Third, we may as individuals be trying to form our own coherent and emotionally satisfying picture of reality, and it is always relevant to see the great ideas and practices of various important cultures and civilizations."[4]

Added to this list is the fact that "before judging people, it is important to understand their beliefs because it is on the basis of these that they act."[5] Closely connected with this is the plural context where varieties of people live together which demands 'to know something of others, so that mutual understanding, though may be not in agreement, may animate community relations.'[6]

Considering these necessities the previous Senate BD curriculum (prior to 2010) placed the following objectives in studying other religions:

"Recognizing the importance of religions in human life and acknowledging that the interaction between religion and ideologies provides the context in which Christian Theological reflection should take place, this department seeks to train a community of students with the necessary skills and tools for such reflection. With this view, the attempt is made.

a) to study the phenomena of religions in society through the scriptures, traditions, rituals, symbols social practices and other constituent elements.
b) to understand religions of India in their classical, modern and contemporary expression, including tribal and village religions.
c) to learn classical languages of Indian religions.
d) to enable students to participate in the struggle for an inclusive human community, overcoming attitudes of narrow fanaticism or shallow friendliness.

---

3 Raimon Panikkar, "Introduction," in *Toward Mutual Fecundation and Fulfilment of Religions*, Varghese Manimala (Delhi: Media House and ISPCK), 2009, p. 15.

4 Ninian Smart, *The World's Religions* 2nd ed. (Cambridge: University Press), 2002, p. 10.

5 Paul G. Hiebert, R. Daniel Shaw and Tite Tienou, *Understanding Folk Religion: A Christian Response to Popular Beliefs and Practices* (Michigan: Baker Books), 2001, p. 21.

6 Ninian Smart, *The World's Religions* 2nd ed. (Cambridge: University Press), 2002, p. 11.

e) to understand and appreciate the religious experience of people of other faiths and overcome misconceptions of beliefs, practices and ways of life of others.
f) to understand the cultural heritage and roots of Indian Christians.
g) to gain new insights for the Christian faith-experience from the religiosity and spirituality of others.
h) to encourage intra and inter-faith dialogue."[7] These objectives are very relevant even today.

Apart from the positive necessities, we need to address the following fear voiced by our Hindu neighbors (Hinduism). In the words of Ravi Tiwari "it feels threatened and in turn, poses the same to the very existence of the followers of other religions, a process we are now experiencing in India."[8] Of course, the fear is the result of unwillingness to accept the changing scenario, which is vivid in the statement that, "the fact of plurality of religion, in which Hinduism is merely one among many, has been very uncomfortable to the propounders of neo-Hindu ideologues."[9]

It has become usual in recent times to emphasize the need for democratic living even in religious matters. Varghese Manimala writes "today if Christianity, or for that matter any religion, had to fulfill its mission there should be a paradigm shift. One of the important values that religions will have to promote is democracy or a reverential attitude for others."[10]

In spite of the fact that religion cannot be replaced by ethics there is also a tendency to reduce the role of religion in human activities. For example it is argued that "we now live in times where our political beliefs are founded on ethical precepts such as democracy, human rights and the rule of law. People no longer need to turn to organized religion in order to organize or stabilize society.

In this age, religion has to stand on its own; which will happen only if the faith in the hearts of its believers is true, solid and complete. The struggle is private and internal, and a need to publicly defend a faith is an implicit admission either a lack of belief in the power of God or of insecurity in the faith of His believers. A strident call for public action to defend a faith may over time serve to undermine the very cause that it claims to plead."[11]

In this context the following realization needs special attention that "traditional religious education, based on scriptures, can leave young people both

7 Senate of Serampore College, *Bachelor of Divinity Degree Syllabus* (Serampore: Senate of Serampore College, 2005), p. 128.

8 Ravi Tiwari, *Reflections and Studies in Religion* (Delhi: ISPCK, 2008), p. 129.

9 *Ibid.*, p. 138.

10 Varghese Manimala, *Toward Mutual Fecundation and Fulfilment of Religions* (Delhi: Media House and ISPCK), 2009, p. 506.

11 Prem Chandavarkar, "Should One be Defending One's Faith at all?," *The Hindu* (Vijayawada), 28th November 2010, p. 12.

ignorant and prejudiced about alternative faiths."[12] In a nutshell, teaching and learning religion in theological institutions require innovations and dynamism to address newly emerging concerns besides the continuing ones.

1.1. Common Humanness

To continue the discussion further, the study of religions need to seriously view the one humanity which is behind all religiosity. Mircea Eliade wrote: "it is simply a matter of not losing sight of the profound and indivisible unity of the history of the human mind. Consciousness of this unity of the spiritual history of humanity is a recent discovery, which has not yet been sufficiently assimilated."[13] In the words of William James, 'the pivot round which the religious life revolves, is the interest of the individual in his private personal destiny. Religion, in short, is a monumental chapter in the history of human egotism.'[14] According to Raimon Panikkar, "what religion needs to do is to make the human beings realize their common humanity and strengthen the bonds of friendship and affection."[15]

Religious studies need to concentrate more in this direction because "in whatever field we work, be it science, technology, medicine, politics, policing, theology, religion or the judiciary, we have to remain in the service of the common man whose well-being is central to all human knowledge and endeavor."[16] Further "Religions need to realize that they are only means; they are not an end in themselves. Human beings are not to be made slaves of religions; rather they must experience freedom *in* religion and freedom *for* religion."[17] To this end the department of religions has its task cut out.

1.2. Religion and Ideologies

As mentioned earlier "it is important for us to recognize secular ideologies as part of the story of human worldview."[18] There is justification for this endeavour. Ninian Smart writes: "before, there is the narrative of the rise and fall of religious cultures in differing parts of the globe; afterwards, we see patterns of interaction, and eventually the emergence of a global civilization, in which inevitably religious

12 Ninian Smart, *The World's Religions* 2nd ed. (Cambridge: University Press), 2002, p. 590.

13 Mircea Eliade, *A History of Religious Ideas*, Vol. 1, translated by Willard R. Trask (Chicago: The University of Chicago Press), 1978, p. xiv.

14 William James, *The Varieties of Religious Experience: A Study in Human Nature* (London: Collier Macmillan Publishers), 1961, p. 381.

15 Raimon Panikkar, "Introduction," in *Toward Mutual Fecundation and Fulfilment of Religions*, Varghese Manimala (Delhi: Media House and ISPCK), 2009, p. 18.

16 A. P. J. Abdul Kalam, "The Joy of Human Life," in *Towards a Culture of Harmony and Peace*, edited by T. D. Singh (New Delhi & Kolkata: Delhi Peace Summit & Bhaktivedanta Institute, 2005), pp. 13-14.

17 Raimon Panikkar, "Introduction," in *Toward Mutual Fecundation and Fulfilment of Religions*, Varghese Manimala (Delhi: Media House and ISPCK), 2009, p. 19.

18 Ninian Smart, *The World's Religions* 2nd ed. (Cambridge: University Press), 2002, p. 10.

and secular worldviews have to learn to adapt to one another."[19] This move is not just for coexistence but for cooperation for common causes. In many cases earnest ideologies have played significant roles in transforming societies and liberating people. Therefore there is an essential need for religious education to explore the possibilities of religions and ideologies cooperating for liberative causes.

1.3. Religion and Theology

Although attempts to strengthen the difference between religion and theology continue to exist, the signs of our times show that there needs to be a closer exchange of data between the two to rationalize their contributions. It is thoughtfully said, "with regard to theology, it is no longer possible to limit the consideration of theological topics to the Christian sphere; we must take into account the questions and answers posed by other religions."[20] This mutual enrichment is a necessity. Eric J. Lot writes about his work that "it has been intended to show that in spite of certain distinctive aims and modes of functioning making it necessary to *distinguish* the theological task within a religious tradition from other forms of systematic investigation found in 'religious studies,' there are also significant and substantial areas of *interdependence* between these two basic approaches."[21] The concern to relate theology and religious data and using religious data for relevant theologizing and mission deserves attention in teaching and learning religions.

1.4. Renewal of Religious Traditions

The meeting of different cultures and traditions often produces new religious movements.[22] That is why "while it remains most important to evaluate founders and early scriptures, we also need to be sensitive to the ways in which religious traditions evolve and form."[23] In other words, there is a distinction between the period or periods of *roots* and those of *formation*.[24] The development of many religions confirms that it is because of crises in depth and the creations that result from them that religious traditions are able to renew themselves.[25] Hence,

19 *Ibid.*, p. 11.

20 Veli-Matti Karkkainen, *An Introduction to the Theology of Religions* (Illinois: InterVarsity Press), 2003, p. 17.

21 Eric J. Lot, *Vision, Tradition, Interpretation: Theology, Religion, and the Study of Religion* (Berlin. New York. Amsterdam: Mouton de Gruyter), 1988, p. 253.

22 Ninian Smart, *The World's Religions* 2nd ed. (Cambridge: University Press), 2002, p. 13.

23 *Ibid.*, p. 26.

24 *Ibid.*, p. 27.

25 Mircea Eliade, *A History of Religious Ideas*, Vol. 1, translated by Willard R. Trask (Chicago: The University of Chicago Press), 1978, p. xiv. (It is enough to cite the case of India, where the tension and despair brought on by the religious devalorization of the Brahmanic sacrifice produced a series of outstanding creations (the Upanishads, the codification of Yogic techniques, the message of Gautama Buddha, mystical devotion, etc.), each one of them constituting a different and daring resolution of the same crisis).

religious study needs to be more sensitive to this aspect and be analytical in nature to address such issues.

1.5. Plurality of Religions

There is a strong reason to consider the plurality of religions as a serious matter for consideration while studying religions. Paul Knitter writes: "it is said that in our present age, religious people have to be religious inter-religiously. To walk one's faith-path, one needs to be walking with others from different paths."[26] John Hick maintains, "I suggest that the best religious account we can give of the global situation is that of a single ineffable Ultimate Reality whose universal presence is being differently conceived and experienced and responded to within the different human religious traditions."[27] To go further "Reality is intrinsically complex, rich, intricate, mysterious."[28] A substantial and meaningful recognition of many religions is not a matter of compromising faith traditions but transcending boundaries while deeply committed to our own. In the words of Paul Tillich "in the depth of every living religion there is a point at which the religion itself loses its importance, and that to which it points breaks through its particularity, elevating it to spiritual freedom and with it to a vision of the spiritual presence in other expressions of the ultimate meaning of man's existence."[29]

In our given context religions need to acknowledge one another as co-travelers towards the Absolute offering mutual support and enrichment.[30] Ninian Smart emphatically suggests 'a pluralistic approach to religious education is best.'[31] Such a painstaking and risky assertion is grounded on the fact that 'religion cannot be shelved to some corners of life and to a few hours of practice; it has to permeate the whole life. As religious pluralism is a gift and a challenge religions need to take it up with earnestness not by its denial but by learning to live with it.'[32] It is fitting to recall here that "we must all remember, very often we tend to forget that religion is an accident of birth except perhaps for that minuscule minority which might adopt it by choice. It is, therefore, essential that we realize that the purpose

26 Paul F. Knitter, *Introducing Theologies of Religions* (Maryknoll, New York: Orbis Books, 2002), p. xi.

27 John Hick, "The next Step beyond Dialogue," in *The Myth of Religious Superiority: Multifaith Explorations of Religious Pluralism,* edited by Paul F. Knitter (Maryknoll, New York: Orbis Books, 2005), p. 12.

28 Paul F. Knitter, *Introducing Theologies of Religions* (Maryknoll, New York: Orbis Books, 2002), p. 7.

29 Paul Tillich, *Christianity and the Encounter of the World Religions* (New York and London: Columbia University Press, 1964), p. 97.

30 Raimon Panikkar, "Introduction," in *Toward Mutual Fecundation and Fulfilment of Religions,* Varghese Manimala (Delhi: Media House and ISPCK), 2009, p. 14.

31 Ninian Smart, *The World's Religions* 2nd ed. (Cambridge: University Press), 2002, p. 590.

32 Raimon Panikkar, "Introduction," in *Toward Mutual Fecundation and Fulfilment of Religions,* Manimala (Delhi: Media House and ISPCK), 2009, p. 14.

and objective of every religion is to foster peace, harmony, brotherhood, and not to quarrel needlessly."[33] Hence, a responsible undertaking of studying religions needs to address the uniqueness of the existence of different religions and their problems and prospects.

1.6. Dialogical Approach

Recognition of the existence and reality of many religions and ideologies is closely linked to one of the concerns expressed in Samartha's *One Christ Many Religions,* i.e. to listen to the experiences and voices of others as well. This he demanded in the context of dialogue between different faith traditions and it finds space in the present academic exercises as well. For example it is said "until now, we have only had representatives of various religions speak to each other in interfaith dialogue; a next step will be taken when Buddhist, Hindu, Taoist and other theologians of religions begin to dialogue and perhaps carry out common research projects."[34]

Such daring considerations require humility because "we can be persuaded by personal experience: and this may indeed be spiritually convincing, but it is a 'soft' reason for belief, in as much as a differing revelation can attract a similar proof. From a public point of view, however much of my belief is hedged by certitude, it is still (and I repeat, from a public point of view) a matter of opinion."[35]

Hence "from this perspective, faith is not something about which to dogmatize, and again it is a matter about which we may enter into dialogue, and should."[36] To deepen the discussion Eric J. Lot writes "if we believe our faith in some way puts us in touch with ultimate realities, then engaging in dialogue with people of similar conviction, even if their faith and its community loyalty identifies them as 'other,' is an essential part of the dialogical life faith calls for. Given the crises of our times, and the frequent violence between religion-based communities, there can be few more urgent tasks than that of dialogical interpretation."[37]

Wilfred Cantwell Smith's view point is relevant here because "Smith recognizes that in each religious tradition 'faith' is interpreted differently; but in that faith is that by which the religious person participates in transcendence,

33 A. M. Ahmadi., "Towards a Global Society," in *Towards a Culture of Harmony and Peace,* edited by T. D. Singh (New Delhi & Kolkata: Delhi Peace Summit & Bhaktivedanta Institute, 2005), p. 18.

34 Veli-Matti Karkkainen, *An Introduction to the Theology of Religions* (Illinois: InterVarsity Press), 2003, p. 354.

35 Ninian Smart, *The World's Religions* 2nd ed. (Cambridge: University Press), 2002, p. 583.

36 *Ibid.*, p. 583.

37 Eric Lott, *Religious Faith, Human Dignity: Dangerous Dynamics in Global and Indian Life* (Bangalore: ATC/UTC), 2005, p. 400.

he sees it as essentially the same in all cultures."[38] He goes on to suggest that "it is this generic quality of 'faith' by which people of all kinds of cultures find a link between the mundane and the transcendent; it thus creates the interaction between these two poles of human existence. Faith, then, is a universal characteristic of humanity, it is the fundamental quality of the religious life, though because it represents more adequately that fundamental quality of human life in all its dynamism, this term 'faith' can supersede 'religion' as the focal category for religious study."[39]

Still further "the study of religion is essentially the study of persons. If faith is central to religious life, then we should look to personal life as 'the locus of faith.'"[40] Therefore "if the locus of faith is person, our goal in the systematic study of religions should be primarily to understand the *inner life of religious traditions.*"[41] On the basis of this "an important task of the professional student of religion, contends Smith, is to *participate in the growing interaction between world cultures and religious traditions* and even to *further activate* this process."[42] Although our new curriculum often implicitly points to these directions, it is essential to be made explicit in our teaching (pedagogy) and make them functional. May be this too is ambitious given the pastoral paradigm, but let us not doubt about its effects in the days to come.

1.7. Tribal and Dalit Religions

E. E. Evans Pritchard writes: "primitive religions are species of the genus religion, and that all who have any interest in religion must acknowledge that a study of the religious ideas and practices of primitive peoples, which are of great variety, may help us to reach certain conclusions about the nature of religion in general, and therefore also about the so-called higher religions or historical and positive religions or the religions of revelation, including our own."[43] Again he declares "indeed I would go further and say that, to understand fully the nature of revealed religion, we have to understand the nature of so-called natural religion, for nothing could have been revealed about anything if men had not already had an idea about that thing."[44] Further 'they provide all the more valuable data for a comparative analysis aiming at determining the essential characteristics of religious phenomena and making general, valid, and significant statements about them.'[45]

---

38 Eric J. Lott, *Vision, Tradition, Interpretation, Theology, Religion, and the Study of Religion,* Mouton de Gruyter, 1988, p. 193.

39 *Ibid.*, p. 193.

40 *Ibid.*, p. 194.

41 *Ibid.*, p. 195.

42 *Ibid.*, p. 198.

43 E. E. Evans Pritchard, *Theories of Primitive Religion* (Oxford; Clarendon Press, 1965), pp. 1-2.

44 *Ibid.*, p. 2.

45 *Ibid.*, 1965, p. 2.

A. M. Abraham Ayrookuzhiel remarks about the dynamism required to understand Dalit religion in India. He writes, "I think if we are serious about the 200 million Dalit community in India regaining their religious status, we should undertake the study of Dalit religious heritage both in its folk form and in its historical form."[46] Since there is a growing reassertion of traditional values particularly in tribal and dalit religions, our learning and teaching of religions need to square out substantial space and program for a deeper understanding of these phenomena so as to explore them and constructively use the findings.

2. Evaluations

In the new BD curriculum the Religions Cluster (Religion, Culture and Society) has been placed as the third cluster from its previous Branch 6. It is a significant pointer to the fact that religious study requires serious consideration in our context. In the previous curriculum, the religion branch was titled as Religion and Society, while the new curriculum has included Culture as well in the title. The broader and useful objectives set forth as introduction to the entire course cluster under religion branch in the previous BD curriculum are replaced with a brief pointer at the beginning of each course. This may raise a question whether the new curriculum has sincerely absorbed all the purposes behind learning and teaching religions in theological colleges.

'Histories and Cultures of India/South Asia Regions,' is a new and ambitious course. Apart from constrains of time, the objectives of the course are praiseworthy, but it may become mere repetition to a History graduate. It may be useful if this course is taught at the first year of BD five year program in the place of Philosophical Foundations where the same is made available to all.

The course on Introduction to Indian Religious Traditions includes two additional religions (Zoroastrianism and Dalit Religion) which also have implications for the teaching load. The suggested methodologies need further consideration because each method is relevant for certain purposes as all the proven methods together constitute the study of religions. It is to be noted that the section on different methods to study religions is avoided in the new curriculum. It may be because it finds a vivid expression under an interdisciplinary course (methodologies). However, the importance of harmonious living together with others for the purpose of engaging them for sustainable existence need more emphasis.

As for Sanskrit language is concerned, no change has been effected, not even an attempt to suggest recent available books. This needs to be addressed positively.

In the detailed study of Hinduism, the text from Upanishads is replaced by the texts from Manusumurti. Objectives like concern for women, tribals, the poor, and Dalits, and interreligious relations laid down for the detailed courses are

---

46 A. M. Abraham Ayrookuzhiel, *Essays on Dalits, Religion and Liberation* (Bangalore: Asian Trading Corporation), 2006, p. 40.

appreciable. The additional requirement of perspectival readings is new, but the authors (resources) mentioned there in need substantial justification.

Under the course 'Modern religio—socio-political Movements in India,' on the section on Hinduism contains a few new titles: Satyashodhak Samaj, Narayana Guru Movement, Prajapati Brahmakumaris. Under Guru Movements, the new titles are: Mata Amritananda Mayi, Baba Ramdev and Sri Sri Ravi Shankar. Under Political Parties, more regional parties are added. The section on Contemporary Issues and the responses of churches is new and comprehensively direction oriented. Including additional topics are encouraging but time management has to be taken in to account.

The detailed study of Primal Religion is removed from the new religion cluster; similarly, Indian Philosophy and Cultural Anthropology. These changes are not in line with the emphasis on the importance of philosophical approach in India. This is also the case with tribal concerns including their methodology.

The courses under Inter-disciplinary section are useful from the point of religions; particularly the course on Methodologies which extensively deals with most of the methodologies used for the systematic study of religions. The course Science and Religion offers the possibility of a dialogue. And Christian Faith and Witness in Pluralistic Societies, is removed from the theology branch and included as a interdisciplinary course in the new curriculum. This is also in line with the purpose of learning and teaching religions in theological institutions.

In the new curriculum, optional courses are reduced. Flexibility is relegated to a tight schedule which robs the expected freedom to choose.

It is left to us to judge whether the above listed changes made and the purposes attempted are met in the new curriculum. Even if these are implicitly referred to, a right pedagogy can help addressing these concerns.

In general, the shift from the old curriculum to the new is minimal in nature. Even then a manageable religion syllabus may be worked out with the consultation of people of other faith traditions. Nevertheless, as listed in the previous pages, if we can pursue teaching and learning other religions, we can achieve the target.

3. Conclusion

While evaluating the new curriculum one has to bear in mind that different strands of thoughts will continue to exist side by side with the favored and the newly emerging ones. Therefore emphasizing one aspect does not mean other aspects are ignored. What is important is to prioritize the relevant concerns.

Every branch of M.Th. study needs to include a course on pedagogy even before the commencement of evaluation of M.Th. curriculum as M.Th. is the basic degree for teaching.

In order to avoid the notion of being 'too ambitious,' clear demarcation between BD and M.Th. courses and standards are necessary to be set. It helps limit the scope of different courses and make it manageable. It can also help in managing the stipulated time frame for different courses.

The emerging view point that many courses are lengthier needs serious consideration. In this regard the senate fraternity should courageously be satisfied with courses in consonance with the time limit permissible to a BD degree course.

Of course the one inalienable factor that has to motivate the religion pedagogy is to ensure that God's Mission is carried out at all circumstances in collaboration even with other religions and ideologies.

Finally to sum up, the pedagogy of religions needs to help religions to be viewed as a vital ingredient in the varied story of humankind's various experiments in living, help grasp the meanings and values of the plural cultures of today's world, help see the great ideas and practices of various important cultures and civilization, help judging people, help animate community relations in plural contexts, help analyze the importance of religions in human life, help interaction between religion and ideologies, help religious communities to participate in the struggle for an inclusive human community, help understand and appreciate the religious experience of people of other faiths, help gain new insights for the Christian faith-experience, help encourage intra and inter-faith dialogue, help avoid fear of Hinduism, help promoting democratic living, help avoiding reduction of religion to mere ethics, helps overcome traditional religious education based on scriptures, help recognizing common humanness, help cooperation between religion and ideologies, help interaction between religion and theology, help see the causes for renewal of religious traditions, help recognize plurality of religions, help promote dialogical approach, help sincere study of tribal and dalit religions and help adequate space for other significant developments.

2

Beginnings of the Science of Religion

Introduction

This paper explores the various factors and persons that were responsible for the establishment of the department of *Science of Religion* with special reference to the contributions of Max Muller who was called the Father of comparative religion. The first part of the paper focuses on the factors, while the second part considers the early founders. And the third part concentrates on the contributions of Max Muller.

1. Science of Religion

Religion has existed since time immemorial with the emergence of human beings on earth. It has had many forms and facts, around rites rituals, goods and gods and goddesses, shrines and temples etc., based on the understanding of reality, creation, births and deaths, sin, forgiveness and so on. Religions have had various emphasis based on the geographic, demographic peculiarities, based on culture, customs, morals and ethics and their understanding. As religious began to consolidate in terms of doctrines, dogmas, temples, rites etc., this distinction for each other became more significant so as to cause the understanding of each religion in its own context. Thus was born the science of religion – to understand a religion systematically in terms of its origins, growth, rites, conception of reality etc., as a science of religion with a possibility to test it against the other, reason, faith and so on. Although humanity and religion are coeval, there had been attempts, perhaps amateur or ostensible, to acquire knowledge about religions other than one's own,[1] from the first century of Christian era. The culmination of

1 Eric J. Sharpe, *Comparative Religion,* A History, Duckworth, 1975, pp. 1-26.

this process was the germination of a new discipline for the systematic or scientific study of religions in the later part of the 19th Century.

Factors Responsible for the Emergence of Science of Religion

Several factors were responsible for the dawn of this new discipline as the science of religion. They were: the Renaissance, the Enlightenment (reformation), geographical discoveries, deists, scientific and intellectual developments, travel accounts, decipherment of ancient texts, the emergence of the enlightenment philosophers, studies in romantic idealism, myth and Folklore.

Reformation

Although the years between 14th century and 17th century[2] are called as the period of Reformation, E. O. James[3] and Waardenburg[4] limit this period to 16th and 17th centuries and perceive the impact of Reformation upon the study of religions. Their perception can be justified because till the emergence of the Reformation, the scripture of Christianity was beyond scientific and systematic scrutiny in comparison with other texts and scriptures, and was far beyond the reach of ordinary people to use, to read and to scrutinize its authenticity. Religious practices however were carried out as said by priests irrespective of their validity. It was only because of the effects of Reformation, while the Reformation itself was due as the outcome of various critical studies, scientific studies etc., scripture and rituals or church practices were questioned. Consequently scripture was studied with the aid of all the critical methods of learning available then.

The spirit of critical study continued in the subsequent centuries. Pertaining to Christianity, the beginning of a scientific study of religion came about for example among others – scholars of Comparative Religions, Phenomenon of religions etc. Julius Welhausean (1844-1918) an Old Testament scholar who asserted that, 'Torah cannot actually have been given by Moses' and also a specific date cannot be assigned to it.[5] Similarly, from the New Testament point of view, "A Scholar like David F. Strauss (1808-1874) had concluded that the whole life of Jesus was a myth: that, as a historical person, he never existed."[6] There emerged soon an intense quest for historical truth about the life of Jesus. The application of historical critical method for the study of scripture itself was, in fact, a courageous act, well ahead of time.

---

2 E. A. Livingstone ED., *The Concise Oxford Dictionary of the Christian Church,* Oxford University Press, New York, 1977. pp. 431-432.

3 E. O. James, *Comparative Religion,* First Published as University Paper back, Methuen & Co. Ltd., London, 1961, p. 15.

4 Waardenburg, *Classical Approaches to the Study of Religion, Aims, Methods and Theories of Research, I: Introduction and Anthology,* Mount, Parries, 1973, pp. 6, 7.

5 *Ibid.,* p. 21.

6 *Ibid.,* p. 25.

Thus began the scientific study of religion in terms of its texts, rituals, beliefs etc., in the light of the socio-political situation since it gave a unique colour to each religion as reason and rationalization took over.

Geographical Discoveries

Along with Reformation, another factor that contributed to the zeal for the study of religion was the geographical discoveries of the sixteenth and seventeenth centuries. These discoveries enabled the West to come in contact with other ways of behavior, thought, and belief; and demanded a broadening of one's views of human nature, culture and religion.[7] As a result, there arose a serious interest to learn about the life and practices of other people around the world. This new interest encouraged further explorations into the so far unknown people and their practices including religions.

Deists

During the 17th and 18th centuries, deists also contributed to the systematic study of religions.[8] They were of the opinion that, the original religion was good and pure, it was only later the priests corrupted it. They also popularized the natural religious quality of humanity against the prevalent idea of revealed religions.[9] The Deists' idea of natural religion was struggling to sail through because of the dominance of the church and its less acceptance among the people. Nevertheless, Deistic thoughts survived, and contributed to the fundamental insight-the ideal of natural religion, to the yet to be established new discipline of the scientific study of religion.

Scientific and Intellectual Developments

Thomas L. Benson writes that, "Scientific and intellectual developments of the seventeenth and eighteenth centuries provided the model for new approaches to the study of religion."[10] Scientific developments, particularly Darwin's theory of evolution had greater impact upon the development of religion as an independent discipline of study.[11] It influenced the thoughts of many great scholars essentially those who advocated an anthropological perspective. They developed their insights in the light of 'linear development of things.' It was commonly assumed that everything, including religion, was moving towards perfection. This notion is very vivid in the works of many later day scholars of religion. Added to this assumption was the critical reasoning prevalent in the academic circles.

---

7 E. O. James, *Comparative Religion, op. cit.,* p. 16.

8 *Ibid.,* p. 16.

9 Thomas L. Benson, *The Encyclopedia of Religion,* vol. 14, p. 65.

10 Thomas L. Benson, *op. cit.,* p. 8.

11 E. O. James *Comparative Religion, op. cit.,* p. 16.

Travel Accounts

After the geographical discoveries, 18th century witnessed the descriptions of other religions by several travelers as they found them across the world. These accounts are not systematic in their presentation. Only a few such works were published. One among them was the work of Charles de Brosses (1709-1777).[12] For him, Fetishism was the earliest form of religion.[13] Commenting on his theory F. Max Muller writes in his *Origin and Growth of Religion*, "all nations, he holds, had to begin with fetishism, to be followed afterwards by polytheism and monotheism."[14] After explaining Brosse's idea of fetish[15] Muller argued, "there is no fetish without its antecedents, and it is in these antecedents alone that its true and scientific interest consists."[16]

Another such work was that of Meiners (1747-1810). He accepted the theory of fetishism but went beyond it and 'stressed the role of human imagination in the development of religious worship.'[17] A similar account was given by Benjamin Constant y de Rebeque (1769-1830). "For Constant, religion is essentially a feeling which is the very foundation of man's nature."[18] The traces of a later psychological approach to the study of religion can be found in his work.

Whatever may be the limitations or criticisms leveled against these initial ventures, the fact remains that, they had sown the seed for the growth of the 'Science of religion.' In these works there are allusions to the early anthropological, sociological and psychological approach to the study of religion.

Decipherment of Ancient Texts

According to Max Muller, "Side by side with the travel accounts of living people, it was the discovery and decipherment of ancient texts that opened a field of research on as yet largely unknown religions."[19] William Jones (1746-1797) studied Sanskrit and compared it with certain European Languages. He "... discovered structural similarities between the two groups of languages and concluded that they belong to one linguistic family."[20] He also found similarities between the Indian Myths and Greek, Roman and Biblical. Through his studies many came in contact with Indian religions and opened up possibilities

---

12 Waardenburg, *op. cit.*, p. 8.

13 F. Max Muller, *Lectures on the Origin and Growth of Religion, as Illustrated by the Religions of India,* Indological Book House, Varanasi (India), 1964, p. 56.

14 *Ibid.*, p. 59

15 *Ibid.*, p. 66.

16 *Ibid.*, p. 98.

17 Waardenburg, *op. cit.*, p. 8.

18 *Ibid.*, p. 8.

19 *Ibid.*, p. 8.

20 *Ibid.*

for further research in Indo-European linguistics and mythology through comparative studies. Another notable scholar in this period and field was Jean Francois Champollion (1790-1832). He was the 'decipherer of the ancient Egyptian hieroglyphic script.'[21] Similar to the impact of the theory of evolution on the study of religion, the results of the study of languages became a reality in the life and contributions of Max Muller. In fact it was this philological research that ultimately constituted the Scientific Study of religion.

German Philosophers

Thomas L. Benson writes, "While the Philosophers of the 18th century Enlightenment in France (e.g., Voltaire) viewed religion as the invention of cunning priests to secure their fears and superstitions, German philosophers were venturing toward a broad and deep understanding of the variety of religions and their historical development."[22] Having taken into consideration the plurality of religions they viewed religions as the out-growth of a natural reasonable religion or as the natural outcome of the general manifestation of Divine grace.[23] They suggested that religions have a historical existence and that religion cannot be studied apart from history.[24] Their two significant insights to the later scientific study of religion were, the common origin of religions and the concept of historical development of religions.

Romantic Idealism

"Another important German contribution to modern approaches to religion was Romantic idealism. As a reaction against Enlightenment thought, it emphasized individuality, feelings, and imagination, and it urged an openness to remote, ancient, mystical, and folk culture and religion."[25] One of its proponents was Friedrich Scheliermacher (1768-1834), a Protestant theologian who assigned religion primarily to feeling that is, the feeling of absolute dependence.[26] In this context, Hegel's contribution is also noteworthy. "For Hegel, the concrete history of religions is the realization of the abstract idea of religion."[27] The third scholar in this brief list is Vico. Vico (1668-1744), the Italian philosopher held that the 'fear of a superior power' was the origin of religion. He perceived this development from polytheism to a spiritual monotheism as a gradual process ruled by divine

21 *Ibid.*

22 Thomas L. Benson, *op. cit.,* p. 65.

23 Waardenburg, *op. cit.,* p. 7.

24 *Ibid.,* p. 9.

25 Thomas L. Benson, *op. cit.,* p. 65.

26 *Ibid.,* p. 66.

27 *Ibid.*

providence.[28] In general Romantic Idealism considers, religion had a common origin, whether it was fear or feeling.

Myth and Folklore

The early part of the 19th century witnessed several studies in mythology. Often the history of religion was compared to the study of myth and comparative religion with comparative mythology. Along with myths, studies in the folklore also influenced the scientific study of religion. Waardenburg writes, "History of religion could now use not only mythology but also folk-lore to its advantage, in this sense Mannhardt had much influence on a scholar like James G-Frazer."[29] Wilhelm Mannhard (1931-1980) was a scholar of European Folk-lore.

In summary Kuncheria Pathil states, "the contact of the West with Islam, the revival of classical antiquity in Renaissance with its aftermath of humanism, and the geographical discoveries of the 15th and 16th centuries with their subsequent colonial and missionary conquests, gave impetus to the study of religions of other lands and peoples."[30] S. Radhakrishnan limits the sources of influence to two: "the development of the science of comparative Religion is due mainly to two factors: the publication and study of the – Sacred Books of the East and the growth of anthropology."[31]

Early Founders

Max Muller in his *Introduction to the Science of Religion* stated, "the Emperor Akbar may be considered the first who ventured on a comparative study of the religions of the world."[32] Nevertheless the real vision for the establishment of an independent discipline for the scientific study of religion was the product of a later part of the 19th century.

One of the pioneers of "Science of Religion" was Cornelis P. Tiele (1830-1902) of Holland. According to Waardenburg "He was one of the first to offer a historical survey of a number of religions based on the study of source materials."[33] In the words of Thomas L. Benson, "Tiele's combined historical work in ancient Near Eastern religions with a systematic interest in religious phenomena and a philosophical search for the essence of religion."[34] The impact of evolutionary thought also reflects his ideas: "In his general view of religion he stressed the

28 *Ibid.*

29 Waardenburg, *op. cit.,* p. 13.

30 Kuncheria Pathil, "Scientific Study of Religions: Some Methodological Reflections", *Journal of Dharma,* Vol. XXI, No. 2, April-June 1996, p. 163.

31 Radhakrishnan, *East and West in Religion,* George Allen & Unwin Ltd., London, 1933, p. 13.

32 F. Max Muller, *Introduction to the Science of Religion,* New Edition, London, 1882, p. 209.

33 Waardenburg, *op. cit.,* p. 98.

34 Thomas L. Benson, *op. cit.,* p. 69.

evolution of the 'religious idea' through the historical forms of religion which represented different stages."[35]

The reason assigned by him for the scientific study of religion was quite simple. In the *Elements of the Science of Religion* he asserted that religion is investigated in order to learn something about it, in accordance with a sound and critical method, appropriate to each department.[36] He advocated a kind of historical method. Still he said, "Yet I believe that the science of religion requires a broader foundation than history in the ordinary sense of the word."[37] Two points are clear. One is that he applied historical approach and the other is that, he felt the need for more approaches for the better understanding of religious phenomena.

Another pioneer who contributed to the development of the scientific study of religion was Pierre D. Chantepie de la Saussaye (1848-1920) of Netherlands. "Chantepie, in his classic *Manual of the Science of Religion* (1887-1889), made an elaborate classification of religious phenomena (Sacred stones, trees, animals, places, times, persons, writings, communities and the like), a forerunner of later phenomenologies of religion."[38] "Besides historical work in his field, he was primarily interested in systematic classification."[39] He is one of the first scholars to speak of phenomenology of religion as a special branch of the study of religion.[40] It is said that his inadequate knowledge of language[41] restricted him as he felt inaccessible to the original sources. Hence he concentrated less on history and more on classification of religion.

Max Muller

The most important of the founders of a separate discipline called 'Science of religion', for the systematic study of religion was the Oxford Sanskritist Friedrich Max Muller (1823-1900). He was called the Father of Comparative Religions. R. W. Brockway says, "Max Muller's Essay in *Comparative Mythology* (1856) was the earliest significant discussion of comparative religion and it could be said that Muller was the father of *Religionswissenschaft* or Religious studies."[42] According to professor J. G. Arapura, without Muller, there could not have emerged the separate discipline for the scientific study of religion: "But for him, comparative religion, history of religion, phenomenology of religion, Relgionswissenschaft, or whatever else it is called, as distinguished from theology, would not have found

35 Waardenburg, *op. cit.,* p. 98.

36 *Ibid.,* p. 97.

37 *Ibid.,* p. 100.

38 Thomas L. Benson, *op. cit.,* p. 69.

39 Waardenburg, *op. cit.,* p. 105.

40 *Ibid.,* p. 105.

41 *Ibid.,* p. 15.

42 R. W. Brockway, "A Critique of Max Muller's Methodology of Mythology." *Journal of Dharma,* Vol. II, No. 4, October 1977, p. 368.

a place in the modern university."[43] Muller declared his commitment and vigor for the establishment of a discipline for the scientific study of religion, as the new science would change the aspect of the world.[44]

Basically Muller was a philologist. In his study of languages he used the comparative method. The same method was later applied to the systematic study of religion. It is said as "Muller's wide knowledge of Indo-European languages, his comparative approach to philology and extension of that method to the study of religion, and his eloquent advocacy of that study as a scientific discipline prepared the way, during his life time, for the establishment of Chairs in the new field in leading European Universities."[45] He was interested in the archaic forms of religion. The reason was that, he wanted to find the origin of religions from the study of archaic forms. R. W. Brockway writes, "Interested in archaic forms of religion, he suggested that contemporary primitives might preserve some very ancient mythologies, rituals, and beliefs which could be taken as survivals from prehistoric times, and that from them one could discern originals."[46]

The aim of establishing the new discipline for the scientific study of religion is summed up by Eric J. Sharpe as "His ultimate aim was to elaborate a complete science of human thought: and this he chose to do in four stages, beginning with the science of language, and passing through the science of mythology and the science of religion to the final goal of the science of thought."[47] In the *Natural Religion* Muller said, 'I want, if possible to show you how the road which leads from the Science of Language to the Science of Mythology and to the Science of Thought is the only safe road on which to approach the science of religion.'

Language

Max Muller's field of interest was philology. His linguistic studies of Indo-European languages using comparative method convinced him that a similar method could be applied to the study of religions. R. W. Brockway says, "Muller approached the study of religion from his knowledge of Sanskrit and other ancient languages."[48] In the words of J. G. Arapura, "Max Muller considers comparative philology as both a tool and model for research in religion. Language and religion are two phenomena that have the closest similarity with each other both originating in the instinctual life of man and exhibiting a remarkable continuity of development."[49] His ever-growing interest was to find out the original forms of

---

43 J. G. Arapura, *Religion as Anxiety and Tranquility, An Essay in Comparative Phenomenology of the Spirit,* Mouton & Co., Netherlands, 1972, p. 31.

44 Arie L. Molendijk, "Tiele on Religion, *Numen,* Vol. XLVI, No. 3, 1999, p. 237.

45 Thomas L. Benson, *op. cit.,* p. 69.

46 R. W. Brockway, "A Critique of Max Muller's Methodology", *op. cit.,* p. 368.

47 Eric J. Sharpe, *Comparative Religion, A History,* Duckworth, London, 1975, p. 40.

48 R. W. Brockway, *op. cit.,* p. 368.

49 J. G. Arapura, *op. cit.,* p. 29.

religions. Regarding his conviction for the commitment, it is said "He held that philological and etymological research can discover the meaning of religion for early men by restoring the original sense to the names of the gods and the stories told about them."[50]

Muller's option for the use of comparative philological method for the study of religion is well explained in his *Chips from a German Workshop* as "the science of Language has taught us that there is order and wisdom in all languages, and that even the most degraded jargons contain the ruins of former greatness and beauty."[51] The same verdict, Muller gave to all religions, irrespective of their status. For him, perhaps, all religions contained same form of truth. Muller says in his *Natural Religion* "Our customs and traditions are often founded on decayed and misunderstood words."[52]

Having understood the difficulty of explaining the ancient concept using modern languages Muller says, "Nay, I believe it can be proved that more than half of the difficulties in the history of religion owe their origin to this constant misinterpretation of ancient language by modern language, of ancient thought by modern thought, particularly whenever the word has become more sacred than the spirit."[53] He further, tells in a very authentic tone that if we want to understand ancient religion, we must first try to understand ancient language.[54]

Myth

Muller's philological skills necessitated him to consider myths from the same perspective. In the words of Waardenburg, "Myths being in his view primarily poetry and phantasy Muller tried to explain their substance by means of natural phenomena, and their terminology by what he called a 'disease of language."[55] J. G. Arapura writes, "Mythology, which was the bane of the ancient world is in truth a disease of language."[56] The concept of 'disease of language' can be explained as "His much-criticized summation of Myth was the result of metaphors derived from impressive experience of natural phenomena and then the taking the figurative for the real."[57]

Understanding myths play a significant role in the understanding of religions and it is clearly indicated by Eric J. Sharpe: "Hence it was and is necessary to penetrate the myths in order to reach the heart of the religion which they

50 Waardenburg, *op. cit.,* p. 85.

51 *Ibid.,* p. 86.

52 F. Max Muller, *Natural Religion,* First Asian Reprint, Asian Educational Services, New Delhi, 1979, p. 385.

53 F. Max Muller, *Introduction to the Science of Religion,* New Edition, London, 1882, p. 32.

54 *Ibid.,* p. 198.

55 Waardenburg, *op. cit.,* p. 85.

56 J. G. Arapura, *op. cit.,* p. 27.

57 Thomas L. Benson, *op. cit.,* p. 69.

conceal."[58] Max Muller was the pioneer to investigate myths in order to find out the hidden meanings of the words applied.

Science of Religion

Max Muller, starting from the science of language passed through mythology and now moved to the science of religion, before reaching the final destination – origin of religion. Before going any further it is necessary that the expression "Science of Religion" is made clear. "Science of religion" is the direct translation of the German expression 'Religionswissenschaft.' Max Muller coined this term.[59] He used this term to denote the new discipline, which he established. It only points to the scientific or systematic study of religions.

The method Muller adopted in the science of religion was comparative and historical. Comparative because of the varieties of data found from various religions and branches of study. He recommended this method from his earlier experience of philological studies. His assumption was that if comparison of languages could facilitate a common origin, the comparison of data from religions should also yield such useful result. It is historical because, his intention was to trace the history of the origin of religions by going back, from the present data.

Today, the terms 'Science of Religion', 'comparative religion' and 'history of religions' are used without much distinction, implying just what Muller intended by the term science of religion. Regarding, 'comparative religion' J. N. D. Anderson contends, "Strictly speaking, the very term is, of course, a solecism, for it is not 'religion' itself, which is 'comparative', but the method of study and approach."[60] He further says, "as such, comparative religion is simply one aspect of the study of religion."[61] He was concerned with the common tendency of many to quickly be immersed in comparison of religions, without adequate knowledge of what they really mean in their specific context. In the words of Ninian Smart, "Quite often what is meant by 'comparative study of religion' is typological phenomenology."[62] For him, this is against what he calls the historical phenomenology.

Max Muller himself perceived such a misuse and said, "Generalization will come in time, but generalization without a thorough knowledge of particulars is the ruin of all sciences, and has hitherto proved the greatest danger to the Science of Religion."[63] Further danger of misunderstood and misused notion of comparative religion is clearly brought out by Frank Whaling that.

---

58 Eric J. Sharpe, *op. cit.,* p. 43.

59 R. W. Brockway, *op. cit.,* p. 108.

60 J. N. D. Anderson, *Christianity and Comparative Religion,* Reprinted, Tyndale Press, London, 1972, p. 7.

61 *Ibid.,* p. 7.

62 Ninian Smart, *Phenomenon of Religion,* Mac Millan, London, 1973, p. 41.

63 Max Muller, *Natural Religion, op. cit.,* p. 350.

> One of the reasons why the term 'comparative religion' came under suspicion was its implied connection with theology. According to this view, the motive for much work in the comparison of religions was not the 'impartial and scientific' desire to establish patterns, similarities and differences, but the theological desire to demonstrate that one's own position was superior, fuller, or more than mundane compared with that of others.[64]

To use the method of comparison meaningfully as Muller intended, it is worth mentioning Michael Pye. In his *Comparative Religion* he states, "the comparative study of religion or 'comparative religion' for short is really a phrase to indicate the study of religion in so far as the student is not confining his attentions to single case-study."[65]

Along with comparative method Muller also used the historical method. The purpose was to find the origin of religion on the basis of the available data. It is different from the strictly historical method called *Religionsgeschichte* (historical study of Religions). But later the original intention was lost. In the words of Ninian Smart, "to complicate matters, it has become usual to substitute the phrase history of religions for the comparative study of religion."[66] Muller himself said "... to my mind, the more interesting, if not the more important part of the science of religion is certainly concerned with what we call the historical development of religious thought and language."[67]

Again it needs to be stressed that Muller used comparative historical method for the scientific study of religion. Later these two methods were used as synonyms for the expression 'Science of Religion.' Because of the unscrupulous use of comparative method, the expression comparative religion is almost vanishing. Because of the ambiguities and disadvantages of the two expressions 'Science of religion' and 'comparative religion', today the term 'history of religion' is used in the place of 'science of religion' for the systematic and scientific study of religion.

The Subject for the Science of Religion

Like other subjects, religion cannot be squared out from the very life of human beings. It is the integral part of humanness. It therefore, cannot be studied subjectively, i.e., "the 'faith of the believer' can no longer be a legitimate subject of the science of religion."[68] Yet human beings have an objectified religious

64 Frank Whaling ed., *Contemporary Approaches to the Study of Religion in 2 Volumes,* Volume I: *The Humanities,* Mouton Publishers, Berlin, 1984, p. 166.

65 Michael Pye, *Comparative Religion An Introduction Through Source Materials,* David and Charles, Newton Abbot, 1972, p. 8.

66 Frank Whaling ed. Vol. I, *op. cit.,* p. 371.

67 F. Max Muller, *Natural Religion, op. cit.,* p. 13.

68 Ursula King, "The debate about the science of religion", edited by Frank Whaling, Vol. I, *op. cit.,* p. 131.

experience to the position of studying it as a subject. "The science of religion investigates religious conception, values and behavior."[69] Ernst Troeltsch has explained it thus: "its great question is the question of the nature of religious phenomena, the question of their epistemological and cognitive import, the question of the value and the meaning of the great historical religious formations."[70] It does not focus upon the essence of religion nor does it create a new religion. In brief, the subject of the science of religion is the objectified subjective experience of human beings.

Data for the Science of Religion

Max Muller, from philological perspective, gives more importance to the scriptures of religion, but with caution. "To the student of religion canonical books are no doubt, of the utmost importance, but he ought never to forget that canonical books too give the reflected image only of the real doctrines of the founder of a new religion, an image always blurred and distorted by the medium through which it had to pass."[71] Going behind this Ernst Troeltsch suggests that, "Very important data are those one-sided or exclusively religious personalities, sects and groups among whom the effects of scientific ways of thinking sit but loosely or are absent altogether, and who also have not yet lost their religious innocence by any struggle against science."[72] For the present student of religion apart from these two, the practical utility of religions in every day life should become a datum.

The Task of the Science of Religion

The task of the science of religion has been termed diversely by scholars. Though, they look different in expression all of them are legitimate from varied perspectives. For Waardenburg, the central task is 'the understanding of other religious.'[73] More understanding of other religions may not be of any help unless it is related to religions as a whole. Y. Masih in his *A Comparative Study of Religions* points out that, "in the opinion of the author of this book, the most important task of comparative study of religions is to find out a principle of unity which will harmonize and balance the claims and counter claims of warring religions into one unity."[74] Though he is dreaming of an unattainable task this is what the scholars of religions in general are striving for.

69 *Ibid.,* p. 131.

70 Robertmorgan and Michael Pye, *Ernst Troeltsch: Writings on Theology and Religion,* Translated and edited, Duckworth London, 1977, p. 88.

71 F. Max Muller, *Introduction to the Science of Religion,* New Edition, London, 1882, p. 53.

72 Robertmorgan and Michael Pye, *Ernst Troeltsch: Writings on Theology and Religion, op. cit.,* p. 91.

73 Waardenburg, Vol. I, *op. cit.,* p. 513.

74 Y. Masih, *A Comparative Study of Religions,* Motilal Banarsidars, Delhi, reprinted, 1993, p. 13.

Another dimension of the task of scientific study of religion is highlighted by Ernst Troeltsch. For him, the purpose of scientific work on religion is entirely and necessarily to influence religion itself.[75] Perhaps, he was concerned with the reformatory work required on the part of many religions including Christianity to which he belonged. A more moderate and useful task of the scientific study of religion is found in the work of Ninian Smart that "an important task in the building of a science of religion is to collect the various key materials which recur in differing religious environment."[76] He wanted to investigate the interaction of such materials in diverse religions. From a religious point of view, it is almost clear that a simple formula of unity is out of place. What is envisaged is to see how similar materials are present in diverse religious expressions. Such an approach could promote healthy inter-religious understanding, without insisting upon unity or without causing damage to any particular religion.

Pattern of Study

Most of the religious studies were carried out by missionaries or missionary minded Christians. Their aim was to exhibit the view that their own religion was true and superior. The philosophers who were interested in the study of religions however heed their own reservations. It is stated that "the 'true believers' studied religions only to laud the superiority of their own and to depreciate those of others, while the skeptics started with the preconception that all religions were false and entertained a simpleminded theory of the nature and origin of religion."[77]

Because of the increasing amount of religious knowledge, the traditional narrow or too general perspectives of religious studies have been ignored and more charitable expectations have penetrated into the realm of scientific study of religion. Kuncheria Pathil has rightly indicated that, "today these 'one-track schemes of development' have been discarded by most of the scholars and emphasis has been placed on understanding the uniqueness of each religion and discovering the basic *structures* of the religious phenomena."[78] This view too limits itself with constraints as it looks for the basic structure of the religious phenomena. This is not a healthy demand. An open expectation is declared by Dr. Radha Krishnan that "for a scientific student of religion is required to treat all religions in a spirit of absolute detachment and impartiality."[79] A similar view is found enhanced in the writing of E. O. James that "Religious phenomena as distinct from spiritual experience must be investigated on their own merits historically and

75 Robertmorgan and Michael Pye, *Ernst Troeltsch: Writings on Theology and Religion, op. cit.*, p. 63.

76 Ninian Smart, *Religion and Truth: Towards An Alternative Paradigm for the Study of Religion*, Mount Publishers, The Hague, 1981, p. 148.

77 Thomas L. Benson, *op. cit.*, p. 64.

78 Kuncheria Pathil, *op. cit.*, p. 163.

79 Radhakrishnan, *East and West in Religion,* George Allen & Unwin Ltd., London, 1933, p. 16.

comparatively independent of any preconceived theories or accepted loyalties."[80] Here the present author affirms the original vision of the science of religion as expected by Max Muller himself.

Objections to the Study of Religion

Dr. Radha Krishnan gives at least three reasons as to why there are objections to the scientific study of religion. These are, seemingly, the fear inherent among those religious people who claim absolutism or superiority. According to him, "One reason for this is that the scientific study of religion is imagined to be a danger to religion itself."[81]

"Another objection is that comparison means resemblance, and if one religion is like another, what happens to the claims of superiority and uniqueness."[82] A third objection is given as "again, it is urged, if comparative Religion tells us that higher religions possess features in common with the low and the primitive, then the inference is legitimate that our religious beliefs are of a degrading and childish character."[83]

Of course these are genuine fears as long as people were not aware of what was happening around the world. As every form of knowledge is available at the doorsteps of every individual, scientific knowledge of religions too should be. It can strengthen and widen the relationship between different religious communities, which were hostile so far on account of non-availability of scientific knowledge of religions.

Max Muller had perceived this objection in advance and answered it as "I do not say that the science of religion is all gain. No, it entails losses, and losses of many things which we hold dear. But this I will say, that, as far as my humble judgment goes, it does not entail the loss of anything that is essential to true religion, and that if we strike the balance honestly, the gain is immeasurably greater than the loss."[84] It is time that the discipline of religion looks beyond the simple objections to fulfill its task of presenting useful facts in order to facilitate a peaceful co-existence among people of different faiths.

Origin of Religion

Starting from language and passing through mythology, Muller established the science of religion. Through the science of religion, he clearly draws every one's attention to two vivid objectives. One is the origin of religion and the other is the type of religions, as he understood.

---

80 E. O. James, *op. cit.,* p. 18.

81 S. Radhakrishnan, *op. cit.,* pp. 15, 16.

82 *Ibid.,* p. 16.

83 *Ibid.,* p. 16, 17.

84 F. Max Muller, *Introduction to the Science of Religion, op. cit.,* p. 8.

Waardenburg summarizes Muller's view of the origin of religion as "Religion proper would have started with an 'immediate perception of the infinite' through nature apart from the senses and reason."[85] This may be an inadequate way of summing up Muller's understanding of the origin of religion because for Muller, not only nature, but the human and self also are the great manifestations. But the presentation of the idea of the 'immediate perception of the infinite' also finds support in Max Muller. Muller in his *Natural Religion* says that, "my chief endeavour is to show that 'religion did not begin with abstract concepts and a belief in purely extra-mundane beings, but that its deepest roots can be traced back to the universal stratum of sensuous perception.'"[86]

According to Max Muller, there are three crucial reasons for tracing the origin of religion. The first one is found in his *Chips from a German workshop,* as quoted by Waardenburg: "Whenever we can trace back a religion to its first beginnings, we find it free from many of the blemishes that offend us in its later phases."[87] According to him, it helps in grasping the original nature of religions.

The second reason is that it helps to understand humanity. It is summarized by Eric J. Sharpe as, "To Max Muller, the attempt to understand religion was an attempt to understand men, and an attempt, to persuade men to understand one another."[88]

In the words of Muller, it enables us to see the development of religions. "Religion is something which has passed, and is still passing through an historical evolution, and all we can do is to follow it up to its origin, and then try to comprehend it in its later historical developments."[89]

From the scientific study of religions Max Muller found that "Nature, man and self are the three great manifestations in which the infinite in some shape or other has been perceived, and every one of these perceptions has in its historical development contributed to what may be called religion."[90] He assigned names to these three manifestations. "I shall distinguish these three divisions as *Physical Religion, Anthropological Religion,* and *Psychological Religion.*"[91]

He wanted to show that these three aspects are found in every religion. However, the amount of importance attributed to a particular manifestation may be varied. In his *Physical Religion* it is stated that, "it must not be supposed that these three phases of natural religion, the *Physical, the Anthropological and the Psychological,* exist each by itself, that one race worships the powers of nature only, while another venerates the spirits of human ancestors, and a third meditate on

85 Waardenburg, *op. cit.,* p. 85.

86 F. Max Muller, *Natural Religion, op. cit.,* p. 141.

87 Waardenbugr, *op. cit.,* p. 88.

88 Eric J. Sharpe, *op. cit.,* p. 44.

89 F. Max Muller, *Lectures on the Origin and Growth of Religion, op. cit.,* p. 21.

90 F. Max Muller, *Natural Religion, op. cit.,* p. 164.

91 *Ibid.*

the Divine, as discovered in the deepest depth of the human heart."[92] As intended, Muller has reached his final destination of finding the origin of religion.

2. Conclusion

Various factors and persons have contributed to the establishment of the 'Science of Religion.' While the science of religion has benevolent objectives, there are objections to it as well. If religions are studied as the founding parents envisaged, the end result would be harmony and fellowship among religions. Although the scientific study of religions is now well developed than originally intended, it needs to be pursued with due respect to the plurality of faith traditions and to the underlying principle of religious harmony among adherents of diverse faith orientations.

92 F. Max Muller, *Physical Religion*, First Asian Reprint, Asian Educational Services, New Delhi, 1979.

3

An Evaluation of the Science of Religion

Early Beginning of the Science of Religion

The beginnings of religion have a hoary past since the advent o human beings on the earth although its conception, doctrines, rites etc., have grown through the ages. However, a systematic and a scientific approach to religion have been modern phenomena. In case of these the science and religion has taken into account is its stride various other factors, circumstances, scientific discoveries etc., to conceptualise religion as a factor to understand the society, the nature of reality, ethos of a culture, the plurality of religions etc. With these developments, the science of religion has taken on many facets of research and approaches to enrich the study.

Different Approaches to the Study of Religion

The 'Science of Religion' was though simple in origin, rich in purpose and privileged to avail the expertise of many other branches of knowledge it opened a vast area of research and study to enrich the phenomena of religious study systematically. As a result many approaches developed for the scientific study of religions. Some of them are: anthropological, sociological, historical, phenomenological and psychological.

Anthropological Approach

Anthropology is the study of human beings and its basis is culture. Anthropologists use the comparative method in order to find what is common to all humanity and 'what is distinctive of particular societies or groups of societies.'[1] They also study

1 Marc J. Swartz and David K. Jordan, *Anthropology: Perspective on Humanity,* John Wiley & Sons, Inc., 1976, p. 2-3.

the beliefs and practices of all human societies and use their data to trace the origin of religions.

E. B. Tylor is generally regarded as the founder of the Anthropological study of religion.[2] For him, religion was not the result of any revelation or supernatural intervention.[3] He propounded the theory of *animism* i.e., "the belief that all living beings and natural phenomena that appear to move or have life (Sun, Moon, Rivers, etc.) have individual spirits (animas), some or all of which are appropriate objects of worship."[4] For him, the earliest stage of religion 'consisted in the belief in souls, present not only in human beings but also in all natural organisms and objects. Tylor saw earlier animistic experience as the irreducible and original source of later religious life.[5]

In turn, R. R. Marett, a disciple of Tylor, proposed '*animatism*' or dynamism or pre-animism as the origin of religion. Marett argued that belief in souls or spirits is the result of reasoning. Before reasoning, there could have been a 'super naturalistic' stage, in which a human recognized an impersonal religious force, which was rather felt than reasoned out.[6] The Melanesian islanders for example, worshiped this supernatural force as Mana, i.e., 'undifferentiated impersonal supernatural force.'[7] In shor,t animatisms is belief in Mana. For Marett, this was the first stage of religion.[8]

For Hebert Spencer, *manism* or ancestor worship is the beginning of religion.[9] This he derived from human's belief in spirits or ghosts.[10] The fundamental assumption is that, just as fear of the living is at the root of political control, fear of the dead is at the root of religious control.[11] E. O. James called it as the 'ghost theory.'[12]

Andrew Langh proposed that the primitives believed in *Supreme beings or high gods* and that could be the earliest form of religion. It was prior to animism.[13]

2 Thomas L. Benson, *The Encyclopedia of Religion,* Vol. 14, p. 69.

3 E. O. James, *Comparative Religion,* First Published as University Paper back, Methane & Co. Ltd., London, 1961, p. 30.

4 Marc J. Swartz and David K. Jordan, *op. cit.,* p. 664.

5 P. S. Daniel, David C. Scott, *et al., Religious Traditions of India,* Indian Theological Library, 1988, p. 21.

6 Waardenburg, *Classical Approaches to the Study of Religion, Aims, Methods and Theories of Research,* I: Introduction and Anthology, Mouton, Paries, 1973, p. 257.

7 Marc J. Swartz and David K. Jordan, *op. cit.,* p. 663.

8 Eric J. Sharpe, *Comparative Religion, A History,* Duckworth, London, 1975, p. 68.

9 F. Max Muller, *Anthropological Religion,* second AES Reprint, Asian Educational Services, New Delhi, 1986, p. 127.

10 Thomas. L. Benson, *op. cit.,* p. 69.

11 Waardenburg, *op. cit.,* p. 29.

12 E. O. James, *op. cit.,* p. 37.

13 Waardenburg, *op. cit.,* p. 240.

He perceived that 'parapsychology has more to say about the nature and origin of religion than rationalistic anthropological theories.

For James G. Frazer, religious activities and attitudes were preceded by the practice of *magic*.[14] Its aim was to master the external environment through human powers. It is easy to conceive that religion and magic function side by side but not magic preceding religion.

Apart from the above views of cultural anthropology, Social anthropology emphasizes the functional aspect of religion. The Diffusionist school insists upon the necessity of studying various cultural circle or layers, which could have been caused by small migrations in order to answer the question of similarities in cultures in different religions.

The general criticism against the anthropological approach is that it is confined to the empirical religious phenomena and does not go to the original religious feeling. The second criticism is that, having studied one or few religions, the anthropologists involve in generalizing the data. There is also the fear of approaching primitive religions with a missionary motive.

Sociological Approach

The original aim of sociology was to find out the 'scientific account of the laws underlying the social fabric.'[15] It is convinced that human institution cannot be based on error and falsehood, otherwise it could not have lasted.[16] By definition "the sociology of religion is the study of the significant, and often subtle, relationships which prevail between religion and social structures, and between religion and social processes."[17] It studies the processes by which religion enters human interaction and how the interaction of persons influences religion.[18] In the words of Joachim Wach, "the sociologist of religion will have to study and to classify with care the typologically different organizational structures resulting from divergent concepts or religious communion."[19] Harvey Carrier therefore writes, "sociology from its very birth showed itself immediately (as being) concerned with the role

---

14 P. S. Daniel, David C. Scott *et al., op. cit.,* p. 21.

15 Michael Hill, "Sociological Approaches" *Contemporary Approaches to the Study of Religion in 2 Volumes,* edited by Frank Whaling, Volume II, Mouton Publishers, Berlin, 1985, pp. 117, 118.

16 W. S. F. Pickering, *Durkheim on Religion, A Selection of Reading with Bibliographies,* New translations by Jacqueline Reading and W. S. F. Pickering, Routledge & Kegan Paul, London, 1975, p. 103.

17 Thomas F. O' Dea, *The Sociology of Religion,* Prentice-Hall, Inc., 1966, p. 117.

18 Richard. Knudten, *The Sociology of Religion an Anthology,* Meridith Publishing Company, New York, 1967. p. 26.

19 Joachim Wach, *Sociology of Religion,* Twelfth Impression, The University of Chicago Press, London, 1971, p. 34.

and the function of religion in the dynamism of societies."[20] It is thus expected that the sociologist will not make any statements about the supernatural in the theories, which attempt to explain or predict religious behavior.[21]

Religion for the sociologists cannot be understood as an extra-social phenomenon.[22] It is the product of society. Hence, "we cannot understand the inner dynamics of a society unless we understand its religion."[23] Max Weber was the first to conceive a systematic sociology of religion.[24] For him, religious behavior can be understood only through its meaning for the individuals concerned[25] and "the most elementary forms of behavior motivated by religious or magical factors are oriented to *this* world."[26]

William Robertson Smith thus argues, on the basis of totemism that sacrifice was a social integrative and conservatively traditional act.[27] For him totemism was the most elementary form of religious life. Emile Durkheim in turn 'associated totemism with the distinction between the realms of the sacred and the profane.' For him, religion is inherently a social reality and hence it should be studied as a response to specific social needs. He says, "the most barbarous and the most fantastic rites and the strangest myths translate some human need, some aspect of life, either individual or social."[28] According K. P. Aleaz, for Durkheim "religion is the essence of the social bond."[29] The only difference between religion and other institutions is that religion distinguishes itself from other human institutions through its fundamental opposition between the profane and the sacred.

---

20 Herve Carrier S. J., *The Sociology of Religious Belonging,* Darton, Longman & Todd, London, 1965, p. 19.

21 Daniel L. Hodges, "Breaking a Scientific Taboo: Putting Assumptions about the supernatural into scientific theories of religion," *Journal for the Scientific Study of Religion,* Volume 13, No. 4, December, 1974, p. 393.

22 Gunter Kehrer and Bert Hardin, "Sociological Approaches," *Contemporary Approaches to the Study of Religion in 2 Volumes,* edited by Fran Whaling, Vol. II. Mouton Publishers, Berlin, 1985, p. 173.

23 Christopher Dawson, *Religion and Culture,* Meridian Books, New York, 1958, p. 50.

24 Joachim Wach, *Sociology of Religion,* Twelfth Impression, The University of Chicago Press, London, 1971, p. 3.

25 Max Weber, *The Sociology of Religion,* Translated by Ephraim Fishchoff, third printing, Beacon Press, Boston, 1964, p. 1.

26 Max Weber, *op. cit.,* p. 1.

27 Thomas L. Benson, *op. cit.,* p. 70.

28 Emile Durkheim, *The Elementary Forms of the Religious Life,* Translated by Joseph Ward Swain, Second Edition, George Allen & Unwin Ltd., London, 1976. p. 2.

29 K. P. Aleaz, *Dimensions of Indian Religion, Study, Experience and Interaction Punthi Pustak,* Calcutta, 1995. p. 20.

Historical Approach

Cornelius Tiele may be regarded as its founder. The protagonists of a strictly historical approach emphasize the use of historical – critical method and insist on factual – descriptive expositions. Ursula king writes: "It was not only the concern of historical truth but also the need to free the study of religion from the dominance of *a priori* theological and philosophical speculation which required a strong insistence on the use of the historical method."[30] The reason being, every religious element is significant only in its own proper context.[31]

Robert D. Baired's definition that history is *the descriptive study of the human past*[32] *holds good if only religion is treated as an integral part of humanity. Muller writes, "there is but one method that leads to really trustworthy and solid results and this is the Historical Method."*[33] For him, "the principle of the historical school is not to ignore the present, but to try to understand the present by means of the past."[34] Practically, the historical approach is burdened with surplus data without adequate 'integration.' Another concern is whether the historian is able to investigate the essential inner meaning of any religious tradition.

Phenomenological Approach

The main task of phenomenological approach is to study the essence of religion by studying various structures of religion. Phenomenology is defined as the systematic discussion of what appears.[35] Further, "the phenomenological method is a way of describing rather than a way of explaining."[36] The first person to outline the principles of phenomenology to investigate the 'essential inner structures of religion'[37] was P. D. Chantepie de la Saussay. In turn, Husserl laid two basic principles of phenomenology. One is *Epoche* i.e., 'bracketing, or suspension of judgment regarding the phenomenal object.' The second is, *eidetic vision,* i.e., 'the intuitive, undistorting grasp of the 'essence' of the object.'

One of the major tasks of phenomenologists is to 'describe the essence of the phenomenon, and not to "locate" it. That is seeking the meaning or essence rather than finding the cause or truth.[38] It means to interpret the symbols in a

---

30 Frank Whaling ed., Vol.1. *op. cit.,* p. 37.

31 UGO Bianchi, *The History of Religions,* E. J. Brill, Leiden, Netherlands, 1975, p. 49.

32 Robert D. Baird, *Category Formation and the History of Religions,* Mouton, Netherlands, 1971, p. 49.

33 F. Max Muller, *Physical Religion, op. cit.,* p. 7.

34 F. Max Muller, *Natural Religion, op. cit.,* p. 278.

35 J. G. Arapura, *op. cit.,* p. 49.

36 Joseph Pabney Bettis, ed., *Phenomenology of Religion, Eight Modern Descriptions of the Essence of Religion,* SCM Press Ltd., London, 1969, p. 6.

37 Eric J. Lott, *Vision, Tradition, Interpretation, Theology, Religion, and the Study of Religion,* Mouton de Gruyter, 1988, p. 179.

38 Joseph Dabney Bettis ed., *op. cit.,* p. 10.

way that enhances the self-knowledge of human beings. Thus a phenomenologist of religions takes a deep interest in studying symbols.[39] However, while the earlier (empirical) phenomenologists though were busy with structures and pattern, the modern historical phenomenologists study the structures and their connection in their specific historical context.[40] Thus the new style phenomenology, "is moving from the search for timeless essences to a search for meaning inside time."[41] Its aim is to trace the intention of the religious phenomena.

For Rudolf Otto the non-rational, which is the opposite of that which can be thought about conceptually is the subject matter of investigation. The unnamed or the non-rational is the *numinous.* It is felt as objective and outside the self. Its nature is '*Mysterium tremendum*', i.e., it grips or stirs the human mind with this and that is the determinate affective state. Conceptually the *mysterium* denotes merely that which is hidden and esoteric, which is beyond conception or understanding, extraordinary and unfamiliar. *Tremendum* is the positive aspect of it. It is not fear in the strict sense. This positive can be experienced only in feeling. It is this feeling which emerged in the mind of primeval human, to be the starting-point for the entire religious development in history. Besides '*mysterium tremendum*', the numinous is 'fascination.' The combination of these two qualities, the daunting and the fascinating, now combine in a strange harmony of contrasts, and the resultant dual character of the numinous consciousness, to which the entire religious development bears witness. The relation between the rational and the non-rational in the end constitute the final meaning of the "Holy."[42]

On the basis of the combination of these two aspects "Religion, he (Otto) argued, has its own autonomous existence as a phenomenon in human experience."[43] Otto's theory is that reason and its limits likewise being set aside, reality manifests itself in consciousness by means of a peculiar numinous sense. He instead of studying the *ideas* of God and religion undertook to analyze the modalities of *the religious* experience.[44] Radin[45] remarks, "awesome" feelings described by Otto are the result of 'economic and psychic insecurity.' Otto however, did not grasp it because of his theological and mystical background.

Nathan Soderblom's major contribution is the idea of "Holiness." He was of the opinion that there may be religions even without God, but none, without

---

39 Ursula King, "Phenomenology" edited by Frank Whaling, Vol. I, *op. cit.,* p. 39.

40 Ursula King, "Phenomenology" edited by Frank Whaling, Vol. I, *op. cit.,* p. 88.

41 K. P. Aleaz, *Dimensions of Indian Religion, Study, Experience and Interaction, op. cit.,* p. 17.

42 Rudolf Otto, *The Idea of the Holy, An Inquiry into the Non-rational Factor in the Idea of the Divine and its Relation to the Rational,* Translated by John W. Harvey, Pelican Books, 1959, pp. 15-45.

43 P. S. Daniel, David C. Scott *et al., op. cit.,* p. 37.

44 Mircea Eliade, *The Sacred and the Profane,* The Nature of Religion, Translated from the French by Willard R. Trask, Harcourt, Brace and Company, New York, 1959, p. 9.

45 Thomas L. Benson, *op. cit.,* p. 74.

the distinction between the holy and the profane.[46] His disciple Friedrich Heiler asserted that all religions are directed towards the Holy. For him, prayer is the heart and center of all religion.[47]

For Gerardus Van der Leeuw, Phenomenology seeks the phenomenon, as such, the phenomenon again is what appears. This principle has a threefold implication: 1. Something exists, 2. This something appears, 3. Precisely because it 'appears' it is 'phenomenology.'[48] When someone tries to explain what appears, then phenomenology arises. Thus phenomenology is the systematic discussion of what appears. Leeuw focused on a wholly other "power" as the object of religious experience. The experience of power varies from people to people. The original experience of the power is more important than the reflection upon it. Finding the original experience of the power is the key aspect of religious study. Leeuw was criticized for devoting his effort to the 'discernment and presentation of timeless types, structures, and essences.' His intuitive method for arriving at his types and structures is far removed from the empirical procedures practiced by modern science and scholarship. Therefore Joachim Wach insisted upon the necessity of some personal religious predisposition in the inquirer, apart from scholarly procedures.

Clarifying further, Mircea Eliade views that a human becomes aware of the sacred because it manifests itself, shows itself, as something wholly different from the profane. For him, the history of religions – from the most primitive to the most highly developed – is constituted by a great number of hierophanies, by manifestations of sacred realities.[49] The sacred and the profane are considered as the two modes of being in the world, rather, 'two existential situations assumed by man in the course of his history.'[50]

Psychological Approach

In this approach the area of investigation will be primarily the mental states, motivations and attitudes found in religious contexts.[51] Regarding this, Erich Fromm writes, the "analysis of religion must not stop at uncovering those psychological processes within man which underlay his religious experience; it must proceed to discover the conditions which make for the development of authoritarian and humanistic character structures, respectively, from which

46 *Ibid.,* p. 74.

47 Waardenburg, *op. cit.,* p. 461.

48 *Ibid.,* p. 412.

49 Mircea Eliade, *op. cit.,* p. 11.

50 Jay J. Kim, "Hierophant and History," *Journal of the American Academy of Religion,* Vol. XL, No. 3, September, 1972, p. 334.

51 P. S. Daniel, David C. Scott *el at., op. cit.,* p. 24.

different kinds of religious experience stem."[52] Since the psychology of religion is more individualistic in nature[53] and it explores human's inner consciousness, it should never slacken in its search for scientific means of doing so.[54]

From the beginning, the psychology of religion follows the observation of religious individuals and the study of traditional content from the history of religion. In other words, "the methods employed by psychologists are those of experiment and observation.[55] Thus the psychological approach to the study of religions considers rituals seriously because "compulsive neurotic patients exhibit numerous forms of private rituals."[56] Again "Religious behavior springs from conscious and unconscious motivation."[57] But one need to be cautioned that religious emotions, sentiments, and dispositions are complex and no single feeling or meaning characterizes all varieties of religious experience.

William James viewed religious experience as involving intense human emotions and feelings directed toward some unseen order, reality, power "Out there" to which the personal stance is adjustment and surrender.[58] A person's religion involves both moods of contraction and moods of expansion of his being, i.e., sorrow and happiness. In order to explain the matter further, he divides the psyche (soul) into two types. One is the healthy soul and the other is the sick soul. Healthy soul is optimistic and the sick soul is pessimistic. In his words, "the completest religions would therefore seem to be those in which the pessimistic elements are best developed."[59] James is criticized for interpreting his cases apart from their socio-cultural context and hardly going into religious history or anthropology.

Sigmund Freud discovered the existence of the personal unconscious and he was able to analyze the major forces within this realm and their influence on consciousness.[60] The unconscious is essentially within us, which is bad, the repressed, that which is incompatible with the demands of our culture and of our higher self.[61] Freud's main insight was that all psychical activity is at first

52 Erich Fromm, *Psychoanalysis and Religion,* Fourth Printing, Yale University Press, New Haven, 1952, p. 52.

53 Paul E. Johnson, *Psychology of Religion,* A Bingdon – Cokesbury Press, New York, No. Date, p. 15.

54 Walter Houston Clark, *The Psychology of Religion, An Introduction to Religious Experience and Behavior,* Second Printing, The Macmillan Company, New York, 1959, p. 29.

55 L. W. Grensted, *The Psychology of Religion,* Oxford University Press, New York, 1952, p. 17.

56 Erich Fromm, *op. cit.,* p. 31.

57 Paul E. Johnson, *op. cit.,* p. 221.

58 William James, *The Varieties of Religious Experience,* Mentor Books, New York, 1958, p. 77.

59 William James, *op. cit.,* p. 139.

60 Waardenburg, *op. cit.,* p. 96.

61 Erich Fromm, *op. cit.,* p. 96.

unconscious.[62] For Freud, religion is the projection of infantile dependencies upon imagined superhuman beings. The dependencies, he called, collective neurosis. He also found that, there were many non-religious motivations, behind all religions aspirations. The infantile dependencies, or the obsessional childhood neurosis, Freud called, the "Oedupus complex." That is why he said religion is illusion. The process of detecting this neurosis is called psychoanalysis. For this Freud chose to interpret dreams. Dreams for him, are the outcome of the suppressed feelings, may be of childhood. It is commented that Oedipus complex may be a more complicated image in our context given that insofar as the father's influence actually has been complex and not simply authoritarian in our own times.[63]

For Carl Gustav Jung, the psyche consists of two parts: Consciousness and the unconscious. The unconscious is older than the consciousness. Again he made a distinction between the personal unconscious and the collective unconscious. Collective unconscious is responsible for religious behavior. The personal unconscious is an accumulation of contents that have been repressed during the life of the individual and is continuously being refined with new materials. The collective unconscious consists entirely of elements characteristic of the human species. The elements of the collective unconscious are called 'Archetypes.' The archetypes are common to all human beings. From the collective unconscious, the archetypes come into the regular course of life. This is religion.[64]

Issues in the Study of Religion

This section will analyze the issues involved in the different approaches to the study of religion. Besides, some of the general interests that concern all the students of religion shall be highlighted. They are such as, definition of religion, who should study religion, nature of data for the study of religion, whether value free judgment of data is possible, issues related to the use of language, specific problems in studying living religions, response threshold, observable and non-observable aspects of religion, hermeneutic and option for a pluralist perspective.

Issues Involved in the Different Approaches to the Study of Religion

With due acknowledgement to the contributions of Max Muller it can be said that, his initial endeavors did not suffer challenges, which are confronted by modern scholars. His openness to accept the significant value of data supplied by other

---

62 Hans Kung, *Freud and the Problem of God,* Translated by Edward Quinn, Yale University Press, New Haven, 1979, p. 20.

63 Leighton Mc Cutchen, "The Father Figure in Psychology and Religions," *Journal of the American Academy of Religion,* Vol. XL. No. 2, June 1972, p. 182.

64 Jolande Jacobi, *The Psychology of C. G. Jung,* 1973 edition, second printing, Yale University Press, 1974, pp. 9 & 35.

branches of learning for the science of religion is in fact applicable. However, a review of scholars approaching the study of religion seems pertinent here.

Anthropologists in their research mostly depended on empirical knowledge and did not penetrate into the real religious realm, which is beyond the empirical phenomena. They were suspected for missionary activities. Their main concentration was upon the primal religions, hence they failed to examine the challenges facing the living religions. They are also blamed for over generalization. Even though most of the primal religious data are in oral form, the anthropologist is handicapped by the lack of understanding in terms of language, at least at the stage of interpretation.

Sociologists have explained religion as a social phenomenon. The real issue is whether religion is responsible for the social institutions or the social structure is responsible for the emergence of religion, because many religious experiences of individuals cannot be explained away by the sociological criteria alone. Some sociologists also perceive some form of supernatural influence upon the religious behavior of the people.

The issue in historical approach is whether the historian of religion will be able to use the abundance of available data to trace the origin of religion. Since the data will be influenced by the values and personal experiences of particular scholars concerned, the historical approach should explore the possibilities of presenting objective facts, which are not hampered by other personal influences.

Phenomenologists are accused for their over dependence on the religious experience of the people. Their quest for various structures, to find out their similarity or differences, involves removing certain phenomena from the original setting. It can lead the scholar to recognize meanings different from what was really intended. Their enthusiasm to find out the essence of religion is a crucial issue because what seems to be the essence of one religion may not find a similar status in other religions.

Studying a few individual cases, psychologists conclude that, certain psychic experience is common to humanity. And this common human nature is responsible for the religious behavior of the people.

General Issues

These are however, issues that concern all the scholars of religions irrespective of their specific approaches. First of such an issue is the definition of religion. Definitions abound, but without any common agreement. The very word 'religion' has thus become a bone of contention because of its implicit Roman religiosity.[65] Also studies have proved that there are religions even without any supernatural element. Thus the question is whether religion has to be defined or not, before attempting to study. As an inadequate definition of religion can affect

65 De Graeve, *New Catholic Encyclopedia,* Vol. 12, p. 240.

the scholar in examining all the available data, an open-ended approach for the definition will be of greater significance for the scientific study of religion.

Secondly, although not now, earlier studies of religions had been dominated by western scholars, presumably with considerable missionary zeal. The main issue, irrespective of advantages and disadvantages, is whether the insider or the outsider should study religion. The convincing answer is honesty in study.[66]

Thirdly, the scholar of religion is over burdened with enormous amount of data because of the emergence of various disciplines and the rapid growth of science and communication. Whether any individual scholar will be able to handle and classify all the data or only one aspect of the data should be focused needs to be examined.

Fourthly, whether one achieves a pure value free objectivity, in the study of religion? Although difficult to say, a student of religion can exercise a more balanced attitude.

Fifthly, since all religious language, symbol, practice etc., are found meaningful only in their proper contexts, can modern language transmit their real content and implications? Textual study of religious traditions can be effective; but the availability of the texts[67] and language[68] scholarship are again a matter of concern.

Sixthly, unlike studying primal religious traditions, living religions pose new challenges.[69] Here, the problem is not data or origin, but how different religions interact and exist side by side in harmony by addressing common issues.[70] In other words, their 'meaning and function in society.'[71] Another issue connected to the study of living religions is "the response threshold," that is, the right of the present day devotee to advance a distinctive interpretation of his or her own tradition.[72]

Seventhly, the academic study of religion, now, is generally concerned with observable data-historical knowledge of the rituals, mythologies, religious communities, ideas, teachings, institutions, arts, and architecture. Beyond the observable there is a non-observable factor. A clear distinction between them

---

66 Henry H. Presler, "How Should we Study Other Religions?" *National Christian Council Review.* Vol. LXXXI, No. 5, May 1961, pp.193, 194.

67 Thomas L. Benson, *op. cit.,* p. 86.

68 Jarich Oosten, "Cultural Anthropological Approaches," *Contemporary Approaches to the Study of Religion in 2 Volumes,* edited by Frank Whaling, Vol. II: The Social Sciences, Mouton Publishers, Berlin, 1985, p. 252.

69 Ursula King, "The Debate about the Science of Religion," *Contemporary Approaches to the Study of Religion in 2 Volumes,* edited by Frank Whaling, Vol. I: The Humanities, Mouton Publishers, Berlin, 1984, p. 149.

70 Geoffrey Parrinder, *Comparative Religion,* George Allen & Unwin Ltd., London, 1962, p. 21.

71 Ursula King, "Phenomenology" edited by Frank Whaling, Vol. I, *op. cit.,* p. 43.

72 Michael Pye, *Comparative Religion An Introduction Through Source Materials,* David and Charles, Newton Abbot, 1972, p. 13.

can resolve many misunderstandings.[73] And "discovering the character of this transcendent focus comprises an important part of the study of a religion."[74]

Eighthly, the bulk of religious data warrants an appropriate hermeneutical principle as religion influences human life at all levels. Otherwise it is impossible to systematically order and account for the variety of religious data.[75]

Ninthly, contrary to the original intention, the increasing connection between religion and theology, and other disciplines pose the challenging question, can the study of religion be called as an area rather than a discipline. In other words, whether a multidisciplinary approach is possible. The answer seems to be affirmative.[76]

Implications for the Indian Context

A scientific study of religion offers many valuable insights to the Indian context. First, it reveals that religion is as old as human history.[77] Secondly, it helps furthering 'free sharing among religions' i.e., interaction among them. Thirdly, it also postulates that 'all our faiths have some value' and the superiority claims of religions becomes untenable[78] and suspicious[79] because in one sense every religion is a true religion in its context.[80] Fourthly, the Indian context requires special approach, not merely western, as she houses major living religions of the world.[81] More over now the nonwestern scholar's study and reflection of their own religion is amply available.[82] There is a clear distinction between the Eastern and Western contexts. In India religion is defined as a way of life.[83] And it is never separated

73 Thomas A. Idinopulos, "The Difficulties of Understanding Religion," *What is Religion? Origins, Definitions & Explanations,* edited by Thomas A. Idinopulos & Brain C. Wilson, Brill, 1998, p. 27.

74 Eric J. Lott, "Approaching Religious Traditions," *Religions Traditions of India,* Indian Theological Library, 1988, p. 3.

75 Ursula King, *op. cit.,* p. 152.

76 Eric J. Lott, *Tradition, Interpretation, Theology Religion, and the Study of Religion,* Moutan de Gruyter, 1988, p. 156.

77 F. Max Muller, *Theosophy or Psychological Religion, Collected Works of F. Max Muller,* Asian Educational Service, New Delhi, Reprinted 1978, pp. 18-37.

78 S. Radhakrishnan, *East and West in Religion,* George Allen & Unwin Ltd., London, 1933, p. 26.

79 S. Radhakrishnan, *Religion and Society,* George Allen & Unwin Ltd., London, 1947, p. 52.

80 F. Max Muller, *Introduction to the Science of Religions,* New Edition, London, 1882, p. 190.

81 Eric J. Lott, "The Science of Religion in an Indian Theological Context," *Bangalore Theological Forum,* Vol. XIII, No. 4, Oct-Dec., 1985, p. 1.

82 Frank Whaling, "The Study of Religions in a Global Context," *Contemporary Approaches to the Study of Religion in 2 Volumes,* edited by Frank Whaling, Volume I: The Humanities, Mouton Publishers, Berlin, 1984, p. 392.

83 S. Radhakrishnan, *The Hindu of Life,* Third Indian Reprint, Blackie & Son Publishers Pvt. Ltd., Blackie House, Bombay, 1979, p. 55.

from daily life. Fifthly, in the context of growing threats to life, religion has a wider and significant role to bring people together and engage them in common concerns.[84]

Sixthly, the scientific study of religion reveals the fundamental, "Unity of Religion."[85] It is already present in religion but we need to realize it.[86] It helps to bring home the idea that religion was one and manifold forms are its existence in diverse cultural contexts. Seventhly, studying religion means studying life.[87] The problem of religion would become vastly complicated if it were to be discretely separated from the problem of people because it has neither essence nor existence nor any kind of being whatsoever apart from people.[88] Focus upon "Life" should become thus the key to the understanding of religious phenomena in India.[89]

Eighthly, the two fundamental aspects for the scientific study of religions from an Indian perspective are "Unity of Religion" and concern for "Life." It is time we shift from the teaching of religion to the study of religion.[90]

Ninthly, there is no distinction between religion and philosophy in India. Thus Dr. S. Radhakrishnan approached religion from the viewpoint of philosophy, contrary to the West.[91] Although the philosophy of religion verifies religious data systematically and logically, it is feared that this approach might become a mere intellectual exercise.[92]

Tenthly, against the original wishes now there is a greater possibility for creative integration between theology and the study of religion.[93] This possibility is promising,[94] hence Indian theology cannot ignore the rich and variety of religious resources.

---

84 S. Radhakrishnan, *Religion & Society, op. cit.,* p. 18.

85 L. W. Grensted, *The Psychology of Religion,* Oxford University Press, New York, 1952, p. 109.

86 Gustan Mensching, *Structures and Patterns of Religion,* Translated by F. Klimkeit and V. Srinivasa Sarma, Motilal Banarsidass, Delhi, 1976, pp. 319, 320.

87 L. W. Grensted, *op. cit.,* p. 15.

88 J. G. Arapura, *Religions as Anxiety and Tranquility, An Essay in Comparative Phenomenology of the Spirit,* Mouton & Co., Netherlands, 1972, p. 39.

89 K. P. Aleaz, *Harmony of Religions: The Relevance of Swami Vivekananda,* Punthipustak, Calcutta, 1993, p. 52.

90 Wilfred Cantwell Smith, "The Study of Religion and the Study of the Bible," *Journal of the American Academy of Religion,* Vol. XXXIX, No. 2, June, 1971, p. 131.

91 Frank Whaling, Vol. I., *op. cit.,* p. 403.

92 Eric J. Lott, "Approaching Religious Tradition," *Religious Traditions of India,* Indian Theological Library, 1988, p. 29.

93 S. Israel, "An Integral Approach to the Study of Religion: Insights from an Indian Christian Perspective," *Bangalore Theological Forum,* Vol. XIX, No. 2, April-June, 1987, p. 104.

94 Eric J. Lott, "The Science of Religion in an Indian Theological Context," *Bangalore Theological Forum,* Vol. XVII, No. 4, October-December, 1985, p. 3.

Conclusion

Max Muller founded the "Science of Religion." Its main task is to study religion scientifically. The scientific study of religion concentrated on the origin of religion. For this the comparative and historical perspectives were applied. The early anthropological theories saw the origin of religion in animism, animatism, manism, supreme beings, magic etc. The anthropologists of religion used a rigorous empirical method, while the sociologists of religion interpreted religion as a social phenomena. The phenomenological perspective found the essence of religion in some 'sacred focus.' And the psychological perspective located religion in human psyche.

The science of religion has to tackle some crucial issues. One of them is whether religion should be defined at all. Whether the insider or the outsider should study religion is another issue. The ever-growing quantity of data raises serious concern to the scholars of religion. The study of living religions faces new issues, which were never a problem to the scholars of primal religions. To avoid all seeming hardships in the study of religion a multi-methodic approach is convincing.

The scientific study of religion offers valuable insights, which are relevant to the specific Indian context. A challenging Indian perspective for the scientific study of religion can be formulated on the basis of these insights. Any relevant perspective for the scientific study of religion should take "Life" as the hermeneutical principle.

It has its positive aspects too. The growing communal conflicts in India can be lessened, if religions are studied scientifically and their findings are made known to their adherents. It will be promising to implement the 'Science of religion' in the regular college curriculum. The Indian pluralistic context demands that every citizen is aware of the findings of the "Science of Religion."

4

A Religio-theo-dialogical Approach to the Science of Religion

Introduction

The hyphenated title of the paper implicitly suggests that the gap between different disciplines, particularly religion and theology can be filled in or at least reduced to a minimum if researches can be pursued keeping in mind the necessity of dialogical existence. The multidisciplinary setting of our seminars, without ignoring our own disciplines, obviously calls for researches leading to this end. I am also compelled to think that the realms of spirited research are still very vast and inspiring. As a student of religion, I have started this exercise beginning from the openness created by the science of religion. As sufficient amount of concentration is dedicated to the possibilities of explaining the interconnectedness between religion and theology, our specific focus to inspire or provoke serious research will continue and the final discussion revolves around the dialogical approach to further the study of the science of religion.

I. Historical Overview

The Reformation opened up a space for critical biblical and theological considerations, followed by the Enlightenment of the 18th century, with its stress on reason and tolerance, leading to an initial openness toward other religious traditions than the Western one.' Romanticism (feeling and nature) in the beginning of the19th century raised questions about the origin and the psychological nature of religion. It led to an openness to the dimension of religious experience and to the reality of experience in general.

With a fascination for the past, there emerged openness to the idea of a common history of humankind, including its religions. There was also openness towards the plurality of cultures and religions. While some considered plurality as a problem, many others considered as enrichment. These led to understand the role of religion in the political, social, and economic life of society in a new way.

Added to this were the technological, social and political transformations of the 19th century Europe that led in the first place, to 'intense spiritual searches' about the nature and destiny of the universe and the human race. There was in some quarters a feeling that Oriental religions had something to say about the nature and destiny of man' [sic]. Thus 'scholarly activity developed to study the distinctive features and facts of foreign cultures and religions.'[1]

There were 'private initiatives' in this direction. Besides, 'amateur or volunteer researchers' worked on materials from foreign or ancient religions. They did not engage in research but read religious texts in translation and followed up what travelers and literary men[sic], missionaries and preachers, explorers and scholar had to tell about religions other than Christianity.' There was a 'longing for the sake of truth and to correct or unmask current wrong opinions and prejudices.'[2]

The 'idealists,' among the scholars, 'had a fundamentally positive appreciation of religion and they held certain ideas about its historical development and its crucial role in society and culture.' There were other scholars who were suspicious of religion as a phenomenon and denied the claims to truth. They were keen to discover the "real" factors operative behind religious behavior and representations such as the impersonal social, political or psychological forces, or the willful manipulation of religions by self-interested political and religious factions and their leaders.' The third group of scholars avoided constructs and did not want to say more than what the results of empirical factual research allowed them to say. In the study of humanities, they kept to themselves the study f philology, textual research and history, in the social sciences to sociological and anthropological description. Instead of spiritualizing or demonizing religion, they restricted themselves to working on verifiable facts and checking hypotheses.[3]

Besides, 'it was the discovery and decipherment of ancient texts that opened a field of research on as yet largely unknown religions.' Thus the founding fathers of the scientific study of religions, concentrated on Mythology and folklore (lower mythology) with the support of philology, and comparative and historical methods. Unlike others, the founding fathers, 'boldly rook religion as their focus of research.'[4] Later the study took support from many other disciplines.

1 Jacques Waardenburg, *Classical Approaches to the Study of Religion* (New York. Berlin: Walter de Gruyter, 1999), vii.

2 Jacques Waardenburg, viii.

3 Jacques Waardenburg, viii-ix.

4 Jacques Waardenburg, viii.

The methods/approaches that followed trod on "more rigorous empirical forms of description' with 'objectivity perhaps as an 'explicit aim,' called hard approaches. They 'did not accept the 'integral science of religion,'[5] which included – sociology, anthropology, psychology. Philosophy, because of its analytical nature, falls in this category. However there is a great deal of convergence and interdependence among these sciences. The social structuring, cultural forms and mental processes became significant factors in deciphering the *hidden* dynamics of religious life.[6] Of course, most of these methods were influenced by the idea of evolution. While this is so, the approaches that looked for a systematic 'science of religion' and gave a more significant role to the 'subjectivity of the participants'[7] fall under the soft method - Phenomenological, comparative and dialogical.

II. Consensus on Various Approaches

A 'general consensus,' among the scholars of religions was that religious phenomena are diverse and wide-ranging that 'no *single* approach is competent to deal exhaustively with everything that constitutes religion without recourse at all to other disciplines or to other forms of approach.' Similarly, religious phenomena 'typically manifest in conjunction with and as part of the historical and human cultural process, in socially institutionalized contexts, or along with psychologically identifiable mental states and patterns of human behavior.' This makes it inevitable and only proper that the dynamics of religion should be investigated from the perspective of the disciplines appropriate to these dimensions of human existence.[8]

III. Outcomes

For the first time 'religion' was considered as a subject of empirical inquiry and 'a human reality' that can be investigated. What was held so far as 'irrational' was now open to rational research. It shows human's very capacity to objectify her/his involvements, social and psychological as well as religious. This objectifying process may start with the category of '**the others**.' Further, no intelligent person could study other people, their culture and religion, without establishing at the same time a '**distance**' also from himself, his past, his surroundings, and his involvements up to now.[9]

Against the 'supernatural origin or essence of religion an appeal was made to reason and experience as sole criteria of truth.' Religious phenomena were 'seen

5 Eric J. Lott, *Vision, Tradition, Interpretation: Theology, Religion and the Study of Religion* (Berlin. New York. Amsterdam: Mouton de Gruyter,1988), 155.

6 Eric J. Lott, *Vision, Tradition, Interpretation: Theology, Religion and the Study of Religion*, 161.

7 Eric J. Lott, *Vision, Tradition, Interpretation: Theology, Religion and the Study of Religion*, 155.

8 Eric J. Lott, *Vision, Tradition, Interpretation: Theology, Religion and the Study of Religion*, 155-156.

9 Jacques Waardenburg, 3.

as natural expressions of human, of which an inventory and further examination would be possible.' The historical and literary critical study of the Bible, the relationship between the Bible and its environment, the historical reality of the sacred history, all amounted to a radical reinterpretation of traditional religion, with 'historical truth' as a new criterion.

Right across different disciplines/methods were attempted soon 'explaining,' the verifiable relationships among religious phenomena. Others strived to 'understanding,' aimed at the meaning of the phenomena studied. Yet others moved in the direction of 'interpretation,' paving a methodological space for philosophy and theological inspiration.[10]

Today, there is a need to develop techniques, methods, questions, and perspectives that are applicable to oral cultures and to the study of all religious cultures. Frank Whaling argues that 'the position of theology is a pivotal one within any discussion of the study and teaching of religion.' He further claims that both religious studies and theology are complementary.[11]

However, critics hold, what has thrived is 'the religious study of religion;' it means the scholar studies her or his own religion or a religion other than his or her own primarily for the purpose or purposes stipulated by the religion studied rather than the purpose or purposes stipulated by the academy.[12] Thus the study 'abandons its own distinctiveness.' To put the matter in a different way, today "the academic study of religion, rather than arising as a field in its own right, has taken inspired and productive paths."[13]

IV. Differences between Religion and Theology

Religious studies cover, in principle, all the religious traditions of the world. As being inherently multi-religious, it uses different approaches and methods. Again it places equal emphasis upon elements in religion, such as social practice, ritual, aesthetics, spirituality, myth, symbol, ethics and so on. It has no particular predilection for doctrines or concepts. The scope is generally wider, more comprehensive, and less focused than theology. But 'the focus is more on the believer and his or her experience or faith rather than on any object of faith.'[14]

It is part of the task of religious studies to be aware of, and to understand, the separate theologies of different religions. The scholar of religion 'will attempt to understand rather than to adopt the confessional stance of the particular tradition concerned.' An important part of the work of religious studies is 'the search for

10 Jacques Waardenburg, 76-77.

11 Frank Whaling, "Theological Approaches," in *Approaches to the Study of Religion*, edited by Peter Connolly (London: The Continuum International Publishing Group, 1999), 227.

12 Sam Gill, "Settled Issues and Neglected Questions in the Study of Religion," *Oxford Journals* (Winter 1994): 966, http://www.jstor.org/stable/1465226, (4 April 2018).

13 Sam Gill, 967.

14 Frank Whaling, "Theological Approaches," in *Approaches to the Study of Religion*, 230.

words and terms to conceptualize transcendence in a general rather than in a particular sense.'[15]

As such, 'Theology is essentially a constructive activity, not a descriptive or expository one.'[16] It is also an 'intellectual activity' with its focus on the concept of "God."[17] Theology as a 'human work' is founded upon and interprets human historical events and experiences. It utilizes humanly created and shaped terms and concepts. Our theological work therefore has to be understood entirely in terms of what we can do on the basis of what is available to us.[18]

Theology as 'faith-articulation' is grounded and committed to a particular sacred tradition 'with its rituals, symbols, myths, scriptures, spiritual discipline, community life and of course its doctrines. Thus 'the primary task of any theology is the *communication of meaning* to those within the tradition.'[19] In that sense, "Christian theology would no longer be the totality of theology but one genus among many others."[20]

In this context, Frank Whaling writes, "the notion of theology in other religious traditions has also tended to emphasize the conceptual element in religion as being more central than matters to do with practice, spirituality or behavior."[21] Therefore, Wilfred Cantwell Smith appeals that 'our conceptualizing, and understanding of each other's concepts, be anchored in history, even for history-transcending and self-transcending concepts such as 'God.' For, the understanding that we seek (theology) 'is not simply of the history of religion, but of that to which the history of religion has at its best been a response.'[22]

Theology 'was not the prerogative of a particular community, it was part of a general education.'[23] In fact, "other cultures have developed in different ways, and the traditions of intellectual reflection have likewise moved down quite different paths."[24] We cannot stop with these differences. We need to move forward honestly acknowledging the differences and searching for ways of integrating both religion and theology.

15 Frank Whaling, "Theological Approaches," in *Approaches to the Study of Religion*, 255.

16 Gordon D. Kaufman, *An Essay on Theological Method*, 41.

17 Gordon D. Kaufman, *An Essay on Theological Method*, 7.

18 Gordon D. Kaufman, *An Essay on Theological Method*, 3.

19 Eric J. Lott, *Vision, Tradition, Interpretation: Theology, Religion and the Study of Religion*, 11.

20 Frank Whaling, "Theological Approaches," in *Approaches to the Study of Religion*, 228.

21 Frank Whaling, "Theological Approaches," in *Approaches to the Study of Religion*, 230.

22 Wilfred Cantwell Smith, *Towards a World Theology* (London: Macmillan, 1989),186.

23 Frank Whaling, "Theological Approaches," in *Approaches to the Study of Religion*, 227.

24 Gordon D. Kaufman, *An Essay on Theological Method*, 7.

V. Relationship between Theology and Religious Studies

Although the boundaries and interests of theology and religious studies are separate, 'the two enterprises intertwine.'[25] Their interrelations, even though complex, do need to be reconsidered.[26] This will fill the gap between the 'oppositional binaries of "religion"- "dogmatic" versus "comparative," "normative" versus "descriptive," and of course "theological" versus "scientific."[27]

In this context, Gordon D. Kaufman notes that, 'theologians should pay close attention to the critical study of religion.' It should be of importance and aid to the theologian and this 'may have profound effects on the way she does theology as well as on her theological conclusions.'[28]

Theology should therefore welcome the contribution of religious studies as necessary to *its own self-understanding* and to the effectiveness of its *self-communication*. As theology cannot function reflectively and contextually in an isolated state of independence from other religious traditions, it cannot be ignorant of the findings of religious studies. In the words of Eric J. Lott, "theology, then, is dependent upon religious studies for greater understanding of other traditions, understanding of the manifold dimensions of their life."[29]

If a theologian of a tradition seeks to respond appropriately to other faiths, she needs to acquire at least a sufficiently authentic understanding of those traditions to ensure a genuine reflective interaction between the visionary centre of the one and the visionary centre of others as expressed in their varied phenomena.[30]

Of late, there has been a deliberate modifying of the theological task from *within* a theological tradition, but 'there has in general *not* been the same attempt to correlate theology with the scientific or systematic study of other religious traditions.' The caution is that there is a need to recognize 'the extent to which there must also be *convergence* if each is to function in ways most appropriate to its own interest.'[31]

VI. Theological Approach

Eric J. Lott writes, "any kind of *normative* as against the purely descriptive approach intended by some sciences of religion is sometimes called a 'theological'

---

25 Frank Whaling, "Theological Approaches," in *Approaches to the Study of Religion*, 236.

26 Eric J. Lott, *Vision, Tradition, Interpretation: Theology, Religion and the Study of Religion*, 220.

27 Reid B. Locklin and Hugh Nicholson, "The Return of Comparative Theology," *Oxford Journals* 78/2 (June 2010): 502, http://www.jstor.org/stable/40666528, (4 April 2018).

28 Joshua Braley, "A Critique of Gordon Kaufman's Theological Method, with Special Reference to His Theory of Religion," *The University of Chicago Press Journal* 88/1 (January 2008): 30-33, http://www.jstor.org/stable/10.1086/522275, (4 April 2018).

29 Eric J. Lott, *Vision, Tradition, Interpretation: Theology, Religion and the Study of Religion*, 233.

30 Eric J. Lott, *Vision, Tradition, Interpretation: Theology, Religion and the Study of Religion*, 231.

31 Eric J. Lott, *Vision, Tradition, Interpretation: Theology, Religion and the Study of Religion*, 5-6.

approach."[32] It is also perceived that a theological approach may have to begin with the fact of the experience of the Transcendent.[33]

As there are 'a number of theological differences *within* religious traditions,' the study of religion should show interest 'in exploring the theologies of different religions in order to understand their core concepts, the different types of theology within each tradition, and the different theological view points within each tradition.[34]

If we are to understand a religious tradition, or a number of religions, then 'the ways in which people of that tradition have expressed *their* understanding of the meaning of their religion is essential.'[35] Further, 'a scientific study of religion needs to give due prominence to the inclusive vision of the tradition's meaning-articulators.' Then "clearly there are many different kinds of interaction possible between Theology and Religions."[36]

Part of the theological approach to the study of religion is to make available to scholars a clear accurate account of the conceptual frameworks of different traditions, bearing in mind that the role and purpose of concepts and of theology differ from tradition to tradition.[37]

Now we shall explore, a few among the many, the ever available dynamic possibilities of expanding the horizons of research in relation to religion from other branches of study, specifically from theology and biblical studies.

1. Reality/Transcendence

In every religious tradition, there is a 'Sacred Focus' that provides the integrating centre to all other dimensions of religious life. Without this basic element there can not be a living religion.[38] It can be called as the 'transcendent Focus, to which all religious activity, ultimately, is oriented, whether seen as personal or impersonal.' For example, "it is amazing that within the same general tradition, Vedanta ...there are different perceptions of the one Transcendent that are so strikingly different."[39]

---

32 Eric J. Lott, *Vision, Tradition, Interpretation: Theology, Religion and the Study of Religion*, 6.

33 Paramananda Divarkar, "Towards an Objective Study of Religion: A Theological Approach," in *Approaches to the Study of Religion*, edited by Harbans Singh (Patiala: Punjabi University, 1999), 61.

34 Frank Whaling, "Theological Approaches," in *Approaches to the Study of Religion*, 243.

35 Eric J. Lott, *Vision, Tradition, Interpretation: Theology, Religion and the Study of Religion*, 10.

36 Eric J. Lott, *Vision, Tradition, Interpretation: Theology, Religion and the Study of Religion*, 14.

37 Frank Whaling, "Theological Approaches," in *Approaches to the Study of Religion*, 237.

38 Paramananda Divarkar, "Towards an Objective Study of Religion: A Theological Approach," in *Approaches to the Study of Religion*, edited by Harbans Singh (Patiala: Punjabi University, 1999), 60.

39 Eric J. Lott, *Vision, Tradition, Interpretation: Theology, Religion and the Study of Religion* (Berlin. New York. Amsterdam: Mouton de Gruyter,1988), 42.

The other paradox is that the more objective we try to be in our assessment of reality the more subjective we become, for we try to be critical and in doing so we impose our criteria, our categories, on reality instead of simply and unquestioningly accepting the reality as it is.[40] Therefore, there is always an enormous scope for constantly attempting to explore newer and relevant understandings of the transcendent focus.

2. God

The other concept that has a huge potential for continuing research from different disciplines is God. Theology (*theos-logos*) is "words" or "speech" about God – "God-talk". All other terms of the theological vocabulary in one way or another qualify, explain or interpret what is meant by "God," or indicate ways in which God is related to or involved in human experience and the human world.

The *concept* of God too 'is shaped and affected by many considerations and must be qualified, defined and redefined in very careful and complex ways if it is to be properly constructed.' It is the most complex and difficult of all concepts, in some ways dependent on and conditioned by all others. God cannot be dealt with independently or in isolation from the rest of the theological vocabulary. It gains its meaning precisely through its connections with other terms and ultimately thus with the whole of human experience.

The actual human speech about God, is rather talk about life and the world, about our deepest problems, about catastrophe and triumph, about human misery and human glory. It is the 'ultimate point of orientation to which all else must be referred.'[41] As the concept of God is in a way idealization of the human, it is possible for humanity to stretch and grow in new directions.[42]

The past makes manifest that God participates in human life, in its grandeur and its dismay. Yet He is available to us not in the past, but today. In order to know Him and His dealings with humankind, our knowledge of Him cannot be that of history's knowing, or even way of knowing, but must be our own.[43] This challenge throws open, never ending possibilities of research and relevant reconstruction, though critical of the very challenges themselves.

3. God's Revelation

The construct, 'revelation of God,' has been created and developed in and through human processes of reflection on life and interpretation of experience. 'Some persons at certain times and places found it useful and meaningful and perhaps even necessary to speak of "God's revelation," in order to make sense of the life and history which they were undergoing.' These terms and concepts

40 Paramananda Divarkar, 60.

41 Gordon D. Kaufman, *An Essay on Theological Method*, 9-13.

42 Gordon D. Kaufman, *An Essay on Theological Method*, 53.

43 Wilfred Cantwell Smith, *Towards a World Theology*, 194.

were developed and employed within the human sphere and thus 'we have them available now for our use.'

The question is about how and why such concepts were created and shaped in the first place, and how they can be sustained and reconstructed now.[44] Revelation is presented in the experiences of certain persons. The appeal to revelation itself 'is in effect an appeal to certain experiences.' Ninian Smart forcefully says, "if religious experience is our ground of faith, then let us not be so narrow as to consider only the experiences of *our* tradition."[45] It is for the new researchers to make God's revelation unique to each tradition and at the same time not to ignore other revelations, and their contributions to our enrichment.

4. Religious Experience

The foundations of theological language are to be found in "religious experience.' To understand a theological language, then, we must locate and describe that particular domain of human experience. 'There is no such thing as a raw pre-linguistic experience of "transcendence." Each "experience" is shaped, delimited and informed by the linguistic symbols which also name it. Without those symbols, these "experiences" would not be available to us at all.[46] There was always an *Experience-reflection-communication.* We *interpret* our experience. We clothe our intuitions in the vestments of one tradition, sometime quite unconsciously.[47] We may be 'committed' to our tradition, but we should be as understanding as possible regarding other faiths, and not make commitment an excuse for prejudice.[48]

Given the different linguistic traditions and histories, reflection on experience and life in other cultures, which have been shaped by other linguistic developments and traditions, use different categories and focuses on different emphases and values. And experience itself in those other cultures, 'is of a quite different sort, with different qualities, values, emphases, meanings.'

Gordon D. Kaufman is of the view that, 'the raw pre-conceptual and pre-linguistic ground of religious experience is simply not available to us for direct exploration, description or interpretation.'[49] Religious studies have got the responsibility of continuously providing data to attempt relevant constructs that will make different departments of studies more accommodative to new ways of understanding religious experience.

44 Gordon D. Kaufman, *An Essay on Theological Method*, 2.

45 Ninian Smart, *World Religions: A Dialogue* (Baltimore. Maryland: Penguin Books, 1960), 14.

46 Gordon D. Kaufman, *An Essay on Theological Method*, 4-5.

47 Ninian Smart, *World Religions: A Dialogue*, 14.

48 Ninian Smart, *World Religions: A Dialogue*, 16.

49 Gordon D. Kaufman, *An Essay on Theological Method*, 7-8.

5. Culture-Tradition-Language

Kaufman argues, 'to suppose that theology is essentially a work of the church and that therefore the theologian can or must accept without question the "faith" of the church' is simple-minded view.' Because, the church's life is imbedded within the society and culture in which it is found. More so the entire vocabulary of the church consists of ordinary words from the everyday language of the people. Their meaning is tied to the life of the culture as a whole and can be grasped only in connection with that broad cultural base and experience.[50]

In reality, religious tradition and language provide the actual foundations of theology. 'All special and technical meanings are variations or developments of the ordinary language building upon it, refining it, transforming it.' It is not restricted either to the language and tradition of a particular community or to the peculiar experience of unusual individuals. Having studied myths, Max Muller said, :that the names of the divinities basically are due to a 'disease of language' which substitutes *numina* for *nomina*, i.e., inflating ordinary names to religious powers or poetic to religious language."[51]

In this setting it is interesting to note that "theology has come to realize that it is not hermetically sealed and that it is itself rendered intelligible by the cultural narratives in which it is embedded. Religious studies, meanwhile, has come to realize that the ideal of the neutral observer is illusory and that the discipline is itself underpinned by certain presuppositions that are themselves more theological than was previously thought."[52]

It is incumbent upon the science of religion to be always cautious about the complexity of the web of issues related to explaining the religious phenomena buried in uncritically accepted concepts. Closely distilled, not purely as it is not possible, research findings can lead towards a more accommodative and dialogical consideration from different branches of study.

6. Faith vs Belief

Harvey Cox distinguishes between faith and belief and writes, 'faith is about deep-seated confidence' and belief on the other hand, is more like an opinion. Beliefs are then more propositional than existential. 'We can *believe* something to be true without it making much difference to us, but we place our *faith* only in something that is vital for the way we live.' He goes on to argue that 'Creeds are clusters of beliefs.' But the history of Christianity is not a history of creeds. It is the story of a people of faith who sometimes cobbled together creeds out of beliefs. It is also the history of equally faithful people who questioned, altered, and discarded those

50 Gordon D. Kaufman, *An Essay on Theological Method*, 3.

51 Jacques Waardenburg, 13.

52 Gavin Hyman, "The Study of Religion and the Return of Theology," *Oxford Journals 72*/1 (March, 2004): 215, http://www.jstor.org/stable/40005883 (4 April 2018).

same creeds. In order to stress the need for faith he demarcates three different periods in the history of Christianity.

He calls the first period of Christianity as "Age[53] of Faith" which began with Jesus and his immediate disciples. It was the time of 'explosive growth and brutal persecution,' and sharing in the living Spirit of Christ with each other. Faith meant hope and assurance in the dawning of a new era of freedom, healing, and compassion that Jesus had demonstrated. To be a Christian meant to live in his Spirit, embrace his hope, and to follow him in the work that he had begun.

The second period is "Age of Belief." Its seeds appeared within a few decades of the birth of Christianity when church leaders began formulating orientation programs for new recruits who had not known Jesus or his disciples personally. Emphasis on belief began to grow, replacing faith *in* Jesus with tenets *about* him.

In the third period, from the third century, ecclesial specialists distilled the various teaching manuals into lists of beliefs. These varied widely from place to place and as the fourth century began there was still no single creed. A wide range of different theologies thrived. At the time of Emperor Constantine he and not the pope was the real head of the church. An energetic movement of faith became a body of required beliefs. It was the beginning 'for every succeeding Christian fundamentalism for centuries to come.' 'Heresy became treason, and treason became heresy.'[54]

The task of all our research work is to ensure the priority of faith to the beliefs. In other words, our calling for research is to initiate a gentle movement from belief to faith.

7. Faith a Universal Category

Wilfred Cantwell Smith writes, a religious person everywhere, has had his or her relationship to God formed primarily by a participation in the on-going historical movement of one or another of the world's religious communities. This relationship is called 'faith.'[55] To understand it better one may consider calling it 'faith in its Christian form,' rather than 'Christian faith.'[56]

Any person's faith is what it is; in interaction with the particular religious context in which that person actually lives. The context during any given century is different from that during any other. It is the same with the religious contexts. However, in the words of Wilfred Cantwell Smith, "it is an observable fact that what happens in the historical process of one religious tradition can be in significant part a function of what happens in the historical process of another."[57]

53 Harvey Cox, *The Future of Faith* (New York. Harper One, 2009), 4.

54 Harvey Cox, *The Future of Faith*, 3-6.

55 Wilfred Cantwell Smith, *Towards a World Theology*, 170.

56 Wilfred Cantwell Smith, *Towards a World Theology*, 114.

57 Wilfred Cantwell Smith, *Towards a World Theology*, 37-38.

For Smith, 'faith and transcendence are universal theological categories.'[58] According to Harvey Cox, faith starts with awe/mystery. Faith is not the mystery but the response to it. And this response 'comes in an infinite variety of forms.'[59] All religions and cultures are responses to the same fundamental mystery, but each perceive and respond in its own way. Cox writes "the various world religions constitute complex codifications of these responses, and they differ from each other in significant respects. This is what makes the study of comparative religion so absorbing. If all religions really *were* essentially the same, it would soon become unbearably boring."[60]

Frank Whaling argues that, in the process of searching for global categories like "global theology of religion," 'particular theologies will not disappear' because 'theology is not solely concerned with doctrines but also with conceptual formulation of other matters, such as ethics.'[61] That is why Wilfred Cantwell Smith writes, "the task of theology is to make rationally intelligible the meaning of human life in faith, and of the world in which that faith is lived."[62]

Faith, in all cultures, is a link between the mundane and the transcendent. Faith creates the interaction between these two poles of human existence. Therefore faith is a universal characteristic of humanity and the fundamental quality of the religious life. Therefore, 'this term 'faith' can supersede 'religion' as the focal category for religious study.'[63] Researching for such categories is essential where plurality is challenged by singularity of ideology/religion.

8. Age of the Spirit

Harvey Cox argues that, we are now in the "Age of the Spirit." Many prefer "Spirit" as their preferred way of speaking of the divine. People who want to distance themselves from the institutional or doctrinal demarcations of conventional religion now refer to themselves as "spiritual" rather than "Religious."[64]

Further, religions are becoming less regional, and less hierarchical. Lay leadership and initiative flourish in all of them. In addition many are becoming less dogmatic and more practical. Religious people today are more interested in ethical guidelines and spiritual disciplines than in doctrines. They are also becoming less patriarchal.

Countries where clerical leadership clings to the older model, churches are empty but where creeds and hierarchies have been set aside to make way of the

58 Wilfred Cantwell Smith, *Towards a World Theology*, 128.

59 Harvey Cox, *The Future of Faith*, 35.

60 Harvey Cox, *The Future of Faith*, 38.

61 Frank Whaling, "Theological Approaches," in *Approaches to the Study of Religion*, 262-268.

62 Wilfred Cantwell Smith, *Towards a World Theology*, 128.

63 Eric J. Lott, *Vision, Tradition, Interpretation: Theology, Religion and the Study of Religion*, 193.

64 Harvey Cox, *The Future of Faith*, 8-10.

Spirit, one senses life and energy.[65] He thus concludes that "all the signs suggest we are poised to enter a new Age of the Spirit and that the future will be a future of faith."[66]

His prophetic commitment provides ample directions to the ever changing dynamics of research orientation, taking into account the signs of the times.

9. Unity of Humankind's Religious History

Wilfred Cantwell Smith discusses 'unity or coherence of humankind's religious history.' For him, 'at one level, this unity is a matter of empirical observation and an historical fact.' 'At another level, it is a matter of theological truth.' He argues further that these two realities exist and there is a 'link between them.'

As there is the unity of humankind and the unity of God there is 'unity of humankind's religious history.' This is not to say that there is unity among 'the religions of the world.' In fact there is no unity even within one so-called 'religion.' The unity that is discussed is not of religion, which is varied, but of 'religious history.' Truth has an historical dimension. Ultimate truth or God is actively involved in the historical arena. The history of religion is the history of men and women's religious life, and especially of their faith. This is 'intrinsically the locus of the mundane and the transcendent, unbifurcated.'[67] Therefore there is no reason to be independent of other religions and theological categories. This is a valid ground to religious studies and theologies to move towards a dialogical approach.

VII. Dialogical Approach

Today, "diverse religious traditions, with their distinct views of reality, and their distinct life-values, have been increasingly brought into inter-penetrative social situations."[68] In the words of Harvey Cox, there is 'the unanticipated resurgence of religion in both public and private life around the globe,' 'fundamentalism is dying' and there is 'a profound change in the elemental nature of religiousness.'[69]

Different religious communities have developed languages peculiar to themselves. The meaning of that language will not be immediately apparent to those who approach it from outside. 'It has to be learnt.' Recognition of this characteristic of religious language is important to any assessment of the practical possibility of inter-religious dialogue.[70]

---

65 Harvey Cox, *The Future of Faith*, 196.

66 Harvey Cox, *The Future of Faith*, 224.

67 Wilfred Cantwell Smith, *Towards a World Theology*, 3.

68 Eric J. Lott, *Vision, Tradition, Interpretation: Theology, Religion and the Study of Religion*, 229.

69 Harvey Cox, *The Future of Faith*, 1-2.

70 Maurice Wiles, *Christian Theology and Inter-religious Dialogue* (London: SCM Press, 1992), 34-37.

'All our language about God is imagistic or symbolic.' 'God is absolute, not the assertions that we make about him.' As per apophatic tradition, 'our firmest affirmations constitute a denial that God shares our human limitations.' And 'the continuation of that emphasis is vital to inter-religious dialogue.'[71]

History is always written by the winners, who also destroy any counterevidence. In terms of canon or heretical writings, we need to bring the same degree of suspicion and expectation we bring to any other primal source. We must know where it came from and how others have struggled to interpret it.[72]

If truth is the goal of religions and not the present possession of every religion, then what is called for is a strongly revisionist understanding of religious belief.[73] Truth that one seeks is to be found not in the history of religion but through it. Truth is humane, not an objective concept. It does not lie in propositions, but what these mean, have meant, to particular persons, and groups. 'In so far as truth is apprehended by persons, it is apprehended within history; yet in so far as it is true, it transcends history.'[74]

Theology too is a product of the historical process and an intellectual activity. A Christian's theology should be informed by hope and by love.[75] Such a theology should be 'perspectival, parabolic and provisional' in consonance with the interpretation of experience within a tradition, the nature of religious language and the changing historical character of human existence.

Perspectival because it necessarily embodies a particular cultural approach to the world. Any revelation finds its expression in the context and thought forms of some specific and contingent cultural tradition. All theology is in that sense perspectival. It is *parabolic* because of the special degree of indirectness with which any language refers to the divine or the transcendent. In this way the concept of 'verbal inerrancy' in relation to theology is false and impossible in principle. *Provisional* draws attention to the new knowledge about the world that is continually coming to light.[76]

Dialogical approach 'necessarily involves seeing the other religion as in some sense a revelation of God from which we need to learn.'[77] Christianity has drawn from other religious traditions so fruitfully. Christianity is thus a 'prophetic religion.' It protests against its own currently established form, written into it. Jesus challenged the contemporary understanding of the Torah's pronouncements.

---

71 Maurice Wiles, *Christian Theology and Inter-religious Dialogue*, 33-35.

72 Harvey Cox, *The Future of Faith*, 170.

73 Maurice Wiles, *Christian Theology and Inter-religious Dialogue*, 43.

74 Wilfred Cantwell Smith, *Towards a World Theology*, 190.

75 Wilfred Cantwell Smith, *Towards a World Theology*, 123.

76 Maurice Wiles, *Christian Theology and Inter-religious Dialogue*, 64-65.

77 Maurice Wiles, *Christian Theology and Inter-religious Dialogue*, 4.

Christianity opened its doors freely to Gentiles as well as Jews.[78] Smith writes "the God whom Christ reveals is a God of mercy and love, who reaches out after all men and women everywhere in compassion and yearning; who delights in a sinner's repentance, who delights to save."[79] May this be our guiding light as our researches proceed from religion through theology and other disciplines and finally to the dialogical.

VIII. Conclusion

Our context is overshadowed by a forceful advocacy of a singular ideology. It demands prudent understanding and interpretation of other traditions and concepts. Dialogically orienting our researches can be one way of offering a loving response to this context. This can help our continuous commitment to a sustainable capability and to the enhancement of the multifariously deprived ones.

---

78 Maurice Wiles, *Christian Theology and Inter-religious Dialogue*, 17-18.

79 Wilfred Cantwell Smith, *Towards a World Theology*, 171.

5

Approaching Faith-traditions in the Indian Context

Introduction

This paper is an attempt to draw insights from the larger arena of scientific study of religions, missiology and secular principles in India to evolve relevant models of Jesus to serve God dynamically in the Indian texture towards a sustainable existence based on the struggles of life. The basic assumption here is that the struggles of life can be a starting point for different faith-traditions to meaningfully contribute to sustainable life. This is not a random thought but a logical conclusion emerging from the analysis of faith-traditions as applied in this paper.

In this process the expression faith-traditions is used mainly in the place of religions to mean religions and at the same time to allow space for some faith-orientations which are not considered as religions in the usual sense of the term religion. Indian context is used to suggest the plural nature of Indian life, particularly in the realms of religions, and to underline the communal facet of events starting from politics and to emphasise the need for religions to cooperate and if possible to work together towards a sustainable existence. The expressions 'struggles of life' and 'sustainable life/existence' are used to accommodate any struggle including theological and content to include the entire aspect of life together with humans.

Since the matter of faith-traditions is the core launch pad, I shall focus largely on the issues emerging from the scientific study of religions. Since these issues are gaining ground in other aspects of study, a graphic reference to two facets-missiology and secularism are made.

1. Insight from the Scientific Study of Religions

A thorough analysis of the major approaches to the scientific study of religions throw open the following challenges. They are: religion is as old as human history; there is in essence a 'unity of religions;' there is a possibility of 'free sharing among religions;' superiority claim of religions is untenable; as India houses many living religions a special approach to study faith-traditions is called for; there is a need for 'integration of theology and religion,' and struggles of life can be a relevant paradigm for varying faith traditions to contribute as resources-spiritual and others towards a sustainable existence.

1.1. Religion is as Old as Human History

The scientific study of faith-traditions reveals that religion is as old as human history.[1] It has survived and continued for several ages and developments. In the process of growth and development, faith-traditions have accommodated newer spiritual insights and human insights depending on the context.

Every faith-tradition was intended to enrich and enhance life in its texture, of course, often not without specific interests. So, much of human elements have entered in to the original and purposeful revelations that for example in India, religions are used for political gain, and domination.

Nevertheless the fact that everyone follows some form of religion and all the faith-traditions have trodden similar paths needs to be accepted.

In this issue, Christians, particularly the theological community, have a responsible role to perform. They have to identify and single out the human-made religiosity and help the people to realize the original revelation and the original relation between God and creation. This, Christians alone, may not be able to do. They have to even join with others or mobilize the help of all fellow religious seekers. This initiative helps in protecting people from the onslaught of personally motivated and communally loaded interpretations of faith-traditions.

As a Christian, one has to maintain her/his faith and conviction in the unique revelation of Jesus Christ. At the same time she/he should help his neighbours to realize the uniqueness of his/her own revelation, while calling attention to the necessity of living together amidst differences, for the sake of wider and meaningful engagement.

1.2. Unity of Religions

The study of religions reveals that there is a basic unity behind the diversity of religions, i.e. "Unity of Religion."[2] This is already present in religions but we need

1 F. Max Muller, *Theosophy or Psychological Religion, Collected Works of F. Max Muller,* Asian Educational Service, New Delhi, Reprinted 1978, pp. 18-37.

2 L. W. Grensted, *The Psychology of Religion,* Oxford University Press, New York, 1952, p. 109.

to realize it.[3] Its realization helps bring home the idea that 'religion was one' and its manifold forms prove its existential presence and application in diverse cultural contexts.

T. Swami Raju puts this fact as "Christians have to continue their search for re-visioning new spiritualities and build up better inter-religious relations. Christians need to express their willingness to accept plurality of faiths and religions."[4]

It is not just enough to understand the unity of religions and accept plurality for the sake of just tolerating the other. This process should be substantial. In Samartha's words, "Mystery provides the ontological basis for tolerance without which it runs the risk of being uncritical friendliness."[5]

Swami Vivekananda always held that 'all religions are branches of the same tree.'[6] He also said 'to a man who has realized, all religions are paths that lead to the same goal'[7] Gandhi's analysis has been put in a nut-shell as "after long study and experience I have come to the conclusion that: (1) all religions are true, (2) all religions have some error in them, (3) all religions are almost as dear to me as my own Hinduism."[8]

Realizing the unity of religions is not to compromise with our own faith-traditions but to be earnestly committed to one's own faith-tradition and at the same time help acknowledge the spiritual and other significances of other faith-traditions. It is like anchoring oneself concretely in his or her faith orientation and use that strength for furthering the spiritual vision of that particular faith tradition, possibly in co-operation with the faith-traditions of others as well. In the words of Swami Vivekananda, "it is only by releasing a flood of enlightened religious feeling that society can be cleansed and men and woman made to grow to their spiritual heights."[9]

John Hick calls for the recognition of the oneness of humanity and the diversity of revelation. He says, "it is clear that we are being called today to attain a global religious vision which is aware of the unity of all mankind before God and which at the same time makes sense of the diversity of God's ways within the

---

3 Gustan Mensching, *Structures and Patterns of Religion,* Translated by F. Klimkeit and V. Srinivasa Sarma, Motilal Banarsidass, Delhi, 1976, pp. 319, 320.

4 T. Swami Raju, "Re-Visioning Theologies: A Multi-Faith Perspective," *The SATHRI Journal* Vol. 2, No. 1 (May, 2008), p. 146.

5 S. J. Samartha, "Commitment and Tolerance in a Pluralist Society", *NCC Review*, Vol. CVI, No. 2, (February 1986), p. 76.

6 D. S. Sharma, *Hinduism Through the Ages* (Bombay: Bharatiya Vidya Bhavan, 1967), p. 122.

7 D. S. Sharma, *Hinduism Through the Ages* (Bombay: Bharatiya Vidya Bhavan, 1967), p. 136.

8 Nirmal Minz, *Mahatma Gandhi and Hindu – Christian Dialogue* (Madras: CLS, 1970), p. 12.

9 D. S. Sharma, *Hinduism Through the Ages* (Bombay: Bharatiya Vidya Bhavan, 1967), p. 122.

various streams of human life."[10] To put it differently, unity of religion and the unity of life behind the diversity of religions need to be accepted and utilized as a relevant paradigm for a sustainable approach.

1.3. Free Sharing among Religions

The scientific study of religions has helped in transcending the religious boundaries and in realizing the necessity of 'free sharing among religions' i.e., interaction among them. Paul F. Knitter highlights the necessity of 'free sharing among religions.' In his words, "somehow, they must meet each other and relate to each other not in order to obliterate or absorb each other but to learn from and help each other."[11]

Jesudason Baskar Jeyaraj writes, "enabling each religious community to accept other communities and seeing the need to work with them are the major challenges today."[12] The purpose of facilitating free sharing or interaction among faith-traditions is necessitated by the demand for working together for sustainable existence.

Mahatma Gandhi has suggested as to how different religions should approach each other. For him, "the correct attitude is one of firm adherence to one's own religion coupled with an equal reverence towards all other religions. It is not simply a question of tolerating other faiths, but of believing that all faiths lead to the same goal."[13] Again he maintained that "Let Hindus become better Hindus, Muslims better Muslims and Christians better Christians."[14] We cannot stop with Gandhi. It is not enough to just have equal reverence for all faith-traditions. It is not enough to be silent so that everyone matures in his/her faith-tradition. The reverence and individual spiritual enhancement should ultimately lead to constructive life sustaining initiatives.

This fact is further substantiated by the view that "in a world haunted by fear and torn by strife what is the need of the moment is a spirit of tolerance and understanding, not the mere grudging admission of other religious views but the glad recognition of the variety of the human mind."[15] Acknowledging the

---

10 John Hick ed., *The Myth of God Incarnate Seventh Impression* (London: SCM Press Ltd., 1985). p. 180.

11 Paul F. Knitter, *No other Name? op. cit.*, p. 6.

12 Jesudason Baskar Jeyaraj, "Nation building with the People of other Faiths: A Need for new Models of Missiological Education," *Mission Today*Vol. X (2008), p. 244.

13 D. S. Sharma, *Hinduism Through the Ages* (Bombay: Bharatiya Vidya Bhavan, 1967), pp. 193-134.

14 Mahatma Gandhi, *Fellowship of Faiths and Unity of Religions,* ed., by Abdul Majid Khan (Madras: G.A. Natesan and Co., No. year), p. 20.

15 Madhukar, "The Role of Religions in Ensuring the Welfare of the People", *Religion and Soeity,* Vol. 42. No. 3 (September 1995), p. 13.

possibility of diversity and its purpose is essential for fruitful co-operation among different faith-traditions.

Wilfred Cantwell Smith highlights the risk of non-cooperation among different faith-traditions. He writes, "unless men can learn to understand and to be loyal to each other across religious frontiers, unless we can build a world in which people profoundly of different faiths can live together and work together, then the prospects for our planet's future are not bright."[16] This is true and obvious in a situation like ours (Indian).

1.4. Superiority Claim Untenable

According to the scientific study of religions 'all our faiths have some value,' and the superiority claims of religions becomes untenable[17] and suspicious[18] because in one sense every religion was a true religion in its context.[19] Each religion is a unique response to the ultimate. Samartha writes, "in the last analysis, religions should be recognized as having responded differently to the mystery of the Ultimate."[20]

Samartha, emphatically and candidly expresses the impossibility of claiming superiority on religious grounds. His consideration is significant to understand other faith-traditions and co-operate with them. His proposal to accept the faith experience of other faith-traditions is expressed in the form of a question: "why then is it necessary to deny the credibility and the genuineness of the religious *anubhava* of neighbours of other faiths?"[21] In another place he argues that "our neighbours too have their answers to the mystery of life and the tragedy of suffering."[22] In the analysis of Samartha, there is no reason to consider other faith traditions as inferior. This is vivid when he says "in terms of spiritual depth, intellectual power, cultural richness, and social solidarity they do not regard themselves in any way inferior to Christians."[23]

---

16 Wilfred Cantwell Smith, "The Christian in a Religiously Plural World", *Christianity and Other Religions, op. cit.*, p. 95.

17 S. Radhakrishnan, *East and West in Religion,* George Allen & Unwin Ltd., London, 1933, p. 26.

18 S. Radhakrishnan, *Religion and Society,* George Allen & Unwin Ltd., London, 1947, p. 52.

19 F. Max Muller, *Introduction to the Science of Religions,* New Edition, London, 1882, p. 190.

20 S. J. Samartha, *The Lordship of Jesus Christ and Religious Pluralism* (Madras: The Christian Literature Society, 1981), p. 23.

21 S. J. Samartha, *Between Two Cultures* (India: Asian Trading Corporation, 1997), p. 151.

22 S. J. Samartha, *The Lordship of Jesus Christ and Religious Pluralism* (Madras: The Christian Literature Society, 1981), p. 2.

23 S. J. Samartha, *The Lordship of Jesus Christ and Religious Pluralism* (Madras: The Christian Literature Society, 1981), p. 3.

Samartha also expresses the wishes of people adhering to other faith-traditions as "neighbours of other faiths also ask humbly and sometimes not so humbly: what about our centers and our names?"[24]

Therefore, there is a necessity to consider newer understanding of religion/God, in the context of many faith-traditions. T. Swami Raju maintains "in our re-visioning of God, we have to reiterate strongly that 'God is impartial' in dealing with human beings irrespective of their class, race, nation or religion."[25]

This perspective and proposal is helpful in the Indian texture as it unambiguously calls for cooperation and not conflict among different faith-traditions. The realistic acceptance of the credibility of other faith-traditions can prompt and lead to the vision of sustainable contributions for which they were originally committed.

1.5. India Needs Special Approach

In India, religion is defined as a way of life.[26] And it is never separated from daily life. Thus, the Indian context requires a special approach in studying other faith-traditions, not merely Western, as she houses major living religions of the world.[27]

There is also not much distinction between religion and philosophy in India. For example, Dr. S. Radhakrishnan approached religion from the viewpoint of philosophy, contrary to the West.[28] Philosophy of religion verifies religious data systematically and logically. It is feared that this approach might become a mere intellectual exercise.[29]

At this juncture, now the nonwestern scholars' study and reflection of their own religion and others are amply available.[30] One thing one can authentically be said that the present generation of scholars in the field of religions has devoted their life and works for generating, nurturing and strengthening inter-religious

---

24 S. J. Samartha, *One Christ Many Religions,* op. cit., p. 18.

25 T. Swami Raju, "Re-Visioning Theologies: A Multi-Faith Perspective," *The SATHRI Journal* Vol. 2, No. 1 (May, 2008), p. 145.

26 S. Radhakrishnan, *The Hindu of Life,* Third Indian Reprint, Blackie & Son Publishers Pvt. Ltd., Blackie House, Bombay, 1979, p. 55.

27 Eric J. Lott, "The Science of Religion in an Indian Theological Context", *Bangalore Theological Forum,* Vol. XIII, No. 4, Oct-Dec., 1985, p. 1.

28 Frank Whaling, "The Study of Religions in a Global Context," *Contemporary Approaches to the Study of Religion in 2 Volumes,* edited by Frank Whaling, Volume I: The Humanities, Mouton Publishers, Berlin, 1984, p. 403.

29 Eric J. Lott, "Approaching Religious Tradition," *Religious Traditions of India,* Indian Theological Library, 1988, p. 29.

30 Frank Whaling, "The Study of Religions in a Global Context," *Contemporary Approaches to the Study of Religion in 2 Volumes,* edited by Frank Whaling, Volume I: The Humanities, Mouton Publishers, Berlin, 1984, p. 392.

relations. They also indicate the danger of communal hatred and the possibility and necessity of taking the plural context seriously.

T. Swami Raju categorically asserts that "no theological education will be of much help, if we do not take into account the religious and communal conflicts that are destroying the very foundations of "integrity in diversity" and "unity in plurality" of our national community and harmonious life among the people of different faiths."[31]

In the context of political parties exploiting religiously sentimental issues to gain mileage, the new approach needs to take into serious consideration many living religions, plurality of faith-traditions, danger of communalism and the possibility of working together for a sustainable existence. It also needs to ask the serious question that whether we want freedom of religion or the extra-constitutional right to convert others.

1.6. Integration of Theology and Religion

At the initial stage of the founding of the department for the scientific study of religions the main objective was to separate this department from theology. But now things have changed completely. From the point of theology, Indian theology cannot ignore the rich and variety of religious resources. Against the original wishes now there is more possibility for creative integration between theology and the study of religions.[32] This possibility is promising.[33] The main issue is to theologically consider the insights gained from the study of other faith-traditions.

It is not for mere theological interpretation of other religious principles or concepts. But it is to take the plurality of religion seriously and formulate theologies addressing the plurality of faith-traditions. Or in other words our theologies cannot miss even a fraction of the fact that there are many faith-traditions and their significance, contribution and willingness to promote sustainable life. Such considerations should find place in our theological language.

Wilfred Cantwell Smith suggested that it is time we shift from the teaching of religion to the study of religion.[34] That is to avoid teaching religions with a set of agenda or motive and to begin to study and understand other faith-traditions to cooperate with them and work with them towards the possibility of promoting sustainable life.

---

31 T. Swami Raju, "Re-Visioning Theologies: A Multi-Faith Perspective," *The SATHRI Journal* Vol. 2, No. 1 (May, 2008), p. 141.

32 S. Israel, "An Integral Approach to the Study of Religion: Insights from an Indian Christian perspective," *Bangalore Theological Forum,* Vol. XIX, No. 2, April-June, 1987, p. 104.

33 Eric J. Lott, "The Science of Religion in an Indian Theological Context", *Bangalore Theological Forum,* Vol. XVII, No. 4, October-December, 1985, p. 3.

34 Wilfred Cantwell Smith, "The Study of Religion and the Study of the Bible", *Journal of the American Academy of Religion,* Vol. XXXIX, No. 2, June, 1971, p. 131.

Still further we also come across the acknowledgment that "religious pluralism has been established today not only as an irreversible historical fact but also as a theological principle."[35] In approaching other faith-traditions the above concerns can no longer be sidelined.

T. Swami Raju substantially underlined the necessity of the integration of theology and religion in India as "keeping the changing contexts of our days in mind, we need to reconsider or review or re-vision our Christian theologies afresh making them relevant in our contemporary context, since the concept of God has become one of the major problems in multi-faith relations."[36]

Not just God alone, but any concern that becomes the barrier for co-operation and working together. It is not debating theological strengths and weaknesses but looking for ways and means to accept the differences on the one hand and at the same time proceeding further towards the goal.

1.7. Strugglers of Life

All the above mentioned insights form the study of other faith traditions are informative and enlightening. The most significant consideration to approach other-faith traditions is the fact that the data from the study of faith-traditions is suggestive of the possibly enhanced contribution the religions could make if 'struggle for sustainable life' is accepted as a common ground to work together. According to Radha Krishnan, in the context of growing threats to life religion has wider and significant role to bring people together and engage them in common concerns.[37]

In our times studying religion means studying life.[38] The problem of religion would become vastly complicated if it were to be discretely separated from the problem of people because it has neither the essence nor the existence nor any kind of being whatsoever apart from people.[39] Hence, focus upon "Life" should become the key to the understanding of religious phenomena in India.[40]

S. J. Samartha states the need for cooperation among religions. In his words, "it is agreed that the most helpful relationship between persons of different faiths

---

35 Kuncheria Pathil, "Christian Approach to other Faiths: A Historical Perspective", NCC Review, Vol. CX, No. 2 (February 1990), p. 67.

36 T. Swami Raju, "Re-Visioning Theologies: A Multi-Faith Perspective," *The SATHRI Journal* Vol. 2, No. 1 (May, 2008), p. 138.

37 S. Radhakrishnan, *Religion and Society,* George Allen & Unwin Ltd., London, 1947, p. 18.

38 L. W. Grensted, *The Psychology of Religion,* Oxford University Press, New York, 1952, p. 15.

39 J. G. Arapura, *Religions as Anxiety and Tranquility, An Essay in Comparative Phenomenology of the Spirit,* Mouton & Co., Netherlands, 1972, p. 39.

40 K. P. Aleaz, *Harmony of Religions: The Relevance of Swami Vivekananda,* Punthipustak, Calcutta, 1993, p. 52.

in the world today must be one of co-operation in pursuing common purposes like justice, peace and human rights."[41]

In the words of Paul F. Knitter, "religions must speak and act together because only so can they make their crucially important contribution to removing the oppression that contaminates our globe."[42] He also suggested that, the "world of suffering, which provides the context or Kairos for dialogue, is all around us."[43] In another place he says "… peace can and must become a common commitment and a common ground for conversation and action."[44] Another insight he provides is that, as the world is facing suffering and want of peace, the world needs salvation i.e. not only in the spiritual sense, but in its comprehensive sense. For this he proposed a soterio-centric approach. But later he said, "working for eco-human justice becomes a common context in which we find ourselves using our different religious stories and symbols."[45] Therefore he suggested the functioning together of liberation theology and theology of religions. He writes "their encounter, may be even their marriage, can bear much fruit for the Christian Churches and the world."[46] This idea has been expounded in his later works. He said, "so people and events in my life have led me, sometimes lured me, to what has become for me the moral obligation to join 'pluralism and liberation' or 'dialogue and global responsibility."[47]

Aloysius Pieris proposed a new paradigm for the Asian context for the religions to work together. It includes three aspects. In his words, "the first is the acknowledgement of a third magisterium, namely, that of the poor; the second is the *liberational thrust* that defines our theology of religions; and finally, the social location of this theology is the Basic Human Communities (BHC)."[48] S. J. Samartha goes deeper into the aspect of social responsibility of the enlightened and writes "unless the Hindu-Christian quest for truth is related to the ongoing life of the community, to the life of people who are struggling, suffering, and dying in the world today, it will remain isolated."[49] These ideas are shared by

41 S. J. Samartha, *Courage for Dialogue: Ecumenical Issues in Inter-religious Relationships* (Geneva: World Council of Churches, 1981), p. 30.

42 Paul F. Knitter, "Toward a Liberation Theology of Religions", *The Myth of Christian Uniqueness*, op. cit., p. 181.

43 Paul F. Knitter, *One Earth Many Religions*, Mutlifatith Dialogue and Global Responsibility (New York: ORBIS, 1996), p. 58.

44 *Ibid.*, p. 66.

45 *Ibid.*, p. 113.

46 Paul F. Knitter, "Religion and Liberation in Defense of a Pluralistic Theology of Religions," *NCC Review*, Vol. CXII, No. 4 (April 1992), p. 229.

47 Paul F. Knitter, One Earth Many Religions, *op. cit.*, p. 11.

48 Aloysius Pieris, *Fire and Water, Basic Issues in Asian Buddhism and Christianity* (New York: ORBIS Books, 1996), p. 156.

49 S. J. Samartha, *Courage for Dialogue*, *op. cit.*, p. 156.

Paul F. Knitter too. He writes that "there is today a growing awareness among religious persons that their religious identity must somehow be related to those common experiences of suffering and global threat."[50] It is to be appreciated that the concern for the poor, among many other significant concerns, has been the key thrust of almost all the contemporary thinkers. And the solution is to be sought from all faith-orientations.

In participating with the struggles of life in order to achieve "Life Sustaining" vision spirituality is the fundamental source of inspiration. Every individual must be rooted and filled with the Sakti or spirit of that particular faith-tradition to which he/she belonged. It is a long process.

It is called in the Indian tradition as the state of "Jivan Mukta." This ideal of Jivanmukta is to help others to come over from their own narrow outlook. The Jivanmuktas consider the world as one, i.e., Vasudevakudumbam. Coming to this stage is a process. The person who is rooted in a particular spiritual foundation can uphold *dharma* towards people, creatures, and the cosmos as a whole.

This realization naturally dawns on a Christian because of his/her intensive commitment to the principles of Jesus. Irrespective of the faith-traditions to which one belongs, every one may have to ask a question-as a human being adhering to a particular faith-tradition, what is distinct in me? Or what is distinct about me? A close observation of life of the people of different faith-traditions can help us learn that every human being is striving to live, rather a better life. A better life is what everyone aspires for. In this stark struggle for life, no individual is better placed because of his/her religious identity. Our endeavor in working for the friendliness of religions is to strengthen life.

This argument can be substantiated with the feeling of a contemporary, humble religions scholar. He writes, "today's dire need of our country is not demolishing and constructing temples/mosques/shrines to God- "the ultimate reality," but to reconstruct healthier and better relations between various human communities. It is not imperative of any religion either to prove which "God" or "deity" is true and authoritative, or whose religion is superior or highly valuable, but how to restore "human dignity" and "peaceful relations" in the midst of a diversity of faiths, oppressive structures, inhuman attitudes and how to meet the basic needs of humankind."[51] Again he states "the dire need of our country today is not demolishing and constructing temples for "God" in the name of either "religious" or "cultural" nationalism, but rather to help human beings – the "image of God," in their basic needs of day-to-day life."[52] The force of the point is

50 Paul F. Knitter, *One Earth Many Religions*, *op. cit.*, p. 57.

51 T. Swami Raju, "Re-Visioning Theologies: A Multi-Faith Perspective," *The SATHRI Journal* Vol. 2, No.1 (May, 2008), p. 138.

52 T. Swami Raju, "Re-Visioning Theologies: A Multi-Faith Perspective," *The SATHRI Journal* Vol. 2, No. 1 (May, 2008), p. 145.

clear. But the stand point requires much more an inclusive and a comprehensive expression.

2. Mission

The above discussions from the point of religions are leading to the conclusion that working for religious cooperation is essential in India because such an approach can be beneficial in many ways.

It is indispensable to note that this concern has captured the attention of missiological paradigm as well. Missiologists agree that a new reading or rereading of the Bible and its dynamic is necessary for newer directions. It may not be a surprise that ecological dimensions are emerging from the great commission (Mark 16:15). Sam Amirtham points out that "the Gospel will offer God's grace to transform not only human nature and human history, but also the whole of nature and all of creation."[53]

Similarly a re-reading or new reading of Bible can offer many more useful insights even to facilitate religious cooperation to work towards sustainable existence.

The bold declaration of Russell Chandran is significant here. He writes, "there is no mission programme which can be copied for all situations. One has to be sensitive to discern what the Holy Spirit tells us about Christ's mission in different contexts."[54]

Such bold visions are found to be materialized in the modern missiological writings. For example, Jesudason Baskar Jeyaraj writes: "Missiological education should relate not merely to one sector of the world but to all the segments including the people of other faiths. The people of other faiths are also partners in the *missio Dei.*"[55]

The mission of the church has a substantial role to play in matters of many faith-traditions. Russell Chandran maintained that, "the church's mission does have a role in relation to the quest for communal harmony and peace and the safeguarding of the secular character of the state in which people of all faiths can live together, enjoying equal rights and without fear of any discrimination."[56]

Although missiology has accepted the significance of inter-religious co-operation it is the traditional frame of mind and thought that obstruct progress.

---

53 Sam Amirtham, "Gospel to all Creation," in *The Good News of Jesus Christ in the Indian Setting,* edited by Dayanandan Francis (Chennai: The Christian Literature Society, 2000), p. 60.

54 J. Russell Chandran, "A Mission Theology for Tomorrow," in *The Good News of Jesus Christ in the Indian Setting,* edited by Dayanandan Francis (Chennai: The Christian Literature Society, 2000), p. 107.

55 Jesudason Baskar Jeyaraj, "Nation Building with the People of other Faiths: A Need for New Models of Missiological Education," *Mission Today* Vol. X (2008), p. 235.

56 J. Russell Chandran, "A Mission Theology for Tomorrow," in *The Good News of Jesus Christ in the Indian Setting,* edited by Dayanandan Francis (Chennai: The Christian Literature Society, 2000), p. 108.

S. Wesley Ariarajah affirms, "our encounter with religions and cultures over several decades has indeed produced new wine. But we have a missiology that cannot take it. New wine needs new wineskins."[57] This is what that is to be considered while approaching other religious traditions in India.

While missiology comes forward with wider facets it is not free from certain challenges. P. S. Jacob writes, "the crucial question for missiologists today is whether Christianity can offer a quality of transformation which is not being offered by other religions."[58] This challenge can be overcome by the conviction that all faith-traditions have something concrete to contribute to inter-religious relations for the sake of pursuing a life sustaining vision.

3. Secularism

It is also significant to remember that the secular principle of our nation is in tune with relation between faith-traditions as against the obvious notion of non-religious or irreligious nature of the state. Neera Chandhoke writes, "it is not surprising that secularism in the Indian polity, as a response to our conditions and mode of thought, came to be conceptualized as *sarva dharma sambhava*, or equality of all religions."[59] The fact that in the Indian constitution the word secular is used to stress the neutrality of the state in relation to religions is further emphasized as "ironically, it is often forgotten that secularism in India had been devised precisely to negotiate interreligious relationships; to grant the freedom of religious belief; to ensure equality of all the religious groups. And to assure the minorities that their identities would be safe."[60]

This notion is capturing attention as modern scholars are grouping secularism as a faith, in order, not to miss any valuable contribution towards sustainable existence launched from the launch-pad of struggles of life. While classifying the various religions as Indian religions, foreign religions, folk religions, T. Swami Raju makes reference to "Other Faiths: Apart from these 'religions,' there are people who have faith in secular visions, and political ideologies like Gandhism, Marxism, Leninism, Maoism, Naxalism and so on."[61]

Such an enthralling attitude from the modern scholars have noteworthy purpose. For example S. J. Samartha writes, the "future of Christianity in India

57 S. Wesley Ariaraja, "Mission in the Context of Cultures and Religions," in *Mission Paradigm in the New Millennium,* edited by W. S. Milton Jeganathan (Delhi: ISPCK, 2000), p. 237.

58 Plamthodathil S. Jacob, "Hindu and Christian: Conversions and Transformations," in *Conversion in a Pluralistic Context: Perspectives and Perceptions,* 108.

59 Neera Chandhoke, *Beyond Secularism, the Rights of Religious Minorities* (New Delhi: Oxford University Press, 1999), 42.

60 Neera Chandhoke, *Beyond Secularism, the Rights of Religious Minorities,* 47.

61 T. Swami Raju, "Re-Visioning Theologies: A Multi-Faith Perspective," *The SATHRI Journal* Vol. 2, No. 1 (May, 2008), p. 139.

lies in liberal Christians combating Hindu fanaticism and at the same time co-operating with liberal Hindus."[62]

J. Russell Chandran maintained that "Churches should find ways of co-operating with organizations and agencies working for secularism, democracy and communal harmony."[63]

Churches and theological educators need to recognize the importance of secular ideology and take special efforts to incorporate those ideals in to ours in the process of obeying the call of God. We also need to learn to work with such ideologies. This is the demand of the context. This is vivid in the statement that "intolerance has manifested itself in the activities of communal political parties which are clearly antagonistic to the entire spirit of the secular State."[64]

4. Jesus is Life-Centered

With the above insights drawn largely from the study of faith-traditions and graphically from Missiology and Secularism we can be sure in our persuasion of theology for the sake of sustainable existence that we need to be always open to the available resources and challenges. In this direction Christians can creatively draw a paradigm from the life and teachings of Jesus Christ.

Jesus came to do the will of God. He came to enrich life. He wanted to obliterate all the religious systems and practices which worked against life. To give life to the needy, Jesus broke away many traditional laws. If laws and practices are not in consonance with the necessities of life, they should be avoided. His main fight was against the 'religions' which functioned at the cost of life and suffering. He was always of the view that religion is for life and life is not for religion.

Jesus wanted religions and religious practices to be life sustaining and not life destroying. Whoever, or whichever faith tradition, is involved in fulfilling the will of God was in the company of Jesus. He said whoever does the will of my father is my brother and sister.[65]

Even if such deeds took place, in an unexpected environment, Jesus appreciated that move. He appreciated the faith of the centurion and said even in Israel there was not such faith.[66] J. Russell Chandran writes, "through re-reading the Gospels we may also learn from Jesus way of drawing attention to the greatness

62 S. J. Samartha, *Between Two Cultures, op. cit.*, p. 160.

63 J. Russell Chandran, "A Mission Theology for Tomorrow," in *The Good News of Jesus Christ in the Indian Setting,* edited by Dayanandan Francis (Chennai: The Christian Literature Society, 2000), p. 109

64 E. C. Bhatty, "Religious Minorities and the Secular State," in *Religious Freedom*, 77.

65 Mark 3:35.

66 Luke 7:9.

of the faith of other people such as the Samaritans, the Syrophoenecian woman and the Roman centurion."[67]

For Jesus, the neighbor[68] is one who involves in life saving activity. That is why, he had to say men would come from east and west, and from north and south, and sit at table in the kingdom of God.[69] To use the words of Jesudason Baskar Jeyaraj, "the Bible does not preach hatred towards the people of other faiths but love and concern for them because they are also created in the image of God as Christians are created."[70] Still further, "we always need to remember as a fact that Jesus Christ never and ever condemned others' faiths and religions."[71]

Another important aspect to note is that "Jesus was definitely opposed to proselitization in the sense of conversion from one religion to another religion, when he said, "Woe to you, Scribes and Pharisees, hypocrites! for you traverse sea and land to make a single proselyte, and when he becomes a proselyte you make him twice as much a child of hell as yourselves"[72] [Matthew 23:15].

Jesus' concern for the needy is outstanding. His selection of people for the reward was on the basis of the amount of service they did to the needy.[73] This is declared in the 'Nazareth manifesto.'[74] He wanted that humanity's relation to the ultimate mystery and to the people around should go hand in hand. He said, 'love the lord and love your neighbor.'[75]

Jesus' main enemies were people who used religion as a mere ceremonial observance, as a means of oppression and as a means to escape from the responsibilities.[76] He wanted to restore Sabbath as a source of life for the needy. He said, 'Sabbath is for man and man is not for Sabbath.'[77] A taunting question he faced was whether to save or destroy life on Sabbath.[78] He proved in his life

67 J. Russell Chandran, "A Mission Theology for Tomorrow," in *The Good News of Jesus Christ in the Indian setting,* edited by Dayanandan Francis (Chennai: The Christian Literature Society, 2000), p. 108.

68 Luke 10:29.

69 Luke 13:29.

70 Jesudason Baskar Jeyaraj, "Nation Building with the People of Other Faiths: A Need for New Models of Missiological Education," *Mission Today* Vol. X (2008), p. 236.

71 T. Swami Raju, "Re-Visioning Theologies: A Multi-Faith Perspective," *The SATHRI Journal* Vol. 2, No. 1 (May, 2008), p. 146.

72 Gnana Robinson, "Life and Mission of the Church," in *The Good News of Jesus Christ in the Indian Setting,* edited by Dayanandan Francis (Chennai: The Christian Literature Society, 2000), p. 121.

73 Matthew 25:35.

74 Luke 4:18-19.

75 Mark 12:30 & 31.

76 Matthew 9:13, 15:6, & Mark 7:11 & Luke 11:42.

77 Mark 2:27.

78 Matthew 12:10, & Mark 3:4, & Luke 6:9.

that, saving the life of the needy (any) is the chief concern of people who are committed to the ultimate Reality, of course, in manifold forms.

The life sustaining persuasion is based on two main convictions. One is the conviction that, all are committed to the ultimate through diverse channels. And the other is that commitment demands that life is strengthened in all possible ways to achieve, harmony, peace, justice and equality for all. S. J. Samartha writes, "for Christians the fight against all that destroys true community, the quest for spiritual resources to under grid all efforts to build community, and the search for the ultimate meaning of truly human existence in community cannot be separated from faith in Jesus Christ."[79]

Above all faith in Jesus is the key to our theological agenda. As we look to Jesus for inspiration let us try to apply the principles of Jesus as he interpreted them in his life time. This paradigm shall be relevant, in conformity with our faith and it shall be life sustaining.

At the same time as a Christian community, we need to acknowledge a purposeful fact that "every religion wishes to show a path to 'realize' reality, and reality is whole. But every person and every religion participates in, enjoys, arrives at, lives in that whole in a limited way. Nobody has a monopoly on the whole, and no one can completely satisfy the human thirst for the infinite and content herself with a part of the whole."[80] This helps us to construct a positive and a wider understanding about all the faith-traditions in the process of relating with others and working with others towards a sustainable existence while unshakably committed to the Jesus-paradigm.

5. Conclusion

In the face of living with communal tensions triggered by terrorizing activities, for one or other purpose, as a theological community we have a responsible role to play as we learn from others and educate others for the challenging tasks ahead in a pluralistic context like India.

The specific call for such a responsible role is emerging from the reality of many faith-traditions that are some time conflicting but at the same time dynamic and willing to relate with the other and work with the other towards an all inclusive sustainable goal.

In this process we need to constantly strive to discern the really religious concerns from the other, accidental or incidental accumulations for the sake of cooperation and working together towards life sustaining vision and mission. This will be further strengthened if we can recognize the unity of real purpose that underlies all the religions in spite of the obvious differences. Once this recognition

79 S. J. Samartha, "Dialogue as a Continuing Christian Concern", *Religion and Society*, Vol. XVIII, No. 1 (March 1971), p. 22.

80 Raimon Panikkar, *The Fullness of Man. A Christophany*, translated by Alfred Dilascia (Maryknoll: Orbis , 2006), p. 157.

is achieved we can move forward in establishing a mutual sharing or a substantial relationship with other faith-traditions for the sake of committing ourselves to struggle for a sustainable existence.

As we progress in this direction we need to be humble about our own faith affirmations which are ultimate and absolute to us, while accepting the possibility of ultimate and absolute faith affirmations, may be in different forms than ours, in other faith-traditions as well. This bold challenge is indispensable to avoid the destructive utility of the power of religions. This is looking beyond the set proposals to approach other faith-traditions in order to address the currently emerging threats to establishing a sustainable existence.

One of the basic signs of embarking on this hard terrain in accordance with our faith commitment to God which, we inherited from the faith in the life and work of Jesus Christ is to instill these acknowledged challenges in our theological formulations which, of course is the interpretation of our faith relevant to the contextual realities. It is not mere Indian Christian theology, but theology resulting from the realistic existence of many faith-traditions. The culmination principle of this process, at least in our times, is the confluence of religious resources towards hammering a paradigm to address the struggles of life in order to seek and establish a sustainable existence.

Creating and involving (in) such a paradigm has become the trend emerging in the present missiological considerations. Although this consideration is not free from challenges, an open approach free from traditional ones to include the other as well, in our study and application, can lead us further.

Positively considering the other and cooperating with the other and working together with the other towards sustainable existence is not only a religious affair, it is not only the missiological consideration of Christians. It is also the inherent and implicit expectation of secularism, at least from the point of the Indian Constitution, which in India cannot be ignored at any level as we work together towards a sustainable existence.

It is not at all surprising that all the afore maintained appeals are the reality of the life and the work of Jesus, which inspire and embolden all of us to advance further in our commitment to serve God purposefully in the given context.

In the end, in our approach to other faith-traditions we should not fail to recognize the basic principles that all are committed to the ultimate through diverse channels and life that needs to be strengthened towards sustainable existence. Above all, faith in Jesus is the key to our theological agenda, as we open ourselves to the truth that there are other faith-traditions as well. The relevant method to approach other faith-traditions, in our context, is "Life Sustaining" based on the "Struggles for Life," which helps crossing the boundaries with purpose and at the same time necessitates safe return and relaxation in one's own faith-tradition. The kinds of struggle and contents of sustainable life are kept open-ended so as to be always open to the newer possibilities.

6

Towards a Theology of Dialogue

Introduction

Plurality of religion is as old as human history but what is new now is religious pluralism. It is the recognition of the real existence of different religions and their history and to sincerely attempt to live together. This process has necessitated the planning and programs of dialogue. Dialogue is not only between different faith traditions but also with ideologies both political or any other for that matter.

In the first place there are many factors that have contributed to the development of "dialogue," particularly interreligious situations. Secondly, there were genuine attempts made long ago since Akbar in the 16th century, whether relevant or otherwise in today's context, by both Catholic and Protestant churches and individual thinkers/theologians which have moved the discussion on dialogue much forward. In the third place, these initial attempts have contributed to some of the major developments in the contemporary debates on dialogue among religions and ideologies. In the fourth place, the paradigm of dialogue is often attacked as a Christian attempt to continue mission, particularly in the Indian context. And finally, it is useful to present a "life sustaining" paradigm to continue practicing dialogue in a multi-faith and ideologies context.

Factors that Contributed Towards Interreligious Dialogue

Humanity has always lived in the midst of many religions and ideologies consciously or otherwise. Now there is a need to willfully develop principles to live together in harmony and fellowship for the larger good of the globe. This was obvious from the later part of the nineteenth century may be because of the following reasons. They can be discussed under general and Indian reasons.

In general, the *European geographical explorations* in the 15th to 17th centuries stimulated a new interest in other religions.[1] It challenged the superiority and relevance of Christianity to be the only world religion. It also encouraged missionary zeal but definitely broadened the understanding of early Christians and missionaries about their relation to the people of other faith-traditions.

Collapse of colonial power, particularly in Asia and Africa, helped revival 'of indigenous cultural and religious values of the people of the liberated nations.'[2] It was 'only a couple of decades after the dismantling of colonialism that both the Vatican (1965) and the World Council of Churches (1971) came out rather reluctantly, with more positive statements about people of other faiths.'[3]

Modern technology, scientific developments and advancements in communication have reduced the world to a *global village*. People of different religious persuasions often come face to face. They are 'exposed to mutual claims and commitments.'[4] Towards the end of the nineteenth century and the beginning of the twentieth century, these developments helped people to encounter each other as never before. Added to this was the 'study of the religious traditions' which 'helped people to change their attitudes to religious traditions other than their own.'[5]

Knowledge of other faith traditions and setting up of *departments of religious studies* in the universities for the study of religions *supplied* Christians, 'for the first time, with full factual information on the other world religions.'[6] John Hick calls this as 'the modern explosion of knowledge among Christians in the West concerning other great religious traditions of the world.'[7] This has become one of the 'greatest challenges to Christian theology today.'[8] It is not just religious

---

1 J. Paul Rajashekar, ed., *Religious Pluralism and Lutheran Theology* (LWF Report 23/24), Geneva, 1988, 11.

2 V. F. Vineeth, "Inter-religious dialogue: Past and Present a Critical Appraisal," *Journal of Dharma,* Vol. XIX, No.1 (January – March 1997), 42.

3 S. J. Samartha, *One Christ Many Religions: Towards a revised Christology* (Bangalore: SATHRI in association with Ward makers, 1992), 3.

4 J. Paul Rajashekar, ed., *Religious Pluralism and Lutheran Theology*, 9.

5 Jose Kuttianimattathil, *Practice and Theology of Interreligious Dialogue* (Bangalore: Kristu Jyoti Publications, 1998), 27.

6 Harold G. Howard, *Religious Pluralism and the World Religions (*Madras: University of Madras, 1983), 25.

7 John Hick, "The Non-absoluteness of Christianity," *The Myth of Christian Uniqueness: Toward A Pluralistic Theology of Religions,* ed. By John Hick and Paul F. Knitter (New York: ORBIS Books, 1987), p. 17.

8 Kuncheria Pathil, "Christian Approach to other Faiths. A Historical Perspective," *N.C.C Review,* Vol. X, No. 2 (February 1990), 66.

knowledge about other religions but also 'knowledge of other religious persons.'[9] The study has helped realize the 'humanity's multi-religious context.'[10]

The *Sacred Books of the East* edited by Max Muller brought to light the *Eastern faith-traditions.* As a result 'there is in the West a growing interest in openness toward Eastern religions.'[11] Thousands of Westerners, especially the young, journey to India each year in quest of religious experiences. 'Hindu ashrams and Buddhist monasteries are built in Western countries, which attract significant number of devotees.'[12] It is also suggested that "inter-Faith Dialogue is the natural outcome and the direct result of the challenging encounter of Christianity with Hinduism, after a hundred and fifty years of missionary activity on the Indian soil."[13]

With the *Rise of Islam* 'the Christian Church was faced for the first time with a new and powerful missionary religion.'[14] Further, 'far from disappearing, the religions of Judaism, Islam, Hinduism, and Buddhism are alive and well in spite of all the Christian missionary efforts.'[15]

Struggle of the oppressed people who belong to different religions and cultures, for a life of freedom, self-respect and human dignity, prompted religions probably to come together and work together.[16] There was also the realization that "the problem of the relations between the religions of the world is decisive in the quest for world peace and community."[17]

From the academic point of view, Ernst Troeltsch in 1902, in his book *The Absoluteness of Christianity and the History of Religions*, 'called into question Christianity's claim to absoluteness.'[18]

Historically, due to the 'the rise of secularism and materialism' after the world wars, the members of the Jerusalem Meeting of the International Missionary

9 Paul. F. Knitter, *No Other Name?: A Critical Survey of Christian Attitudes Toward the World Religions*, (London: SCM Press Ltd, 1985), 3.

10 Jacques Dupuis, *Jesus Christ at the Encounter of World Religions,* Translated from the French by Robert R. Barr, First Indian Edition, (New Delhi: Intercultural Publications, 1996), 3.

11 Owen C. Thomas ed., *Attitudes Toward Other Religions: Some Christian Interpretation* (London: SCM Press Ltd, 1969), 10.

12 Jacques Dupis, *Jesus Christ at the Encounter of World Religions,* Translated from the French by Robert R. Barr, First Indian Edition, (New Delhi: Intercultural Publications, 1996), 4.

13 CH. Sreenivasȧ Rao., ed., *Inter-faith Dialogue and World Community* (Madras: CLS, 1991), 14.

14 Owen C. Thomas ed., *Attitudes Toward Other Religions: Some Christian Interpretation* (London: SCM Press Ltd, 1969), 11.

15 Harold G. Coward, *Religious Pluralism and the World Religion* (Madras: University of Madras, 1987), 15.

16 S. J. Samartha, *One Christ Many Religions: Toward A Revised Christology,* 2.

17 Owen C. Thomas ed., *Attitudes Toward Other Religions: Some Christian Interpretation* (London: SCM Press Ltd, 1969), 4.

18 Jose Kuttianimattathil, *Practice and Theology of Interreligious Dialogue*), 29.

Council called on the followers of other religions to cooperate with them to fight against these evils.[19]

Although India witnessed a negative Christian attitude towards people of other faiths, 'the freedom struggle brought together large number of Hindus, Muslims and Christians.'[20]

Orthodox Approaches

It is true that Christian attitude towards other religions has always been evolving and accordingly Catholic and Protestant churches have responded. These responses, though, in early stages, orthodox in nature have yielded scope for more relevant and positive approaches leading to dialogue, there were hurdles to be crossed over.

Christianity, even from 'apostolic times,'[21] attempted to influence other religions, often shrewdly. Such attempts continued during the second and third centuries of the Common Era. It took a back seat for almost one thousand five hundred years and "in the nineteenth century it began to appear again as an issue of major importance for the church and in our day it is perhaps more vital than ever before."[22] The missionary attitude to Hinduism during the early part of 19th century was 'one of stark hostility.'[23] It, of course, changed at the end of the century.

The traditional *Catholic attitude* toward other faith-traditions as found in the Declaration of the Council of Florence (1438-45) is that "there is no salvation outside the Church."[24] The Second Vatican Council (1962-65) decided more positively and declared that "She therefore urges her sons, using prudence and charity, to join members of other religions in discussions and collaboration. While bearing witness to their own Christian faith and life, they must acknowledge those good spiritual and moral elements and social and cultural values found in other religions, and preserve and encourage them."[25] This helped the Indian Church to be open and encouraged the initial efforts of Indian Christians to relate with others.

---

19 Jose Kuttianimattathil, *Practice and Theology of Interreligious Dialogue*, 32.

20 Jose Kuttianimattathil, Practice and Theology of Interreligious Dialogue , 23.

21 A. C. Bouquet, *The Christian Faith and Non-Christian Religions* (New York: Harper and Brothers, 1958), 335.

22 E. C. Dewick, *The Gospel and Other Faiths* (London: The Canterbury Press, 1948), 11.

23 Marcus Braybrooke, *The Undiscovered Christ, A Review of Recent Developments in the Christian Approach to the Hindu* (Madras: CLS, 1973), 1.

24 Valson Thampu, "Christian Spirituality in a Religiously Plural Context," *NCC Review*, Vol. CIX. No. 1 (January 1989), 4.

25 John Hick and Brain Hebblethwaite, ed., *Christianity and Other Religions, Selected Readings* (Great Britain: Fount Paperbacks, 1980), 82.

The *Protestants* too maintained that there was no salvation outside Christianity. Only in the first International Missionary Council in Edinburgh in 1910, for the first time, they discussed the 'missionary approach to other religions.'[26] The Commission for the International Missionary Council 'reiterated its conviction that the Christian attitude to Hinduism, notwithstanding the elements which the Christian must reject, should be one of understanding and sympathy.'[27] The Second IMC at Jerusalem in 1928 paid a major attention to secularism and the relation between older and younger churches. However, 'in spite of these stated new priorities, when the preparatory meeting listed the priority issues for commission work, Christian relationship to other faith was at the top.'[28] There was also a demand 'to respect the religious sentiments of the people of other religions.'[29] The next missionary conference at Tambaram in 1938 was dominated by Hendrik Kraemer's *The Christian Message in a Non-Christian World.* His radically negative attitude towards other religions was vehemently criticized by the Indian theologians. The subsequent IMCs followed a more positive outlook about others. The *World Council of Churches* adopted a positive attitude towards others. It formed a subunit called "Dialogue with people of living faiths and ideologies," in 1977 and WCC issued a set of guidelines for dialogue with the people of living faiths and ideologies.

Theological Standpoints Prior to Dialogue

Alan Race categorized these theological developments as Exclusivism, Inclusivism and Relativism.

Exclusivists hold that, 'only one's own religion is true and good; others are erroneous, false or evil.' For Karl Barth, 'Christianity was revelation and all other religions are religions.' He held that "religion is unbelief,"[30] and the Church is the locus of true religion because it is founded on the basis of revelation. Following Barth, Hendrik Kraemer suggested "Biblical Realism," i.e., the Church is revealed in the Bible and is absolutely true. He claimed, 'as the Christian faith is the crisis of all religions, so the Christian ethic is the crisis of all ethic and ethics.'[31] In contrast

---

26 Eeuwout Klootwijk, *Commitment and Openness: The Inter-Religious Dialogues and Theology of Religions in the Work of Stanley J. Samartha* (Zoeetermeer: Bockencentrum, 1962), 103.

27 Wesley Ariarajah, *Hindus and Christians: A Century of Protestant Ecumenical Thought* (Michigan: William B. Eerdmas Publishing Company, 1991), 27.

28 Wesley Ariarajah, *Hindus and Christians: A Century of Protestant Ecumenical Thought* (Michigan: William B. Eerdmas Publishing Company, 1991), 32.

29 CH. Sreenivasa Rao, ed., *Inter-Faith Dialogue and World Community* (Madras: CLS, 1991), 21.

30 Karl Barth, "The Revelation of God as the Abolition of Religion," *Christianity and Other Religions*, ed., by John Hick and Brain Hebblethwaite, 35.

31 H. Kraemer, *The Christian Message in a Non-Christian World*, (London: The Edinburgh House Press, 1938), 88.

to W. E. Hocking's 'reconception' he held the 'theory of discontinuity'[32] in line with Karl Barth. David Lochhead held 'God's activity in Jesus Christ cannot be equivalent to any other act.'[33] A. C. Bouquet maintained that Christianity 'is the true and best of all faith, rich in marvelous recuperative powers and in the capacity for objective self-criticism.'[34] Ajith Fernando viewed that 'the Christian approaches the unbelievers with a sense of authority wholly derived from God whose word he proclaims.'[35]

Inclusivist/fulfillment model considers that 'all religions are inspired and empowered by God but find their fulfillment only in one religion or saviour.' T. Slater, who laid the foundation for fulfillment theology, said, 'all those noble and true in the non-Christian religions would be taken over into Christianity for their complete fulfillment.' J. N. Farquhar (*The Crown of Hinduism*), demanded 'the death of Hinduism in order to give place to Christianity.' William Miller, the Principal of Madras Christian College envisaged this fulfillment to take place, 'not by replacement or extinction of Hinduism but through the simultaneous development of all higher religions along with Christianity into a world religion with Christ as the centre.'[36] Karl Rahner said, 'the religious people who are outside the visible Christianity are "anonymous Christians."[37] Kenneth Cragg moved forward from the 'unknown Christ' or the 'anonymous Christ' of other faiths and said 'they know him by their own naming.'[38] Hans Kung argued, 'though the religions of the world are ways of salvation for their followers, their salvation will have to be confirmed finally by the saviour of the world, Jesus Christ through communion with him.' Paul Tillich 'affirmed that the crucified Jesus is the most valuable criterion for discerning God's activity within the non-Christian religions.'[39] Heinz Robert Schlette held "the ordinary ways of salvation represented by the religions lead to the one living God, it is true, but, relatively speaking they are paths through the darkness while the extraordinary way of special sacred history, that is to say now, the Church, is one which leads through clear light."[40] Jacques Dupuis was also of the opinion that "far from fostering exclusivism,

32 Marcus Braybrooke, *The Undiscovered Christ,* 3.

33 David Lochhead, *The Dialogical Imperative, A Christian Reflection on Inter-faith Encounter* (New York: ORBIS Books, 1988), 17.

34 A. C. Bouquet, *The Christian Faith and Non-Christian Religions,* 15.

35 Ajith Fernando, *The Christian's Attitude Towards World Religions* (Mumbai: Gospel Literature Services, 1980), 158.

36 CH. Sreenivasa Rao, ed., *Inter-Faith Dialogue and World Community* (Madras: CLS, 1991), 19.

37 Karl Rahner, "Christianity and the Non-Christian Religions," *Christianity and Other Religions,* ed., by John Hick & Paul F. Knitter, 75.

38 Kenneth Cragg, *The Christ of Other Faiths* (Great Britain: ISPCK, 1986), 4.

39 CH. Sreenivasa Rao, ed., *Inter-Faith Dialogue and World Community,* 30- 31.

40 Heinz Robert Schlette, *Towards a Theology of Religions* (London: Burns & Oates, 1966), 104.

Christian Christocentrism is capable of integrating, in their difference, all religious experiences into a truly Catholic – inclusive and universal theology."[41]

Most of the inclusivists hold either to the uniqueness of Jesus Christ or Christocentrism. Some argue for universality of Jesus while others say, 'Christ is the answer to the aspirations of the world.' Hence, Eeuwout Klootwijk asked, "When we start from inclusivist premises, can any dialogue between people of different faiths be a real dialogue."[42]

Relativist view holds that all religions are equal and that lead to the same goal. Hence the question of uniqueness does not arise here. Arnold Toynbee the famous historian advocated a relativist view. For him, all religions come from God and they represent some fact of God's truth. He wrote, "I think that it is possible for us, while holding that our own convictions are true and right, to recognize that, in some measure, all the higher religions are also revelations of what is true and right."[43] And "we should recognize that they too are light radiating from the same source from which our own religion derives its spiritual light."[44] Ernst Troeltsch was another scholar who held the relativist perspective in his refined scholarly works.

A. Pushparajan is of the view that 'Christianity should accept equality of all religions.'[45] Arvind Nirmal criticized the relativist approach as "any talk of a radical relativization of all religions' tends to undermine religions."[46] According to Panikkar relativism 'overlooks the concrete and historical religious situation of real people.'[47] P. D. Devanandan, (*Preparation for Dialogue)* was also critical of it. S. J. Samartha, says, "the affirmation that all religions are the same makes little room for critical interaction between them."[48]

Theologies that Led to Dialogue

It was the pluralist theology that culminated in interreligious dialogue. It holds that 'the different religions are unique, thereby necessitating mutually critical and enriching dialogue.' Pluralism seeks 'mutual recognition of one another's

41 Jacques Dupuis, *Jesus Christ at the Encounter of World Religions,* 247.

42 Eeuwout Klootwijk, *Commitment and Openness: The Inter-Religious Dialogues and Theology of Religions in the Work of Stanley J. Samartha*, 10.

43 Arnold Toynbee, *Christianity Among the Religions of the World* (London: Oxford University Press, 1958)), 99-100.

44 Arnold Toynbee, *Christianity Among the Religions of the World,* 99-100.

45 Pushparajan, "Prospects of Christian Dialogue with other Religions," *Journal of Dharma,* Vol. VIII, No. 3. (July – September 1983), 330.

46 Arvind P. Nirmal, *Heuristic Explorations,* (Madras: CLS, 1990), 75.

47 Raimundo Panikkar, *Unknown Christ of Hinduism,* New edition, (Bangalore, Asian Trading Corporation, 1982), 75.

48 S. J. Samartha, "Commitment and Tolerance in a Pluralistic Society," *NCC Review,* Vol. CVI, No. 2 (February 1986), 75.

truths and values, in order for truth itself to come into proper focus.'[49] Pluralism 'rejects the claims of any particular responses to be absolute,'[50] and "pluralism is not synonymous with tolerance toward a multitude of opinions. Pluralism climaxes in acknowledging the unimaginable, that which is absurd for me and, to a certain degree, unbearable to me."[51] John Hick says, Pluralism includes the process of 'transformation of human existence from self-centeredness to reality-centeredness'[52] that is manifestly taking place among religions. In Paul F. Knitter's "unitive pluralism," "each religion will retain its own uniqueness, but this uniqueness will develop and take on new depths by relating to other religions in mutual dependence."[53] K. P. Aleaz's 'pluralistic inclusivism' envisages that 'richness of religious experience grows by mutual giving and receiving.'[54] My humble appeal is for a 'life sustaining pluralistic'[55] paradigm.

In general 'pluralists call for mutual enrichment; cooperation; and the sharing of religious resources.'[56] Samartha went to the extent of saying that "the rejection of religious pluralism is a more serious form of injustice than the merely economic."[57] Critics say 'pluralism as a category simply does not exist, only another form of exclusivism.'[58] However, the pluralists have underlined the necessity for religions to cooperate and work together for the common good which calls for interreligious dialogue.

Inter-Religious Dialogue a Christian Initiative

Although, pluralists paved the way for dialogue, "It was Pope Paul VI who in his encyclical Ecclesiam Suam, employed for the first time the term 'dialogue' to

49 Alan Race, *Christians and Religious Pluralism: Patterns in the Christian Theology of Religions* (London: SCM Press Ltd, 1983), 148.

50 S. J. Samartha, *Between Two Cultures* (India: Asian Trading Corporation, 1997), 190.

51 Raimond Panikkar, *A Dwelling Place for Wisdom*, Trans. By Annemarie S. Kidder (Louisville: Westminister Press, 1993), 85.

52 John Hick, *Problem of Religious Pluralism* (… : The Macmillan Press Ltd., 1985), 91.

53 Paul F. Knitter, *No Other Name?*, 9.

54 K. P . Aleaz, *Theology of Religions* (Calcutta: Moumita Publishers and Distributors, 1998), 193.

55 S. Robertson, *Bhakti Tradition of Alvars and Theology of Religions* (Kolkata: Punthi Pustak, 2006), 281-286.; S. Robertson, *Approaching Religion in a Pluralistic Context* (Bangalore: BTESSC, 2011), 128-134.; S. Robertson, "Life-sustaining Pluralistic Perspective," *Asia Journal of Theology*, Volume 18, Number 2 (October 2004), 374-397.; S. Robertson, "Religion as Life-sustaining-A Pluralistic Perspective," *Religion and society*, vol. 51, No. 1 (March 2006), 1-20.; S. Robertson, "Pluralism Defended?," *Dharma Deepika*, Issue 29, Volume 13, No. 1 (January-June 2009), 35-48.

56 Eeuwout Klootwijk, *Commitment and Openness: The Inter-Religious Dialogues and Theology of Religions in the Work of Stanley J. Samartha*, 12.

57 S. J. Samartha, *One Christ Many Religions*, 2.

58 Gavin D' Costa, "The Impossibility of a Pluralist View of Religions," *Religious Studies*, Vol. 32, No. 2 (June 1996), 232.

designate the "new attitude" which the Second Vatican council had adopted.[59] P. D. Devanandan, initiated dialogue in India in its narrow sense. For Samartha, "Dialogue is an attempt to understand and express our particularity not just in terms of our own heritage but also in relation to the spiritual heritage or our neighbours of other faiths."[60] More vividly, "Dialogue is part of the living relationship between people of different faiths and ideologies as they share in the life of community."[61] Further "The dialogue which is called for is a face to face existence of living together and struggling together as we seek community."[62] He warned "It will be unwise to form 'a religious alliance' against ideologies in order to save and to perpetuate traditional religious institution."[63]

Dialogue requires openness that 'others have something to say to us – that we need to listen as well as speak.'[64] Harold G. Coward writes, 'it is the way of dialogue, and not theological bulldozing,' that is required of Christian in today's pluralistic world.[65] Samartha writes, "Inter-religious dialogue, carefully prepared and practiced can help people to respond to the dangers of religious fundamentalism not just on the political but on the religious level as well."[66] In the words of Raimundo Panikkar, "the way to peace is neither isolation nor competition, but through dialogues."[67]

For Panikkar, 'the context of dialogue, is not the narrowly specific "religious" field but the arena of life, the daily struggle for justice, peace, happiness.'[68] J. Rusell Chandran, says, 'one of the important objectives of dialogue will be our common quest for a just society free from all forms of oppression and marginalization.'[69]

---

59 A. Pushparajan, *From Conversion to Fellowship,* 47.

60 S. J. Samartha, *Courage for Dialogue*, 99.

61 S. J. Samartha, *Dialogue as a Continuing Christian Concern*, 11.

62 S. J. Samartha, "Courage for Dialogue: An Interpretation of the Nairobi Debate," *Religion and Society* Vol. XXIII, No. 3. (September 1976), 35.

63 S. J. Samartha, "Dialogue as a Continuing Christian Concern" in *Christianity and other Religions,* 159.

64 John B. Cobb, Jr., "Dialogue," *Death or Dialogue*? Ed. By Leonard Swidler, John B. Cobb Jr., et al., (London: SCM Press, 1990), 2.

65 Harold G. Coward, *Religious Pluralism and the World Religions*, 40.

66 S. J. Samartha, "The Future of Inter-religious Dialogue: Threats and Promises," *Journal of Dharma,* Vol. XIX, No. 1 (January-March 1997), 83.

67 Raimundo Panikkar, "Foreword" in *Hindu-Christian Dialogue: Perspectives and Encounters* (New York: Orbis Books, 1990), 9.

68 Raimundo Panikkar, "Foreword" in *Hindu-Christian Dialogue: Perspectives and Encounters* (New York: OBRIS Books, 1990), 9.

69 J. Russel Chandran, "Mission in Today's Pluralistic Context," *NCC Review*, Vol. CXIV, No. 5 (May-June, 1994), 360.

Dialogue cannot be pursued unless considered from a 'life sustaining perspective,'[70] which Jesus practiced.

Christians fear that "in the case of dialogue with believers in other traditions there is danger that sympathetic appreciation of their concerns may lead to compromise of faith itself."[71] Another fear is 'dialogue with men of other faith is a betrayal of mission and disobedience to the command to proclaim the Gospel.'[72] Another perception is that 'dialogue has so far tended to favour the dominant class and not the poor.'[73]

Inter-Religious Dialogue as Perceived By Others

There is a perception among people of other faiths and ideologies that 'dialogue is simply a new and subtle Christian tool for mission that is being forged in the post-colonial era'[74] and "there is always the fear of hidden agendas."[75] Sita Ram Goel opines, "'dialogue' does not seem to be a sincere attempt at reconciliation; on the contrary, it is only a strategy for survival on the part of Christianity" and he appealed that "It is high time for the Christians theologies to come down to earth and recognize every person's right to seek truth and salvation in his or her own way."[76] It is endorsed by S. J. Samartha as "Neighbours of other faiths also ask humbly and sometimes not so humbly: what about our centers and our names?"[77] Paul J. Griffiths says Christians have 'not learned to listen very carefully to what members of' other communities say.[78]

The Buddhist response to Christian initiated dialogue is a 'responsible participation I the conviction that the message of the Buddha has a distinctive contribution to make to the world today.'[79] Now Muslims have a seemingly positive attitude towards dialogue that they 'attempt to work out a theology of

70 S. Robertson, *Bhakti Tradition of Alvars and Theology of Religions,* 281-286.; S. Robertson, *Approaching Religion in a Pluralistic Context,* 128-134.; S. Robertson, "Life-sustaining Pluralistic Perspective," *Asia Journal of Theology,* 374-397.; S. Robertson, "Religion as Life-sustaining- A Pluralistic Perspective," *Religion and Society*, 1-20.; S. Robertson, "Pluralism Defended?," *Dharma Deepika*, 35-48.

71 John B. Cobb Jr., "Dialogue," in *Death or Dialogue*, 3.

72 S. J. Samartha, "Dialogue as a Continuing Christian Concern," in *Christianity and Other Religions*, 62.

73 Jose Kuttianimattathil, *Practice and Theology of Inter-religious Dialogue* (Bangalore: Kristu Jyothi Publications, 1995), 118.

74 S. J. Samartha, "Dialogue as a Continuing Christian Concern," in *Christianity and other Religions*, 3.

75 S. J. Samartha, *One Christ Many Religions,* 16.

76 Sita Ram Goel, *Hindu of Hindu – Christian Encounters* (New Delhi: Voice of India, 1989), 4-5.

77 S. J. Samartha, *One Christ Many Religions,*18.

78 Paul J. Griffiths, *Christianity Through Non-Christians Eyes* (New York: ORBIS Books, 1998), 3.

79 S. J. Samartha, *One Christ Many Religions*, 31.

dialogue based on Islam even as Christians are seeking to develop a Christian theology of dialogue.'[80]

These developments strengthen the commitment for real dialogue pursued and inspired by religions and ideologies while persuading openness to go beyond the narrow constrains of religions and ideologies without dishonoring their commonalities and differences for a 'life sustaining' dialogue.

Life Sustaining Dialogue

It is obvious that there is an overwhelming commitment for interreligious dialogue if initiated for the sake of addressing common concerns that affect the earth. Wilfred Cantwell Smith writes that, "Unless men can learn to understand and to be loyal to each other across religious frontiers, unless we can build a world in which people profoundly of different faiths can live together and work together, then the prospects for our planet's future are not bright."[81] S. J. Samartha asserts, "It is agreed that the most helpful relationship between persons of different faiths in the world today must be one of co-operation in pursuing common purposes like justice, peace and human rights."[82] Paul F. Knitter opines that people and events in my life have led me, sometimes lured me, to what has become for me the moral obligation to join 'dialogue and global responsibility.'[83]

Religions must speak and act together in dialogue 'to removing the oppression that contaminates our globe,'[84] to discuss the 'world of suffering,'[85] to establish 'peace,'[86] to work for 'eco-human justice,'[87] 'to learn from and help each other'[88] and to help the 'poor.'[89] Dialogue can help correct the perceptions that 'religions continue to be more effective at motivating wars than peace,'[90] it is 'used

80 S. J. Samartha, *One Christ Many Religions,* 24.

81 Wilfred Cantwell Smith, "The Christian in a Religiously Plural World", *Christianity and Other Religions*, 95.

82 S. J. Samartha, *Courage for Dialogue: Ecumenical Issues in Inter-religious Relationships* (Geneva: World Council of Churches, 1981), 30.

83 Paul F. Knitter, One Earth Many Religions, 11.

84 Paul F. Knitter, "Toward a Liberation Theology of Religions," *The Myth of Christian Uniqueness*, 181.

85 Paul F. Knitter, *One Earth Many Religions*, Mutlifatith Dialogue and Global Responsibility (New York: ORBIS, 1996), 58.

86 Paul F. Knitter, *One Earth Many Religions*, Mutlifatith Dialogue and Global Responsibility (New York: ORBIS, 1996), 66.

87 Paul F. Knitter, *One Earth Many Religions*, 113.

88 Paul F. Knitter, *No other Name*?, 6.

89 Aloysius Pieris, *Fire and Water, Basic Issues in Asian Buddhism and Christianity* (New York: Orbis Books, 1996), 156.

90 Paul F. Knitter, "Inter-religious Dialogue and the Unity of Humanity," *Journal of Dharma* Vol. XVI, No. 4 (October – December 1992), 284.

as handmaidens to political interests'[91] and it is used as a tool for communal riots motivated by nonreligious considerations too.

Life Sustaining Vision

The 'life sustaining dialogue' demands that every individual or community must be rooted and filled with the Sakti or spirit of their particular religion or ideology while being open to learning from each other and working with each other even with differences. It is a long, laborious and sacrificial process comparable to the notion of "Jivan Mukta" in the Indian setting that considers the world as one, i.e., *Vasudevakudumbam* where concern for the lives of others is the sign of spiritual maturity attained in and through interreligious and inter ideological dialogues. This process takes spiritual inspiration for dialogue seriously because the person who is rooted in the spiritual foundation can be the upholder of *dharma* towards people, creatures, and the cosmos as a whole. This realization dawns on a Christian because of his/her intensive commitment to the principles of Jesus.

A close observation of life of the people of different traditions can teach us that every human being is striving to live. A better life is what every one aspires for. No one wants to enslave himself/herself to poverty or suffering of any kind. In this struggle for life, rather better life, no individual is comfortably placed because of his/her religious identity. Interreligious/ideological dialogue is an unavoidable tool to realize the multifaceted potential of humanity to establish a 'life sustaining vision.' Our endeavor in working for the friendliness of religions is to strengthen life. Life sustaining vision of dialogue is the tangible solution for religious harmony, peace and prosperity.

The Church has the responsible mission of facilitating cooperation between religions and ideologies through a selfless dialogue which is symbolized in the death of Jesus on the cross with the firm hope of glory. One has to be strong in his/her faith and conviction for effective and fruitful dialogue.

Jesus came to enrich life, to obliterate all the religious systems and practices which worked against 'life.' To give life to the needy, Jesus broke away many traditional laws. He was always of the view that religion is for life and life is not for religion. Hence, a 'life sustaining vision of dialogue' can help religions and ideologies to explore their best for a sustainable life.

91 S. J. Samartha, "Inter-religious Relationships in the secular State," 62.

7

Towards a Life Sustaining Pluralistic Perspective

1. Introduction

Human beings never lived without practicing one or another form of religion. They always attempted to comprehend the ultimate mystery in manifold forms, as their intellect and cultural context permitted.

Thus, the plurality of religion is as old as human history. However, our times have witnessed a shift from the plurality of religions to religious pluralism. That is, religious pluralism has become a significant subject matter concerned with all religions. It is not just accepting the diversity of religions but venturing to fuse a cooperative relationship among religions in order to actualize the real purpose, of religions-protecting and enhancing life. It is not uniformity but unity without losing individuality.

This paradoxical context of our time devolves Christianity to formulate a theology of religions relevant to pluralistic contexts in the light of the life and work of Jesus Christ who was committed to the ultimate mystery on the one hand and the life sustaining situation on the other. Hence, exploring the possibilities for a life sustaining pluralist perspective is the immediate task of any contemporary and relevant Christian theology of religions.

It is necessary because the global religious context and new sciences have brought different peoples, cultures, and religions much closer than ever before. People are face to face with traditions once foreign and alien to them.

The specific Indian context, particularly the neo-Hindu assertion reveals that each religion needs to be left unintervened because each is complete and sufficient enough for the votaries to attain the purpose of religion. And no religion or religious person has anything significant, which the other religions or religious persons do not possess.

The ever increasing misuse of religions for extremist purposes and political gains and the large scale human made disasters, which threaten the existence of life on the planet earth require that religions should be united without damaging the differences for the sake of life itself. This is possible only in a life sustaining pluralistic perspective. It enables of different religions to address the issues, which challenge and threaten life as a whole.

2. What is Life Sustaining Pluralistic Perspective?

As Christians are committed to Jesus, who promoted a life sustaining vision and the present realities of the world demand a life sustaining pluralist perspective, it is essential to expound it further.

Beyond religion, culture, language, race, geography, climate, history etc., the common core of humanity is life. It is unfortunate that often religions are used to separate people and destroy life rather than uniting and strengthening. Such untoward developments need to be countered at all levels. It is possible if, life the only uniting principle across religious boundaries is taken in to the heart of inter religious endeavors.

Each individual is earnestly engaged in the daily struggles of life. This striving is not specific to any single religious community. Struggles of life may vary from person to person, yet every one is struggling to live. The struggle for existence is a day-to-day reality. No single being can escape the stark reality of life – happiness, sorrow, poverty, sickness etc. In other words, the struggles of life-threats and challenges concern every one beyond religious boundaries. Therefore the struggle for existence can bring people of all walks of life, who are committed to the genuine quest for the mystery, together for common action in order to sustain life.

An analysis of ordinary life will reveal that, human beings are striving to make a better life. Similarly every collective effort of humanity including religious, is devoted to sustaining life in all its possible fullness or committed to achieve a better life on the planet earth. The problem of religious pluralism too, will not be applicable unless it concentrates on the issues confronting life, besides the other regular objectives. It is not just human life, but human life in relation to the rest of creation. Arvid P. Nirmal writes, "the primary object of any theology is certainly the concept of God, but we need to recognize the fact that the primary datum for doing theology is human life."[1]

Religions have always embarked on the way to support and strengthen life in many ways. The moral and spiritual nature of humanity distinguishes it from other forms of life. The program of inter-religious understanding cannot be substantial if it ignores the necessity of a strong spiritual and ethical foundation.

---

1 Arvind P. Nirmal, Heuistic Explorations, Madras, C.L.S., 1990, p. 98.

Of course, today, religions are used for selfish reasons. To restore the pristine purity of religion, there should be a sound theology of religions. A sound, relevant and contemporary theology of religions should emerge from the concrete religious and ethical commitment of the individuals. So, that it can evolve a lasting and a fruitful solution to the current threats and challenges of life. The problem of the current world is lack of genuine and strong spiritual life. Only those who are spiritually mature alone will be able to see the commonality of life beyond all the human-made differences. They alone will be able to realize the equality and the significant dynamic nature and purpose of human life.

It is established beyond doubt that reality is not plural but it has been understood in manifold forms in consonance with the cultural backgrounds. The diverse understanding of the mystery is manifested in various forms of religions. As the reality is a mystery, humanity cannot be divided on religious grounds. Religions are the different, humble and modest attempts of people who lived in diverse circumstances-culture, climate, language, geography, etc., to understand the one mystery, which is still beyond conceptualized dimensions.

It is necessary therefore to accept the plural structure of reality. It is not that reality is plural but the one reality can be understood in manifold forms. Plurality of religions is thus purposeful. They are testimonies to the incomprehensible and the transcendental nature of the mystery besides its immanence. Different religions are independent in their own rights. But they cannot function in isolation, if they have to serve the real purpose of enhancing human life at a time when the world is torn with religious strife of all shorts and degrees.

As practical life and religion are intertwined, the issues related to life cannot be approached in isolation from the rich religious resources at our disposal in the form of many religious traditions. Any solution that ignores the significance of spiritual foundation for life and the problems threatening it will be incomplete. Hence, it is necessary that the issue of religious pluralism be pursued from a life sustaining pluralistic perspective, which is the result of one's earnest commitment to the ultimate mystery. Here, concern for life and commitment to the quest for the ultimate mystery go hand in hand in order to gather all the dynamic religious resources without any discrimination, for the promotion of a better life in harmony with God's creation.

Participation in the struggles of people and commitment to the ultimate mystery are the two sides of the same coin. They make a complete paradigm. One without the other is incomplete, counterproductive and unacceptable. Insisting on the one and sidelining the other is risky. One who is committed to the mystery will not slack in his/her responsibility to life and its paradoxes. Without an intimate relation with the mystery one's concern for the life of the other will be shallow and short lived.

It needs to be noted that the theology of religions pursued from a life sustaining pluralist perspective is committed to friendship and co-operation among religions without interfering in the personal religious interest of the individual. It is committed to life and its realities. It seeks a friendly cooperation between religions to pool their resources to sustain life at all levels. Religions are to guard life. If they fail to do so, they cease to be religions. As the challenges to life are increasing, one or two religions alone cannot save them in isolation. To protect and enhance life, all religions should work together without losing their individuality and differences. This is possible only if a theology of religions is developed from the 'life sustaining pluralistic perspective,' which reflects its ontological base in the mystery.

3. Premises of Life Sustaining Pluralistic Perspective

3.1. Mystery as the Center

The primary premise of life sustaining pluralist perspective is the mystery. Treating the ultimate as the mystery is the only answer to the diverse forms of religiosity of humanity to which life alone is the uniting/common principle. Commitment to the genuine quest for the better understanding of mystery automatically calls for concrete concern for life. Concern for life without commitment to the mystery will be short lived. Thus these two are inter- connected.

Scholars who are committed to the problem of religious pluralism are convinced that the ultimate reality is beyond the comprehension of human beings and therefore, it is a mystery. Paul F. Knitter writes, the 'divine mystery which we know in Jesus and which we call *Theos* or God, is ever greater than the reality and message of Jesus.'[2] Panikkar explains this mystery from a pluralist point of view as "pluralism dethrones monism, and with it monotheism. Reality does not need to be transparent and intelligible in itself."[3] In the words of S. J. Samartha, "... religions should be recognized as having responded differently to the mystery of the ultimate."[4] Further, "a sense of mystery provides a point of unity to all plurality."[5] This point of unity holds all religions together with a common purpose. Without a sense of this point of unity, the scope of religious pluralism shall remain bleak.

This is the meeting point of the horizontal and vertical dimensions of Christian theology of religions. Vertically, the theology of religion revolves around the mystery and horizontally the mystical root inspires people of all faiths to actively engage in the struggles of humanity. Thus the unceasing quest for the mystery is the ontological uniting point and the contemporary energizer for a life sustaining pluralistic perspective.

---

2 Paul F. Knitter, *Jesus and the Other Names*, New York, Orbis, Books, 1996, p. 9.

3 Raimon Panikkar, *A Dwelling place for Wisdom*, Trans. by Annemarie S. Kidder, Louisville, Kentucky, Westminister/John Knox Press, 1995, p. 85.

4 S. J. Samartha, *The Lordship of Jesus Christ and Religious Pluralism*, Madras, The Christian Literature Society, 1981, p. 23.

5 S. J. Samartha, *One Christ Many Religions, op. cit.*, p. 5.

3.2. Jesus is Life - Centered

Jesus was both God-centered and life-centered. Life-centered because he always subjected himself to the will of God. He repeated that he came to do the will of God. Jesus, because of his intimate relation with God, called Him father. This father-hood of God is the way God is addressed by Christians. But the Reality is still a mystery beyond the nomenclature 'father.' The mystery is the axis around which all faith-traditions revolve to seek meaning.

Jesus was life-centered. He wanted religions and religious practices to be life sustaining and not life destroying. Whoever, or which ever faith tradition, is involved in fulfilling the will of God was in the company of Jesus. He said 'whoever does the will of my father is my brother and sister.'[6] Even if such an action took place, in an unexpected environment, Jesus appreciated. Jesus esteemed the faith of the centurion and said 'even in Israel there was not such faith.'[7] For Jesus 'the neighbor'[8] is one who involves in life saving activity. That is why, he had to say 'men will come from east and west, and from north and south, and sit at table in the kingdom of God.'[9]

Jesus' concern for the needy is outstanding. His selection of people for the reward was on the basis of the amount of service they did to the needy.[10] This is what, is declared in the 'Nazareth manifesto.'[11] He wanted that humanity's relation to the ultimate mystery and to the people around should go hand in hand. He said, 'love the lord and love your neighbor.'[12]

Jesus' main enemies were people who used religion as a mere ceremonial observance, as a means of oppression and as a means to escape from the responsibilities.[13] He wanted to restore Sabbath as a source of life for the needy. He said 'Sabbath is for man and man is not for Sabbath.'[14] A taunting question he faced was 'whether to save or destroy life on the Sabbath.'[15] He proved in his life that, saving the life of the needy is the chief concern of people who are committed to the ultimate reality, of course, in manifold forms.

Thus any inter religious venture need to work on these two dimensions. One is the conviction that, all are committed to the ultimate through diverse channels.

6 Mark 3:35.

7 Luke 7:9.

8 Luke 10:29.

9 Luke 13:29.

10 Matthew 25:35.

11 Luke 4:18-19.

12 Mark 12:30 & 31.

13 Matthew 9:13, 15:6, & Mark 7:11 & Luke 11:42.

14 Mark 2:27.

15 Matthew 12:10, & Mark 3:4, & Luke 6:9.

And the other is that, that commitment demands that life is strengthened in all possible ways to achieve, harmony, peace, justice and equality for all.

3.3. Life Struggle-Threats and Challenges

The next premise of life sustaining pluralist perspective is life. That is, the struggles of life-the challenges and threats, which life as a whole confronts in manifold forms. These are common to every individual beyond the boundaries of religions. Every one can join in the fight against the odds of life as religious convictions and differences cannot intervene in the process. As life is common for all, religious cooperation can be effected on the premise of life, because life is the same but religions are many.

Life's realities are the real testing ground of one's commitment to the ultimate mystery and his or her life sustaining vision of life, which is the reflection of one's genuine submission to the continuous quest for the real knowledge about the ultimate mystery.

3.4. Love the Linking Point

Life is prior to religion. Religion adds meaning to life. But both life and religions find their ontological root in the mystery. The connecting point between the one life and the many religions is love. It is the love of God that motivates love for all living beings. And the sincere concern for life at large deepens one's commitment to the ultimate mystery. The love of God brings people closer to God and closer to the struggles of life. It is *agape* that produces philial love.

4. Promise and Prospects of Life Sustaining Pluralistic Perspective

4.1. It is Based Upon the Life and Work of Jesus Christ

The paradigm for life sustaining pluralist perspective is found in the life and work of Jesus Christ. All through his life, he was life-centered, that is, he dedicated his life to sustain the life of others in all possible ways. His concern for the value of life was the result of his commitment to his father, who is understood as a mystery in the Indian context. He was always conscious about his responsibility to the father and acknowledged the people, who involved in such responsibility as his brothers, sisters and mother irrespective of their backgrounds. Thus, life sustaining pluralist perspective is a great promise to Christian theology of religions and prospective to the Indian context, which witnesses the intricacies of an intensively pluralist context.

4.2. The Real Purpose of Religions is Upheld

Religions are to protect and strengthen life in all possible ways. Jesus wanted that all forms of religious observances-sabbath, offering, law etc., should not become a hindrance to life-giving or life-saving acts. When inter religious cooperation is pursued from the point of life sustaining pluralist perspective, the struggles and concerns of people take precedence over other formal observances. Be they poverty, sickness, disasters, caste hierarchy, women's concerns, ecological imbalance or any other issue.

Once Swami Vivekananda said, 'the crying evil in the East is not want of religion, but want of bread.'[16] He saw God in man and said, "since God dwells in man, He can be worshipped by serving man."[17] Similarly, "Gandhi always appealed to the religion of humanity underlying all religions."[18] Thus the life sustaining pluralist perspective promises commitment to one's own religion and offers prospective service to life as reflection of God's love.

4.3. Plurality of Religions Accounted For

Any model that is used to bring about unity and fellowship among religions should take into account the fact that each religion is unique on its own merit and at the same time it could relate with the other. In other words, a balance should be established to maintain the individuality of religions on the one hand and the unity of religions on the other. The unity is not uniformity or monolithic structure, but the collective efforts of individual religions without losing their individual identity. Gandhi said, "the correct attitude is one of firm adherence to one's own religion coupled with an equal reverence towards all other religions. It is not simply a question of tolerating other faiths, but of believing that all faiths lead to the same goal."[19] Again he said, 'let Hindus become better Hindus, Muslims and Christians better Muslims and Christians.'[20]

The promising aspect is that the life sustaining pluralist perspective treats different religions as various attempts of people to comprehend the ultimate mystery through the ways and means familiar to them in their own context. It is prospective because it pursues inter religious cooperation with the assumption that unity of religions is possible without losing individuality and differences. In other words, there is scope for diversity of religions on the one hand and unity of religions without uniformity on the other.

4.4. Convergence of Spirituality and Life

The life sustaining pluralist perspective is the convergence of deep spirituality, which is the result of one's paramount religious conviction and commitment for establishing better life, which is the reflection of one's intense relation with the ultimate mystery. Without deeper spiritual footing the theology of religions would remain a mirage. For Ramakrishna Paramahamsa "it is only by releasing

---

16 D. S. Sharma, *op.cit.* p. 151.

17 Swami Gokulananda, 'Vivekananda – Unifying Vision and Mission and our Response', *N.C.C. Review*, Vol. CXIII, No. 8, [September 1993], p. 507.

18 Nirmal Minz, op. cit., p. 50.

19 D. S. Sharma, *op. cit.*, pp. 193, 194.

20 Mahatma Gandhi, *op. cit.*, p. 20.

a flood of enlightened religious feeling that society can be cleansed and men and women made to grow to their spiritual heights."[21]

According to Gandhi, "religion is best propagated by the noble lives led by its followers."[22] For him, "preaching the Gospel means to live the Gospel."[23] Again he said, "religion can be defended only by the purity of its adherents and their good deeds, never by their quarrels with those of other faiths."[24] This is the need of the hour in India. The life sustaining pluralist perspective promises a concrete spiritual foundation for the theology of religions on the one hand and looks for prospects in its efforts to transform the life of people, who adhere to varieties of religious experiences on the other.

4.5. Mission of the Church

People of other faiths categorise the reconciliatory and confidence building effort of the Church in a pluralist society as indirect ways of conversion. Thus a theology of religions proposed from life sustaining pluralist perspective can convey the message that Christian initiatives are not for conversion but to create awareness among people about the need for cooperative action among religions to avert the misuse of religions and to consider the possibilities of creatively utilizing the dynamic potentials of religions. It is not to convert people from one religion to the other but extending invitation for people of all walks of life to a change of attitude towards people of different faiths and the realities of life. Of course, in a developing society, change of religion is the freedom and fundamental right of the individual concerned according to his or her conviction and necessity. We need a change of attitude but not religion.

Such an approach promises a possibility for the furtherance of the great commission of the Lord relevant to the context. Its prospect is the hope that all religions will be sensitive to the problems of life and function to actualize the supreme expectations of religions in the day to day life.

5. Why Life Sustaining Pluralistic Perspective?

5.1. Global Context

There were remarkable changes in the global context from the fifteenth century onwards. These changes resulted from the impact of geographical explorations, advancement in science and communication technology and the collapse of colonial power. The geographical explorations, starting from the fifteenth century onwards, expanded the horizon of human knowledge. They revealed that, there were diverse people, faiths, cultures etc., in the world. These discoveries 'stimulated

21 D. S. Sharma, *op. cit.,* p. 122.

22 *Ibid.*, p. 193.

23 Nirmal Minz, *op. cit.,* p. 47.

24 Mahatma Gandhi, *op. cit.,* p. 46.

a new interest in other religions'[25] among the people, who once thought that there was no other religion besides their own. The interest was to learn other religions and see their difference from Christianity.

Scientific developments brought tremendous change in communication technology, including transport. They reduced the distance between people at all levels-information of all shorts including religious. V. F. Vineeth writes, 'our world has been reduced to a 'global village' and contact with men of other faith has now become a day-today reality for many, both in the East and in the West.'[26] It is not a mere contact with the other, but a chance to learn from the other and exchange ideas, especially, religious. In the words of J. Paul Rajashekar, "...people from different religious traditions have not only come into greater contact but are also being exposed to mutual claims and commitments."[27] This situation is a challenge for the missionary religions.

Added to these two was the collapse of colonial power. Discoveries revealed the realities of the expanded globe. Communication reduced the distance of the globe and brought them together. It was the break of colonial power that provided adequate freedom at all levels. There emerged the 'revivalism of indigenous cultural and religious values of the people of the liberated nations.'[28] It affected the Church as well. According to S. J. Samartha, 'it was only a couple of decades after the dismantling of colonialism that both the Vatican (1965) and the World Council of Churches (1971) came out rather reluctantly, with more positive statements about people of other faiths.'[29]

These developments created the awareness that humanity can no longer be separated on the basis of faiths and creeds. In short, these developments enabled the people to move from the plurality of religions to religious pluralism. That is, it is not just accepting the existence of many religions, but working towards the cooperation of religions for the sake of better life.

5.2. Religious Context

The urgency for the Church to respond to the challenge of religious pluralism was captured by the scientific study of religions. It helped 'the first time Christian scholars with full factual information on the other world religions.'[30] According

25 J. Paul Rajasekar, ed., *Religious Pluralism and Lutheran Theology (LWF Report 23/24)*, Geneva, 1988, p. 11.

26 V. F. Vineeth, "Interreligious Dialogue: Past and Present a Critical Appraisal," *Journal of Dharma*, Vol. XIX, No. 1, (January – March 1997), p. 42.

27 J. Paul Rajasjekar, ed., *Religious Pluralism and Lutheran Theology, op. cit.*, p. 9.

28 V. F. Vineeth, *Journal of Dharma, op. cit.*, p. 42.

29 S. J. Samartha, *One Christ Many Religions; Towards a Revised Christology*, Bangalore, SATHRI in Association with Wordmakers, 1992, p. 3.

30 Harold G. Howard, *Religious Pluralism and the World Religions*, Madras, The Dr. S. Radhakrishnan Institute for Advanced Study in Philosophy, University of Madras, 1983, p. 25.

to John Hick, "perhaps the most important factor has been the modern explosion of knowledge among Christians in the West concerning the other great religious traditions of the world."[31] In the words of Kuncheria Pathil, 'discovery of the other faiths and the recognition of their role in the universal salvific plan of God is perhaps the greatest challenge to Christian theology today.'[32] It changed the perception of Christianity about other religions. Harold G. Howard writes, "no longer can Christians view Hindus, Buddhists and Muslims as heathens living in far off lands to be converted by Christian missionaries."[33]

Along with the knowledge of other faith traditions, there was 'a knowledge of other religious *persons.*'[34] This is to say that adhering to a particular faith tradition does not change the natural course of events in life. In other words, discriminations on the basis of religions is unwarranted for. Paul F. Knitter writes about others that, "they are normal happy human beings, getting their jobs done, raising their families as well, perhaps better, than we, and living lives of love, of service, of commitment."[35]

It is not just the knowledge of many religions and many people that was brought to light but also it revealed the 'multi religious context of humanity'[36] everywhere. This is to say that plurality of religions is natural and that cannot be ruled out. What can be done is that the plurality of spiritual traditions may be enabled to work together to face the threats and challenges that the globe is facing.

The other challenges to Christianity are the 'growing Western interest and openness toward Eastern religions.'[37] Jacques Dupuis writes, "while thousands of Westerners, especially the young, journey to India each year in quest of religious experiences Christianity has apparently denied them, Hindu ashrams and Buddhist monasteries are built in Western countries, attracting no insignificant number of devotees."[38]

The missionary nature and monotheistic structure of the fast growing Islam was another challenge to Christianity. In the words of Owen C. Thomas, "with

---

31 John Hick 'The Non-absoluteness of Christianity,' *The Myth of Christian Uniqueness; Toward a Pluralistic Theology of Religions*, ed. By, John Hick and Paul F. Knitter, New York, ORBIS Books, 1987, p. 17.

32 Kuncheria Pathil, 'Christian Approach to Other Faiths, A Historical Perspective,' *N.C.C. Review,* Vol. CX, No. 2 (February 1990), p. 66.

33 *Ibid.*, p. 25.

34 Paul F. Knitter, *No Other Name?: A Critical Survey of Christian Attitudes Toward the World Religions*, London, SCM Press Ltd., 1985, p. 3.

35 *Ibid.*, p. 3.

36 Jacques Dupuis, *Jesus Christ at the Encounter of World Religions*, Translated from the French by Robert R. Barr, First Indian Edition, New Delhi, Intercultural Publications, 1996, p. 3.

37 Owen C. Thomas ed., *Attitude Toward Other Religions; Some Christian Interpretations*, London, SCM Press Ltd., 1969, p. 10.

38 Jacques Dupuis, *Jesus Christ at the Encounter of World Religions, op. cit.*, p. 4.

the rise of Islam the Christian church was faced for the first time with a new and powerful missionary religion."[39]

The scientific study of religions revealed that no religion could be treated as absolute, because there are elements of truth in every religion. Added to this was the critical study of the New Testament, which questioned the authenticity of some of the unique claims of Christians.

5.3. New Sciences

The modern scientists are convinced that, even in science, there is nothing called the truth. It 'changes' always. This idea is reflected in modern philosophy as well. According to Paul F. Knitter "the catch phrase is that we are not in a state of being but in a state, or better a process of becoming."[40] It means, including religion nothing is static. His main argument was that, science, philosophy, sociology, economics and politics of contemporary world indicate that, the global scenario demands the co-operation of all to face the common challenges. His list of challenges is 'starvation and malnutrition, economic inequality, dwindling resources, exploitation and poverty, official flouting of human rights and nuclear weaponry.'[41] In order to avoid the possible irresponsible question of the few he writes, "to be religious and to be serious about it one must, generally belong to a religion."[42]

There is a great awareness among sincere people of all religious traditions to be a member of a particular religion in order to be a member of wider religious family for the sake of establishing a better community life.

5.4. Response From India

5.4.1 Reaction From Hindu Thinkers

C. V. Mathew takes the readers way back and says "in short, by the middle of the 19th century we see the slow but steady emergence of a resistant Hinduism in the national context."[43] It should be kept in mind that Hinduism does not subscribe to a single line of thought pattern in matters of religion. Yet their aversion to the Christian missionaries and the superior claims of Christianity is uniform.

39 Owen C. Thomas ed., *Attitudes Toward Other Religions; Some Christian Interpretations, op. cit.*, p. 11.

40 Paul F. Knitter, *No Other Name?; A Critical Survey of Christian Attitudes Toward the World Religions, op. cit.*, p. 7.

41 *Ibid.*

42 *Ibid.*, p. 13.

43 C. V. Mathew, *The Saffron Mission [A Historical Analysis of Modern Hindu Missionary Ideologies and Practices]*, New Delhi, ISPCK, 1999, p. 56.

5.4.1.1. Swami Dayananda Saraswati

His reaction to Christianity and Christian mission is stated as, "Dayananda firmly believes that the world would be better of without such an ensnaring and superstitious faith as Christianity."[44] Paul J. Griffiths quotes extensively from the *Light of Truth* to show similar reactions. Regarding the birth narrative of Jesus Christ, Dayananda said, "only people in a state of barbarism can believe them."[45] Jesus' temptation proves that 'He is not omniscient.' Referring to the preaching of Jesus he argued that if only righteous could be saved what is the use of Jesus. Again he said, if all will be punished according to their deeds why preach about salvation. For Swamy Dayananda Saraswati, Christianity is not at all necessary for the Indian soil. He writes, rather using a harsh expression, as "in a country where no trees are seen to grow, even the–castor oil plant is considered to be the biggest and the best tree, in like manner in a country where none but the ignorant savages lived, Christ was rightly considered a great man but Christ can be of no count among the learned and wise men of the present day."[46]

5.4.1.2. Swami Vivekananda

Swami Vivekananda had great respect for the teaching of Jesus Christ, but not for Christianity as a religion. He said about Jesus that "He was unfettered, unbound Spirit."[47]

Paul J. Griffiths quotes from '*Christ the messenger*', to explain the grievances of Swami Vivekananda about Christianity. For Vivekananda, Christians have ignored the teachings of Christ and insist upon the divinity of Jesus Christ. Their argument looks, 'if you credit the master you will be saved; if not, there is no salvation for you.' Thus for Vivekananda, "...the whole teaching of the Master is degenerated and all the struggle and fight is for the personality of the Man."[48]

His reaction to Christian propagation was so vehement that for him Christianity 'failed to satisfy the spiritual longing of the educated and scientific folks.'[49] He also said that, "what the nation wants is a religion of strength based on the inherent divinity of the human soul, and not a religion of weakness teaching that man is a born sinner."[50] This, of course, is his attack upon the Christian doctrine of sin.

---

44 *Ibid.*, p. 74.

45 Paul J. Griffiths, *Christianity Through Non-Christian Eyes*, Fifth Printing, New York, Orbis Books, 1998, p. 198.

46 *Ibid.*, p. 201.

47 Paul J. Griffiths, *op. cit.*, p. 210.

48 *Ibid.*, p. 213.

49 C. V. Mathew, *The Saffron Mission (A Historical Analysis of Modern Hindu Missionary Ideologies and Practices)*, Delhi, ISPCK, 1999, p. 128.

50 D. S. Sharma, *op. cit.*, p. 155.

Swami Vivekananda's view of religions is stated as "let us, therefore, find, God not only in Jesus of Nazareth but in all the Great ones that have preceded him, in all that came after him, and all that are yet to come... They are all manifestations of the same infinite God."[51]

5.4.1.3. Mahatma Gandhi

D. S. Sharma writes, 'like every true Hindu, Gandhi believes that all religions are branches of one and the same tree-the Tree of Truth.'[52] Nirmal Minz states, "all religions, he held, are appropriations of Satya under the condition of cultural limitation and human finitude... They are equal in the sense that no single religion has the absolute or exclusive truth."[53] Further, "it is my conviction that all the great faiths of the world are true, are God-ordained and that they serve the purpose of God and of those who have been brought up in those surroundings."[54] Gandhi believed, "as all religions were rooted in faith in the same God, all were of equal value, while each was specially adapted to its own people."[55] He has put in a nut-shell his view as "after long study and experience I have come to the conclusion that: [1] all religions are true, [2] all religions have some error in them, [3] all religions are almost as dear to me as my own Hinduism."[56]

Apart from the acceptance of the empirical realities of religion he also talked about a philosophical view that "the one Religion is beyond all speech."[57] For him, "God [Truth] is one and so humanity also is one."[58]

Mahatma Gandhi had a distinct understanding of Christianity, Christ and the activities of Christians although he had not much good to speak about Christians. But he declared that, "though I took a path my Christian friends had not intended for me, I have remained forever indebted to them for the religious quest that they awakened in me."[59]

Gandhi always accused Christians of busy in preaching, but never practice what they preach. "Christians generally seemed to him to be rather poor disciples of their master."[60] The reason for his dislike over Christianity is stated as "in those days Christian missionaries used to stand in a corner near the high school and

---

51 Paul J. Griffiths, *op. cit.,* p. 214.

52 D. S. Sharma, *Hinduism Through the Ages*, Bombay, Bharatiya Vidya Bhavan,1967, p. 193.

53 Nirmal Minz, *Mahatma Gandhi and Hindu-Christian Dialogue*, Madras, C. L. S,1970, p. 23.

54 Nirmal Minz, *op. cit.,* p. 24.

55 Mahatma Gandhi, *Fellowship of Faiths and Unity of Religions*, Ed. by Abdul Majid Khan, Madras, G. A. Natesanand Co., No. year, p. 20.

56 *Ibid.*, p. 12.

57 Mahatma Gandhi, *op. cit.,* p. 17.

58 Nirmal Minz, *op. cit.,* p.1.

59 Paul J. Griffiths, *op. cit.,* p. 225.

60 Mahatma Gandhi, *op. cit.,* p. 19.

hold forth, pouring abuse of Hindus and their gods. I could not endure this."[61] The reasons for further dislike are worded as, "surely, thought I, a religion that compelled one to eat beef, drink liquor, and change one's own clothes did not deserve the name. I also heard that the new convert had already begun abusing the religion of his ancestors, their customs and their country. All these things created in me a dislike for Christianity."[62] Of course, this is what he heard about a person who was converted to Christianity. It cannot be the right presentation. Nevertheless, certain facts everyone must learn. They are regard for culture, nation and religion of others.

He firmly believed that it was not necessary for him to become a Christian in order to get salvation. He said "it was impossible for me to regard Christianity as a perfect religion or the greatest of all religions."[63] The main reason is that the pious lives of Christians did not give him anything that the lives of men of other faiths had failed to give.

Mahatma Gandhi's view of Jesus Christ can contribute to the formulation of a viable Christology in India. For him, "Jesus was a great teacher of humanity but not the only begotten son of God… He is as divine as Krishna, Rama, or Mohammed."[64] For Hindus, Jesus is one among the teachers of *dharma*, and not the only teacher of *dharma*.

He also accepted 'Jesus as a model not the only model.'[65] It is also to be noted that Mahatma Gandhi never considered Jesus as the perfect man. He says, "I could accept Jesus as a martyr, an embodiment of sacrifice, and a divine teacher, but not as the most perfect man ever born."[66] No doubt Mahatma Gandhi has put Christians in a challenging task.

According to him, "religion is best propagated by the noble lives led by its followers."[67] "Preaching the Gospel means to live the Gospel."[68] Again he said "religion can be defended only by the purity of its adherents and their good deeds, never by their quarrels with those of other faiths."[69] This is the need of the hour in India.

Mahatma Gandhi has suggested as to how religions should approach each other. For him, "the correct attitude is one of firm adherence to one's own religion coupled with an equal reverence towards all other religions. It is not simply a

61 Paul J. Griffiths, *op. cit.,* p. 217.

62 *Ibid.*

63 Paul J. Griffiths, *op. cit.,* p. 224.

64 Nirmal Minz, *op. cit.,* p. 39.

65 Mahatma Gandhi, *op. cit.,* p. 19.

66 Paul J. Griffiths, *op. cit.,* p. 224.

67 D.S. Sharma, *op. cit.,* p. 193.

68 Nirmal Minz, *op. cit.,* p. 47.

69 Mahatma Gandhi, *op. cit.,* p. 46.

question of tolerating other faiths, but of believing that all faiths lead to the same goal."[70] Again he said, 'let Hindus become better Hindus, Muslims and Christians better Muslims and Christians.'[71] Working to this end can be the right mission of Christians in India. To go still further is to ask them to work together with others for the healing and well-being of humanity.

Another remarkable contribution of Mahatma Gandhi for religious pluralism is the acceptance of common humanity. "Gandhi always appealed to the religion of humanity underlying all religions."[72] He always disbelieved the illusion of forming one single religion. He believed in the harmony of religions. Once he said, "if the Hindus believe that India should be peopled only by Hindus, they are living in a dreamland."[73]

5.4.1.4. Dr. Radhakrishnan

He was of the opinion that Hinduism does not lack anything. From the point of religious pluralism he was thinking of an absolute, which is active and present in all revelations. For him, "such an absolute is the ground of transcendental unity as well as historical differences of religions."[74]

Similarly, 'Radhakrishnan had a vision of the religion of the spirit which he proposed as a possible solution to the problem of religious pluralism in the world.'[75] Being an Indian, he too subscribes to the view that all religions are the same. And they lead to the same goal. In summary Hindus consider Christ as one of the revealer and Christianity one of the revelations. Hinduism lacks nothing, which Christianity is in hold of.

5.4.1.5. Buddhism and Islam

Despite the theological differences between Buddhism and Christianity there had been dialogue between them. In the words of S. J. Samartha, "the Buddhist response to Christian initiated dialogue is not one of confrontation and controversy, but of responsible participation in the conviction that the message of the Buddha has a distinctive contribution to make to the world today."[76]

The traditional Muslim response to religious pluralism was negative. They understood the western missionary work as power play. "They think that Christian missionaries from the West came to destroy the religion of Islam and help the

70 D. S. Sharma, *op. cit.,* pp. 193, 194.

71 Mahatma Gandhi, *op. cit.,* p. 20.

72 Nirmal Minz, *op. cit.,* p. 50.

73 Mahatma Gandhi, *op. cit.,* p. 1.

74 Bibhuti S. Yadav, 'Vaisnavism on Hanskiung: A Hindu Theology of Religious Pluralism,' *Religion and Society,* Vol. XXVII, No. 2 [June 1980], p. 32.

75 C. H. Sreenivas Rao ed., *Inter-faith Dialogue and World Community,* Madras, CLS, 1991, p. XXXII.

76 S. J. Samartha, One Christ Many Relgions, *op. cit.,* p. 31.

foreign powers, especially the British, to conquer and subjugate India."[77] At times they demanded that all missionaries from the Islamic states to be removed in order to strengthen Christian-Muslim relations.

Now there is a positive attitude towards Christianity. S. J. Samartha points out that "a significant response to Christian initiatives is the Muslim attempt to work out a theology of dialogue based on Islam even as Christians are seeking to develop a Christian theology of dialogue."[78]

On the whole, the people of other faith-traditions were unhappy with the way Christianity was insensitive to their feelings, perceptions and requests. Thus it is necessary that Christian theology of religions ventures to propose a new paradigm, which is life oriented without involving in wordy tussles.

5.5. The Urgency of the Problem

5.5.1. Religious Extremism

The original life sustaining vision of religions is lost in the contemporary world. Often religions are misused. One such misuse is religious extremism. It is identified that, "for whatever the root cause, religious extremism is fast turning out to be the most potent source of violence and human suffering in the world today."[79]

Today, religions are used as a pretext for war, terrorism, power, and in short for selfish purposes of a few. They shatter the pluralist vision of religion and use religions to divide people rather than uniting. In the words of Paul F. Knitter, "still today the battle cries of Protestants and Catholics in Northern Ireland, of Muslims and Jews in the Middle East, of Buddhists and Hindus in Sri Lanka, of Sikhs and Hindus and Muslims in India are sad testimonies that religions continue to be more effective at motivating war than peace."[80]

Another growing tendency is to attribute religious colors to general riots. In the words of A. Pushparajan "many non-religious factors very often influence the riots. However it is undeniable that the riots have been colored by religious considerations."[81]

5.5.2. Politicization of Religion

A specific Indian requirement is that, religion should be saved from politicization. It is said, "the RSS fears of Islamisation and now the Christianisation of India belong to the world of make believe. They serve the purpose of the consolidation

77 Sam V. Bhajjan, 'Muslim – Christian Dialogue in India,' *N.C.C. Review*, Vol. CVII, No. 9 [October 1987], p. 547.

78 S. J. Samartha, *One Christ Many Religions, op. cit.*, p. 24.

79 *The Hindu*, 'Religions for Peace', Chennai, September 4, 2000.

80 Paul F. Knitter, 'Inter-Religious Dialogue and the Unity of Humanity,' *Journal of Dharma*, Vol. XVI, No. 4, (October – December 1992), p. 284.

81 A. Pushparajan, *From Conversion, to Fellowship; The Hindu Christian Encounter in the Gandhian Perspective,* Allahabad, St. Paul Publications, 1990, p. 18.

of the Hindu vote bank and the politics of Hindu Rashtra."[82] In the words of S. J. Samartha, "religions are used as handmaidens to political interests."[83]

The reason for such deterioration is the outcome of greed for power. In order to grab power, thousands of lives are rooted out, in the name of safeguarding religions. Religions and gods are meant to protect humanity. But now humanity is championing the cause of protecting religions and gods in order to exploit the innocence of thousands of souls. Added to this are the crafty fabrications in the form of conflict between majority and minority religions.

5.5.3. Life is at Peril

At the global level, life the only factor common to all living beings is threatened from various human made disasters. Nuclear war, economical imbalance, poverty, disease, corruption, ecological degradations, gender discriminations etc., are not the problems of one religious community. The persistence of these threats can make life difficult in the planet earth. Life can be saved from these threats only by the co-operative and conscious efforts of all people across religious boundaries. Therefore, there is an urgent need for co-operation between religions. Wilfred Cantwell Smith writes, "unless men can learn to understand and to be loyal to each other across religious frontiers, unless we can build a world in which people profoundly of different faiths can live together and work together, then the prospects for our planet's future are not bright."[84] Paul F. Knitter writes "religions must speak and act together because only so can they make their crucially important contribution to removing the oppression that contaminates our globe."[85] In the words of S. J Samartha, "it is agreed that the most helpful relationship between persons of different faiths in the world today must be one of co-operation in pursuing common purposes like justice, peace and human rights."[86]

The growing misuse of religions and the increasing threats to life call for committed action from people of all faiths to restore the original purpose of religions and to bring about closer fellowship among religions from the point of life-struggles, threats and challenges.

---

82 Ram Puniyani, 'Thou Shall be Banished,' *The New Indian Express*, Chennai, October 12, 2000.

83 S. J. Samartha , *Inter-Religious Relationships in the Secular State*, p. 62.

84 Wilfred Cantwell Smith, 'The Christian in a Religiously Plural World,' *Christianity and Other Religions, op. cit.*, p. 95.

85 Paul F. Knitter, 'Toward a Liberation Theology of Religions,' *The Myth of Christian Uniqueness, op. cit.*, p. 181.

86 S. J. Samartha, *Courage for Dialogue: Ecumenical Issues in Inter-Religious Relationships*, Geneva, World Council of Churches, 1981, p. 30.

5.6. Task Ahead for Christianity

5.6.1. Alloy Suspicion

The Christian attempts for co-operative action of religions are looked at with suspicion. S.J. Samartha writes that there is "always the fear of hidden agendas."[87] Further, "the suspicion that dialogue may be used for purposes of Christian Mission is an ever present fear among neighbors of other faiths."[88] Conforming this, Sita Ram Goel maintains that "the "dialogue" does not seem to be a sincere attempt at reconciliation; on the contrary, it is only a strategy for survival on the part of Christianity."[89] He called indigenization, inculturation etc., as fraud and said "it is high time for the Christian theologies to come down to earth and recognize every person's right to seek truth and salvation in his or her own way."[90] Writers like, Arun Shourie have interpreted all the contributions of Christians in India as efforts of proselytization.

5.6.2. Time to Listen

Most initiatives for inter religious relations have come from Christians. S. J. Samartha, while discussing the issue of dialogue, writes, "in all these the initiatives have invariably been Christian although in recent years some meetings have been organized by others as well."[91] Nevertheless, he has devoted a full chapter in his *One Christ Many Religions* to reflect upon the responses of people of other faith-traditions to the Christian initiated dialogue etc. In his own words, "neighbors of other faiths also ask humbly and sometimes not so humbly: what about our centers and our names?"[92] E. C. Dewick says 'to-day the claim of Christianity to be the final and perfect religion for the whole world is being sharply challenged by a large number of people.'[93]

This is a pertinent issue, which should be addressed by all who are sincerely committed to the problem of religious pluralism. Paul J. Griffiths had to say that,

> Christians have said a great deal about how they see Buddhists, Hindus, Jews, and Muslims and about what place they are prepared to allot the members of these Communities in God's plan for human salvation;

---

87 S. J. Samartha, One Christ Many Religions, *op. cit.,* p. 16.

88 *Ibid.*, p. 22.

89 Sita Ram Goel, *History of Hindu – Christian Encounters*, New Delhi, Voice of India, 1989, p. IV.

90 *Ibid.,* p. X.

91 S. J. Samartha, *One Christ Many Religions op. cit.,* p. 15.

92 *Ibid.,* p. 18.

93 E. C. Dewick, *The Gospel and Other Faiths*, London & Edinburgh, The Canterbury press, 1948, p. 13.

> they have as yet not learned to listen very carefully to what members of these Communities have said and are saying about them.[94]

Of late, there is a remarkable change in the approach of people of other faith-traditions towards Christians. Earlier they listened to what Christians said. Even in the 19th century many accepted the greatness of Jesus Christ but not Christianity. This too is challenged. The reason for the resistance to the Christian initiated dialogue is that this is an attempt to continue traditional Christian claims.

5.6.3. Christianity Introspects

Earlier, Christians thought that they could easily convert the whole humanity to Christianity with the help of a few missionaries. To their dismay "today Christians are recognizing that far from disappearing, the religions of Judaism, Islam, Hinduism, and Buddhism are alive and well in spite of all the Christian missionary efforts."[95]

Another failure is that in attempting to change the world, Christianity perpetuated exploitation and oppression on a large scale. The best example is the crusades. Again, Christianity was always knit together with colonial activity. Further Christianity was insensitive to the injustice of the world, especially to the Jews. This is categorically stated as, "the picture would be very different if Christianity, commensurate with its claim to absolute truth and unique validity, had shown a unique capacity to transform human nature for the better."[96]

The same idea is expressed with strong words as "the Holocaust that took place in the country that gave birth to the Reformation, the first use of the atom bomb, and the more recent threats to humanity because of environmental pollution and the shadow of nuclear annihilation hanging over all life, have raised profound moral and spiritual questions about the credibility of Christianity."[97] S. J. Samartha's introspective question was "if Christianity was unable to prevent these horrors in countries over which it held sway for so many centuries, why export it to people in other countries who live by other faiths?"[98] Thus there is a great need for reconceptulising Christian understanding of other religions as to make it more life centered.

94 Paul J. Griffiths, *Christianity Through Non-Christian Eyes, op. cit.*, p. 3.

95 Harlod G. Coward, *Religious Pluralism and the World Religions*, Madras, The Dr. S. Radhakrishnan Institute for Advanced Study in Philosophy, University of Madras, 1983, p. 15.

96 John Hick, 'The Non-Absoluteness of Christianity', *The Myth of Christian Uniqueness, op. cit.*, p. 17.

97 S. J. Samartha, *One Christ Many Religions; Toward a revised Christology, op. cit.*, p. 2.

98 *Ibid.*, p. 2.

5.6.4. New Context for Co-operation

Paul F. Knitter writes that "this world of suffering, provides the context or Kairos for dialogue."[99] Overcoming this suffering and establishing peace is the concern of religions. Thus he writes further that, "…peace can and must become a common commitment and common ground for conversation and action."[100] His wider plan of action was comprehensively called the soterio-centric approach. But later he said, "working for eco-human justice becomes a common context in which we find ourselves using our different religious stories and symbols."[101] He was of the opinion that the liberation theology and theology of religions should work together in meeting the challenges of life. He wrote "their encounter, may be even their marriage, can bear much fruit for the Christian churches and the world."[102] How amazing is his progress from unitive pluralism to thus far!

Paul F. Knitter has made it very clear that theory and action should go hand in hand. It is not mere relationship among religions that is important, but the culmination of that relationship in the form of constructive action for the sustenance of life. This, he relates to his living experience. He says "so people and events in my life have led me sometimes lured me, to what has become for me the moral obligation to join "pluralism and liberation" or "dialogue and global responsibility."[103]

Aloysius Pieris proposed a new paradigm for the theology of religions in the Asian context. His main contribution was that he brought to light the importance of considering the poor as the target of any theology. Because in Asia there are many religions and cultures at the same time there are many poor. His paradigm consisted of three aspects. "The first is the acknowledgement of a third magisterium, namely, that of the poor; the second is the *liberational thrust* that defines our theology of religions; and finally the social location of this theology is the Basic Human Communities (BHCs)."[104] It is true that, any contemporary theology of religions should be based upon life and its realities *i.e.,* the struggles of life. This is the earnest vision of the many Indian Christian theologians of religions.

---

99 Paul F. Knitter, *One Earth Many Religions, Multifaith Dialogue and Global Responsibility*, New York, ORBIS, 1996, p. 58.

100 *Ibid.,* p. 66.

101 *Ibid.,* p. 113.

102 Paul F. Knitter, 'Religion and Liberation in Defense of a Pluralistic Theology of Religions', *N.C.C Review,* Vol. CXII, No. 4 (April 1992), p. 229.

103 Paul F. Knitter, *One Earth Many Religions, op. cit.,* p. 11.

104 Aloysius Pieris, *Fire and Water, Basic issues in Asian Buddhism and Christianity*, New York, Orbis Books, 1996, p. 156.

6. Conclusion

The current global situation requires that religions be united without losing their individuality and differences for the sake of presenting and promoting better life for all. A viable paradigm for such an undertaking is the life sustaining pluralist perspective. It does justice to the many forms of religion on the one hand and struggles of humanity on the other. This is also in consonance with the life and mission of Jesus Christ, to which the Church is expected to bear witness.

S. Robertson

8

Politics and Religion in India
An Analysis

Introduction

The simple thesis of this paper that religion and politics were never purely or completely separated in India, in spite of the contributions of modernity and hence it is necessary to strive hard to separate them as secularism seems to be more viable in a pluralistic context. While working towards this direction, it may also be asked how best positive religious insights can guide political wisdom.

To drive this point, I shall attempt a sketchy and a graphic historical development of the process of secularization leading to the formulation of secularism and the secular state. While attempting to do so, I shall also highlight the never-ceasing influence of religion on politics and how politicization of religion takes place.

To prove the thesis I shall analyze the role of the Congress party, the emergence of the Muslim League and religious-interest organizations leading to the formation of BJP. Considerable space shall be devoted to the patterns in which BJP attempts to subscribe to communal politics. Before concluding the analysis, the areas and issues that need to be considered and addressed are taken up.

1. Traditional Society

The ideological component in traditional societies was provided almost entirely by religion; as such secular political ideologies did not exist, and the legitimacy of the ruler was based on religious ideas. The religio-political system was an integrated system in which the ruler, clergy, religious ideology, religious norms of behaviour, and coercive governmental power were combined in order to maximize the stability of the society.[1]

It is also often true that "in the intricately woven fabric of traditional systems, the political functions of the clergy were no less important than the religious role of the king."[2]

In general, the sway of religion over politics was noteworthy in traditional societies because religion is a mass phenomenon, politics is not; but religion can be used to make politics meaningful. Religious values are also an important influence on political culture, and they can predispose individuals and societies toward certain patterns of political life.[3]

The preponderance of religion over politics in specific traditional societies has been challenged in the modern society. Here there is a conscious, but often unsuccessful, attempt to distinguish between religion and the other aspects of life. To understand this phenomenon it shall be appropriate to circumscribe the situation in the modern period.

2. Early Modern Period and Modern Period

The term modern period or modern era is the period of history that succeeded the Middle Ages (which ended approximately 1500 AD). Before underlining the characteristics of Modern era it is necessary to note the characteristics of early modern period a subdivision within the modern period. Of course, making a watertight distinction between these two eras is not possible.

2.1. Early Modern Period

The early modern period is a term used by historians to refer to the period approximately from AD 1500 to 1800, especially in Western Europe. It is marked by the first European colonies, the rise of strong centralized governments, and the beginnings of recognizable nation states that are the direct antecedents of today's states in what is called Modern times.

Also, the early modern period is characterized by the rise to importance of science, the shrinkage of relative distances through improvements in transportation and communications and increasingly rapid technological progress, secularized civic politics and the early authoritarian nation states. Further, capitalist economies and institutions began their rise and development.

The early modern period also saw the rise and beginning of the dominance of the economic theory of mercantilism. As such, the early modern period represents the decline and eventual disappearance, in much of the European sphere, of Christian theocracy, feudalism and serfdom.

1 Donald Eugene Smith, *Religion and Political Development* (Boston: Little Brown and Company, 1970), p. 57.

2 Donald Eugene Smith, *Religion and Political Development*, p. 58.

3 Donald Eugene Smith, *Religion and Political Development*, p. xii.

2.2. Modern Era

The modern era begins with the 19th century, and includes World War I, World War II, and the Cold War. It has been a period of significant development in the fields of science, politics, warfare, and technology. It has also been an age of discovery and globalization. During this time the European powers and later their colonies, began a political, economic, and cultural colonization of the rest of the world.

The modern era is closely associated with the development of individualism, capitalism, urbanization and a belief in the positive possibilities of technological and political progress. The brutal wars and other problems of this era, many of which come from the effects of rapid change, and the connected loss of strength of traditional religious and ethical norms, have led to many reactions against modern development.

Although modernity and post modernity have some commonalities, a salient distinction between the two needs to be underlined as people now speak of post-modernity. This is found in the American Heritage Dictionary. It describes the meaning of postmodern as 'of or relating to art, architecture, or literature that reacts against earlier modernist principles, as by reintroducing traditional or classical elements of style.'

Having underlined the salient characteristics of these different historic eras, it is appropriate now to begin to discuss the process of separation between religion and politics starting with the Reformation and concentrating on the developments in the 19th century in order to focus on secularization.

3. Reformation and After

Almost invariably, religion and politics are inseparable in their ability to arouse strong emotion. This was no doubt true during the 17th century when there was a drastic change in how both religion and politics were perceived by the European society. Through either the Protestant Reformation or the Counter Reformation, governments gained control over the religion their state practiced and religious tolerance became more prevalent. Religion was also used as a means to legitimize the nobles' power struggles, thus gaining public support for their conflicts.

To put it differently, "the contemporary nation-states of the West evolved out of a medieval religiopolitical system of Catholic integralism. The medieval synthesis was cracked open by the Reformation and Renaissance; nationalism challenged the religious basis of political community, and the secularization conflicts of individual states occupied an important place in Western history right up to the present time."[4] Since the days of Luther, political and national convictions outweighed religious convictions in Europe.

4 Donald Eugene Smith, *Religion and Political Development*, p. 3.

After the Protestant Reformation and the Counter Reformation, the states of Europe gained almost complete control over Church hierarchy. Governments benefited from this new acquisition, as they gained all the property the Church previously controlled in their country. However, religious alignment often led to conflicts.

Religious ideals were often used as a rallying point to build power bases for political agendas. Oliver Cromwell, an army commander (supported parliamentary party) used religion, during the English Civil War, to strengthen the spirit of his New Model Army, which was unbeatable against the King's forces. During the Thirty Years War, the Holy Roman Emperor fought against the Protestants.

Through the integration of religion into the politics of the day, the common people supported the power struggles of the nobles, and religious toleration became common. This pattern of diversity and compromises continues even today.

Roughly, from the first decades of the nineteenth century traditional systems came under external attack.[5] The integral relationships also came under powerful attack.[6] The impact of the attack was that it cracked open the integralist nature of society.[7] As a result "from that time to this, the secularization of the polity has been the most fundamental structural and ideological change in the process of political development."[8]

4. Secularization

The tem Secularization was first used at the end of the thirty years war in Europe, 1648, to refer to the transfer of Church properties. It generally refers to people of transformation by which a society migrates from close identification with religious institutions to a more separated relationship. It is also the name given to a general belief about history, namely that the development of society progresses toward modernization and lessening dependence on religion as religion loses its position of authority. In other words, it is the detachment of a state or other body from religious foundations.

In expressly secular states like India, it has been argued that the need was to legislate for toleration and respect between quite different religions, whereas the secularization of the West was a response to intra-Christian tensions between Catholicism and Protestantism.

To be very specific, "starting with the disruption of traditional religiopolitical systems, the secularization of polities is a major aspect of *differentiation*, separating the political from the religious structures. Religious symbols, leaders, and

5 Donald Eugene Smith, *Religion and Political Development,* p. 10.

6 Donald Eugene Smith, *Religion and Political Development,* p. 60.

7 Donald Eugene Smith, *Religion and Political Development,* p. 10.

8 Donald Eugene Smith, *Religion and Political Development,* p. 2.

organizations served as vehicles to bring the masses into the political process, producing *mass participation*."[9]

In such contexts, "Secularization involves the separation of the polity from religion; legal and constitutional recognition is given to the fact that the political system does not derive its legitimacy from religion, and the symbols and structures which linked the two are destroyed. Secularization involves the expansion of the polity at the expense of religion as major areas of social life (education, law, economy, and so on) pass from religious regulation to the jurisdiction of the state. Secularization involves the transformation of political culture as politically relevant values assume a secular orientation. Nationality and nationalism displace religious notions of political community, and secular ideologies develop a legitimating power of their own. Finally, in a few countries which have undergone violent revolutions, secularization extends to state domination of religion, narrowly defined, with efforts to eradicate or drastically alter its very core."[10]

Precisely, "the secularization of the polity is the political consequence of the disruption of the traditional religiopolitical system."[11] Generally, "Western imperialist regimes in Asia and Africa have been powerful secularizers."[12] In some instances their impacts are accepted without modifications. For example, "In a number of cases the independent states proceeded to ratify the polity-separation secularization which had been forcibly imposed by their former colonial rulers. The constitutions of India and Ceylon, for example, made no mention of special status for any religion and clearly outlined the structure of a secular state."[13]

In general, secularization is characterized by (1) the *separation* of polity from religious ideologies and ecclesiastical structures, (2) the *expansion* of the polity to perform regulatory functions in the socio-economic spheres which were formerly performed by religious structures, and (3) the *translation* of the political culture to emphasize nontranscendent temporal goals and rational, pragmatic means, that is secular political values. In the context of a participant and competitive political system, with universal suffrage and opposition political parties, however, the secularization of political culture becomes a much more problematical enterprise. Thus we can add to the first three aspects; (4) the *dominance* of the polity over religious beliefs, practices, and ecclesiastical structures.[14]

Mostly "liberal regimes, with varying degree of democratic political participation, have accounted for a great deal of the secularization which has taken place throughout the third world."[15]

9 Donald Eugene Smith, *Religion and Political Development*, p. xii.

10 Donald Eugene Smith, *Religion and Political Development*, p. 11.

11 Donald Eugene Smith, *Religion and Political Development* , p. 12.

12 Donald Eugene Smith, *Religion and Political Development*, p. 88.

13 Donald Eugene Smith, *Religion and Political Development*, p. 95.

14 Donald Eugene Smith, *Religion and Political Development*, pp. 85-86.

15 Donald Eugene Smith, *Religion and Political Development*, p. 90.

Although, it is evident that secularism and secular state are the products of the secularization process, the point is true that, politics and religion never completely get separated. This is obvious from the fact that on many occasions religious functionaries emerged as powerful political leaders. As the politics of mass participation has increasingly become a reality, religious political parties have appeared.[16]

5. Secularization and the Secular State

The process of secularization of politics led to the development of Secular state in India. Neera Chandhoke writes, "Secularism as a creed that the state should treat all religions equally, was adopted by the Indian National congress as one of its core principles, simply because it was moral, relevant, and appropriate for the needs of our society."[17]

Having taken into careful consideration the plural structure of the Indian society in all aspects of life, the preamble of the Indian Constitution envisages justice, liberty, equality and fraternity to all the citizens of India.[18] The above definite assertion is possible because of the meticulous insertion of the word 'secular' in the preamble of the Constitution.[19] However, the critiques argued for the non-necessity of the inclusion of the word secular on the flimsy and covet ground that India is secular in nature (Hinduism is secular).[20] In the opinion of anti-secular proponents, the word secular is Western and it was used to fight against the pope and hence it is not relevant to India.[21]

The necessity of separating religion and politics is explained in one of the judgments regarding the meaning and scope of the word secular as "the neutrality of the state would be violated if religion is used for *political* purposes and advocated by the political parties for their political ends. An appeal to the electorate on grounds of religion offends secular democracy (para 128). Politics and religion cannot be mixed (para 131). If a State Government does this, it will be a fit case for application of Art. 356 of the Constitution against it (para 365

16 Donald Eugene Smith, *Religion and Political Development,* p. 3.

17 Neera Chandhoke, *Beyond Secularism, the Rights of Religious Minorities* (New Delhi: Oxford University Press, 1999), p. 41.

18 P. L. John Panicker, "Marginalization of Minorities: Anti-conversion Bill," in *Inter-Play of Religion, Politics and Communalism,* edited by Samson Prabhakar (Bangalore: BTESSC/SATHRI, 2004), p. 61.

19 Durga Das Basu, *Introduction to the Constitution of India,* 19th ed. Reprint (Nagpur: Wadhwa and Company, Law Publishers, 2003), 27.

20 Pannalal Dhar, *India and Her Domestic Problems: Religion State and Secularism* (Calcutta: Punthi-Pustak, 1993), p. 63. The author of the book purposely used small 'm' for Muslims.

21 M. S. Golwalkar, *Bunch of Thoughts,* 3rd ed., Reprint (Bangalore: Sahitya Sindhu Prakashan, 2000), p. 162.

(10))."[22] It is evident that in spite of substantial guidelines communal politics is gaining momentum in India.

Meera Nanda writes, "the future of secular societies depends upon the cultivation of secular culture."[23] Despite the fact that secularism is essential for the preservation of plurality in India, people who hold on to the traditional mix of politics and religion argue against it even after witnessing many ugly communal unrests.

5.1. Critiquing Nehru

According to critiques, Nehru introduced secularism for the first time in 1952 General Election de-linking politics from religion. In 1976, during the Emergency it was incorporated into the Preamble of the Constitution of India to appease the disgruntled Muslims.[24] For instance, "the Jana Sangh hated Jawaharlal Nehru, the most committed and articulate of secularists."[25] For the opponents, "Nehru broke up the relationship of Hinduism with politics."[26] The critiques are unjustified as a secular framework is inevitable to the Indian plural context.

It cannot be wished away that "Secularism as a peculiarly modern concept, aligned to the equally modern concepts of equality and freedom, was an integral part of the project of modernity that India began her post-independence life with."[27] Nevertheless, in contrast to the prevailing form of secularism the anti-secular forces argue, "Gandhiji's Ram Rajya is based on that concept of toleration and universality which form the bed-rock of positive secularism that BJP advocates. In this positive secularism there is no appeasement of minorities."[28] It needs to be reiterated that the vision of Gandhi had no commonality whatsoever with the present Hindutva communal ideology.

5.2. Secular State

One could also argue that, nowhere in the Constitution of India has the term "secular" been used to signify the character of the State. The fact is that, "nevertheless it embodies the idea of a secular State."[29] The role and place of religion in Indian secularism is amply established. E. C. Bhatty maintains that

22 Durga Das Basu, *Introduction to the Constitution of India*, pp. 116-117.

23 Meera Nanda, *The Wrongs of the Religious Right: Reflections on Science, Secularism and Hindutva* (Haryana: Three Essays, 2005), p. 61.

24 Pannalal Dhar, *India and Her Domestic Problems: Religion State and Secularism,* p. 80.

25 A. G. Noorani, "Fractured Democracies," *Frontline* (December 1, 2006), 84.

26 Pannalal Dhar, *India and Her Domestic Problems: Religion State and Secularism*, p. 80.

27 Neera Chandhoke, *Beyond Secularism, the Rights of Religious Minorities*, 50.

28 Pannalal Dhar, *India and Her Domestic Problems: Religion State and Secularism*, 56.

29 E. C. Bhatty, "Religious Minorities and the Secular State," in *Religious Freedom*, edited by J. R. Chandran, and M. M. Thomas, (Bangalore: The Committee for Literature on Social Concerns, 1956), p. 74.

"a secular State is neither religious nor anti-religious. It is neutral in religious matters. Not that it is indifferent to the religious welfare of its citizens."[30] P. N. Sapru writes, "a secular state is not an unethical state. The basic ethical ideas are much the same in all religions."[31]

One of the basic expectations in a secular state is the separation of religion and state or religion and politics. In other words, the essential basis of a modern secular State is the institutional separation of State and religion. While the State limits itself to the promotion of the secular welfare of the people, religious life is considered as intimately personal.

5.3. Challenges to Secularism/Secular State

Politicization of religion is the major challenge a secular state has to face. It is very painful to notice "intolerance has manifested itself in the activities of communal political parties which are clearly antagonistic to the entire spirit of the secular State."[32] M. P. Raju states "the dreams for a secular India soon started to vanish with the growth of a kind of neo-fanaticism as part of Hindu revivalism and cultural nationalism."[33]

There is a great need to protect the secular principle of our nation. In the words of E. C. Bhatty, "we have to guard against political religious communalism gaining strength and stifling religious freedom and destroying the secular State."[34] This is a dangerous trend because religious elements influence politics and politics uses religious elements.

Although, secularization and secularism were significant hallmarks of the modern era, the influence of religion on politics was not completely vanquished. This continuity in discontinuity or seemingly inseparable relation between religion and politics needs to be analyzed thoroughly in order to determine the magnitude of conflicts resulting from the mixing of religion and politics particularly in India.

6. New Role of Religion in the Modern Period

It can be argued that "in a modern colonial semi-colonial or independent democratic society people are less religious but religion tends to become politics oriented."[35] In other words, "Religion on account of its powerful emotional appeal has often sought to be dragged into political and social arenas by various

30 E. C. Bhatty, "Religious Minorities and the Secular State," in *Religious Freedom*, p. 74.

31 P. N. Sapru, "Religious Freedom and Civil Liberties," in *Religious Freedom*, edited by J. R. Chandran, and M. M. Thomas, (Bangalore: The Committee for Literature on Social Concerns, 1956), p. 5.

32 E. C. Bhatty, "Religious Minorities and the Secular State," in *Religious Freedom*, p. 77.

33 M. P. Raju, *Religious Conversion: Legal Implications* (Delhi: Media House,1999), p. 34.

34 E. C. Bhatty, "Religious Minorities and the Secular State," in *Religious Freedom*, p. 86.

35 Sunita Gangwal, *Minorities in India: A Study in Communal Process and Individual Rights* (Jaipur: Arihant Publishing House, 1995), p. 187.

interest groups."[36] In the political arena, religion was no longer oriented towards faith, rational or irrational, but towards evolving a religious identity, a primordial consciousness for its political utility.[37]

In India, the political orientation of religion began with the consolidation of the British rule after the failure of the war of Independence of 1857. Then onwards, one's identity as a Hindu or Muslim was more important than one's true religiosity or actual faith in religion. Jinnah, the Supreme leader of the Muslim League was an archetypal model of such a Muslim stand. So was Savarkar, the archetypal Hindu of similar mould.[38]

It was during the freedom struggle that a sense of separatism was injected in the minds of Hindus and Muslim middle classes which were instrumental in articulating their respective political ambitions. The elites of both the communities freely made use of religion, culture and language for this purpose.[39] Still further, religions were being reinterpreted to provide ideological support for political systems seeking to increase their *capacity* to direct socio-economic change.[40]

6.1. Power

According to general theories, the incarnation of religion in various forms in the political sphere is based upon the principle that power comes from God. It is said, "The exercise of power is at the center of the polity and in virtually all cultures power is an attribute of divinity."[41] Even those who hold power are considered to be divine or agents of the divine being.[42]

This may not be true in the current Indian scenario where respect for the transcendental is not the driving force for using religion for political mileage. The main principle is to grab power at any cost, including the lives of many minority religious communities which are vulnerable in nature due to numerical disadvantage. In other words, the present mixing of religion and politics is to polarize the people on the grounds of majority-politics and creating communal hatred among people of different religions.

36 Sunita Gangwal, *Minorities in India: A Study in Communal Process and Individual Rights*, p. 187.

37 Sunita Gangwal, *Minorities in India: A Study in Communal Process and Individual Rights*, p. 187.

38 Sunita Gangwal, *Minorities in India: A Study in Communal Process and Individual Rights*, p. 187.

39 Sunita Gangwal, *Minorities in India: A Study in Communal Process and Individual Rights*, p. 188.

40 Donald Eugene Smith, *Religion and Political Development*, p. xii.

41 Donald Eugene Smith, *Religion and Political Development*, p. 6.

42 Donald Eugene Smith, *Religion and Political Development*, p. 7.

6.2. Politicization of Religion

Communally obsessive leaders know well that "in traditional societies, religion is a mass phenomenon, politics is not; in transitional societies, religion can serve as the means by which the masses become politicized."[43] This is the reason why "Individual clerics or religious functionaries have made great impact on the political scene in a number of countries."[44]

Prominent lay politicians who have effectively utilized religious symbols have been found in all religious traditions. Among the important Hindu nationalists were: Tilak, who used religious festivals for anti-British propaganda; the Bengal terrorists, who identified Mother India with the goddess Kali whose worship required bloody sacrifices (political assassinations); and Gandhi, whose elaborate theory of nonviolent resistance, rooted in Hindu concepts, also spurred the Indian national movement. Jinnah used Islamic symbols to intensify the Indian Muslims' sense of separate national identity and, on this basis, demanded a separate state, Pakistan.[45]

Also of concern are the religion-oriented interest groups of a predominantly lay character. The RSS ideology holds to the concept of a Hindu Nation and urges the creation of a Hindu State in which the religious minorities would be relegated to the status of foreigners. Although, RSS has concentrated on the indoctrination and paramilitary training of youth and has never entered politics directly, it has provided much of the leadership and organizational strength to the Jana Sangh.[46]

Interest groups and political parties have been formed to further communal interests. In the case of Pakistan, a new state was created for a minority religious community.[47] At the same time it cannot be ignored that "In societies characterized by religious pluralism, each community may become in some sense a political actor. Religious communities become politicized in conflict situations where the real issues are frequently social, political, and economic. Religion derives its chief importance from its function as a symbol of group identity and self-esteem."[48]

6.3. Patterns of Politicization

It follows then that the notion of *conflict* is central to our understanding of the nature of politics. At the practical level, "Politicization – the drawing of people into active participation in the political process – takes place as people become conscious of conflicts which are perceived as relevant to their lives."[49] When the

43 Donald Eugene Smith, *Religion and Political Development*, p. 124.

44 Donald Eugene Smith, *Religion and Political Development*, p. 127.

45 Donald Eugene Smith, *Religion and Political Development*, p. 128.

46 Donald Eugene Smith, *Religion and Political Development*, p. 132.

47 Donald Eugene Smith, *Religion and Political Development*, p. 136.

48 Donald Eugene Smith, *Religion and Political Development*, p. 136.

49 Donald Eugene Smith, *Religion and Political Development*, p. 144.

principle of conflict is instilled in the mind of the people, "Politicians, clerical and lay, are engaged in manipulating religious symbols as one technique in the struggle for power, sometimes cynically but more often through the same process of rationalization by which interests become disguised as principles in politics everywhere."[50]

Along with the conflict of misusing religious interests, we must recognize still another kind of conflict-the conflict of political interests which cuts across, and in some cases clearly dominates, the conflicts over ostensibly religious issues.[51]

The Hindu-Muslim conflict leading to the partition of India in 1947 is the classic example. After Independence and Partition, Hindu-Sikh tensions became a prominent feature of politics in the Punjab. A militant Sikh political party, the Akali Dal, sought to mobilize the entire community behind the demand for a separate Sikh state within the Union of India. After the movement for the creation of linguistic states developed, the Sikh demand assumed the form of an agitation for a Punjabi-language state, which involved the partition of the then bilingual (Punjabi and Hindi) state of Punjab. While language constituted the official basis and justification for the demand, which was conceded in 1966, the motivating force behind it was clearly religious and communal. In any event, the creation of a Punjabi-language state also meant the creation of a Sikh-majority state, which was the real point of the agitation.[52]

From the middle of the nineteenth century down to Gandhi, social reform was a predominant nationalist motif. The liberal Moderates in the Congress thought in terms of an Indian nation. In the 1920's, however, illiberal communalists such as V. D. Savakar began to speak of a "Hindu Nation." It helped the emergence of some sense of a Hindu community.[53]

In general, "Politicization in the third world has been significantly furthered by various ideological conflicts involving religious and political belief systems. These are conflicts not only of general world views but of blueprints for society."[54]

In order to analyze the process of politicization of religion in India it is necessary to start with the Congress party. It is interesting to note that its secular vision was challenged by communally charged members and significantly the Congress also had attempted to play religious sentiments for its advantage, intentionally or otherwise. The real opponents of secularization process later emerged as advocates of religious political parties. This can be discussed after analyzing the Congress.

50 Donald Eugene Smith, *Religion and Political Development*, p. 145.

51 Donald Eugene Smith, *Religion and Political Development*, p. 145.

52 Donald Eugene Smith, *Religion and Political Development*, p. 147.

53 Donald Eugene Smith, *Religion and Political Development*, pp. 148-49.

54 Donald Eugene Smith, *Religion and Political Development*, p. 157.

7. Indian National Congress

Started in 1885, the Indian National Congress was not intended to be a political party but an annual gathering, speaking on behalf of social groups. However, roughly from the last decade of the 19th century onwards, the radical ideology of the young leaders like Tilak challenged the moderate Congress. While the moderates, the old generation leaders had a secular outlook in politics, the young leaders who were known later as the extremists invoked the help of religion for arousing national, patriotic and political feeling among Hindus.[55] As a result, the nature of Indian nationalism changed and the growing tension between Hindus and Muslims began to surface.[56]

7.1. Tilak

Lokamanya Bal Gangadhar Tilak introduced religious-nationalism in Indian politics and his ideology influenced many others as well. People like Veer Savarkar who later became known for the ideology of Hindutva and K. B. Hedgewar, the founder of Rashtriya Swayamsevak Sangh are the best examples of this.[57] In other words, "He was a pace setter for the use of religious fundamentalism in Indian politics, in that he supplied a thought–structure for politics based on religious ideology, which later became an acceptable norm for many a politician."[58]

Tilak utilized the *Ganapati* festival and a festival in the name of Shivaji, the celebrated Maratha ruler who withstood the Muslim invasion of Deccan, to galvanize Hindus. This is the first example of using religion for political gains, in the context of the freedom struggle.

7.2. Gandhi

Opposed to Tilak's Hindu religious nationalism which was based upon religious intolerance, Mahatma Gandhi envisaged nationalism based upon inter-religious relationship in India. Gandhi envisioned an India where Hindus and Muslims could live harmoniously and work for the welfare of each other.[59] The utility of religion by Tilak and Gandhi was diametrically opposed to each other. One used religion for hatred and the other used it for harmony.

In view of Gandhi's application of religion, he is often proclaimed as the spiritual father of Indian secularism. For Gandhi, secularism was considering all religions as equal.[60] He also had to encounter the nationalists who believed

55 M. T. Cherian, *Hindutva Agenda and Minority Rights: A Christian Response* (Bangalore: Centre for Contemporary Christianity, 2007), p. 98.

56 M. T. Cherian, *Hindutva Agenda and Minority Rights: A Christian Response*, p. 99.

57 M. T. Cherian, *Hindutva Agenda and Minority Rights: A Christian Response*, p. 99.

58 M. T. Cherian, *Hindutva Agenda and Minority Rights: A Christian Response*, p. 100.

59 M. T. Cherian, *Hindutva Agenda and Minority Rights: A Christian Response*, p. 105.

60 M. T. Cherian, *Hindutva Agenda and Minority Rights: A Christian Response*, p. 106.

in Hindu state and the majority Hindu' rule over religious minorities.[61] In fact, "There was a strong move by Hindu fundamentalists groups for making Hinduism the state religion of India. Gandhi repudiated such ideology."[62]

However, Gandhi is often criticized for his use of religion for political purposes, because, he used religious idioms and phrases to explain his political philosophy. He saw a close relationship between politics and religion. He used religious idioms and practices, sometime even Islamic practices like *Ramadhan*, fasting, prayers and religious anecdotes to advance his struggle for freedom and to mobilize the masses on the basis of religious symbols. However, most of the symbols used by Gandhi were from Hinduism. Yet, it needs to be emphasized that his concept of religion was entirely different from that of the proponents of Hindu Nationalism and Muslim Nationalism.[63]

While Gandhi was fighting for freedom of India, he was also concerned with the emancipation of the different sections of the population like the Muslims and Dalits.[64] Gandhi asked for Swaraj because "Gandhi seems to have understood that rushing the agenda of freedom and self-determination of the nation, without first resolving the great potential and manifest conflicts within-among the Hindus and Muslims and Hindus and Dalits-would jeopardize the very cause of freedom."[65]

It needs to be admitted that "Amidst serious contestations and efforts to construct the nation along the lines of the Hindi-Hindu-Hindustan slogan, the combination of the Gandhian and Nehruvian streams posited 'unity-in-diversity' as the essence of Indian nationhood."[66]

7.3. Jawaharlal Nehru

Aditya Nigam writes, "The ideology of secular-nationalism as the ideology of the postcolonial nation-state in India is closely related to the figure of Jawaharlal Nehru, the first prime minister of the Indian republic."[67] He had to choose that noble path because of the two decades of Hindu-Muslim conflict which preceded Independence and which led to the partition of the subcontinent. Various elements in Nehru's thought strongly confirmed the commitment to secularism, but it was above all the fundamental sociological fact of religious pluralism which dictated

61 M. T. Cherian, *Hindutva Agenda and Minority Rights: A Christian Response*, p. 108.

62 M. T. Cherian, *Hindutva Agenda and Minority Rights: A Christian Response*, p. 110.

63 M. T. Cherian, *Hindutva Agenda and Minority Rights: A Christian Response*, p. 112.

64 Aditya Nigam, *The Insurrection of Little Selves: The Crisis of Secular-Nationalism in India* (New Delhi: Oxford University Press, 2006), p. 38.

65 Aditya Nigam, *The Insurrection of Little Selves: The Crisis of Secular-Nationalism in India*, p. 38.

66 Aditya Nigam, *The Insurrection of Little Selves: The Crisis of Secular-Nationalism in India*, p. 38.

67 Aditya Nigam, *The Insurrection of Little Selves: The Crisis of Secular-Nationalism in India*, p. 69.

the policy.[68] The alliance of religion and politics was the most disturbing issue for Nehru. and, "He saw the danger of communalism in independent India."[69]

Nehru constantly worked to show that India, timeless and eternal, had always been an ocean of tolerance and an exemplar of openness, ever willing to absorb different cultures.[70] He was always true to the reality of many cultures in India.

7.4. Ambedkar

Ambedkar was committed to the cause of the Dalits and hence "he vehemently refuses to accept the givenness of the nation, such as was sought to be constructed by the Congress."[71] Similarly he refused to take the working class as given. That is why "It is well-known that when he formed his first political party in 1936, he called it the Independent *Labour* Party."[72] From the point of Indian politics, Ambedkar's efforts were in line with bringing in the concerns of the Dalits, but surely not communal as he found that the social evils in India was the outcome of Hindu religion.

7.5. Indira Gandhi

Originally, the Congress party was committed to secular principles, but "It is with the return of Indira Gandhi in 1980, after the failure of the Janata experiment, however, that we can begin to see the changes in Congress politics clearly."[73] It has been noted and meticulously documented by various scholars in recent years that this turn in Congress politics was defined by an overarching move to cater to Hindu majoritarian sentiments. The process received a major fillip with the assassination of Indira Gandhi, after which the Congress then led by her son Rajiv Gandhi, openly utilized Hindu 'fears.' His notorious statement in response to the massacre of Sikhs that 'when a big tree falls, the earth shakes,' was a clear and a blatant admission of the fact that thenceforth, the party would have no qualms

---

68 Donald Eugene Smith, *Religion and Political Development*, p. 92.

69 M. T. Cherian, *Hindutva Agenda and Minority Rights: A Christian Response*, p. 121.

70 Aditya Nigam, *The Insurrection of Little Selves: The Crisis of Secular-Nationalism in India*, p. 75.

71 Aditya Nigam, *The Insurrection of Little Selves: The Crisis of Secular-Nationalism in India*, p. 245.

72 Aditya Nigam, *The Insurrection of Little Selves: The Crisis of Secular-Nationalism in India*, p. 244.

73 Aditya Nigam, *The Insurrection of Little Selves: The Crisis of Secular-Nationalism in India*, p. 118.

in using majoritarian sentiments to the maximum.[74] In fact the emergence of the Hindu right as a major political force belongs to this phase.[75]

7.6. Rajiv Gandhi

According to Arun Nehru, formerly one of Rajiv Gandhi's close confidantes and advisors, the Congress High Command had taken a decision in early 1986, to 'play the Hindu card.' The Muslim Women's Bill was passed to play the Muslim card; and then came the decision on Ayodhya to 'play the Hindu card.' Rajiv's biographer, Nicholas Nugent, also notes that in August 1989, Nehru hinted in an interview that Rajiv also arranged the televising of Hindus worshipping at the newly unlocked shrine. In 1989, Rajiv initiated his party's campaign for the Lok Sabha elections, by ritually breaking a coconut at Ayodhya and claiming that only the Congress could usher in the utopia of *Ram Rajya*. The role of the Rajiv led Congress in making possible the foundation-stone laying ceremony (the *shilanayas*), at Ayodhya, is known to have been one of the most dangerous episodes in this game of placating the Hindu communal platform.[76]

It was only in the course of the build-up to the Babri Masjid crisis in the late 1980s, that sections of the Muslims started moving away from the Congress. The episode of the Shah Bano judgment and the subsequent surrender to 'fundamentalist' Muslim pressure by Rajiv Gandhi, went hand in hand with the *shilanyas*, or the foundation-stone-laying ceremony at Ayodhya, that was accomplished under the Congress. If pandering to 'majority Hindu' sentiments in dealing with the Akalis in Punjab had led Indira Gandhi to practically stigmatize the entire Sikh community, Rajiv Gandhi managed to do so with the Muslims, when he began his 1989 election campaign from Ayodhya with the slogan of *Ramrajya*. The crowning event came with the demolition of Babri Masjid, under the watchful eyes of the Congress government under Narasimha Rao. All day long the dance of destruction went unchallenged, leaving little doubt where the Congress government's sympathies lay.[77]

It is very obvious that even the best secular wisdom of the Indian leaders were challenged by communal politics. Religion continued to stake claim in several important decision making processes. Although, the Congress desired to be secular in its early phase, many of the religiously oriented congress men diluted that wishes. Subsequently, the Congress itself had attempted to utilize religious

74 Aditya Nigam, *The Insurrection of Little Selves: The Crisis of Secular-Nationalism in India*, p. 119.

75 Aditya Nigam, *The Insurrection of Little Selves: The Crisis of Secular-Nationalism in India*, p. 120.

76 Aditya Nigam, *The Insurrection of Little Selves: The Crisis of Secular-Nationalism in India*, p. 120.

77 Aditya Nigam, *The Insurrection of Little Selves: The Crisis of Secular-Nationalism in India*, p. 316.

sentiments. To put it simply, secular vision was always either challenged as in the early part of the Congress or misused as in the latter part of the Congress. Consequently the religious orientation and religious influence on political parties came out distinctively.

8. Religious Political Parties-Communal

The communal political party arises in response to the actual or latent conflict of a religiously pluralist society. In British India, the Muslim League, founded in 1906, and the Hindu Mahasabha, founded in 1923, sought to articulate and champion the interests of their respective communities which, both were convinced, were being ignored, harmed, or betrayed by the leadership of the Indian National Congress which professed secular nationalism. The major Hindu party since Independence has been the Jana Sangha, which maintains a definite anti-Muslim bias despite the existence of liberal elements within the party.[78]

Communal parties always promise protection of communal interests. For example, "The political expression of Hinduism, it is clear, is dominated by two basic expressions: the *laity* and *communalism*. Religious functionaries, individually or collectively, have played no significant political role; on the other hand, there have been very prominent lay spokesmen for Hinduism in the political sphere. Hindu interest groups and political parties have not concerned themselves with developing a Hindu ideology for modern society but have been strongly oriented toward defending the interests of their community in communal conflict."[79] This will be clearer as the discussion of the Hindu communal politics progresses.

8.1. Muslim

Reference has already been made to the fact that, in British India the Muslim League, founded in 1906, demanded a separate nation for Muslims resulting in the partition of India. Many Muslims would not prefer to be ruled by Hindu principles as the Muslims believe that Allah is the almighty ruler of the universe whose sovereign transcendence over all creation is absolute.[80] The original Islamic vision is the complete fusion of religious and political authority in the Prophet and his successors. As separate clerical class, the *ulama*, was developed to interpret the comprehensive sacral law[81] soon, in most Muslim countries the legal and judicial functions of the *ulama* were virtually eliminated.[82]

In India, an organization known as the *Jamiat-ul-ulama-i-Hind* was founded in 1919 to give guidance to the Indian Muslims in religious and political matters. It cooperated with the Indian National Congress in the struggle against

78 Donald Eugene Smith, *Religion and Political Development*, p. 137.

79 Donald Eugene Smith, *Religion and Political Development*, p. 141.

80 Donald Eugene Smith, *Religion and Political Development*, p. 46.

81 Donald Eugene Smith, *Religion and Political Development*, p. 8.

82 Donald Eugene Smith, *Religion and Political Development*, p. 48.

British rule and, since Independence, it has continued to act as the spokesman for Muslim interests in relations with the government.[83] One unpleasant fact is that the secularization of law in the Muslim countries has produced one of the most serious conflicts of modernization.[84]

8.2. Hindu

To begin with, "The traditional Hindu religio-political system was dominated by a theory of the sacral caste order of society."[85] On the contrary, the communal political orientation using Hindu sentiments may implicitly continue to press for caste, but explicitly herald to protect the religious interests and sentiments of Hindus. This can be analyzed as follows.

8.2.1. Arya Samaj

A brief mention about Arya Samaj is made here as its concerns will repeat in the subsequent discussions. Arya Samaj was started in 1875 in Bombay by Swamy Dayananda Saraswati from Kathiawar in Gujarat. The major area of its work was Punjab. Its watchword was 'Back to the Vedas.' The origin of the Samaj is significant as it heralded the birth of the first reactionary movement against the modernist.[86] Dayanand contended that the kings of *Arya varta*-India enjoyed universal sovereignty up to five thousand years ago.[87] Return to that utopian golden age should be the motivational force to unite the Hindus together against the interests of the minority religious communities.

In a nutshell, Arya Samaj was a fundamentalist organization working for the establishment of a Hindu nation and the revival of the Hindu spirit through various means-*Shuddhi* and *Sanghatan.*[88]

8.2.2. Hindu Mahasabha

Founded in 1915, the Sabha did not emphasize political involvement in the beginning because its leaders were simultaneously members of the Indian National Congress. However, it declared its aim to maintain the protection and promotion of Hindu culture and Hindu civilization for the advancement of *Hindu Rashtra.*[89] While Arya Samaj could evoke a fear psychosis among Hindus and called them for a return to the scripture and to the Vedic golden age, the new movement

---

83 Donald Eugene Smith, *Religion and Political Development*, p. 48.

84 Donald Eugene Smith, *Religion and Political Development*, p. 50.

85 Donald Eugene Smith, *Religion and Political Development*, p. 8.

86 M. T. Cherian, *Hindutva Agenda and Minority Rights: A Christian Response*, p. 163.

87 M. T. Cherian, *Hindutva Agenda and Minority Rights: A Christian Response*, p. 170.

88 M. T. Cherian, *Hindutva Agenda and Minority Rights: A Christian Response*, p. 174.

89 M. T. Cherian, *Hindutva Agenda and Minority Rights: A Christian Response*, p. 176.

challenged Hindus to consolidate the Hindu nation, heralding the beginning of nationalism based on religious fundamentalism.[90]

The founding of Hindu Mahasabha became a reality as a reaction to the formation of the Muslim league.[91] It mobilized the Hindus to form an exclusive Hindu political party. It also started to canvas for Hindu nationalism as against the secularism of the Congress party.[92] The growth of the Mahasabha was marked by the adoption of the *Shuddhi* and *Sanghatan* invented by the Arya Samaj.[93] Aggressive militancy was another feature of Hindu Mahasabha.[94]

The Sabha came to prominence during the tenure of Vinayak Damodar Savarkar.[95] Like Dayananda, he found encouragement from an utopian past glory, which he wanted his people to achieve in the future. The ideology of the Hindu Mahasabha (HMS) put forth by Savarkar was known as '*Sangahatan*' or Hindu Nationalism. *Sangahatan*, otherwise known as Hindu unity was his goal."[96] Savarkar went to the extent of threatening and sometimes challenging Muslims, with the fate of the Jews under Hitler's rule in Germany.[97]

The movement was thus highly motivated by political undercurrents, aiming at the establishment of an exclusively Hindu nation. The cardinal principle of Hindu Mahasabha was always the unity of Indians as a single culture, and single religion.[98] Though it was meant to be a political organization, it was more religious than political in its activities. Politics linked with religion was the pattern of its functioning.[99] A crucial point of importance is that the idea of a Hindu Nation stood in contrast to the idea of a composite, territorially defined political entity that developed among the secular nationalists.[100]

8.2.3. Bharatiya Jana Sangh (BJS)

The major Hindu political party in India since Independence has been the Jana Sangha, which maintains a definite anti-Muslim bias despite the existence of liberal elements within the party.[101] The context of the origin of the party itself was complex. Assassination of Gandhi and the ensuing legal struggles of RSS-were badly in need of a political party.

90 M. T. Cherian, *Hindutva Agenda and Minority Rights: A Christian Response*, p. 175.

91 M. T. Cherian, *Hindutva Agenda and Minority Rights: A Christian Response*, p. 175.

92 M. T. Cherian, *Hindutva Agenda and Minority Rights: A Christian Response*, p. 177.

93 M. T. Cherian, *Hindutva Agenda and Minority Rights: A Christian Response*, p. 177.

94 M. T. Cherian, *Hindutva Agenda and Minority Rights: A Christian Response*, p. 183.

95 M. T. Cherian, *Hindutva Agenda and Minority Rights: A Christian Response*, p. 177.

96 M. T. Cherian, *Hindutva Agenda and Minority Rights: A Christian Response*, p. 182.

97 M. T. Cherian, *Hindutva Agenda and Minority Rights: A Christian Response*, p. 183.

98 M. T. Cherian, *Hindutva Agenda and Minority Rights: A Christian Response*, p. 178.

99 M. T. Cherian, *Hindutva Agenda and Minority Rights: A Christian Response*, p. 187.

100 M. T. Cherian, *Hindutva Agenda and Minority Rights: A Christian Response*, p. 178.

101 Donald Eugene Smith, *Religion and Political Development*, p. 137.

Shyama Prasad Mukherjee, a former Hindu Mahasabha member, one of the ministers of the Nehru Cabinet openly criticized Nehru for his pro Muslim stand and resigned from the Cabinet. Mukherjee was looking for a political platform to air his views. As Hindu Mahasabha was already vanishing from the political parlance, it seemed good for him to start a new party. Shyam Prasad Mukherjee's ambition got materialized through the help of RSS as Bharatiya Jana Sangh. As Mukherjee was in full agreement with RSS in the articulation of Hindu *Rashtra*, Golwalkar lent some of his faithful lieutenants for the political task. Consequently, by October 1951, a national level political party named Bharatiya Jana Sangh (BJS) was inaugurated in Delhi with Swayamsevaks as the main working body. This was the beginning of the RSS involvement in Indian politics.[102]

Although, BJS was started as a reactionary and opposition political movement against the Congress policy of minority appeasement and secularism, Jana Sangh was not a success in the political scenario till it merged with the Janata Party after the Emergency (1975). Due to inner conflicts, the Janata government fell in 1979 and on 5th April 1980 Jana Sangh was revived with a new name Bharatiya Janata Party (BJP) with more RSS ethos. A senior leader of the erstwhile BJS, Atal Bihari Vajpayee became the founding President of the new party.[103]

8.2.4. Bharatiya Janata Party (BJP)

It is baffling that, "Communalist ideology and communal politics have not declined as many modernizers expected. On the contrary today it is on the offensive, particularly with the BJP aggressively promoting its Hindutva-ideology."[104] In spite of its predecessors' opposition to secularism as a state policy, the BJP emerged with a new formulation, 'positive secularism' against Nehruvian secularism.[105] BJP's cynical approach to secularism is obvious as positive secularism envisages suppression of religious minorities under the Hindu majority rule.

It was in the late 1980s that the BJP started emerging as a serious contender for power at the Centre. For a period after the collapse of the Janata government in 1979, the BJP went through a process of reinventing itself. Reluctant to go back to the Jana Sangh past, the party made desperate efforts to gain an acceptable and inclusive character. It sought to establish continuity with the Janata Party legacy, not simply by adopting the new name of the Bharatiya Janata Party, but importantly, by emphasizing the link with the Gandhian legacy of the former by declaring its commitment to 'Gandhian socialism.'[106]

---

102 M. T. Cherian, *Hindutva Agenda and Minority Rights: A Christian Response*, pp. 217-18.

103 M. T. Cherian, *Hindutva Agenda and Minority Rights: A Christian Response*, p. 218.

104 Gabriele Dietrich & Bas Wielenga, *Towards Understanding Indian Society* (Tiruvalla: Christava Sahitya Samithi, 2003), p. 180.

105 M. T. Cherian, *Hindutva Agenda and Minority Rights: A Christian Response*, p. 219.

106 Aditya Nigam, *The Insurrection of Little Selves: The Crisis of Secular-Nationalism in India*, p. 120.

In July 1980, Ram Jethmalani with the support of Sikkander Bakht, 'introduced a Bill in the Lok Sabha that would once again legalize religious conversion. His justification for this initiative was the need to dispel anxieties engendered by O. P. Tyagi's Freedom of Religion Bill and to give credibility to the secularist image that the BJP wanted to promote.[107]

During this period, the BJP concentrated on raising mass issues like price rise. In fact, it is interesting that the Meenakshipuram conversion was hardly noticed publicly by BJP at that time. The conversion took place on 19th February, 1981.[108]

The well-wishers of the BJP did not like its soft and apparently non-communal approach. In fact, in mid-1984, Bal Thackeray told correspondents that the BJP was 'also following the same policy of Indira Gandhi' and that it had also 'started wooing the Muslims.'[109]

Unlike its predecessors, the main objective of BJP was to capture political power in order to implement Hindutva ideology. Therefore, "BJP took up the issue of the construction of Ram temple in Ayodhya as a political agenda to come to power."[110] It is alarming that "BJP, the present political organization of the Sangh Parivar seeks political mileage by dividing the nation on communal lines."[111] Its communal canopy has become true in the recent years in its attack against Christianity. Similarly, in all the recent political programmes of the BJP, there was always a tinge of communal element.[112]

8.2.4.1. Hindu Nationalism

The Hindu communal politics spreads through a form of strange nationalisms, while Nationalism in India was born in the dual moment of its struggle against colonial domination and the encounter with modernity.[113] Again, Nationalist discourses are discourses of modernity *par excellence*.[114] On the contrary "Hindu nationalism was always a strong opponent of Indian nationalism: the nationalism advocated by Nehru and Gandhi."[115]

107 Aditya Nigam, *The Insurrection of Little Selves: The Crisis of Secular-Nationalism in India*, pp. 120-21.

108 Aditya Nigam, *The Insurrection of Little Selves: The Crisis of Secular-Nationalism in India*, p. 121.

109 Aditya Nigam, *The Insurrection of Little Selves: The Crisis of Secular-Nationalism in India*, p. 121.

110 M. T. Cherian, *Hindutva Agenda and Minority Rights: A Christian Response*, p. 223.

111 S. Robertson, *Freedom of Religion a Human Rights Issue* (Bangalore: SATHRI, 2007), p. 117.

112 S. Robertson, *Freedom of Religion a Human Rights Issue*, p. 118.

113 Aditya Nigam, *The Insurrection of Little Selves: The Crisis of Secular-Nationalism in India*, p. 37.

114 Aditya Nigam, *The Insurrection of Little Selves: The Crisis of Secular-Nationalism in India*, p. 36.

115 M. T. Cherian, *Hindutva Agenda and Minority Rights: A Christian Response*, p. 219.

In spite of the marked differences between the nationalisms of the secularists and the Hindu fundamentalists, the latter wanted the nation to be divided and the people to be subjugated on religious grounds. The intrinsic purpose of this obnoxious nationalism is to make India Hindu in the primordial way.[116] There is no progressive element in it. The Hindu-nationalists do not stop with ridiculing the credibility of secular nationalism; they go to the length of backtracking people to the false glory of yore.[117]

8.2.4.2. Religious Nationalism

While Hindu nationalism bargains for Hindu India, religious nationalism takes recourse to certain religious elements and presents them as inspirational to nationalism while ignoring the existential realities of life. Religious nationalism helps the Parivar to elevate the religion of the majority and put down others.[118] In a way, religious nationalism helps the Parivar to shift the focus of attention from real issues to abstract and trance-mundane concepts.[119]

The Sangh Parivar also envisages that this religious nationalism can pave way for world unity. Unfortunately, communal forces that promote religious nationalism divide the people within a nation. When it is impossible to establish harmony within a nation, how can such an idea bring about world unity?[120]

Another utter false promise the Parivar assures is that, accepting religious nationalism in India on the basis of religious insights can pave way not only for world unity but also for human welfare.[121] A society stigmatized with caste discriminations will definitely be skeptical of such welfare.

If Hindu religious nationalism can bring about brotherhood where is the necessity for asking other religious communities to leave this country? What is the need for asking other religious communities to subject themselves to the whims and fancies of the majority religion? Where is the need to venerate Hindu Heroes?[122]

Added to these are the other nationalisms promoted by Hindutva Ideology such as: Motherland Nationalism, Caste Nationalism, Cultural nationalism, Language nationalism and Territorial Nationalism. What India needs is Commitment for Real and United Nationalism.

How RSS a Hindu religious affiliate contributes to the influence of BJP can be discerned from the following finding that, in Chhattisgarh's Baster (district) region a changed socio-religious character of the tribal population has

116 S. Robertson, *Freedom of Religion a Human Rights Issue*, p. 129.

117 S. Robertson, *Freedom of Religion a Human Rights Issue*, p. 130.

118 S. Robertson, *Freedom of Religion a Human Rights Issue*, p. 134.

119 S. Robertson, *Freedom of Religion a Human Rights Issue*, p. 135.

120 S. Robertson, *Freedom of Religion a Human Rights Issue*, p. 135.

121 S. Robertson, *Freedom of Religion a Human Rights Issue*, p. 135.

122 S. Robertson, *Freedom of Religion a Human Rights Issue*, p. 136.

also impacted the voting pattern, the beneficiary being the Bharatiya Janata Party (BJP). The BJP is now reaping the rewards of a long campaign by the various outfits of the Rashtriya Swayamsewak Sangh (RSS). This tribal support has greatly strengthened the party in the State. Right from the 2003 Assembly elections, the tribal vote has been polled in favour of the BJP and the trend is likely to continue in 2009, unless something dramatic happens. The changed politics has become more evident in the recent past with tribals shifting their support from the Congress to the BJP.[123]

The other organizations that can be analyzed for the influence of religion on politics are Shiv Sena, Ram Sena, Akali Dal, etc.

8.3. Christian Response

Whether we like it or not Christians also have started to use religion as a tool to mobilize political power. Rather than communalizing, Christians need to work with secular minded people, because the fact is that all Christians do not belong to one single political affiliation. They are members of different political orientation. Hence, it is difficult to be prescriptive. Christians can work towards strengthening secularism and democracy and motivate people to actively involve in the electoral process.

9. Issues

The major concern in politicization of religion is that "Whether it is Hindus or Muslims or anyone who uses religion for political purposes, all of them are contravening the constitutional provisions of secularism in India."[124] Using religion for political gains is against civility. It promotes the debate between modernity and traditional mind set.

Further, "Communalizing politics amounts to constant tension and threat to peaceful and harmonious living."[125] It leads to polarization of communities on the basis of majority and minority; promotes communal disharmony; encourages hatred towards each other and hatred towards communities. The unfortunate Ayodhya tragedy, the horrifying communal carnages in Gujarat, the ill-fated Christians in Kandamal, vandalizing churches and properties in Mangalore and Bangalore are other examples.

Varun Gandhi's hate speech, inciting hatred towards communities just for votes and Ashok Sahu's (M.P. candidate of BJP, in Kandamal) communal speech against Christians are the vivid manifestations and risks of communal politics.

A painful outcome of communal politics is the suffering and inconveniences inflicted upon the minority religious communities. In other words, "Due to such communal political orientations, minority religious communities, particularly the

---

123 Aarti Dhar, "The Hinduised face of Bastar's tribals," *The Hindu*, 14 April 2009, p. 17.

124 S. Robertson, *Freedom of Religion a Human Rights Issue*, p. 183.

125 S. Robertson, *Freedom of Religion a Human Rights Issue*, p. 183.

Muslims, are irritated and frustrated. This situation will have adverse effect on the polity of India."[126]

This situation helps proliferation of minority-majority conflicts resulting in the suppression of minority rights and trying to root them out by terrorizing them through communal atrocities-killings, burning of worship places and houses. The influence of religion on politics thus seriously affects the religious freedom of the minority communities.

10. Conclusion

In the traditional societies the sway of religion on the politics was an accepted principle. The modernity discourses have brought in secularization and secular polity mainly through colonialization. Yet the fact remains in India that secularization and communalization of politics exists simultaneously. Religion is used by politicians to galvanize support for them, as it facilitates mass mobilization.

Although the Congress was a secular party in its early phase, in its latter stage, it was a mix of secular as well as communal politics. Soon the purely secular commitment of the Congress came under the attack of the religious radicals.

Consequently the religious radicals formed political parties to implement religious programs. The dangers of the failures of the process of secularization and secularism are really a matter of concern.

In order to fight the communal political affiliates, without disturbing the genuinely religious sentiments of the committed people a consideration of Gandhian model may be beneficial. We need to fight against communal politics. It is against the Constitution and it is against the beauty of plurality in India as Nehru conceived.

126 S. Robertson, *Freedom of Religion a Human Rights Issue*, p. 185.

9

Freedom of Religion and Peace Building

Introduction

This paper suggests that freedom of religion is a Constitutional privilege of all the citizens of India besides it being one of the basic human rights, and flawless practice of freedom of religion is an imperative to any peace initiative. The following discussion will start considering the Constitutional and human rights basis for freedom of religion, which is essential to peace initiatives and explains the possible role religion can play in peace building. Before doing so a glimpse at a few relevant constituents of freedom of religion and peace are graphically highlighted.

Freedom of religion implies one's freedom to freely choose or abandon his or her choice of religion subject to the Constitutional and legal provisions of her/his State. Any discussion on the freedom of religion in India is grounded on the premise that every individual has the freedom to convert to any religion but no one has the right to convert others. What is asked in this discussion is freedom of religion which leads to peace and harmonious living and not freedom to convert others.

Among the many meanings of the word peace, the following are worth remembering from the point of this paper. Peace is the state prevailing during the absence of hostilities; a treaty or an agreement to end hostilities; harmonious relations or a state of mutual harmony between people or groups; the normal freedom from civil commotion and violence of a community or cessation of or freedom from any strife or dissension; the general security of public places or public security and order. Peace also represents a larger concept wherein there are healthy or newly-healed interpersonal or international relationships, safety in matters of social or economic welfare, the acknowledgment of equality and fairness in political relationships and, in world matters. Reflection on the nature of peace is also bound up with considerations of potential causes for its absence: insecurity, social injustice, economic inequality, political and religious radicalism, and acute nationalism.

1. Indian Constitution and Freedom of Religion

The starting point for discussion on freedom of religion and peace building is the Constitution of India and from here we reach out together to higher grounds where freedom of conscience and sensitive tolerance make for an equal and open dialogue.[1]

The Indian Constitution unambiguously guarantees freedom of religion to all the citizens of India and the Constitution is supreme in India. It is also significant that the Indian Constitution is most comprehensive, well researched, and uniquely balances unity in diversity. It has also perceived the possible conflicts between the religious majority and minorities.

The framers of the Indian Constitution have taken freedom of religion as an inescapable component of the Indian Constitution. The inculcation of freedom of religion in the Indian Constitution is spontaneous. The untainted vision of the founders of the Indian Constitution had been to provide justice to all the citizens, equality of people before law, freedom of thought and religion, and protection to the minorities.

1.1. Preamble

Although the Preamble of the Indian Constitution is nonjusticeable, it guides the rest of the Constitution. It directs the interpretation of the Constitution. The Preamble guarantees to the citizens of India, particularly religious minorities, **justice, liberty, equality and fraternity.** This guarantee is further strengthened by the incorporation of the principles of secularism and democracy in the Preamble. No doubt the Constitutional guarantee is often challenged and distorted. Nevertheless the inherent pluralistic principles of the Constitution always protects the vulnerable as situation warrants. Hence, to discuss freedom of religion we need to mention the principles of Secularism and democracy.

1.1.1. Secularism

The inclusion of the word Secular in the Preamble has clarified and empowered the neutrality of the State on religious matters. The state does not interfere in religious matters in a secular state. Although, the word secular is not defined in the Constitution its implications are vivid in some of the judgments. Accordingly, the state shall be neutral in the matters of religion and religion should not be used

1 Rudolf C. Heredia, "Mission as Text in Context: Religious Conversions in Contemporary India," *Vidyajyoti Journal of Theological Reflection* 73/7 (July, 2009), p. 6.

for political ends. Secularism gains unequivocal acceptance as earnest religious bodies realize the possibility of living together with other religious communities rather than hating the other. Even after knowing that India needs secularism, people who do not subscribe to the secular values of the Indian Constitution search for flimsy and unrealistic reasons to go against it.

For example, anti-secular advocates blame Nehru for introducing secularism in the Indian Constitution. For them, otherwise India would have accepted a majority religion as the state religion. They also make a distinction between Indian secularism and western secularism and argue that western secularism is not relevant to India. To their perception, the efforts of all those who are asking for or adhering to secular principles are pseudo secularists. Blaming and trying to eliminate the principle of an universally accepted secular principle, they come up with a positive secularism which means religious minorities should subject themselves to the designs of the religious majority, and the religion of the majority assumes first place and others second.

While erroneous interpretations are a challenge, it cannot be undermined that the essential basis of a modern secular state is institutional separation of state and religion. Politicization of religion is a major threat to secularism. Another challenge is politico-religious communalism which is the present form of religious influence on political matters. Accepting the reality of plurality and upholding secularistic principles in order to work for peace is stated as "Religious tolerance is best supported by a social pluralism and secularism, which opens spaces for diverse religious traditions in society."[2]

1.1.2. Democracy

Democracy is closely connected with secular state and hence related to freedom of religion. Only a democratic form of government can assure freedom of religion to all its citizens based on the democratic principles of equality and justice. Equal respect for other's view is one of the crucial principles of freedom of religion and democracy. The democratic value loaded in the Indian Constitution is another proof of Constitutional guarantee for the freedom of religion. When freedom of religion is uninterruptedly realized, its consequential peace is possible only through a democratic acceptance of each other.

It is said "Today if Christianity, or for that matter any religion, had to fulfill its mission there should be a paradigm shift. One of the important values that religions will have to promote is democracy or a reverential attitude for others."[3]

---

2 *Ibid.*, p. 12.

3 Varghese Manimala, *Toward Mutual Fecundation and Fulfilment of Religions* (Delhi: Media House and ISPCK), 2009, p. 506.

2. Citizenship

The Indian Constitution is pregnant with the potentials for freedom of religion and peace building. This is reflected in the articles on citizenship because the Constitution does not provide for class or grade of citizenship in India. The basis of citizenship in our country is not religion but residence in the territory known as India. But, this rudimentary fact is often undermined. People who do not have faith in secularism and democratic principles describe the citizenship of minorities as secondary which is unconstitutional, against the freedom of religion and opposed to any form of peace initiatives, on the basis of equality and justice for all. More dangerous than this is the altercation that those who do not prescribe to the majority religious persuasions are secondary citizens and need to leave the country.

Whereas the Constitution wants peaceful coexistence on the basis of equality and justice, people who desire to perpetuate inequality and injustice on the basis of majority-minority polemic are a threat to freedom of religion and establishment of peace.

3. Fundamental Rights

The other provision of the Constitution which guarantees freedom of religion which is essential for peace building is the fundamental rights found in part III of the Indian Constitution. These rights prevent any form of discrimination, particularly on the basis of religion. The Constitution is vocal in matters that are infringing peace.

The fundamental rights authentically and firmly enable people to ask for and stand by their, choice of religion. Article fifteen prohibits discrimination on the basis of religion, race, caste, sex or place of birth. Article sixteen guarantees equality to all in terms of opportunity (employment), irrespective of religious affiliation. Article nineteen protects freedom of speech and expression, besides many other individual rights. Article twenty one protects the life and personal liberty of all citizens.

Article twenty five confers freedom of conscience and free profession, practice and propagation of religion. This discussion is of the view that article 25 of the Indian Constitution does not guarantee the right to convert another person although it is often claimed that the said article includes such a provision. In other words, article 25 guarantees freedom of religion and freedom of individuals to convert to any religious/ideological persuasions; and not the freedom to convert others. Some often see conversion as a means to liberation. It is acceptable as far as the individuals prefer to do so. Contrary to the freedom of religion enshrined in the Indian Constitution, Christian Dalits are denied their rights and privileges on the basis of religion, particularly new religion which they accepted.

Article twenty six guarantees freedom to manage religious affairs. Article twenty seven prohibits payment of taxes for promotion of any particular religion.

It implies public funds shall not be used for the promotion of any specific religion. Article twenty eight is about freedom to attend to religious instruction or religious worship in certain educational institutions. Article twenty nine protects minorities' culture and their admission into state maintained educational institutions. Article thirty confers on the minorities the right to establish and administer educational institutions.

The contention that freedom of religion is one of the basic prerequisites for peace building includes the responsibility that the minorities are sensitive to the sentiments of others.

While the fundamental rights are misinterpreted, for instance, the word propagation includes the right to convert others or when fundamental rights are interpreted as undue advantage to specific groups, freedom of religion and its resultant peace initiatives are challenged.

4. Directive Principles

It is a known fact that inequality and injustice are responsible for the prevalence of opposite of peace. An awkward manifestation of injustice and inequality is the form of denial of freedom of religion which pervasively works against peace. Thus, from the perspective of peace and freedom of religion, the idea of equality of citizens is implicit in the directive principles (Part IV A) of the Indian Constitution. It is worth realizing the fact that the directive principles are guidelines to the states to ensure the welfare of citizens based on justice and equality in social, political and economic life. Although nonjusticeable, the directive principles are there to guide the states to frame policies in consideration with equality and justice. When the states fail to do so and opt for communal strategy, inequality and injustice will prevail and freedom of religion and peace initiatives will be relegated to the back seat.

5. Fundamental Duties

Another provision of the Indian Constitution which vouchsafes equality, justice, peace and harmony is the fundamental duties. They aim to promote harmony and the spirit of common brotherhood amongst all the people of India transcending religious, linguistic and regional or sectional diversities. Article 51-A casts duty on every citizen to promote communal harmony and the spirit of brotherhood among all people of the country. The main thrust of the fundamental duties is preservation and strengthening of harmonious living in India. In other words, peaceful coexistence based on the promotion of communal harmony is the overflowing implications of fundamental duties.

The assumption freedom of religion is intrinsic to peace building without discriminations, inequality and injustice is the major theme emerging from the Constitutional provisions related to freedom of religion and peace building. The obvious inference is that if peace is at stake it is not the problem with the

Constitution but with people who oppose peace and promote inequality, injustice and hatred among people of different persuasions, religious or otherwise. It is our dharma to facilitate environment conducive to uphold Constitutional rights so that peace may be envisaged.

6. Human Rights

From the Constitution we need to move towards civil society[4] where freedom of conscience and sensitive tolerance make for an equal and an open dialogue. It can play an active role in considering freedom of religion as a human rights issue.

Freedom of religion which is one of the prerequisites for peace is a basic human rights according to the universal declaration of human rights. It is noteworthy that the Indian Constitution was influenced by human rights concerns. The universal declaration of human rights emphasizes the importance of freedom of religion especially to the minority communities in the world. Denial of freedom of religion amounts to denial of basic human rights. It is very important to underline the fact that religious rights are the means to realize other rights of the minority groups. Hence, the issue of freedom of religion is closely connected with human rights. If we respect fundamental rights we regard human rights as well. The point of caution is that in the UN's declaration of human rights "religious freedom now emphasized the right to change or maintain one's faith, not the right to convert or proselytize other."[5]

Denial of freedom of religion emerges only when the majority communities are unwilling to recognize equality and justice to the entire fabric of society. This causes a peace-less situation. And hence any consideration for a peace initiative need to underline the fact that freedom of religion in India is not only a Constitutional provision it is also a universal human right essential for peace and other freedoms. Therefore, "To maintain peace and harmony, the State must act strongly and decisively against all who break the law."[6]

7. Challenges to Freedom of Religion

7.1. Non-acceptance of Plurality

Unfortunately communal and fundamental organizations and political outfits utilize the religious sentiments of the people to gain political mileage and challenge the rights of religious minority communities in terms of freedom of religion, which in turn makes peace a remote reality. For example, the Hindutva ideology is a major threat to freedom of religion and peace.

---

4 Rudolf C. Heredia, "Mission as Text in Context: Religious Conversions in Contemporary India," *Vidyajyoti Journal of Theological Reflection* 73/7 (July, 2009), p. 6.

5 *Ibid.*, p. 17.

6 S. M. Michael svd, "Religious Violence in Orissa: Issues, Reconciliation, Peace and Justice," *Mission Today* xi/3 (July-September 2009), p. 258.

The problem with this ideology is rather than promoting Hindu religious values it uses Hinduism as a vehicle to forcefully infiltrate Hindutva Ideology. The ideology lacks acceptance as it harps on age old customs and practices and attempts to rationalize them. As inequality and injustice are the main evils working behind the disturbance of peace, principles that promote inequality and injustice-caste, poverty should not be rationalized and justified.

In a plural and secular state exclusive interpretation of the aspects of culture, nationalism etc., is a threat to harmony and peace. In this connection Nationalisms-cultural, religious, linguistic, caste, majority and Hindu are alleged to be fabricated to impoverish freedom of religion offered to the minorities.

The majority complex and non-acceptance of plurality are behind all the communal disturbance is vivid in India. Ravi Tiwari writes: "The fact of plurality of religion, in which Hinduism is merely one among many, has been very uncomfortable to the propounders of neo-Hindu ideologues."[7] Paradoxically they also fear that they might lose numbers if freedom of religion and peace prevail. Hence "It (Hinduism) feels threatened and in turn, poses the same to the very existence of the followers of other religions, a process we are now experiencing in India."[8]

Another unfounded fear is that the minorities will form separate nations within India. Added to this is the perception that the reservation given to the minorities is a political conspiracy.

Attempt to clothe re-conversion with nationalism is another dangerous threat to freedom of religion and peace. Jesus said, "Woe to you scribes and Pharisees, hypocrites! For you traverse the sea and land to make a single proselyte, and when he becomes a proselyte, you make him twice as much a child of hell as yourselves (Matt. 23:15 RSV)."

The religious minority community is also often accused of disrespecting Hindu religion, culture, nation, religious heroes, etc. This in fact is the reason for nurturing hatred between minority and majority communities, which is detrimental to any peace initiative.

Another pretentious effort to curb freedom of religion and endanger peaceful coexistence is the so called freedom of religion bills. Although, the title is freedom of religion the purpose is to thwart religious freedom and peaceful coexistence.

The present role of religion in politics is disturbing. It does not directly involve in politics but non-religious people use it for certain advantages. It is risky as it camouflages the uncritical mass and sentimentally manipulates the people.

7.2. Inequality and Injustice

It has already been repeatedly maintained that inequality and injustice prevent peace. Varghese Manimala points, "The imbalance-imbalance of economy,

---

7 Ravi Tiwari, *Reflections and Studies in Religion* (Delhi: ISPCK, 2008), p. 138.

8 *Ibid.*, p. 129.

imbalance of development appalling poverty in the midst of affluence, power concentration in the hands of a few, etc. – that we find in the world of today is hardly helpful for the building up of peace."[9]

Elements disturbing the possibility of peace are also a threat to progress. It is said "The key for progress is fairness in world affairs, the development of a new world vision concerned with the have-nots, and improved knowledge of different cultures and religions."[10] It is further emphasized that, "...the current world disorder results in part from ignorance about civilizations-unawareness or selective memory of the past and lack of perspective for the future- and in part from the economic misery and political injustices experienced by the have-nots, which represent some 80 percent of the world's population all across the globe and in different civilizations. These are the barriers for achieving the advanced state of world order, and if we can overcome them, we will reach the optimum-a dialogue of civilizations."[11]

Another aspect of peace highlighted in the graphic explanation of peace is social security. That is, "If we believe that the world is becoming a village because of information technology, then in that village we must provide social security for the less privileged, or it may promote a revolution."[12]

One single threat that is core to the non-availability of peace is poverty resulting from inequality and injustice. It is emphatically stated that, "Poverty and hopelessness are sources for terrorism and disruption of world order. Better communication and partnerships will end the divide between "us" and "them."[13] Felix Wilfred remarks, "Today, the threat to peace is caused not by terrorism and organized crimes alone. The pervasive threat to peace is caused by poverty."[14]

In the context of Kandamal it is said, "Without justice and fairness, we cannot have peace and reconciliation."[15] Swami Agnivesh points out: "Peace without justice will be simply a euphemism for reinforcing the social and economic status quo."[16]

---

9 Varghese Manimala, *Toward Mutual Fecundation and Fulfilment of Religions* (Delhi: Media House and ISPCK), 2009, p. 527.

10 Ahmed Zewail., "Dialogue of Civilizations: Making History through a New World Vision," in *Towards a Culture of Harmony and Peace,* edited by T. D. Singh (New Delhi & Kolkata: Delhi Peace Summit & Bhaktivedanta Institute, 2005), p. 24.

11 *Ibid.*, p. 25.

12 *Ibid.*, p. 36.

13 *Ibid.*, p. 24.

14 Felix Wilfred, *Religion and Culture for Social Amity* (Bangalore: ECC, 2006), p. 15.

15 S. M. Michael svd, "Religious Violence in Orissa: Issues, Reconciliation, Peace and Justice," *Mission Today* xi/3 (July-September 2009), pp. 257-258.

16 Swami Agnivesh., "Promotion of Peace through Social Justice," in *Towards a Culture of Harmony and Peace,* edited by T. D. Singh (New Delhi & Kolkata: Delhi Peace Summit & Bhaktivedanta Institute, 2005), p. 185.

8. Religion and Peace Building/Initiatives

As the constitutional provisions and human rights concerning freedom of religion are challenged due to intolerance, inequality and injustice for the sake of gaining political mileage, religions need to function dynamically in order to establish peace. Needless to say religions need to function freely and dynamically freedom of religion is mandatory. Real religious freedom facilitates mutual respect and cooperation among religious communities in order to establish peace. Freedom of religion for peace initiative also implies harmonious living with other communities and respect for the other.

8.1. Living Together

Paul F. Knitter writes, "It is said that in our present age, religious people have to be religious interreligiously. To walk one's faith-path, one needs to be walking with others from different paths."[17] Raimon Panikkar suggests, "Religion is "orthopraxis" and it cannot be shelved to some corners of life and to a few hours of practice; it has to permeate the whole life. As religious pluralism is a gift and a challenge the religions need to take it up with earnestness not by its denial but by learning to live with it, and …find ways and means for mutual fecundation and fulfillment."[18] Such a benevolent notion emerges when one is deeply committed to build peace from the perspective of religions. A deep involvement for the cause of peace calls for change in our perceptions. Paul F. Knitter affirms, "Study, prayer, interreligious dialogue, and action to promote justice, peace, liberation, and the integrity of creation have changed me."[19] He also maintains, "A new way of understanding other religions implies a new way of understanding Christianity."[20] It is further reiterated, "Freedom of conscience demands that boundaries be kept porous, as indeed most borders will be in a globalizing world."[21]

8.2. Pluralist Perspective

While harmonious living and mutual respect for others are essential constituents of peace, a pluralist perspective also will be helpful. It is clearly stated: "Religious pluralism is the proper attitude that promotes religious freedom and freedom of religions, it encourages respect for the free expression of one's religious beliefs and

---

17 Paul F. Knitter, *Introducing Theologies of Religions* (Maryknoll, New York: Orbis Books, 2002), p. xi.

18 Raimon Panikkar, "Introduction," in *Toward Mutual Fecundation and Fulfilment of Religions*, Manimala (Delhi: Media House and ISPCK), 2009, p. 14.

19 Paul F. Knitter, *Introducing Theologies of Religions* (Maryknoll, New York: Orbis Books, 2002), p. 4.

20 *Ibid.*, p. 13.

21 Rudolf C. Heredia, "Mission as Text in Context: Religious Conversions in Contemporary India," *Vidyajyoti Journal of Theological Reflection* 73/7 (July, 2009), p. 7.

respect for the right of each person to associate with others and to organize with them for religious purpose."[22]

A pluralist perspective also helps overcoming constrains within one's own tradition. For example, "Not only is the freedom to follow one's religious law important, equally important is the freedom to transcend those laws. In this way, the understanding of religious enlightenment is ultimately supportive of the understanding of religious freedom as pluralism."[23]

8.3. Interior of Religion (Mystery)

The principle of pluralist perspective can be substantial if the approach to the ultimate is pursued with humility because of its unfathomable and infinite greatness. In the words of Paul Tillich, "The way is to penetrate into the depth of one's own religion, in devotion, thought and action. In the depth of every living religion there is a point at which the religion itself loses its importance, and that to which it points breaks through its particularity, elevating it to spiritual freedom and with it to a vision of the spiritual presence in other expressions of the ultimate meaning of man's existence."[24] It is also true that, "There needs to be a true transcendence of religion, the ability to go beyond one's religion and reach out to others in an active pro-existence and only then we can be called religious in the true sense of the term, otherwise we tend to be fundamentalists."[25]

In this context our understanding of the ultimate may need reconsideration because "Reality is intrinsically complex, rich, intricate, mysterious."[26] In the words of John Hick, "I suggest that the best religious account we can give of the global situation is that of a single ineffable Ultimate Reality whose universal presence is being differently conceived and experienced and responded to within the different human religious traditions."[27]

The mystical/ultimate/reality beyond the temporal expressions can be a base for working together for peace. It does not mean that there shall be only one single religion.

---

22 Jove Jim S. Aguas, "Religious Pluralism and Freedom of Religion," *Journal of Dharma* 31/1 (January-March 2006), p. 80.

23 Warayuth Sriwarakuel, "Religious Freedom," *Journal of Dharma* 31/1 (January-March 2006), p. 49.

24 Paul Tillich, *Christianity and the Encounter of the World Religions* (New York and London: Columbia University Press, 1964), p. 97.

25 Raimon Panikkar, "Introduction," in *Toward Mutual Fecundation and Fulfilment of Religions,* Varghese Manimala (Delhi: Media House and ISPCK), 2009, p. 14.

26 Paul F. Knitter, *Introducing Theologies of Religions* (Maryknoll, New York: Orbis Books, 2002), p. 7.

27 John Hick, "The Next Step Beyond Dialogue," in *The Myth of Religious Superiority: Multifaith Explorations of Religious Pluralism,* edited by Paul F. Knitter (Maryknoll, New York: Orbis Books, 2005), p. 12.

It is not just enough to follow pluralism and accept limitation before the beyond, in order to contribute to peace religions need to co-operate and support each other. Raimon Panikkar suggests: "The idea of a universal religion appears not to be feasible, and in the given situation religions need to acknowledge one another as co-travelers towards the Absolute offering mutual support and enrichment."[28]

8.4. Dialogue

To live together we need to follow the principle of pluralism which in turn leads to a mystical beyond which could accommodate most of the religio-ideological traditions. This recognition calls for a dialogical living and working among the many faith traditions. In the words of Raimon Panikkar, "Truth although one is multifaceted and we can only have a glimpse of some of the aspects of the truth, as the world famous story of the blind men and the elephant indicates. We are conditioned by our perspectives, attitudes and culture; and what is needed is that we accept these limitations and cooperate with others in the search for Reality."[29] A sincere dialogical initiative can bring about peace. John Hick writes, "Dialogue between the faiths must continue on an ever-increasing scale. But the only stable and enduring basis for peace will come about when dialogue leads to a mutual acceptance of the religions as different but equally valid relationships to the Ultimate Reality."[30] Sincerity in dialogue is imperative for a positive result. In the words of Ravi Tiwari, "No experience of dialogue is worthy if it is conducted, or engaged in, without sincerity and integrity of purpose."[31] The urgency of peace is emphatically stated as "People of various religious affiliations have to join hands even if their leaders fail to support them in the peace building effort; otherwise the future of the world is in great danger."[32]

8.5. Human Rights

Freedom of religion is a human rights issue and when it is treated as a human right issue the possibility of working towards peace will be easier for the simple reason that "Human rights and religion are interrelated in connection with the freedom of religion."[33] Felix Wilfred suggests the following steps: "Religion can play a

28 Raimon Panikkar, "Introduction," in *Toward Mutual Fecundation and Fulfilment of Religions,* Varghese Manimala (Delhi: Media House and ISPCK), 2009, p. 14.

29 *Ibid.*, p. 15.

30 John Hick, "The next Step beyond Dialogue," in *The Myth of Religious Superiority: Multifaith Explorations of Religious Pluralism,* edited by Paul F. Knitter (Maryknoll, New York: Orbis Books, 2005), p. 12.

31 Ravi Tiwari, *Reflections and Studies in Religion* (Delhi: ISPCK, 2008), p. 186.

32 Varghese Manimala, *Toward Mutual Fecundation and Fulfilment of Religions* (Delhi: Media House and ISPCK), 2009, p. 527.

33 *Ibid.*, p. 515.

significant role by involving itself in the dynamics of peace. First of all, no social harmony is possible without recognition of the dignity and rights of people. By defending human rights Christianity will effectively champion the cause of peace in the Asian societies. Secondly, Christianity could become an active force in developing the values and attitudes which the creation of peace requires. Thirdly, the contribution Christianity could make is to instill the spirit of dialogue as an indispensable and effective method for the promotion of peace. The contribution at these levels will bring Christianity into dialogue and cooperation with other religious traditions of Asia."[34]

Peace initiatives are a very necessary contribution when religions can make it possible, apart from their regular functions. The necessity of peace building is indicated as "Just as protection of human rights should be a treat concern of the religions so also today's world torn asunder by wars and conflicts calls for a big and urgent task of peace building."[35] While calling attention to consider freedom of religion as a human rights concern, "One important factor that has to be recognized by all is the basic freedom of every human being and this includes also the freedom of religion. This is a freedom that is granted by all civilized nations of the world, and especially those nations where democracy is the form of government. While we assert for ourselves a freedom to embrace the religion which we believe to be of divine origin, we cannot deny an equal freedom to those whose minds have not yet yielded to the evidence which has convinced us."[36]

8.6. Humanness

It is again crucial from the point of religious contribution to peace that one has to understand the commonality of human race that is behind all the differences. This fact is clearly stated as, "In spite of all constraints and complexities it must be possible for people of goodwill to come together on the common ground of our basic humanity, protected by a regime of human rights and affirmed in a commitment to fundamental duties."[37] To move further, "Freedom of religion is clearly one of the most basic rights of human beings, for it is rooted in the nature of what they are. It is, perhaps, for this reason that the challenges to this freedom have also been often regarded as violations of what it is to be a human person."[38]

A comprehensive way of understanding humanness is found in the expression of A. P. J. Abdul Kalam: "In whatever field we work, be it science,

34 Felix Wilfred, *Religion and Culture for Social Amity* (Bangalore: ECC, 2006), p. 16.

35 Varghese Manimala, *Toward Mutual Fecundation and Fulfilment of Religions* (Delhi: Media House and ISPCK), 2009, p. 522.

36 *Ibid.*, p. 560.

37 Rudolf C. Heredia, "Mission as Text in Context: Religious Conversions in Contemporary India," *Vidyajyoti Journal of Theological Reflection* 73/7 (July, 2009), p. 6.

38 William Sweet, "Freedom of Religion from Tolerated Practice to Human Right," *Journal of Dharma* 31/1 (January-March 2006), p. 28.

technology, medicine, politics, policing, theology, religion or the judiciary, we have to remain in the service of the common man whose well-being is central to all human knowledge and endeavor."[39] This conviction is the crux if religions earnestly seek to contribute to peace building.

Another important insight that will help peace building is that, "We must all remember, very often we tend to forget that religion is an accident of birth except perhaps for that minuscule minority which might adopt it by choice. It is, therefore, essential that we realize that the purpose and objective of every religion is to foster peace, harmony, brotherhood, and not to quarrel needlessly."[40] To establish peace each religious persons need to ask the genuine question, what could have been my standpoint had I been born in another religion than the one I am following.

If the above principles are not viewed seriously, religions need to concentrate on them. It is suggested that, "What religion needs to do is to make the human beings realize their common humanity and strengthen the bonds of friendship and affection. If religions become a barrier in this mission of theirs they should have the courage to disown such fake religions and religious leaders, and work for the true religion where people will realize themselves as brothers and sisters with a common mission to work, and effect the liberation of man."[41]

A further insight in this direction is, "Religions need to realize that they are only means; they are not an end in themselves. Human beings are not to be made slaves of religions; rather they must experience freedom *in* religion and freedom *for* religion."[42] To put the matter into perspective, we need to realize that "Tolerance towards principles of other religions, respect of human rights and the rights of minorities must be the basis of peaceful coexistence."[43]

9. Conclusion

One of the prerequisites for any form of peace building efforts is freedom of religion which is often challenged by the majority-minority conflicts resulting in gross injustice and inequality. Prevalence of injustice and inequality causes

---

39 A. P. J. Abdul Kalam, "The Joy of Human Life," in *Towards a Culture of Harmony and Peace,* edited by T. D. Singh (New Delhi & Kolkata: Delhi Peace Summit & Bhaktivedanta Institute, 2005), pp. 13-14.

40 A. M. Ahmadi., "Towards a Global Society," in *Towards a Culture of Harmony and Peace,* edited by T. D. Singh (New Delhi & Kolkata: Delhi Peace Summit & Bhaktivedanta Institute, 2005), p. 18.

41 Raimon Panikkar, "Introduction," in *Toward Mutual Fecundation and Fulfilment of Religions,* Varghese Manimala (Delhi: Media House and ISPCK), 2009, p. 18.

42 *Ibid.*, p. 19.

43 Ezekiel Issac Melekar., "Concept of Judaism," in *Towards a Culture of Harmony and Peace,* edited by T. D. Singh (New Delhi & Kolkata: Delhi Peace Summit & Bhaktivedanta Institute, 2005), p. 19.

hostilities. At this juncture nonreligious bodies using religious sentiments for other than religious reasons add fuel to the fire.

The commitment of Indian Constitution to establish justice and equality which are basic to peace and peaceful coexistence often comes under the attack of misrepresentation and misinterpretation generating willful disturbances.

It is important that we need to follow the constitutional commitment to establish communal harmony and fraternity which help peace building. It is also our basic duty to contribute towards facilitating a conducive atmosphere for the principles of the Constitution to function.

Poverty which is the net product of injustice and inequality of all sorts is the main challenge for the peace initiatives. It needs to be countered by opposing the plans for any form of dominance; and allowing healing to take place.

As the freedom of religion a Constitutional and human rights guarantee is a basic requirement for peace building, religions need to learn to live together by accepting and respecting each other. It can be possible if we approach the ultimate as mystery and consider our knowledge of it as partial. Once the source of superiority claims is properly understood dialogical activities among varying faith-traditions towards peace initiatives become meaningful.

In order to make peace initiatives relevant and positive our dialogical endeavors need to rest on human rights concern based upon the common humanness behind all the apparent differences and undertakings in a sustainable way.

10

Alienating Strangers

Introduction

A Stranger is a person whom we do not know, a person who is in a place that he/she has not been before, an unfamiliar person, a foreigner, alien, outsider, visitor, guest and a new arrival. The unique condition of us is that there is an ongoing attempt to make us strangers in our own country. People are on the move for various reasons – migrating, immigrating and emigrating. It is also alarming that people migrate because of religious persecution. Religion which is supposed to unite but it brews strangers and often excludes them and that is our concern. This paper is a modest attempt to highlight the process of 'brewing strangers' that are attempted at various levels and to appeal for vigilance and involvement to counter them in our context.

Hindutva Ideology

The process of making Indians aliens in India began with the emergence of Hindutva ideology conceived by the RSS. Hindutva is not Hinduism.[1] It embraces all the departments of thought and activity of the whole Being of the Hindu race.[2] It is not a word but a history.[3] The first essential feature of Hindutva is securing Hindusthan/Hindu Rashtra/Hindu nation or the land of Hindus.[4] In brief,

1 Vinayak Damodar Savarkar, *Hindutva: Who is a Hindu?*, 6th ed. (New Delhi: Bharti Sahitya Sadan, 1989), 4.

2 Vinayak Damodar Savarkar, *Hindutva: Who is a Hindu?*, 4.

3 Vinayak Damodar Savarkar, *Hindutva: Who is a Hindu?*, 3.

4 Vinayak Damodar Savarkar, *Hindutva: Who is a Hindu?*, 82.

Hindutva is a communal and a majoritarian ideology committed to Hinduvise India at the expense of other faith traditions.

According to Hindutva, Hindus 'are not only a nation but also a race-jati,'[5] and it excludes the votaries of every other faith traditions as foreigners labeling them as enemies and secondary citizens. In the words of M. S. Golwalkar, "we are Hindus even before we emerge from the womb of our mother. We are therefore born as Hindus. About the others, they are born to this world as simple unnamed human beings and later on, either circumcised or baptized, they become Muslims or Christians."[6]

"Hindutva is a politics of RSS combine. It aims to work for the agenda of Hindu Nation (Rashtra)."[7] The idea that was stationary for some time is now actively reemerging as the majority NDA government is at the Centre. The Hindutva ideology is based on inclusion and exclusion.

Hindu Rashtra

Hindutva's intriguing distinction between territorial/geographical nationalism and religious (Hindu) nationalism is a way of making Indians alien in India. Assimilating others or destroying others and 'establishing a Hindu nation is called as world Mission of RSS.[8]

The Hindu Rashtra 'stands not only for political and economic unity but also for cultural and religious unity.'[9] Praveen Togadia has asked the "Hindus of the country to become one and prepare the way for Hindu Rashtra."[10] The darker side of the notion of Hindu nation is, often 'Hinduism became the symbol of nationalism' and 'indeed, it is an ideology which consigns a few hundred million non-Hindus to second-class citizenship.'[11]

That is why Suchitra Vijayan says "religious nationalism" is a genuine fear among the country's minorities.' Religious nationalism excludes the notion of a secular state, and denies equal participation of those who do not identify with the dominant religion.' Further, 'the disastrous marriage between religion and nationalism will ultimately subvert the values that have held this nation together.'[12]

---

5 Vinayak Damodar Savarkar, *Hindutva: Who is a Hindu?*, 84. (jati from jan).

6 M. S. Golwalkar, *Bunch of Thoughts*, 3rd ed., Reprint (Bangalore: Sahitya Sindhu Prakashan, 2000), 117.

7 Ram Puniyani, "Choosing My Religion: *Ghar Wapsi* and Freedom of Religion," *NCC Review* CXXXV/06 (July, 2015), 9.

8 M. S. Golwalkar, *Bunch of Thoughts*, 9.

9 M. S. Golwalkar, *Bunch of Thoughts*, 129.

10 "Development without Hindu Rashtra is of No Use: Togadia," *The Hindu* (Vijayawada), 27 January 2015, 10.

11 "The Missing Conservative Intellectuals," *The Hindu* (Vijayawada), 25 July 2015, 10.

12 "Rewriting the Nation State," *The Hindu* (Vijayawada), 17 March 2015, 9.

The Hindu nationalists reject plurality,[13] and "while the whole country during freedom movement stood up and participated in the movement for independence and for secular democratic India, RSS kept aloof from this movement as its goal was Hindu nation."[14]

The RSS leaders have even suggested that 'let the Constitution be re-examined and re-drafted, so as to establish this unitary form of Government.'[15] Even "both the RSS 'Prayers' and 'Oath' mandatory for its cadres, demand establishment of a Hindu rashtra."[16] These are strategies to make people outsiders in their own country.

Constant Attempt to Challenge Our Hold

The RSS, since its inception in 1925, has been working towards a Hindu nation in spite of India's diversities. However, the inherent secular character of the Indian Constitution even before the inclusion of the word secular in the Preamble of the Constitution in the year 1976 by virtue of 42nd amendment of the Constitution has protected India from such communal agenda. The inclusion of the word "secular" testifies to the fact that there were elements working against the secular principles of the nation. In one of the Republic Day (2015) advertisements of the Union Government, the facsimile of the Preamble of the Constitution was shown without the words "Socialist" and "Secular." BJP leaders defended it saying that it was the facsimile of the original Constitution which was signed on 26th January, 1950, where the words "Socialist" and "Secular" were not mentioned.

It cannot be an inadvertent omission because even the Union Minister for Information technology, Ravi Shankar Prasad, suggested a debate on this issue. This is also in line with the argument that had been advanced when Vajpayee was the Prime Minister that the Constitution needed a comprehensive review.[17] The paradox is that the 'Justice Venkatachelliah commission he had appointed did not suggest deletion of the words Secular and Social even if they had been adopted by parliament in the years of the State of Emergency.'[18]

It is the re-emergence of the ideas of M. S. Golwalkar who said 'the word 'secular' is nowhere to be found in our Constitution.'[19] Further these are reflections of RSS aspiration to replace the Indian Constitution with *Manusmriti*. The *Organizer* in an editorial on November 30, 1949, complained, that 'in our

13 M. S. Golwalkar, *Bunch of Thoughts,* 156.

14 Ram Puniyani, "Choosing My Religion: *Ghar Wapsi* and Freedom of Religion," *NCC Review* CXXXV/06 (July, 2015), 9.

15 M. S. Golwalkar, *Bunch of Thoughts,* 3rd ed., Reprint (Bangalore: Sahitya Sindhu Prakashan, 2000), 227.

16 Shamsul Islam, "Hindutva in Hurry," *Indian Currents* XXVII/30 (27 July-02 Aug, 2015), 30.

17 John Dayal, "Raj Dharma in 2015," *Indian Currents* vol. xxvii/5 (02-08 February. 2015), 33.

18 John Dayal, "Raj Dharma in 2015," *Indian Currents* vol. xxvii/5 (02-08 February. 2015), 33.

19 M. S. Golwalkar, *Bunch of Thoughts,* 162.

constitution there is no mention of the unique constitutional development in ancient Bharat.'[20]

All attempts to destabilize the principle of a 'secular state' with any other alternative in the Indian setting is a deliberate plot to make sections of the nation strangers and it is also an indicator that suggests that the government is refusing to be neutral in religious matters. It is unthinkable that India a secular state is tormented to accept Hinduism as the State religion. Nehru is blamed for disallowing Hinduism becoming a National religion. Had it happened, imagine the number of strangers India would have witnessed. The sad fact is that this notion is again slowly echoing in the conversations of many BJP leaders.

Curbing Freedom of Religion

The Indian Constitution unambiguously guarantees freedom of religion to all the citizens of India. Even before the insertion of the word 'secular' in the preamble, Article 25 guaranteed freedom of conscience, and the freedom to profess, practice and propagate any religion as one of the fundamental rights. The call for a national debate on article 25 is a well calculated plot to paralyze freedom of religion in India.

President Mukherjee in his republic day address (2015) said, "we have always reposed our trust in 'equality' where every faith is equal before the law."[21] Indian civilization has celebrated pluralism, advocated tolerance and promoted goodwill between diverse communities. These values need to be preserved with utmost care and vigilance.[22]

US President, Obama spoke in clear terms to a crowded audience of mostly young people in New Delhi that 'upholding Article 25 of the Indian Constitution is the responsibility of government, but it's also the responsibility of every person.'[23]

Freedom of religion is a fundamental 'universal human rights' as well. On the strength of absolute majority in the Parliament, Union Home Minister Rajnath Singh called for a national debate on 'conversion.' It is a well calculated attempt in continuation with 'the then Prime Minister, Atal Bihari Vajpayee's (a RSS trained Swayamsevak) demand for a debate on the conversion.[24] It is to shut freedom of religion for the minorities thereby alienating many sections of the nation.

It is more disturbing that elements within the BJP government are creating disturbing situations to bring in debate on freedom of religion and enact an anti-conversion law thereby depriving the religious minorities their right to profess, practice and propagate their own religion. What is at stake is the freedom to

---

20 Shamsul Islam, "Hindutva in Hurry," *Indian Currents* XXVII/30 (27 July- 02 Aug, 2015), 30.

21 John Dayal, "Raj Dharma in 2015," *Indian Currents* vol. xxvii/5 (02-08 February. 2015), 32.

22 John Dayal, "Raj Dharma in 2015," *Indian Currents* vol. xxvii/5 (02-08 February. 2015), 32.

23 Kay Abey, "Obama's Parting Shot," *Indian Currents* vol. xxvii/5 (02-08 February. 2015), 28.

24 Ram Puniyani, "Choosing My Religion: *Ghar Wapsi* and Freedom of Religion," *NCC Review* CXXXV/06 (July, 2015), 7.

choose any religion and the ones who willfully chose religion of their choice are treated as foreigners in their own land.

In most important discussions the word deliberately chosen to debate is 'conversion' instead of 'freedom of religion.' 'Where is the place for people volunteering and adopting another religion, like Ambedkar and so many others?' 'Where is the place for choice of one's religion in a democratic society believing in 'freedom of religion and conscience?'[25]

We are Indians. The choice of religion is our fundamental right. We are almost called strangers in our own country because we chose a religion of our choice.

Democracy as Majority Religious View

Democracy helps religious minorities to express their concerns and grievances in a peaceful, acceptable and parliamentary way. India 'cannot remain a democracy without allowing its citizens the freedom to practice a religion of their choice.'[26]

It is the gentle spirit of democracy that even the numerically insignificant find space to bring in their concerns. This golden rule is diluted by arguing that 'the spirit of democracy at its 'best is nowhere more fully recognized and practiced than in the age-old Hindu tradition.'[27] Comparing democracy with Hinduism is mockery but risky as well.

It is falsely claimed that "in a democracy the opinion of the majority has to hold the sway in the day-to-day life of the people. As such it will be but proper to consider the practical conduct of the life of majority as the actual life of the national entity. From this point of view also, efforts to uplift the life of Hindus is national and not communal."[28]

These are the claims and goals of RSS and we see them taking shape at many levels. It is also a fact that 'in any given national context, the more politically dominant a religion, the greater its capacity to undermine democratic values.'[29]

The deliberately worked out strategy of the RSS to compare democracy with the majority Hindu view is a clever strategy to degrade the numerically vulnerable. Religious majority cannot replace political majority and do away with minorities.

Polarization on Religious Basis

'Mobilizing the masses using religion and religious symbols for political ends started along with the Independence movement (Bharat Matha). And 'almost

---

25 Ram Puniyani, "Choosing My Religion: *Ghar Wapsi* and Freedom of Religion," *NCC Review* CXXXV/06 (July, 2015), 22.

26 "Secularism is Not a Policy Option," *The Hindu* (Vijayawada), 19 February 2015, 8.

27 M. S. Golwalkar, *Bunch of Thoughts,* 337.

28 M. S. Golwalkar, *Bunch of Thoughts,* 165.

29 "The Missing Conservative Intellectuals," *The Hindu* (Vijayawada), 25 July 2015, 10.

fifty years later, the Ayodhya Ram Janmabhoomi campaign employed similar strategies to mobilize popular support for its vision of Hindu nationhood.'[30]

It is now a reality that election manifestos of some political parties include highly inflammable and sensitive and controversial religious issues. It is also becoming a reality that just before elections communal riots are instigated. It was seen in Uttar Pradesh before the general elections. Gujarat became a BJP stronghold, presumably, after an ugly communal clash. Another new trend that has developed is to make provocative communal attack on minority communities.

RSS has floated various organizations with exciting names to strengthen Hindu numerical strength in the places of neglected tribal and *adhivasi* people. These bodies work overtime to bring in other religious communities as well. In reality, these have changed the voting pattern of India which has gone in favour of the BJP. Alienating and "the targeting of minorities has played an important role in polarizing the communities, in consolidation of the majoritarianism politics in various ways."[31]

In order to polarize on majority and minority lines a false notion is created that the religious minorities disrespect Hindu religion, culture, nation, religious heroes, etc.

Hindu Culture

The beauty of Indian culture is its plurality (of cultures). Religion is an integral part of any culture. Talk of monoculture, rather majority culture, in place of multi-culture is another source of alienating strangers. We are faced with the claim that the Hindu Rashtra 'stands for cultural and religious unity'[32] and 'our concept of Hindu Nation is 'essentially cultural.'[33] Accepting other progressive and civilizing cultural aspects are dismissed as, spiritual subjection.'[34]

It implies that only a particular set of teachings, morals, standards and practices are the final and similar other resources do not have relevance. The followers of such resources, because minority in number, have to adhere to the norms of the majority otherwise they do not find place in India. We hear news that Ramayana and Mahabharata should be given centrality but not Koran and Bible. Similarly, the unique tribal 'culture and norms are undermined and rejected'[35] saying that they have to return to their original Hinduism.

30 "Rewriting the Nation State," *The Hindu* (Vijayawada), 17 March 2015, 9.

31 Ram Puniyani, "Choosing My Religion*: Ghar Wapsi* and Freedom of Religion," *NCC Review* CXXXV/06 (July, 2015), 10.

32 M. S. Golwalkar, *Bunch of Thoughts,* 129.

33 M. S. Golwalkar, *Bunch of Thoughts,* 34.

34 M. S. Golwalkar, *Bunch of Thoughts,* 42.

35 Ram Puniyani, "Choosing My Religion*: Ghar Wapsi* and Freedom of Religion," *NCC Review* CXXXV/06 (July, 2015), 5.

RSS accuses the minority religious communities that they do not respect Indian culture. Jawaharlal Nehru refuted such notion and wrote 'a Buddhist or Jain in India is a hundred per cent product of Indian thought and culture, yet neither is a Hindu by faith. It, is, therefore, entirely misleading to refer to Indian culture as Hindu culture.' Further, 'it is incorrect and undesirable, to use 'Hindu' or 'Hinduism' for Indian culture.'[36]

The danger of Hidutva ideology is that for the sake of merely preserving outdated and inhuman customs and practices many reforms and transforming efforts are discouraged and disturbed.

One Language

Language is the vehicle that carries the rich resources of different religious traditions. Any effort to promote one language and undermine the value of other is another form of alienating strangers. There is a need in India even to credit the religious resources that mainly depend upon oral traditions.

Hindutva glories about Sanskrit as 'our mother-tongue'- the tongue in which the mothers of our race spoke and which has given birth to all our present tongues. Our gods spoke in Sanskrit, our sages thought in Sanskrit, our poets wrote in Sanskrit. All that is best in us-the best thoughts, the best ideas, and the best lines- seeks instinctively to clothe itself in Sanskrit.[37] It is assumed that, one day "as a solution to the problem of 'lingua franca', till the time Sanskrit takes that place we shall have to give priority to Hindi on the score of convenience."[38] Recently I watched a TV news where a central minister urged the people to sign in Hindi.

The revolutionary contributions of Tamil literature and Dravidian contributions for social change and political discourse are adversely portrayed saying a foreign missionary falsely propagated in Tamilnadu, that 'Tamil culture, Tamil language and everything Tamil differed fundamentally from the rest of the Bharatiya culture, language, etc., and that the Tamilians formed an independent nation by themselves.'[39]

Growing announcements about celebration of 'Sanskrit week' and all out effort of the government to promote Sanskrit is a worrying sign. It is wrongly proclaimed and even defended by the Supreme Court that Sanskrit can be given special status as all the important wisdom and teachings of India are in it. It is untenable that Hindu religious literatures are equated with Indian literature. Sanctifying and promoting a particular language and ignoring others can lead to alienating the linguistic minorities.

---

36 Jawaharlal Nehru, *The Discovery of India*, Centenary Edition (Delhi: Oxford University Press, 1989), 75.

37 Vinayak Damodar Savarkar, *Hindutva: Who is a Hindu?*, 95.

38 M. S. Golwalkar, *Bunch of Thoughts*, 112.

39 M. S. Golwalkar, *Bunch of Thoughts*, 217.

Home Coming/Ghar Vapsi/Reconversion

The effort of converting people back to Hinduism is called Home coming/Ghar Vapsi/Reconversion/Suddhi, etc. It was a process that began with Dayananda Saraswathi and continues even to this day. This is a definite attempt to reconvert people to Hinduism from the religions where the Dalits, Adhivasis, tribals, discriminated and neglected of this country found liberation, respect and acceptance. For the RSS, 'this is only a call and request to them to understand things properly and come back and identify themselves with their ancestral Hindu way of life.'[40] Here religious conversion is mixed up with nationalism and culture.

The program of reconversion is aimed at increasing the number of Hindus and minimizing the minorities from the point of votes. It is true that the 'Sang Pariwar is disturbed by the thought that if the flow of the depressed castes into other religions is allowed to continue, their status as the majority might get overturned in the recent future."[41]

Security concern is often attributed to other forms of religious mobility. For example, "conversion of Hindus into other religions is nothing but making them succumb to divided loyalty in place of having undivided and absolute loyalty to the nation."[42] In reality, forced reconversion is an attempt to make sections of Indian society secondary to the majority community. It is said "in a fascist religious state, minority religions can only continue as secondary, in the mercy of the majority religion."[43] Attempt to clothe re-conversion with nationalism or culture is another process of alienating strangers.

Communalizing History and Education

We are faced with the RSS aspiration of rewriting Indian history and Hinduvising the educational system. The notion behind such an aspiration is that the existing histories are based on different periods (Hindu, Mughal, British, etc) and the education system in vogue is not based on Indian (Hindu) values. The new history is expected to be in line with the heroes (mainly religious) of India and the education system is to be framed after the Hindu literatures.

The background of the new history is that 'Hindus are the only people who have succeeded in preserving their history which began from the Vedas.'[44] It

40 M. S. Golwalkar, *Bunch of Thoughts,* 129.

41 TM Yesudasan, "Ghar Wapsi: The Invitation of Fascism," *Aikyatha* Quarterly (January-March, 2015), 18.

42 M. S. Golwalkar, *Bunch of Thoughts,* 170.

43 TM Yesudasan, "Ghar Wapsi: The Invitation of Fascism," *Aikyatha* Quarterly (January-March, 2015), 18.

44 Vinayak Damodar Savarkar, *Hindutva: Who is a Hindu?*, 6th ed. (New Delhi: Bharti Sahitya Sadan, 1989), 93.

is Hindu religious history rather than Indian history, wherein Hindu heroes are interpreted as saviors of this nation.[45]

Similarly, the new discourse about Godse is 'a political maneuver, aimed at rewriting the history of the Indian polity, and its principles of secular, pluralistic statehood.' Hence it is true that "India's future lies in pluralism, parity, reasonable and principled cosmopolitanism and not with settling scores in history."[46] A Hindu history in place of Indian history is a calculated effort to distort the real historical process and to perpetuate the process of systematically making us guest in our own country.

'Many have charged the NDA with not just saffronising but also degrading the country's premier institutions by appointing under qualified candidates to the post.' It is also called "the closing of the Indian mind." An ideology which relegates a few hundred million non-Hindus to second-class citizenship can ever form the basis of serious scholarship.[47]

For Amartya Sen, 'the obvious danger of the saffronisation project is challenging the principle of scientific enquiry and terming anything rational as anti-Hindu.'[48] Further, "the appointment of Hindutva proponents and sympathizers at the helm of various educational, cultural and research institutions makes one to conclude that ideology has taken precedence over efficiency and competence under the new dispensation."[49]

It is true that 'the BJP Government in Gujarat, MP, Rajasthan and Haryana are introducing Hindu religious texts in schools and making Saraswati Vandana and surya namaskar Hindu rituals compulsory.'[50] The entire exercise is aimed at imposing a particular point of view without space for other views.

Muslims and Christians

Often the patriotism of Muslims in India is suspected.[51] Another allegation is that there is no true religion in them, they are only trying to further their political ambitions.[52]

Christians in India are also subjected to criticism like, "together with the change in their faith, gone is the spirit of love and devotion for the nation."[53] They

---

45 Vinayak Damodar Savarkar, *Hindutva: Who is a Hindu?*, 45.

46 "Rewriting the Nation State," *The Hindu* (Vijayawada), 17 March 2015, 9.

47 "The Missing Conservative Intellectuals," *The Hindu* (Vijayawada), 25 July 2015, 10.

48 Shamsul Islam, "Hindutva in Hurry," *Indian Currents* XXVII/30 (27 July-02 Aug, 2015), 29.

49 Suresh Mathew, "At the cost of merit," *Indian Currents* XXVII/30 (27 July- 02 Aug, 2015), 5.

50 Irfan Engineer, "Preamble, Secularism and Constitution," *NCC Review* Vol. Cxxxv /1 (January-February, 2015), 37.

51 M. S. Golwalkar, *Bunch of Thoughts,* 185.

52 M. S. Golwalkar, *Bunch of Thoughts,* 189.

53 M. S. Golwalkar, *Bunch of Thoughts,* 125.

are accused of 'keeping themselves aloof from the freedom struggle.'[54] They are also warned that, if the Christians do not subscribe to the ideology of Hindutva 'they will remain here as hostiles and will have to be treated as such.'[55]

Savarkar includes Jains, Buddhists and Sikhs as inheritors and partakers in the legacy of Hinduism, but he clearly excludes Islam and Christianity as foreign ideologies. Therefore, hatred is often manufactured against them 'through riots, destruction of religious sites, organizing religious conversion camps, beef bans, rewriting textbooks, censoring works of history, literature and fiction that challenge the 'Hindu' version of history, appropriating political icons, and raising monuments.'[56]

To form a Hindu nation with one culture and one language Christian and Muslim presence is an obstacle. Hence, Hindutva groups concentrate on infiltrating the notion that the forefathers of Muslims were Hindus that they should return to the Hindu fold as self-respecting persons.[57]

Too many attacks on the minority religious communities (mostly Christians) take place because 'the message went around in a subtle manner that 'our' government will ensure that the culprits will 'get away,' law will be made to sleep over these incidents.[58] False propagations, false accusations and willful attacks are engineered to alienate sections of the nation.

The claim of the Hindutva advocates that the Muslim population will overtake Hindu, and therefore Hindu women should give birth to many children has fallen flat with the news that "India's Muslim population is growing slower than it had in the previous decades, and its growth rate has slowed more sharply than that of the Hindu population, new Census data show."[59] Projecting others as a future threat for political prospects is another way of alienating strangers.

Gate at the Border

It is clear that the process of alienating strangers is at the centre of the Hindutva ideology propagated and supported by RSS and now vigorously voiced by some members of the ruling party. It is not to sound an alarm, not to create panic, but to be cautious of the process of us being considered as 'persons that they do not know,' a new arrival, unfamiliar person, foreigner, alien, outsider, visitor and guest in our own country. And hence there is a need to go to the gate at the border.

Normally a gate protects people within against invaders. Besides, at any ancient city gate important business transactions were made (place of Public

54 M. S. Golwalkar, *Bunch of Thoughts,* 159.

55 M. S. Golwalkar, *Bunch of Thoughts,* 194.

56 "Rewriting the Nation State," *The Hindu* (Vijayawada), 17 March 2015, 9.

57 M. S. Golwalkar, *Bunch of Thoughts,* 143.

58 Ram Puniyani, "Choosing My Religion: *Ghar Wapsi* and Freedom of Religion," *NCC Review* CXXXV/06 (July, 2015), 10.

59 "Muslim Population Growth Slows," *The Hindu* (Vijayawada), 26 August 2015, 1.

market), public deliberation took place, law court was convened (administration of justice), Public announcements were heralded, prophets frequently delivered the messages and criminals were punished outside the gate.

To protect ourselves from the seeming invasion, to do our normal transactions as natural Indian citizens, to voice our concerns, to seek justice, to listen government schemes and announcements, to listen to the prophetic voices and to bring the guilty to the book we need to approach all the possible gates. The following are a few seemingly promising gates. We are constantly provoked to become strangers and forced to stand at the gate. It is our strong hope that the gate will not disappoint.

Legal Remedies

Religious freedom is essential for equality before others and the law. Without justice and fairness to all the citizens of the country sections of the nation will be relegated to assumed secondary level of existence.

We live in a country where worship places are razed to the ground by a mammoth mob under the leadership of communal political leaders, in the full view of cameras and security personnel. No one is punished. Thousands of people belonging to a particular religious community are killed under the banner of communal conflicts and their responsibility can not be exactly fixed. An increasing number of elected members of the Parliament make provocative and communally loaded statements and go unpunished.

It is also a fact that most of the sensational and crucial court verdicts are made in consideration of the majority religious sentiments. Though it is rare, "Justice is a necessary precondition for the existence of unity and harmony at every level of society."[60]

Although the possibilities are bleak, we have to tightly hold on to the gate of Justice. This is the prophetic vision. The minorities of the country with one voice should constantly struggle for equal justice for all, as the example used by Jesus, of a woman approaching a wicked judge and he then reluctantly delivers justice to her. All issues that affect equality to minorities need to be legally addressed. This is the strongest gate available to us in spite of the failures. How do we utilize the full potential of this gate needs to be carefully worked out in collaboration with all the minorities, progressive ideologies and political parties.

Legislative Process

Another possible gate for our protection is the legislative system. It is difficult to use this gate as there is less number of legislative members from minority communities compared to the larger number from the majority community. Court rulings that are not exactly suitable for egalitarian and respectable status in the country can be revisited only through the legislative process.

60 Zena Sorabjee, "Interfaith Education," in *Towards a Culture of Harmony and Peace,* 126.

For example, the Supreme Court has ruled that the freedom of religion bills legislated by different states do not infringe on the freedom of religion. In reality these bills have made the choice for Freedom of Religion more difficult and complicated. As human beings are becoming more civilized and global the possibility to change religion should become simple and individual's affair without government interference as long as it does not violate the Constitution of India. A secular legislature alone can prevent dubious debates.

The Supreme Court had earlier declared special status to Sanskrit as the ancient Indian literatures are in Sanskrit. This shows the subjective consideration of issues and the unpalatable nature of the verdict in our context. It requires a legislative process to set right matters. Similarly the presidential order disallowing government privileges to Scheduled Caste Hindus converted to Christianity needs a bold legislative correction. A united Christian persuasion along with other minorities, political parties and ideologies can be of help to achieve this end. It is necessary to find out ways and means to appeal to the secular legislators to set things right. The process of alienating strangers will become more acute if we do not wisely access this gate. It is not easy but we need to sincerely engage until we are able to convince.

Human Rights and Humanness

Along with the gates of legal and legislative process the wider 'human rights' and 'common humanness' aspects have to be carefully explored. As per UN declaration, freedom of religion is a fundamental human right. It guarantees dignity and rights of the people. Freedom of religion is same to all. Hence, as we seek freedom of religion we also respect other's freedom of religion.

Freedom of religion is clearly one of the most basic rights of human beings, "It is, perhaps, for this reason that the challenges to this freedom have also been often regarded as violations of what it is to be a human person."[61] Our constant vigil through state, national and international human rights organizations shall be of great help.

This is in continuation with the recognition of humanity's 'humanness.' What is common to all is humanness and religion is a choice. A. P. J. Abdul Kalam wrote, "in whatever field we work, be it science, technology, medicine, politics, policing, theology, religion or the judiciary, we have to remain in the service of the common man whose well-being is central to all human knowledge and endeavor."[62]

Realization of a common humanity behind the multiplicity of differences help celebrate plurality and avoid denigration of minority communities. Poverty,

---

61 William Sweet, "Freedom of Religion from Tolerated Practice to Human Right," *Journal of Dharma* 31/1 (January-March 2006), 28.

62 A. P. J. Abdul Kalam, "The Joy of Human Life," in *Towards a Culture of Harmony and Peace,* 13-14.

health, education, unemployment, malnutrition, terrorism are some of the concerns that require the collective efforts of all communities. Rather than alienating the numerically vulnerable, efforts should be in place for collectively dealing with these situations.

It is significant that "In spite of all constraints and complexities it must be possible for people of goodwill to come together on the common ground of our basic humanity, protected by a regime of human rights and affirmed in a commitment to fundamental duties."[63] It helps to promote a harmonious and peaceful coexistence with mutual respect in our context.

Creating Awareness

Apart from these collective and broad approaches there needs to be a proactive and concentrated effort from minority communities to prevent alienating strangers. We may use our communication and educational channels to expose the hidden scheme of making us strangers in our own country. The nation should be made aware of the process of alienating us already initiated by the advocates of Hindutva through various means. Wise, meaningful and innovative use of social/media is helpful in this regard.

Often, the 'development slogans' have the mesmerizing and often blinding effects upon the real schemes that are working behind the many dubious announcements and commitments. We need to overcome passivity to disillusion religious majority centered developments ruthlessly blindfolding the younger generation of India from being vibrant to the realities of India.

It has to be made loud and clear that there are already forces at work to make India a Hindu nation, to equate time tested political and government institutions and instruments with Hinduism, to equate majority religious ambitions with 'political majority', to promote one culture, religion, language, values, etc., in the place of many, to facilitate inappropriate reconversions to strengthen Hindu Majority vote, to vilify the religious minority communities and to replace knowledge, scholarship and scientific enquiry and reasoning with Hindutva ideology.

Clear distinction should be made known between the 'spiritual quest' on the one hand and 'politicization of religion' and 'polarizing communities on religious grounds' on the other. This is so significant in the context of growing communal conflicts that dominate pre-election scenarios.

There is also a need to expose the pseudo religiosity of BJP which has come out in public, in the case of meat ban in Maharashtra during the Jain festival.

63 Rudolf C. Heredia, "Mission as Text in Context: Religious Conversions in Contemporary India," *Vidyajyoti Journal of Theological Reflection* 73/7 (July, 2009), 6.

Here, "A philosophy of tolerance is caught in a politics of intolerance and this is ironic."[64]

While we strive against these 'backward looking', insulting and enslaving schemes and their effect on us, the minority communities cannot shrink in their spirit and efforts in nation building and transforming India.

Conclusion

I have highlighted, not the entire, but a few challenges that are at hand for the minorities to be vigilant and active in our commitment to the Church and society. The programs suggested both broad and active are not the whole range of solutions. May God enlarge our wisdom to stand up to the occasion.

64 Shiv Visvanathan, "The Pseudo–Religiosity of the BJP," *The Hindu* (Vijayawada),16 September 2015, 10.

11

A Critique of Rev. Dr. K. P. Aleaz's Theological Contributions

Introduction

As I embark to discuss here the theological contributions of Aleaz, let me start with his insights on his definition of religion, the preferential method to study religions, theology of religions underlying pluralism, pluralistic inclusivism, relational convergence of religions and the connection between religion and culture.

Following his contributions to the religious studies, I shall focus on his contributions to Indian philosophy by underlining his consideration of *pramanas*, Advaita, Christian response to Indian philosophy and Indian Christian philosophy.

Next in that order is his interpretation of theology, mainly focused on Indian Christian theology, Eastern Christian thought and Dalit theology. His proposal for an Indian spirituality however, is no less a significant contribution. Aleaz's bent of knowledge and commitment can further be drawn from his important constructs like Jesus, Gospel and proclamation and mission.

1. Religions

Aleaz's theological contribution need to be discussed in the first place under the title religions, as he is a professor of religions. Under this heading his contribution to the field of religion can be analyzed.

1.1. Defining Religion

As opposed to the customary way of defining religion, Aleaz suggests a novel and a relevant approach which the modern students of religions ought to take into consideration. He says, 'the meaning of religion has to be understood today in terms of an evaluation of the history of ones own religion by its fruits.'[1] Again he says "rather than evaluating other faiths in terms of one's own faith we are entering an era where we will evaluate our own faith in terms of the positive aspects of other faiths."[2] His focus is on that fact where religion needs to be fruitful and thus needs to take into account the positive contributions of other religions to enrich itself. His supplement to the existing considerations about the definition and meaning of religion has its background in the earlier notion that Christianity alone will be the final religion.

Added to the above two insights are the views that all religious experiences are authentic in their own context and the plurality of religious expressions is natural. He writes "our point is, all the expressions of all the religious experiences are authentic in their own realm. Plurality in experience and expression is something natural to religions and we should take note of this point in our understanding of what religion is."[3]

Another important lesson is that expressions of the same religious experience can also vary. In the words of Aleaz, "in our understanding of what religion is, we should note that expressions of the same religious experience can vary and also religious experiences are numerous, all being authentic in their own realm."[4]

The contributions of Aleaz in defining religion is appropriate as it is not concerned with the content of religion rather with the applicability and possibility of relating one religion with the other while upholding the reality of many religions. This proposal is put forward keeping in mind the possible relational convergence of religions from the perspective of pluralistic inclusivism. His contribution would have become more outstanding had it emphasized the need for religions to focus upon life sustaining issues.

1.2. Methodology

Although, there are different approaches to study religions Aleaz suggests for an integrated approach consisting sociological, social anthropological and philosophical methods. In his own words, "Sociological and social anthropological approaches as well as philosophical approach together may constitute an integral Indian approach to the study of religion."[5] He is also of the view that such an integrated approach can take into account even the primal religions.[6] The underlying authentic assumption in this attempt is harmony of religions or relational convergence of religions. This has been stated as "the integral Indian

1 K. P. Aleaz, *Dimensions of Indian Religions*, 1995, p. 2.

2 *Ibid.*, p. 2.

3 *Ibid.*, p. 283.

4 *Ibid.*, pp. 299-300.

5 *Ibid.*, p. 299.

6 K. P. Aleaz, *Religion in Christian Theology*, 2001, p. 7.

approach to the study of religion" conceived as "dialogical in its essence on the basis of a vision of relational convergence of religions."[7]

The reason for selecting the sociological approach is to explain the connection between religion and society; socio-anthropological approach is to highlight the human aspect of religion and society; and philosophical approach is to show that in India religion and philosophy are interconnected. As Indian philosophy is undertaking the orderly arrangement of religious elements, its contribution to the scientific study of religion is an issue. Although, one may discern the life sustaining vision to be implicit in the selection of the other two methods, Aleaz has not spelt it out explicitly. It may also be argued that, rather than confining to these approaches a historical study of the religions will be helpful to understand the general significance and limitations of religions. This will further strengthen dialogical relation between religions.

1.3. Theology of Religions

On the basis of the dialogical existence of religions or relational convergence of religions from the perspective of pluralistic inclusivism, Aleaz has developed his theology of religions. For him, "theology of religions signifies the particular way in which one conceives other faiths in terms of one's own faith."[8] Again he writes, "theology of religions enquires into how from the perspective of one's own religious faith, a person can account for the diversity of the world's religious quest and commitment."[9] Still further, "the issue of the relationship between one's own religious faith and other faiths is the focus of attention in theology of religions."[10]

From these it is clear that theology of religions is concerned with how one conceives other faiths in terms of one's own faith, how one accounts for the reality of many religions and how one relates with the others. In fact in his definition of religion Aleaz has given priority to other religious insights in understanding one's own faith-tradition. Here on the contrary he focuses how one can relate with the other from his or her own standpoint. That is, the focus has moved from the other to one's own faith tradition.

Hence, it may be correct to say that, theology of religions is the study of the ways in which a person understands faith-traditions other than his or her own and how he or she relates his or her tradition with others.

In the pursuit of relational convergence of religions Aleaz has missed a significant aspect of the definition of theology of religions, that, not only faith traditions but ideologies also contribute to the life sustaining relational convergence of religions. Hence it may be appropriate to maintain that, theology of religions is not just confined to religions alone. It is concerned with ideologies

7 K. P. Aleaz, *Dimensions of Indian Religions*, 1995, p. 299.

8 K. P. Aleaz, *Harmony of Religions: The Relevance of Swami Vivekananda*, 1993, p. 233.

9 K. P. Aleaz, *Theology of Religions: Birmingham Papers and Other Essays*, 1998, pp. 227-228.

10 *Ibid.*, p. 168.

as well. Its main aim is to interpret various faiths and ideologies in a way to build up a constructive relation between them, without disregarding the unique differences, for working towards a common goal, i.e., a life sustaining vision.

1.3.1. Pluralism

Aleaz's own proposal is to accept pluralistic inclusivism as the right approach to the theology of religions. Nevertheless, he is comfortable with the strand of pluralism as well. He writes, "the Pluralist perspective maintains that other religions are equally salvific paths to the one God."[11] This definition can raise a crucial question as to how does pluralism account for religions which do not believe in the existence of God. Another shortcoming of the definition is that the role of other ideologies is undermined by excluding them. The school of pluralism, no doubt, has a place for all religions which believe in God, religions which do not believe in God and ideologies which are constructively contributing towards life sustaining pluralistic perspective.

Aleaz is of the view that "in the religious history of India we notice Hinduism accepting religious pluralism theologically."[12] One can also recall without doubt that the predominant Hindu perception of other religions is relativism. Aleaz himself writes "in the view of Neo-Vedanta which reinterprets Advaita, each religion is a path leading to the same goal."[13] It is also obvious at present that the hardcore Hindu fundamentalist and communal representation is nowhere near pluralism.

Yet Aleaz goes on to suggest that, "Hindu culture accepts religious pluralism theologically through the concepts of *adikara bheda* and Advaita."[14] This assertion needs reconsideration as the present day politicized Hinduism is committed to a communally charged one monolithic Hindu culture.

In support of his position, Aleaz argues that "the pre-Diamper (pre1519) St. Thomas Christians upheld Pluralism in theology of religions."[15] His appreciation and aspiration for the pre-Diamper days need to take in to account the increasing intolerant attitude of some sections of Christianity against other religions.

1.3.2. Pluralistic Inclusivism

Aleaz's agreement however, with pluralist interpretation of religions no way disturbs his unyielding preference for pluralistic inclusivism. This is evident as he writes, "Pluralistic Inclusivism can be conceived as a viable Indian Christian theology of religions in the context of dialogue."[16] Aleaz also points out that 'the pre-Diamper

11 *Ibid.*, p. 170.

12 K. P. Aleaz, *Harmony of Religions: The Relevance of Swami Vivekananda*, 1993, p. 236.

13 K. P. Aleaz, *The Gospel of Indian Culture*, 1994, p. 286.

14 *Ibid.*, p. 286.

15 K. P. Aleaz, *Dimensions of Indian Religions*, 1995, p. 285.

16 *Ibid.*, p. 283.

(pre1519) St. Thomas Christians upheld the perspective of Pluralistic Inclusivism in social life.'[17] It implies that one can be pluralist in terms of theology of religions and pluralistic inclusivist in terms of social life.

Since pluralistic inclusivism is Aleaz's own construct, it is necessary to further understand this principle. According to him, "Pluralistic inclusivism inspires each religious faith to be pluralistically inclusive, i.e., on the one hand each living faith is to become truly pluralistic by other faiths contributing to its conceptual content and on the other hand inclusivism is to transform its meaning to witness the fulfillment of the theological and spiritual contents of one's own faith in and through the contributions of other living faiths."[18]

Two important insights emerge from the above explanation. One is that every religion should become pluralistic with the contributions of other religions and the second is that the inclusivistic tendencies of the religions should seek fulfillment from the contributions of other religions. This of course is in contrast to the traditional way of thinking that all other religions will be fulfilled in Christianity. These are, in fact, the radical proposals of Aleaz against the existing tendencies that if a religion is pluralistic it positively considers other religions and if it is incluvisistic it seeks the fulfillment of other religions. In the words of Aleaz, "in Pluralist Inclusivism, both Inclusivism and Pluralism undergo change in their previous meanings. It makes Pluralism inclusive and Incluvism pluralistic."[19]

A major outlook on pluralistic incluvism is obvious in Aleaz's writing from the point of Advaita that "Pluralistic Incluvism is an attempt to make Christian faith pluralistically inclusive, i.e., the content of the revelation of God in Jesus is to become truly pluralistic by other faiths contributing to it as per the requirement of different places and times and it is through such pluralistic understanding of the gospel that its true inclusivism is to shine forth. Here pluralism transforms itself to focus on its centre which is God as God in the universally conceived Jesus and inclusivism transforms itself to bear witness to the fulfillment of the Christian understanding of Christ in and through theological contributions from people of other faiths."[20] Aleaz's elucidation looks speculative and inconceivable from the point of some of the traditional claims of Christianity.

His proposal that other faiths will contribute to the Christian faith according to the situation is hard to digest for an ordinary mind. Similarly, universal Jesus cannot be understood except from the point of Advaita. The underlying assumptions behind this bold proposal is stated as "the basic affirmation here is that there is a possibility of the fulfillment of the theological and spiritual contents of one's own faith in and through the contributions of other living faiths."[21] The

17 *Ibid.*, p. 285.

18 K. P. Aleaz, *Harmony of Religions: The Relevance of Swami Vivekananda*, 1993, p. 234.

19 K. P. Aleaz, *Theology of Religions: Birmingham Papers and other Essays*, 1998, p. 172.

20 *Ibid.*, p. 172.

21 *Ibid.*, p. 172.

doubt that may arise here is that, how is it possible for Aleaz to seek a universal Jesus while arguing for pluralistic inclusivism?

It was already maintained that Pluralistic Inclusivism in reality is the approach of dialogue for the simple reason that as in dialogue in pluralistic inclusivism each religious faith receives from other religious faiths new insights regarding its own conceptual content.[22] It may be asked if dialogical approach is the same as pluralistic inclusivism what is the necessity for galvanizing pluralistic inclusivism?

Another point is that in Pluralistic Inclusivism 'religious resources of the world are conceived as the common property of humanity.'[23] This is further explained as "all religious experiences and traditions are simultaneously ours. We do not have any one particular religious tradition alone as our own and other as belonging to others. All are mine as well as all are for all others. All belong to all. It is a religious perspective in which while remaining in one's own religious faith-experience, one can consider other faiths as one's own, as the common property of humanity, for a more and more blessed and enriched life. Here the otherness of the other is negated."[24] Aleaz is correct in considering all the religious resources of the universe as the common property of humanity. But, this concern needs to be addressed in the realm of freedom of religion where every individual should be entitled to follow the religion of his or her choice.

Another aspect is that, in Pluralistic Inclusivism "there is social justice maintained in the realm of religious experiences by sharing with those who do not have, but this is entirely different an attitude from that of imposing upon others forcibly what they do not want. Pluralistic Incluvism always maintains humility to see that others have better things than us. The superiority of others is always affirmed in it, rather than claiming our own superiority."[25]

Aleaz's unwavering commitment to Pluralistic Inclusivism thus draws resources not only from Hinduism but also from the Syadvada or Anekantavada of Jainism. His assumption is that pluralistic inclusivism contributes to the relational convergence of religions.

1.3.3. Relational Convergence of Religions

Aleaz envisages 'a relational convergence of religio'[26] through pluralistic inclusivism. In other words, 'Pluralistic Incluvism gives birth to relational convergence of religions.'[27] His dedication to promote pluralistic inclusivism is vivid in his declaration that "for the last twenty five years I have been pleading

22 *Ibid.*, p. 322.

23 *Ibid.*, p. 1.

24 *Ibid.*, p. 176.

25 *Ibid.*, p. 184.

26 *Ibid.*, p. 1.

27 *Ibid.*, p. 173.

for the relational convergence of the thoughts and experiences of diverge religious faiths in terms of a particular perspective in theology of religions which I call pluralistic inclusivism."[28]

What is relational convergence of religions and its content can be deduced from his writing that "an important aspect of relational convergence of religions is mutual conversion. Being born in a religion does not mean that we should die in that religion in the same way as we were born. We can get converted into the true spirit of once own religion and in that very conversion get converted into another religious experience as well."[29] Aleaz should not be misunderstood as promoting conversion from Christianity to other religions. He always maintained that the words proselytizing and conversion should not be confused. His priority is to see a conversion or change of attitude in a person in the light of the contributions of other religions. This is to say, to develop a positive attitude towards others while being critical of one's tradition.

This aspect is illustrated as "for example, if the gospel of God in Jesus has to emerge from the hermeneutical context of India, we can rightly say that Indian Christians are in a process of converting to the Indian religio-cultural context."[30] Aleaz's explanation looks difficult, but the simple point is that the Gospel should be relevant to the context. This is further made clear as "in the very conversion to Jesus in India, there is a conversion to the religio-cultural context of India, effecting thus a double conversion and this hints at the possible relational convergence of religious experiences."[31]

Aleaz, no doubt, allows space to consider that "inter-relation as well as relational convergence of religion is a possibility."[32] That is, if it is not existent there we can go for it, in that direction.

1.4. Religion and Culture

In connection with the relation between religion and culture, Aleaz argues that 'the basic feature of Indian culture is its integral relationship with Indian religions.'[33] He further states, "religious enlightenment constitutes the fundamental source of creativity for Indian culture and the Indian psyche."[34] He is also of the opinion that "there was no imposition of Aryan culture on the existing Indian cultures, but only a diffusion of it through an acculturation process."[35]

28 K. P. Aleaz, *A Convergence of Advaita Vedanta and Eastern Christian Thought*, 2000, p. xv.

29 K. P. Aleaz, *Theology of Religions: Birmingham Papers and other Essays*, 1998, p.180.

30 *Ibid.*, p. 180.

31 *Ibid.*, p. 180.

32 K. P. Aleaz, *Dimensions of Indian Religions*, 1995, p. 2.

33 K. P. Aleaz, *The Gospel of Indian Culture*, 1994, p. 1.

34 *Ibid.*, p. 287.

35 *Ibid.*, p. 284.

Aleaz's respect for Indian heritage is admirable, but it cannot be ignored that as there are many religions, there are many cultures. Similarly the infiltration of Aryan influence including culture in various spheres of Indian life cannot be denied. It is true that there is a connection between religion and culture in India as elsewhere. But, promoting one religious culture as the Indian culture is dangerous and it is no way different from communalist tendencies. In fact, the Sangh Parivar in India is arguing for a single monolithic Hindu culture, although mere Hindu culture is not Indian culture.

Of course, Aleaz perceives a double gospel emerging from Indian culture. According to him, "one is the gospel of integral relation between religion and culture, resulting in cultural symbiosis and a composite culture through an ongoing interaction between religions. The second meaning of the gospel of Indian culture points to an understanding of the gospel of God in Jesus emerging from the Indian culture or rather the Indian hermeneutical context which in reality goes beyond the scope of the previous Christian concepts like 'indigenisation' or 'inculturation.'"[36] The third gospel of Indian culture for Aleaz is 'the gospel of interreligious harmony and integration.'[37]

The two gospels-gospel of composite culture and the gospel of God in Jesus emerging from the Indian hermeneutical context are limited to the outcome of the confluence of Christianity and Hinduism. But the fact remains that India has many cultures and many religious traditions/gospels. Aleaz also graphically reflects, without emphasizing the many religions and cultures, the possibility of inter-religious harmony.[38] He also asserts, as indicated earlier, theologically Hindu culture accepts religious pluralism as it is vivid in the principles of *adikara bheda* and Advaita.[39]

In the view of Aleaz, 'the most important feature of Indian culture is its integral relationship with Indian religions.'[40] He calls this relationship as Advaitic.[41] And affirms Advaita cannot be tied down to the narrow boundaries of any one particular religion. It stands for unity and universality in the midst of diversities. As a result it can very well function as a symbol of Indian composite culture.[42] The possibility of this suggestion may be questioned.

Aleaz, almost in line with the Sangh Parivar, claims, "it was its cultural unity based on religion that held India together historically as one."[43] Again, "the

36 *Ibid.*, p. 2.

37 *Ibid.*, p. 283.

38 *Ibid.*, p. 283.

39 *Ibid.*, p. 286.

40 *Ibid.*, p. 283.

41 *Ibid.*, p. 283.

42 K. P. Aleaz, *Christian Thought Through Advaita Vedanta,* 1996, p. 1.

43 *Ibid.*, p. 1.

survival of the political unity of India is based on its cultural unity within which there persists a 'core' of religion to which the sense of Advaita or 'not-twoism' makes an enduring contribution."[44] The Advaitic explanation and political unity based upon cultural unity may amount to communal and fundamental nature. Such notions are disadvantageous to Indian context. Aleaz also needs however to analyze the dangers lurking behind such notions.

It is a fact that India does not have one single culture. It houses many cultures. Unity in diversity is the principle that keeps India going. Seeking for a religious culture based upon Hinduism is the communalist blunder of religionised political parties in India. Hindu culture cannot be considered as Indian culture. Cultures can exist side by side by mutual respect and interaction. Whether cultures can create a composite culture is a difficult question.

2. Philosophy

Having analyzed Aleaz's contribution to theology from the point of religious studies, now his theological contributions in terms of Indian philosophy can be discussed. It is obvious that he is an ardent advocate of Advaita Vedanta of Sankara. Before underlining some of his creative and radical constructs in line with Advaita, his understanding of the six *pramanas* (Sources of Knowledge)[45] of Indian philosophy can be discussed.

2.1. Pramanas

Aleaz is sentimental in using the six *pramanas* in Indian Christian theology. As he finds a close integration of reason and revelation in the *pramanas*, Aleaz considers giving total freedom to the Pramanas of Indian Philosophy to function as Indian Christian *Pramanas*. His sentiments are expressed as, "we receive the *Pramanas* of Indian Philosophy totally as they are; neither do we reject them nor do we reinterpret them to suit a pre-formulated Christian epistemology."[46]

Aleaz's devotion to the *pramanas* is understandable. At the same time we cannot encourage an uncritical application of them in Indian Christian theology. A positive consideration of the *pramanas* is possible if they can serve as tools of interpretation.

Aleaz's reverence for the *pramanas* is so serious that he maintains "one cannot add some more *pramanas* just like that to the list of the six got fixed through centuries of investigation by the best minds of India;..."[47] This is, in fact, his reaction to A. J. Appasamy's proposal to consider sabha (church) as a *pramana* and Paul Gregorios' interpretation of *sabda* as tradition. Another

44 K. P. Aleaz, *A Convergence of Advaita Vedanta and Eastern Christian Thought*, 2000, p. xvi-xvii.

45 Perception-*pratyaksa*, inference-*anumana*, scripture or verbal testimony-*sabda*, comparison-*upamana*, postulation-*arthapatti*, and non-cognition-*anupalabdhi*.

46 K. P. Aleaz, *The Role of Pramanas in Hindu-Christian Epistemology*, 1991, p. 4.

47 *Ibid.*, p. 119.

suggestion is, experience (Anubava) cannot be confused with, perception and it cannot be considered as a *pramana*.

Aleaz also complains that the Indian Christian theologians have not considered using all the six *pramanas*. Nonetheless, in his positive declaration Aleaz maintains "it is our conviction that the construction of a Christian epistemology has to take place from the very use of the Indian Philosophical *Pramanas*."[48] This dedicated acceptance leaves with questions such as, can we accept the *pramanas* uncritically, can't we modify some of them, and can't we add new *pramanas*. In fact we cannot and should not blindly accept them and use them because they are also human products and all of them are not used by all schools of thought in India.

Whereas it is insightful to learn that even in the *pramanas* there is a close integration of reason and revelation, Aleaz's contention that there cannot be any other *pramanas* than the accepted ones and that Indian Christian philosophy has to be developed from within the *pramanas*, can be subjected to further scrutiny.

As theologies today are down to earth realities, Aleaz needs to reconsider some of the claims. Our approach should be from below and the struggle for sustenance-based. In this connection, the *pramanas* may not be of absolute help to us.

2.2. Advaita/Sankara

Philosophically Aleaz is oriented towards Advaita Vedanta of Sankara. It may be because of his perception that 'Advaita is neither monism nor pantheism, but gives value and meaning to jiva and the world.'[49] It may be also because for him, "the proclamation of Sankara is that the Atman as Pure Consciousness and Witness pervades, illumines and unifies the whole world, the whole of history and the entire human personality, giving significance to world and history as well as meaning and purpose to human life on earth."[50]

The intention behind the choice is that for Aleaz, the Advaita Vedanta is helpful to understand God, world and life as not separate entities but as one reality understood at different levels. Another current is that, Advaita Vedanta principle that the reality is one without the second, is a convenient vehicle to emphasise religious harmony. Of course, as Aleaz is for relational convergence of religions, he could promote Advaita, but it may not be appropriate to declare that this is the only viable option. Although it is not his intention, it is implied that other philosophical and theological constructs are insignificant compared to Advaita Vedanta.

48 *Ibid.*, p. 4.

49 K. P. Aleaz, *Religion in Christian Theology*, 2001, p. 1.

50 *Ibid.*, p. 2.

Still further, Aleaz is convinced that "Advaita Vedanta makes Christian faith-experience new and refreshing."[51] This is an extraordinary claim in pursuing the good cause of religious harmony. Not all Indian thinkers have taken up this position. At the same time it needs to be remembered that there are constant appeals to Vedanta to be refreshed in the light of Christianity. Hence, it may be fitting to consider every religion as a whole and explore the possibilities of working together towards a life sustaining vision on the strength of varying spiritual resources.

From the point of other religions and issues, Aleaz has accepted Advaita as the only philosophical system acceptable to all Hindus and other religious communities. He is also reflecting the notion that Advaita alone has solutions to all the problems in theology, religion and society. This is stated as "through the Advaita Vedantic understanding that each idea of god is but a stage in the religious journey, tolerance and acceptance of all different religions become natural and spontaneous for a Hindu."[52] The meritorious point deserving appreciation is Aleaz's commitment in pursuing religious harmony. At the same time there should be room to account for the different strands of Hindu understandings, because one of the salient aspects of Hinduism is its principle of Adikarabheda and istadevata. I am sure Aleaz will not disagree.

Aleaz's faithfulness to Advaita facilitates much broader prospects to Advaita. According to him, Vedanta transcends all religious boundaries.[53] But, the fact that Advaita Vedanta has its background in the Siva tradition cannot be forgotten. Its universalistic tinge is welcome, but it cannot be made obligatory on all other religious communities and even on the Hindus who would subscribe to the various other interpretations available in their own tradition.

2.3. Christian Response to Indian Philosophy

Aleaz's 'Christian Responses to Indian Philosophy,' is based on his commitment to the pluralistic context of India. He is of the opinion that an analysis of the responses of Christian thinkers to the philosophical systems of India will be the first step in this direction.

According to Aleaz, Krishna Mohan Banerjea and Nehemiah Nīlakantha Sastri Goreh responded to all the major doctrines of the six philosophical systems and presented Christian concepts to be superior to them. Nehemiah Nīlakantha Sastri Goreh's approach is exclusive because he entirely disagreed with the six systems of philosophy in the light of his Christian understanding to the extent of suggesting that they are in error.

51 *Ibid.*, p. 10.

52 K. P. Aleaz, *Harmony of Religions: The Relevance of Swami Vivekananda*, 1993, p. 240.

53 K. P. Aleaz, *Christian Thought Through Advaita Vedanta,* 1996, p. 1.

Aleaz emphasizes that in Christian response to Indian philosophy, the relation between reason and revelation warrants special consideration. He also appeals that all the scriptures should be accepted as revelations.

The growth of Navyanyaya within the Nyaya system as presented by John Vattanky tries to remove the blame of atheistic tendency of the original school. Along with Aleaz, John Vattanky maintains that it is not possible to separate religion and philosophy or reason and revelation in the Indian systems of thought.

Aleaz is concerned that some Christian thinkers have misunderstood, and confused *yoga* philosophy with other general expressions of *yoga*. For him, the main principle that '*Yoga* means only separation of the soul from matter and not any union or communion of the soul with God' is often distorted in the Christian usage. While constantly pointing out this mix-up, Aleaz amply credits the number of scholars who are trying to relate Yoga with Christian experiences.[54]

In the view of Aleaz, Francis X. D'Sa has approached Mimamsa Philosophy without relating to the Christian thought but highlights the eternal character of *Sabdah* and its significance in life. Aleaz is perturbed to see that instead of creatively using the Mimamsa insight of *sabdah* in biblical hermeneutics, Francis X. D'Sa suggests Kkavyasastra's Dhvani method of interpretation.[55]

Aleaz attempts to compare and contrast Dhvani of Kavyasastra (Poetics) with *sabdah* (pramana), to suggest a biblical-theological hermeneutics in India. While proposing that, insights from *dhvani* can enrich *sabdah* method of interpretation, Aleaz, on the basis of Vedantians consideration of Sabdah, prefers the application of *sabdah* method in India.

Coming to the Christian thinkers who have responded only to Vedanta, Aleaz is content with those positive responses and suggests that a Christian philosophy is in the making. His conviction, almost uncritical, without considering those who have followed to other ways of relating and interpreting the gospel is that Advaita is the hermeneutical context of India and Advaita enriches Christian faith experience.

In this context, Aleaz presents the Jaina principle of Syadvada as a helpful philosophical principle in the context of many religions and to pursue religious harmony. In spite of a few negative Christian responses to Indian philosophy, Aleaz's aim is to cull out resources from all the positive Christian responses to the Indian philosophical systems to initiate an Indian Christian Philosophy.

2.4. Indian Christian Philosophy

Aleaz's priority is to suggest a Christian philosophy based upon Indian philosophy, specifically anchored on the six *pramans* (sources of valid knowledge). The seeming possibility of this process is conveyed by highlighting the concomitant connection present between reason and revelation in Indian philosophy. Added

54 K. P. Aleaz, *Christian Responses to Indian Philosophy*, 2005.

55 K. P. Aleaz, *Christian Responses to Indian Philosophy*, 2005.

to this is the accent supplemented to the sublime fact that "Indian philosophy is an applied discipline for human transformation and not a merely theoretical one."[56] His conviction is that Indian philosophy can potentially address the plural context of India particularly from the point of pluralistic inclusivism.

Although a strong advocate of Advaita, Aleaz views A. J. Apppasamy's creative use of Ramanuja's philosophy to interpret Christian faith as one of the positive resources for Indian Christian philosophy.[57]

Aleaz is very emphatic that of all the Indian philosophical schools, it is Sankara's Advaita Vedanta that is found resourceful in providing support for an Indian Christian philosophy. Aleaz has used this principle to interpret Jesus. To cite one example, "Jesus is the most beautiful representation of the ever-existing integral relation between god and creation, which includes humans."[58]

The proposal that the *Sabda-Dhvani* method of biblical-theological hermeneutics can explore the possibility of having diverse interpretation of scripture is positively educative. According to Aleaz 'his endeavors to bring out the significance of Sabda method of understanding and interpretation in Biblical-theological hermeneutics stands out as though feeble, a single-handed effort.'[59]

3. Theology

In terms of theology, Aleaz's contributions are tinged with the theology of Eastern Church. For him, "theology primarily is not a conceptual exercise based on 'revealed premises', but an expression of true Christian experience."[60] His definition of theology is in league with the Eastern tradition as it is conspicuously clear from the statement that 'theology is the spontaneous and thankful praise of God; it is our experiential relationship with God.' His reliance on the Eastern tradition directly comes to him as "Christian theology for the East is always a means; a means to attain union with God or deification."[61]

In short, theology for Aleaz is the expression of one's God experience, or one's relation with god. He also feels that various faith experiences/expressions may be encouraging to the faith community. That is "it is the faith experience of the community which gives authority and validity to theological propositions."[62] He also reiterates that the Church has given him the freedom to express his viewpoints freely and these kinds of free expressions in the Church create theology.

56 K. P. Aleaz, *For a Christian Philosophy From India: Cambridge Teape Lectures – 2005, 2006.*

57 K. P. Aleaz, *Christian Responses to Indian Philosophy*, 2005.

58 K. P. Aleaz, *For a Christian Philosophy From India: Cambridge Teape Lectures – 2005, 2006.*

59 K. P. Aleaz, *For a Christian Philosophy From India: Cambridge Teape Lectures – 2005, 2006.*

60 K. P. Aleaz, *A Convergence of Advaita Vedanta and Eastern Christian Thought*, 2000, p. 67.

61 *Ibid.*, p. 76.

62 *Ibid.*, p. 106.

3.1. Indian Christian Theology/Thought

In continuation with his **definition** of theology and taking clue from Eastern Christian tradition, Aleaz defines Indian Christian theology as "according to Indian thought, theology is a mode of being, theology is participating in being and here Eastern Christian thought comes close to Indian thought."[63] Unlike the previous definition, his commitment for radical insights in theology is reflected in his definition of Indian Christian theology that "Indian Christian thought is a conversion of Christian thought to the Indian religio-cultural context."[64] For him, this conversion is the result of one's conversion to Jesus and he calls it as double conversion.

In contrast to interpreting the Christian truth using Hindu or other religious categories, Aleaz feels Christian theology should be converted to the Indian religio-cultural context as Christians are already converted to Jesus. Of course, in order to interpret our own faith we need not go to the extent of professing other convictions. We can do it efficiently if we give up aggressive and antagonistic attitude to other religions. Connected to this is developing a positive approach to other faith traditions.

With regard to the **sources** of Indian Christian theology, Aleaz maintains that Indian Christian theology has accepted the Indian philosophical principle of relation between reason and revelation. For him, this connection is provided by the Indian *pramanas*. At the same time it is to be remembered that the present developments in Indian theology is not in league with the proposal that the insight emerging from the Indian *pramanas* should be used in Indian Christian theology. In other words, the newly emerging Indian contextual theologies are not in line with Aleaz's thinking. Against this challenge Aleaz asserts that Advaita Vedanta best explains Dalit theology.

From the point of Upanishads and Advaita Vedanta, securing the oneness of God and the rest is the **main thrust** of Indian Christian theology. This is explicit in Aleaz's presentation of God and Jesus. For example, "from the Indian Christian interaction with the Upanisadic thought, we may note that the Upanisads can give guidance not only in the Indian Christian conceptions of God and Jesus, but even in acquiring new insight related to the Indian Christian understandings of human person and the world."[65]

On the basis of Advaita Aleaz argues, "there is an inseparable relation between humans and Nature because the material world as well as the material body are constituted by the same five elements (Pancabhuta) and each indria (sense-organs) is composed of the same element, the quality of which is sensed by

63 *Ibid.*, p. 80.

64 K. P. Aleaz, *Theology of Religions: Birmingham Papers and other Essays*, 1998, p. 9.

65 K. P. Aleaz, *Dimensions of Indian Religions*, 1995, p. 286.

it."[66] No doubt, the consideration of Aleaz is loaded with ecological implication, but pursuing Indian Christian theology from Advaita is only one of the many approaches.

Of course, Aleaz is of the view that Indian Christian theologians are slowly recognizing the fact that Advaita enriches their faith-experience particularly in matters of God, humans, creation and deeper meaning of the person and function of Jesus. He explains the relation between God and Jesus as "according to Vedantic Christology the central lesson of the life of Jesus to an Indian is the undermining of the false antithesis between human person and God. Jesus had a non-dual relation with God the Father and he is inspiring all the humans also to have the same relation with God through the renunciation of the lower self."[67] While recognizing the fact that even without the aid of Advaita many theologians have explained the relation between God and Jesus similar to Advaita, the real question here is, are we in a position to see what religious category explains the Christian categories better or, are we in a context to gently and honorably accept the marvel of plurality of religions.

3.2. Eastern Christian Thought

Having analyzed Aleaz's understanding of Indian Christian theology, now we can move on to his perception of Eastern Christian thought. In the Eastern Church theology is a means to attain union with God/deification.[68] Union with God or deification implies not participating in the essence of God but the energy of God. With the insights from Advaita, Aleaz is inclined to accept that God can be explained as essence and energy. At the same time no one may forget that the final reality is still beyond and is a mystery.

Aleaz finds an intimate relation between Advaita and Eastern Christian theology. According to him, "both Advaita Vedanta and Eastern Christian theology proclaim that theology is a mode of being, is participation in being. There is no theology apart from realization."[69] In other words, theology is the experience of divine-human unity.

Besides the connection between Advaita and Eastern Christian thought, Aleaz convincingly states that Advaita can help develop Eastern Christian theology. He writes "the basic contention is that Advaita Vedanta of Hinduism can dynamically enrich eastern Christian thought in its further developments."[70] It is not just his statement but he takes initiatives to invite Advaita to enrich the Eastern Christian thought.[71] It is more interesting that he is inviting Advaita to

66 *Ibid.*, p. 289.

67 K. P. Aleaz, *The Gospel of Indian Culture*, 1994, p. 293.

68 K. P. Aleaz, *A Convergence of Advaita Vedanta and Eastern Christian Thought*, 2000, p. 76.

69 *Ibid.*, p. 130.

70 *Ibid.*, p. xvi.

71 *Ibid.*, p. xix.

assist Eastern Christian theology in reformulating its theology, so that the resulting new creative Christian theological insights will benefit the Eastern Church, the Church in general and even other living religious faith traditions.

Whether his conviction is right, the invitation extendable, beneficial to the Eastern Church, Christianity and other religions needs to be answered by the Church, although Aleaz asserts that the Church has given him the freedom to express himself freely. One pertinent issue is, whether such an uncritical acceptance of Advaita is permissible in the wider context of newly emerging theologies. From the point of religions as well, the Vaishnava Bhakti tradition condemns Sankara and Advaita.

3.2.1. Eastern Christian Thought, God-Creation

Aleaz's earlier point that the Eastern church upholds that there is a distinction in God between essence and energy of God is made clear as "the Orthodox Christian tradition draws a distinction between the essence, nature or inner being of God, on the one hand, and power, His/Her energies, operations or acts of grace, life and power, on the other."[72] In other words, "if the essence signifies the radical transcendence of God, the energies point to his immanence and omnipresence."[73] This goes well with the Advaita view of Brahman and Isvara.

The Eastern Christian idea of human beings is that "a human person's very nature is truly itself only in as much as it exists 'in God' or 'in grace.'"[74] This is to say that there is a close connection between God and humanity. In other words, 'while human beings can do nothing without God, God does nothing, regarding goodness, righteousness and holiness, without human co-operation.'[75] Although, Aleaz is particular about the meeting and supporting of Eastern Christian thought and Advaita, here a kind of Visistadvaita principle in operation.

In the Eastern Christian thought, the union of human and God is further explained in terms of deification. As stated above, human union with God or deification takes place at the level of the energy of God but not in the essence of God.[76] This union is illustrated with the example of the union between Jesus and God. For example, 'in Jesus there is a 'communication' of the divine and human 'energies.'[77]

Again a more Advaitic form of interpretation is echoed in the explanation of God realization or God knowledge. Aleaz maintains "the more we are able to participate in God, the more God becomes unknowable."[78] This is in line with the

72 *Ibid.*, p. 3.

73 *Ibid.*, p. 4.

74 *Ibid.*, p. 44.

75 *Ibid.*, p. 45.

76 *Ibid.*, p. 6.

77 *Ibid.*, p. 6.

78 *Ibid.*, p. 66.

Vedantic notion that a fully realized person cannot explain his experience because he has become Brahman. The same tempo is maintained in explaining knowledge. For example it is said, "the very realization of His/Her incomprehensibility is a knowledge."[79] It is not the ordinary knowledge but the ultimate knowledge which is superior to all other knowledge. For example, 'we should remember that the goal of apophatic theology is not God as object, but God as subject or union with God.'[80] Aleaz's acceptance that 'in the Eastern Christian thought God is understood as Mystery,'[81] is much more open and conducive to theology of religions than Advaita realization. Here, Aleaz's invitation may have to experience reconsideration.

The Eastern Christian understanding of creation is also explained in line with the Advaita that "creation is the work of will, and consequently is not coeternal with God."[82] Having said that creation is not the essence of God the principle of time is explained as "in God's thought eternally, creatures exist only potentially. Their actual existence occurs in time."[83] In other words, creation is not fully separate from God, although it is not the essence. The manifestation of creation was the conceptual beginning of time.

Another surprising thought is that human beings are mediators between creation and God in whatever capacity permissible. It is maintained that "Eastern thought upholds the mediatory role of human presence in creation. Humanity's vocation is to be the mediator or the frontier being mediating between the material and the spiritual between the secular and the sacred, between God and creation."[84] The reason may be that "according to Orthodox world-view, God has formed two levels of created things neotic and material. Human person alone exists in both levels at once."[85] Creation cannot be viewed separately from God. The integral relation between God and creation is metaphorically stated as "Christ is symbol of the integral relation that exists between God and creation."[86]

Again an Advaitic understanding is utilized to explain the image of God. For example, "it is the humanity together with the material creation that constitutes the ultimate image of God."[87] Then Aleaz moves to explain the theological speculations of image and likeness with the Eastern Christian framework. He writes, "the image of God is the essence of human person while 'likeness' points

79 *Ibid.*, p. 67.

80 *Ibid.*, p. 78.

81 *Ibid.*, p. 79.

82 *Ibid.*, p. 17.

83 *Ibid.*, p. 18.

84 *Ibid.*, p. 35.

85 *Ibid.*, p. 38

86 *Ibid.*, p. 19.

87 *Ibid.*, p. 20.

to the ethical being of human person."[88] This falls within the parameters of his explanation that in the fall human did not miss the essence but the ethical aspect. In spite of the bent of Vedantic influence Aleaz tends to accept that the Christ event has restored humanity and creation together. It is said "human person's restoration in Christ is simultaneously a restoration of the cosmos to its original beauty."[89] The thought is comprehensive as it includes the restoration of cosmos as well. But the difficulty is as Aleaz is averse to atonement-theories based explanation of the Christ event, how it is possible to come to this conclusion.

Aleaz's conviction that the Advaita needs to be invited to help Eastern Christian theology to formulate its theology is challenging. Certain areas are pointed as opportunity for Advaita to assist Eastern Christian thought. One such realm is 'the unknowability of Brahman' which 'helps Eastern Christian theology to go deeper into the dimensions of apophatic theology.'[90] Another point of help is 'the Advaitic interpretation of Brahman/Atman as Pure Consciousness enlightens Eastern Christian interpretation of God.'[91] Still further Aleaz feels that 'the Advaita Vedanta provides deeper insights regarding the energies and operations of God in creation for the further development of Eastern Christian thought."[92] This is further substantiated as "Advaita Vedantic understanding of creation further enlightens the creation ex nihilo interpretation of Eastern Christianity."[93]

The difficulty associated with Aleaz's invitation to Advaita to assist Eastern Christian thought is that Christianity ceases to be Christianity. Of course Aleaz may be well pleased with it. But, the best possible approach may be to accept each theologies/philosophies as they are and then explore the possibilities of cooperation from the adherents to challenge common issues that threaten life as a whole.

3.2.2. Eastern Christian Thought, Fall-Restoration

The main point of emphasis here is that sin is not an inherited quality but an inherited morality that is, 'in Greek patristic thought original sin was viewed not as inherited quality but as inherited morality.'[94] This means certain adjustments and disciplines can set things right.

In contrast to the theological perception that in the fall humanity has lost God's image Aleaz maintains "according to it (Orthodox Theology), though the

88 *Ibid.*, p. 24.

89 *Ibid.*, p. 91.

90 *Ibid.*, p. 129.

91 *Ibid.*, p. 145.

92 *Ibid.*, p. 146.

93 *Ibid.*, p. 171.

94 *Ibid.*, p. 91.

divine image in human person was obscured, it was not obliterated."[95] Similarly his response to the view that after the fall humans have completely lost the freewill means, "fall has not destroyed a person's free choice, but only restricted it."[96] With regard to the loss of image and freewill in the fall, Aleaz is of the view that they are not completely obliterated but obscured. This may be nearer to the Advaitic understanding of ignorance. His explanation is in absolute continuity with his thought that what humanity and the creation long for is restoration of the image and will to the first level.

For Aleaz, the Eastern tradition considers that evil entered into the world through the will. Therefore, 'evil is not a nature, but a condition.'[97] This is vividly explained as "the real source of evil in the world is the inappropriate exercise of free will, of self-determination, causing a separation of humans from God."[98]

Since evil attempts to de-link from God, restoration means re-establishing the link. Aleaz makes a distinction between the approach of Jesus and created beings. In order to restore communication, Jesus descended to the earth hence the created beings have to take the opposite direction of ascendancy. In the words of Aleaz, "the path which Christ, the divine Person took, was that of a descent towards created being and taking upon himself of our nature. If that is so the path of created person has to be that of ascent, a rising up towards the divine nature by means of union with uncreated grace communicated by the Holy Spirit."[99]

In Aleaz's view, human person's restoration through Christ is effected by the involvement in the Church and sacrament. He writes, "in the church and through the sacraments our nature enters into union with the divine nature in the hypostasis of the Son, the head of his mystical body."[100] It is also superficially suggested that "Eucharistic worship of the Orthodox occurs when the Spirit transports us into the presence of the heavenly throne."[101] Therefore it is treated as 'an act of freedom, love and joy.'[102] It is not just the Church and sacrament but also the Church's liturgy has a part to play in this ascension. This he writes as, "Eastern liturgy is the passage from this world into the world to come, it is a procession and ascension to the Kingdom."[103]

95 *Ibid.*, p. 26.

96 *Ibid.*, p. 37.

97 *Ibid.*, p. 26.

98 *Ibid.*, p. 45.

99 *Ibid.*, p. 11.

100 *Ibid.*, p. 10.

101 *Ibid.*, p. 98.

102 *Ibid.*, p. 99.

103 *Ibid.*, p. 110.

In the process of restoration to the original status Aleaz envisages that the entire cosmos will be restored.[104] How he will invite Advaita here is not clear because Aleaz maintains that the Church, sacraments and the liturgy directly facilitate the upward mobility. This also may go against his definition of pluralistic inclusivism and relational convergence of religions. It will be worthwhile if he admits directly that other worship places, sacraments and liturgies have similar effect.

3.2.3. Eastern Christian Thought-Deification

Eastern Christian thought in general conceives salvation as deification.[105] The implications of deification are stated as "Deification points to communion with God and that communion is one's destiny since the individual's creation is according to God's 'image and likeness."[106] In other words it is 'a rising up towards the divine nature by means of union with uncreated grace communicated by the Holy Spirit.'[107] The theological significance of this process is pointed out as "in the theology of the Eastern Church, the person of the Holy Spirit, the giver of grace is always distinguished from the uncreated grace or energy which he confers."[108]

The deification process is engineered in the heart. According to Aleaz, "the ascetic tradition of the Christian East considers the heart as the centre of the human being…thus the heart is the source of all intellectual and spiritual activity."[109] The functioning of the process is energized by prayer (Jesus Prayer).[110] In the words of Aleaz, "the ceaseless prayer of the heart can lead a person out of lusting after things of the earth. It can make a person firmly grounded in memory of God alone."[111]

The deification actualized by grace and prayer does not deprive humanness from people. For example, "the patristic tradition stands for a god-centered humanism where deification does not suppress humanity but makes human person truly human."[112] This is further supported by the theory that "apart from tears of repentance there is thus another level of tears in the spiritual tradition of Eastern Christians namely the tears of compassion…"[113] Aleaz will be justified if only the deification goes beyond humanism to include the entire creation,

104 *Ibid.*, p. 19.

105 *Ibid.*, p. 33

106 *Ibid.*, p. 13.

107 *Ibid.*, p. 11.

108 *Ibid.*, p. 11.

109 *Ibid.*, p. 52.

110 Lord, Jesus Christ, Son of God, have mercy upon me/Jesus, son of god, have mercy upon me/ Lord, Jesus Christ, have mercy upon me.

111 K. P. Aleaz, *A Convergence of Advaita Vedanta and Eastern Christian Thought*, 2000 p. 63

112 *Ibid.*, p. 68.

113 *Ibid.*, p. 21

because he also has maintained that "Integral God-human-nature relationship (cosmotheandrisam) is the gospel of both Vedic and Vedantic dharma."[114]

3.2.4. Eastern Christianity and Religions

According to Aleaz, Advaita helps the Eastern Church to reformulate her Christian experience. This new experience can benefit people of all living religious faiths.[115] He is of the view that "the St. Thomas Christians in their glorious history upto the end of 16th c. had very positive approach to their neighbour's faith, i.e., Hinduism, which is identified today through an analysis of the Acts and Decrees of the Synod of Diamper of 1599."[116] He is also of the view that "St. Thomas Christians upheld Pluralism in the theology of religions. They had the vision to see that a Hindu can be saved in his/her own dharma."[117]

It is understandable that Aleaz is striving to usher in the Church, a pre Diamper attitude towards other religions, particularly Hinduism. He also appreciates the pluralistic stand of the pre Diamper Church that Hindus could be saved in their own religion. Earlier also it was shown that he has no problem with the pluralistic school. If he is comfortable with pluralism what is the necessity for pluralistic inclusivism.

3.3. Dalit Theology and Advaita Vedanta

Aleaz is often viewed with suspicion as promoting Brahmanic worldview. But, time and again he proves the other way. He challenges Dalit theologians to draw lessons from the neo Vedanta of Vivekananda. His argument is that the Dailts should revolt against the Brahmins and not against Advaita. They should take the neo Vedantic insights of One Innermost Atman, equality and justice. He writes, "if the Dalit theologians today hold that the suffering of the Dalits should be the basis or starting point of Dalit theology, Swami Vivekananda through his practical Vedanta is inspiring them to add to it the basis of the One Innermost Atman shared by all alike as well. The practical Vedanta through its message of equality and social justice stands for the cause of the Dalits. The Dalits need not revolt against Advaita; rather their revolt has to be against those upper castes who are ignorant of the teaching of equality of Advaita."[118] It looks as if Aleaz suggests that the original proponents of Advaita did not understand Advaita well.

Aleaz is not only suggesting new lessons from Vedanta but also sees the possibility of convergence between Advaitic theology and Dalit theology and

114 K. P. Aleaz, *Dimensions of Indian Religions*, 1995, p. 121.

115 K. P. Aleaz, *A Convergence of Advaita Vedanta and Eastern Christian Thought*, 2000, p. xix

116 *Ibid.*, p. xviii.

117 *Ibid.*, p. xviii.

118 K. P. Aleaz, *Harmony of Religions: The Relevance of Swami Vivekananda*, 1993, p. 242.

argues, "Advaita can provide deeper foundations for Dalit theology and Dalit theology can make Advaitic theology, a people's theology."[119]

Aleaz is emphatic that this possibility was actualized in the life and work of Sri Narayana Guru and therefore Dalit theologians should not ignore it. He writes, "Sri Narayana Guru is specially significant for the contemporary Indian context as in his life and thought we notice a wonderful coming together on Dalit and Advaitic theologies, something which the Indian Dalit theologians who project Dalit theology as a counter theology, have to carefully take note of."[120]

Aleaz's attempts to demonstrate the examples of Swami Vivekananda and Sri Narayana Guru that 'Advaita theology is not anti-Dalit theology, rather on the one hand Advaita can provide deeper foundations for Dalit theology and on the other it is Dalit theology that proclaims Advaita Vedanta practically.'[121] Of course it may be a bitter pill for Dalit theologians to swallow.

4. Indian Spirituality

In the understanding of Aleaz, "Spirituality is our recognition of the involvement of the spirit in us and in the whole creation."[122] Another significant dimension of the definition of spirituality is being available to God. In Aleaz's phrase 'spirituality implies being open to reality in all its dimensions.'[123] Another deeper dimension of spirituality is the response of the self to the rest. It is said, "spirituality represents the total response of the self to the self-world-God trio."[124] Aleaz writes about the comprehensive content of spirituality as "a wholesome spirituality has three aspects namely passion for justice, compassion for people and communion with God."[125] In short, spirituality includes the recognition of the involvement of the spirit, being open to the reality, self's response to the rest and passion for justice, compassion for people and communion with God.

Coming to the model spirituality Aleaz writes, "Jesus is the supreme example to show that there is no spirituality of an exclusive vertical dimension. His was a humanizing spirituality, a life-sustaining spirituality which has to mould and lead us."[126] The life sustaining aspect left in the previous attempts of definition and explanations is included here. Whether the life sustaining is inclusive of the entire God's creation is to be clarified. As poverty is the outcome of all forms of injustice, no definition of spirituality will be all inclusive unless it addresses the

119 K. P. Aleaz, *Dimensions of Indian Religions*, 1995, p. 291.

120 K. P. Aleaz, *Religion in Christian Theology*, 2001, p. 2.

121 K. P. Aleaz, *For a Christian Philosophy From India*: *Cambridge Teape Lectures – 2005, 2006*, p. 151.

122 K. P. Aleaz, The Quest for Contextual Spirituality, 2004, p. 11.

123 *Ibid.*, p. 21.

124 *Ibid.*, p. 22.

125 *Ibid.*, p. 26.

126 *Ibid.*, p. 11.

issue of poverty. In the words of Aleaz, 'there can be no spirituality without an active concern for the poor.'[127] Again he says a "Christian spirituality is lived by one who has the spirit of Christ."[128] It is a call to follow the life of Christ and not a call for christocentric paradigm.

Aleaz is earnestly committed to a contextual Indian Christian spirituality. He wants Christian spirituality to be inclusive and plural. He is also talking about a Christo-centric spirituality. The content of such a spirituality, for him, should be, a life-sustaining spirituality, which is people-centered, Christ-centered and pluralist in nature.

He also sees the possibility of forming a relevant Indian Christian spirituality by culling resources from other religious tradition as well. In his own words, "a contextual Christian spirituality is the focus, receiving insights from spiritualities of sister religious faiths."[129] In this direction he finds the first meeting point in Namajapa. He writes "Namajapa or prayer of the name is a meeting point of the spiritualities of Hindu and Christian traditions."[130] Aleaz also establishes Christians can glean resources form Sufiism as well. In the words of Aleaz, "Islam has immensely contributed to spirituality through Sufism from which Christianity can profit much. The Sufis laid stress on the interior spiritual life, on knowledge of God by experience (kashf) rather than by pure reasoning."[131] He also finds resources for a spirituality of pluralism in Jaina tradition. It is maintained, 'Syadvada stands for a spirituality of pluralism in theology of religions and thus contributes ideologically to the harmony of religions.'[132] Aleaz's intention to gather resources from Indian religious resources is a courageous attempt to make Indian spirituality wider and inter-religious.

5. A Few Salient Constructs

Certain constructs of Aleaz deserve special mention as they are quite radical, innovative and provocative as well. Here we shall discuss Aleaz's explanation of Jesus, Gospel and proclamation and Mission.

5.1. Jesus

Aleaz is convinced that "the Hindu religious experience and thought categories can really enrich Christian faith experience and also bring out new meanings regarding the Christian notion of God as well as the person and function of Jesus."[133] Hence, in understanding and explaining Jesus, Aleaz takes support from

127 *Ibid.*, p. 27.

128 *Ibid.*, pp. 27-28.

129 *Ibid.*, p. 9.

130 *Ibid.*, p. 29.

131 *Ibid.*, p. 32.

132 *Ibid.*, p. 84.

133 K. P. Aleaz, *Dialogical Theologies: Hartford Papers and Other Essays*, 2004, p. 122.

the Advaita Vedanta. He writes, "our method is to give complete authority to the authentic writings of Sankara in order to explain 'who Jesus is.'"[134] Aleaz has already maintained that a deeper meaning of the person and function of Jesus are emerging from within Advaita Vedanta.'[135] The point here is that, Aleaz finds the Advaitic principles are helpful to explain the relation between God and Jesus and the rest.

Aleaz is of the opinion that the connection between Brahman and Jiva is helpful in understanding and explaining Jesus, because 'it provides the best framework in the construction of an understanding of Jesus.'[136]

This is further supplemented as "Jesus, the human representative is a reflection (abhasah) of the Supreme Self like the semblance of the sun in water (jalasuryakadivat). Jesus as reflection of the Supreme Self conforms to the characteristics (dharmanuyayi) of the extrinsic denominators of Jesus, but according to the supreme sense the Self does not have these characteristics. There does not occur any change (parinamah) in the Self due to Jesus' reflection."[137] More elaborately, "as representative Jiva, Jesus has no separate reality for himself; his reality lies in sacrificing himself and finding his reality in Brahman. Jesus in particular form is unreal (akaravisesatoanrtam); he is real only in his own form which is the form of Being (svatah sanmatrarupataya satyam)."[138] Like the Jiva which has no other existence apart from Brahman, Jesus has no existence apart from God. This may go well with the notion that the Word became flesh or God descended in human form to rescue creation. At the same time it will be in disagreement with the notion that God sent his only begotten son to save the creation.

Aleaz, in contrast to the formal Christian belief, maintains that "the symbol 'Son' cannot express the depth of the relation between Jesus and Brahman; name and form (namarupa) would be a better symbol; and India suggests this through Sankara's Advaita Vedanta."[139] The real Advaitic interpretation is that "Jesus, the representative name and form pre-existed in Brahman as unmanifested name and form (avyakrtanamarupah); as the potential seed (bijasaktih). Being the representative of the whole humanity, Jesus is the representative name, form and action of the whole humanity."[140]

Another insight is in 'Aleaz's Jesulogy, Brahman is the cause, Jesus is the effect. Jesus, the effect existed in Brahman, the internal reality-providing (upadanakaranam) as well as efficient cause (nimittakaranam) even before

134 K. P. Aleaz, *Christian Thought Through Advaita Vedanta*, 1996, p. 90.

135 *Ibid.*, p. 212.

136 *Ibid.*, p. 90.

137 *Ibid.*, p. 95.

138 *Ibid.*, p. 98.

139 *Ibid.*, p. 96.

140 *Ibid.*, p. 96.

he took birth in this world.'[141] This idea particularly can be helpful in clearly understanding the relation between Jesus and God.

Aleaz disagrees with the atonement form of interpretation of Jesus. He writes "human sacrifice was a Jewish idea and to fit the gentle and loving Jesus into Jewish beliefs, the idea of human sacrifice in the form of atonement or as a human scape goat, by Christianity, was really unfortunate."[142] This contention is elaborated as "we may have to qualify atonement theory as a Jewish Christian interpretation of the meaning of Jesus which makes no sense to Indians. That is the reason as an alternative understanding of the function of Jesus, in our Jesulogy we are explaining Jesus elaborately as the expression of the all pervasive, illuminative and unifying power of the Supreme Self; as the expression of the eternally present human liberation. Also we are showing that the function of Jesus is to show us the supreme Brahman which is Pure consciousness, as the Witness and Self of all. Such an understanding, we believe, can be a meaningful conception of the function of Jesus as far as Indians are concerned."[143] Aleaz insists that in every aspect of Jesus we should recognize Brahman. This he puts as "the person of Jesus proclaims that if we identify any aspect of his person as Brahman, we are in ignorance; but if we identify in every aspect of his person Brahman and Brahman alone, we have come to the experience who he truly is."[144]

Aleaz does not stop with saying that we should see Brahman in every aspect of Jesus, but goes on to suggest that "the mission of Jesus was to communicate to humanity the uniqueness of Brahman as the only illuminative principle."[145] As Aleaz immerses in the current of Advaita, he admits that, our hermeneutical context is plural and Advaita is just one such hermeneutical context. His openness to other strands of thought is clear when he says that "the resources of God, which were available to Jesus, are open to all and if we struggle as he did, we will develop the God in us."[146] Aleaz in his quest for Indian Jesus can also do justice to similar interpretations put forth by other eminent theologians, from different perspectives.

5.2. Gospel

As Aleaz is committed to Indian Jesuology, he also has an Indian version of the Gospel. According to him, Gospel emerges from the Indian culture-one emerges from the interaction between religion and culture, another emerges from the interaction of religions and yet another emerges from the hermeneutical context

141 *Ibid.*, pp. 96-97.

142 *Ibid.*, p. 99.

143 *Ibid.*, p. 99.

144 *Ibid.*, p. 98.

145 K. P. Aleaz, *A Convergence of Advaita Vedanta and Eastern Christian Thought*, 2000, p. 253.

146 K. P. Aleaz, *For a Christian Philosophy From India: Cambridge Teape Lectures – 2005*, 2006.

of India.[147] He is also of the opinion that 'the understanding of Jesus emerging from the Indian hermeneutical context only ratifies the harmony and integration that exist between religions in India as well as the resultant Indian composite culture.'[148] It is to be underlined that in order to be more relevant Aleaz needs to recognize plurality of cultures in India. Similarly, overemphasizing the connection between religion and culture may not be conducive in the context of communal politics and fundamentalist thinking.

According to Aleaz, the religio-cultural context, which is the hermeneutical context, of India will decide the 'gospel of God in Jesus.'[149] He also says religious pluralism is a hermeneutical context and it will contribute to the content of the Gospel.[150] In a nutshell, for Aleaz, "the gospel of Indian culture is the gospel of interreligious harmony and integration."[151] This deserves acceptance.

He also gives reason for this transition as "the gospel is not pre-formulated, but is in the process of formulation through the guidance of Hindu and other religious experiences."[152] Aleaz envisages a conversion to the new Gospel. For him, Indian Christian theology is this conversion.[153] It may be appealing, if our initiatives are in the direction of addressing newly emerging life-threatening issues, rather than compressing everything to the religio-cultural jacket.

Aleaz's call for the Gospel emerging from the hermeneutical context of India has a provision for the gospels of other religions which are also the resultants of the Indian hermeneutical context. He writes, "though our strife is for the experience of the one Gospel of the One God/Reality in the vision of a relational convergence of religions, gospels as experienced by people of other faiths have to be affirmed as significant, as a primary step."[154] Here, Aleaz's openness to other faiths and his call for relational convergence of religions are vivid.

The full development of his thought in this direction is found when he includes the contexts of globalization. He writes, "Gospel has to emerge from the hermeneutical context, from the experience of the oppressed and suffering people due to globalization on the one hand and from the diverse enriching religious experiences of human kind on the other."[155]

---

147 K. P. Aleaz, *The Gospel of Indian Culture*, 1994, p. 2.

148 *Ibid.*, p. 2.

149 K. P. Aleaz, *Theology of Religions: Birmingham Papers and other Essays*, 1998, p. 180.

150 *Ibid.*, p. 8.

151 K. P. Aleaz, *The Gospel of Indian Culture*, 1994, p. 283.

152 K. P. Aleaz, *Theology of Religions: Birmingham Papers and other Essays*, 1998, p. 180.

153 *Ibid.*, p. 180.

154 *Ibid.*, p. 8.

155 K. P. Aleaz, *Religion in Christian Theology*, 200, p. 13.

5.3. Proclamation & Mission

Aleaz feels Pauline presentation of salvation explanation is not relevant to the present context, because 'today we do not find any of the atonement theories-the conception of salvation as being brought about by Jesus' death as an atonement to God for human sin-as attractive or convincing.'[156] This contention is in view of the Hindu notion that every one is responsible his or her deeds.

His commitment and dedication for the cause of religious harmony is clear when he writes, "a Christian has to proclaim the liberative elements in other religious faiths seeking forgiveness for the damage done in the past by way of oppression, destruction of local religions and cultures as well as misinterpretations."[157]

Coming to Christian mission, he calls for a reconception. This reconception is based upon his contention that Christianity also receives insights from other religious traditions, mainly Advaita. Therefore, against the formal superiority claims, Aleaz maintains, "this receiving aspect is proposed today as the thrust of an Indian Christian theology of mission."[158] It is emphatically stated as "Christian faith in India must stop proselytizing and encourage conversion."[159] This is not conversion from one religion to other but conversion to Jesus and religio-cultural context.

His commitment to the cause of Advaita is obvious as he says 'the Indian Christian mission in this context is to present the gospel as Advaita Vedanta.'[160] Here he has reduced the Gospel only to proclaim that Advaita is the Gospel.

It does not deprive Aleaz's comprehensive understanding of mission. For example, he writes "a Christ-centered humanism has the best opening of making its impact in the Indian dialogic social existence."[161] He has not failed to find a place for women. He writes, "We also noted the point that the essential values of any religion can contribute to the education and development of women in India."[162]

Aleaz's understanding of proclamation and mission is quite distinct. But, they simply reflect his commitment to inter-religious relation or relational convergence of religions from the point of pluralistic inclusivism, deriving insights from Advaita.

156 *Ibid.*, p. 13.

157 *Ibid.*, p. 11.

158 K. P. Aleaz, *Dimensions of Indian Religions*, 1995, p. 292.

159 K. P. Aleaz, *Theology of Religions: Birmingham Papers and Other Essays*, 1998, p. 350.

160 K. P. Aleaz, *Dimensions of Indian Religions*, 1995, p. 294.

161 *Ibid.*, p. 285.

162 *Ibid.*, p. 290.

6. Conclusion

Aleaz's definition/meaning of religion would be substantial had it emphasized the need for religions to focus upon life-sustaining issues. Further, the life-sustaining implications present in the methodology should become explicit. Aleaz's definition of theology of religions is focused on the pursuit of relational convergence of religions. Yet it needs to have space for religions and ideologies which believe in the non-existence of God, yet committed to the life-sustaining relational convergence of religions.

Although proponent of pluralistic inclusivism, Aleaz is sympathetic with the school of pluralism. His evaluation of pluralism can also include the necessity of considering the ideologies and atheistic religions that contribute to common causes. In the light of the relativist school, Aleaz's view that Hinduism stands for religious pluralism needs reconsideration. His expectation of the return of the pre-Diamper Christianity cannot ignore the growing exclusivistic tendencies of the churches. Other related questions are how does pluralistic inclusivism and universal Jesus go together.

Considering the entire religious resource of the universe as a common property of all may well fit within the parameters of freedom of religion/human rights rather than pluralistic inclusivism. Relational convergence of religions in the frame work of pluralistic inclusivism is not the solution to all issues, but it is the life-sustaining vision that leads to relevant solution. Promoting one particular thought pattern alone, for strengthening religious relations may lead to another form of exclusivism.

Over emphasis of the connection between religion and culture may shelter communal ideologies and fundamentalist thinking. Pursuing a composite culture, in the place of multi culture, may lead to mono-culture which is not Indian at all. Likewise, promoting the assumption that there is connection between culture and politics in India can also bring about adverse consequences in the line of Sangh Parivar's ideology. Hence, there is a great need to reiterate the fact of many religions and many cultures in India. Accepting Hindu culture as Indian culture is incorrect.

Aleaz's uncritical acceptance and application of Indian philosophical *pramanas* for the construction of Indian Christian philosophy is not in consonance with the spirit of the present theological developments. His respect for Advaita on the basis of its world-God-life relation cannot draw the conclusion that Advaita is the only way to relational convergence of religions. Aleaz's overemphasis on Advaita, is not in conjunction with his idea that 'even within the same school of religious experience (Swami Ram Tirtha and Sister Nivedita) there is the possibility of divergent expressions.'

In the definition, sources and the main thrust of Indian Christian theology, the Advaitic elements flow profusely. It also needs to be noted that many Christians in India connect Advaita with the symbol of oppression.

Aleaz's presentation of Eastern Christian thought of God and creation, supposed to be from Advaita point of view, swings among, Advaita, Visistadvaita and Eastern mystery. His invitation to Advaita to assist Eastern Christian thought is the outcome of the concerns that Aleaz is addressing.

In Aleaz's presentation of the fall and restoration, the proposal for descent and ascent is comprehensive as they have space for the entire cosmos but there is no role for Advaita because Church, sacrament and liturgy are quite conclusive in their role to the members of the Church.

Whether salvation as deification comprehends the Advaitic God-human-nature composition is a legitimate question. Aleaz's anticipation for the pre-Diamper days, i.e., pluralism, does not synthesise with his constant appeal for pluralistic inclusivism. Parallel to this is the position of Aleaz that Advaita best suits Dalit theology, in the context of Dalit theologians' protest against Advaita.

Most advanced and comprehensive form of thought is found in Aleaz's proposal for Indian Christian spirituality where he ventures the life-sustaining model of Jesus or Christo-centric model. Here he comes explicitly and declares that other religions can contribute to Indian Christian spirituality.

Having concluded that the Christian understanding of 'Son' does not explain the meaning of Jesus, Aleaz is of the view that Hindu categories, particularly Advaita, can explain Jesus well. He does not accept the Pauline presentation of Jesus as the atonement on the cross. For Aleaz, the mission of Jesus is to present Brahman as the whole.

In contrast to other places, Aleaz's call for the emergence of the Gospel from the hermeneutical context of India has provision for other faiths, as they can produce their gospel from the texture.

Aleaz's original and radical insights in relation to religious harmony or relational convergence of religions from the perspective of pluralistic inclusivism shines as he declares that our proclamation is not atonement theories, but the truth in other religions. For him, proclamation of the truth in other religions is not enough but also we need to ask for forgiveness from other religious communities for the damages we have done to them. This is what he calls as Mission of reconception or conversion. Apart from other pleas, Aleaz also feels that Christ-centerd humanism is relevant and any good understanding of religion must have place for the liberation of women.

One may be tempted to say that Aleaz has concentrated on Advaita and applied this paradigm in all his ideas, rather than aspiring for a systematic and gradual development of theological thinking. It may be also alleged that rather than promoting Kingdom values Aleaz has worked for the promotion of other religious values limiting himself to a select few concerns.

Besides the above observations there are many constructive insights in the theological contributions of Aleaz. To start with, his consideration that religions have to be defined on the basis of their fruits is constructive from the point of

Indian realities. Added to this is the appeal to develop positive consideration about the positive aspects of other religions. Aleaz's broader perspective is clear as he states that all religions are authentic in their own context and plurality of religions is natural. More comprehensive is the view that expressions of the same religious experience can vary according to the context.

The major shift in Aleaz's definition of religion is from content to applicability of a religion to the texture. The underlying expectation in his integral method to study religion is religious harmony or relational convergence of religions. Correspondingly, in his definition of theology of religions, the focus has moved from the other to one's own faith tradition. The magnitude of pluralistic inclusivism is that all religions become pluralistically inclusive and inclusivistically pluralist.

One of the radical thoughts of Aleaz is that Christian faith receives insights from other religions. His openness to dialogical approach while upholding pluralistic inclusivism conveys that in the ultimate analysis all are seeking for religious harmony.

Other new thoughts are that all the religious resources of the universe is common property of all and others will be viewed as superior to us, in pluralistic inclusivism. In the relational convergence of religions there is mutual conversion and the context will decide the content of the Gospel of God in Jesus for India.

Aleaz's uncritical acceptance of other religious insights is the revelation of his urge for religious harmony and respect for other religious traditions. He asserts that no one else has attempted an Indian Christian philosophy based on *pramanas*, Advaita and very specially *sabda-dhvani* method, which is relevant for biblical interpretation.

An unselfish struggle for religious harmony is vivid in his invitation and request to Advaita to assist Eastern Christian thought. His hope for the pre-Diamper approach to people of other faiths is his commitment for the Church to come forward with openness in relation to other religions.

Aleaz's Indian Christian spirituality based on inclusion of resources from Indian religions, his interpretation that Jesus is the reflection of Brahman, and his view that the Gospel has to emerge from the religio-cultural context of India are courageous proposals. His ultimate dedication to religious harmony is fully embedded in his view of proclamation and mission.

12

Emerging Challenges to Christian Presence and Witness in India

Introduction

This chapter is an attempt to explain Hindutva as propagated and practiced by RSS ideologues and its challenges for Christian witness in India as BJP the political arm of RSS is at the Centre with absolute majority. In the first place, I graphically describe the various attempts that are underway to communalize the nation and its various instruments against religious minorities particularly, Christians, without excluding the Muslims. And in the second place some issues are highlighted, without causing panic, to reflect upon.

Hindutva, Hindu and Hinduism

A sketchy definition of these three terms can vividly reflect the tone and purpose of them being revived and reinforced. To start with, 'Hindutva is a derivative word from Hindu and it is not identical with Hinduism.'[1] 'Hinduness' is the expression more close to it. Hindutva embraces all the departments of thought and activity of the whole Being of Hindu race.[2] It is not a word but a history.[3] The first essential goal of Hindutva is securing Hindusthan/Hindu Rashtra/Hindu nation or the land of Hindus (geographical).[4] In brief, Hindutva is a communal and majoritarion ideology and not a religion.

1 Vinayak Damodar Savarkar, *Hindutva: Who is a Hindu?*, 6th ed. (New Delhi: Bharti Sahitya Sadan, 1989), 4.

2 Vinayak Damodar Savarkar, *Hindutva: Who is a Hindu?*, 4.

3 Vinayak Damodar Savarkar, *Hindutva: Who is a Hindu?*, 3.

4 Vinayak Damodar Savarkar, *Hindutva: Who is a Hindu?*, 82.

In the light of Hindutva ideology, 'a Hindu is the one who looks upon India as his Fatherland (Pitribhu), who inherits the blood of that race whose first discernible source could be traced to the Vedic Saptasindhus, who has inherited and claims as his own the culture of that race as expressed chiefly in their common classical language Sanskrit and represented by a common history, a common literature, art and architecture, law and jurisprudence, rites and rituals, ceremonies and sacraments, fairs and festivals; and who above all, addresses this land as his Holyland (Punyabhu), as the land of his prophets and seers, of his godmen and gurus, the land of piety and pilgrimage.[5] Hindus 'are not only a Nation but also a race-jati.'[6] There is a false assumption that 'at some future time the word Hindu may come to indicate a citizen of Hindusthan and nothing else.' Whoever does not uphold these characteristics are considered against them.

Jawaharlal Nehru disagreed with these ideas and wrote, "the word 'Hindu' does not occur at all in our ancient literature. The first reference to it in an Indian book is, I am told, in a *Tantrik* work of the eighth century A.D., where Hindu means a people and not the followers of a particular religion. But it is very clear that the word is a very old one, as it occurs in the Avesta and in old Persian."[7]

However, Hindutva derogatively distinguishes Hindus from Christians and Muslims in India and places them second to Hindus as "we are Hindus even before we emerge from the womb of our mother. We are therefore born as Hindus. About the others, they are born to this world as simple unnamed human beings and later on, either circumcised or baptized, they become Muslims or Christians."[8]

From the point of Hindutva, "Hinduism means the system of religious beliefs found common amongst the Hindu people."[9] And "Hinduism is only a derivative, a fraction, a part of Hindutva."[10] Although protecting Hinduism and Hindus is the main agenda of Hindutva, its objectives are multifaceted and they will unfold as the paper progresses.

Hindu Rashtra

In order to undo with the nationalistic and patriotic leaders and their contributions towards Indian nation, and to usher in a Hindu nation, Hindutva terms Territorial/Geographical Nationalism as 'anti-Britishism' and says it is different from true patriotism and nationalism. The efforts to maintain unity

5 Vinayak Damodar Savarkar, *Hindutva: Who is a Hindu?*, 6th ed. (New Delhi: Bharti Sahitya Sadan, 1989), 115-116.

6 Vinayak Damodar Savarkar, *Hindutva: Who is a Hindu?*, 84. (jati from jan).

7 Jawaharlal Nehru, *The Discovery of India*, Centenary Edition (Delhi: Oxford University Press, 1989), 74.

8 M. S. Golwalkar, *Bunch of Thoughts*, 3rd ed., Reprint (Bangalore: Sahitya Sindhu Prakashan, 2000), 117.

9 Vinayak Damodar Savarkar, *Hindutva: Who is a Hindu?*, 102-103.

10 Vinayak Damodar Savarkar, *Hindutva: Who is a Hindu?*, 3.

in diversity are caricatured as 'it was the scheming Britisher who planted in our minds perverted notions of nationhood in a bid to break the proud and defiant spirit of the Hindus.'[11] Again "the first thing he taught was that this was one great 'continent' and not a country; and we are not one people and one nation.'[12]

The present maladies, of India like corruption, disintegration, are the outcome of the present form of nationalism which was adopted in the place of a natural living nationalism (Hindu).[13]

Therefore there is an upsurge now to establish a Hindu nation or Hindu Rashtra in the place of the nation India. The declaration "Territorial nationalism has verily emasculated our nation and what more can we expect of a body deprived of its vital energy?"[14] is a vivid evidence to the communal schemes of Hindutva which is undertaken by the RSS. Golwalkar writes, 'the Rashtriya Swayamsevak Sangh has resolved to fulfill this age-old national mission; verily this is the one real practical world mission- if ever there was one.'[15]

The Hindu Rashtra 'stands not only for political and economic unity but also for cultural and religious unity.'[16] Vishwa Hindu Parishad leader Praveen Togadia rejected the discourse of development without "Hindu Rashtra." He said, development would be of no use if Hindus were not "safe" at home. He asked the "Hindus of the country to become one and prepare the way for Hindu Rashtra." He also provocatively said, "development is important, but what will be its use when Hindus won't be there at homes, and like Hindus in Kashmir, they are thrown out of their motherland."[17]

The very proposal of a Hindu Nation based on the foregone stories and ideals contrary to unity in diversity is a concern for religious communities, particularly, for Christian witness in India.

Hindu Culture

Hidutva ideology assumes a monoculture in the place of multi-culture in India. In the words of Golwalkar "our concept of Hindu Nation is not a mere bundle of political and economic rights. It is essentially cultural. Our ancient and sublime cultural values of life form its life-breath. And it is only an intense rejuvenation of the spirit of our culture that can give us the true vision of our national life, and a fruitful direction to all our efforts in solving the innumerable problems

11 M. S. Golwalkar, *Bunch of Thoughts,* 156.

12 M. S. Golwalkar, *Bunch of Thoughts,* 134.

13 M. S. Golwalkar, *Bunch of Thoughts,* 78.

14 M. S. Golwalkar, *Bunch of Thoughts,* 149.

15 M. S. Golwalkar, *Bunch of Thoughts,* 9.

16 M. S. Golwalkar, *Bunch of Thoughts,* 129.

17 "Development without Hindu Rashtra is of No Use: Togadia," *The Hindu* (Vijayawada), 27 January 2015, 10.

confronting our nation today."[18] Accepting other progressive and civilizing cultural aspects is dismissed as "there can be no greater national humiliation than to be a mere carbon copy of others. Let us remember that blind imitation is not progress. It only leads us to spiritual subjection."[19]

There is no possibility at all to propose a monoculture in India. Nehru saw the possibility of an Indian culture and not a Hindu culture and wrote "a Buddhist or Jain in India is a hundred per cent product of Indian thought and culture, yet neither is a Hindu by faith. It, is, therefore, entirely misleading to refer to Indian culture as Hindu culture. In later ages this culture was greatly influenced by the impact of Islam, and yet it remained basically and distinctively Indian."[20] Further "it is, therefore, incorrect and undesirable, to use 'Hindu' or 'Hinduism' for Indian culture, even with reference to the distant past, although the various aspects of thought, as embodied in ancient writings, were the dominant expression of that culture."[21]

The danger of this communal program is that for the sake of merely preserving age old customs and practices many reforms and services may be hampered. And age-old social evils, that were annihilated or reformed with hard labor, may again pop up.

One Language

Hindutva is against the development of non-Sanskrit languages and rich resources embedded in them. It glories in Sanskrit as 'our mother-tongue-the tongue in which the mothers of our race spoke and which has given birth to all our present tongues. Our gods spoke in Sanskrit, our sages thought in Sanskrit, our poets wrote in Sanskrit. All that is best in us-the best thoughts, the best ideas, and the best lines-seeks instinctively to clothe itself in Sanskrit.[22] Further, "Sanskrit is to this day one of the greatest cementing factors of our national life."[23] It is assumed that, one day "as a solution to the problem of 'lingua franca', till the time Sanskrit takes that place we shall have to give priority to Hindi on the score of convenience."[24]

The pride and prestige of other languages is wrongly twisted with other issues. For example, "the formation of linguistic states has given one more handle to politicians to work up linguistic chauvinism in the minds of people."[25] Again,

18 M. S. Golwalkar, *Bunch of Thoughts,* 34.

19 M. S. Golwalkar, *Bunch of Thoughts,* 42.

20 Jawaharlal Nehru, *The Discovery of India*, 75.

21 Jawaharlal Nehru, *The Discovery of India*, 75.

22 Vinayak Damodar Savarkar, *Hindutva: Who is a Hindu?*, 95.

23 M. S. Golwalkar, *Bunch of Thoughts,* 112.

24 M. S. Golwalkar, *Bunch of Thoughts,* 112.

25 M. S. Golwalkar, *Bunch of Thoughts,* 114.

"the poisonous theory of linguistic states has aggravated the claims for 'right of self-determination' and 'right of secession.'"[26]

The revolutionary contributions of Tamil literature and Dravidian contributions for social change and political discourse are adversely portrayed saying a foreign missionary falsely propagated in Tamilnadu, that 'Tamil culture, Tamil language and everything Tamil differed fundamentally from the rest of the Bharatiya culture, language, etc., and that the Tamilians formed an independent nation by themselves.[27] Hindutva ideology suggests that 'the theme present in the *Tirukkural* is the same old Hindu concept of *catuvidha-purushartha*'[28] and not a distinct value.

There are innumerable dialects in India which do not have a script. Every ethnic group wishes to have its own language. Our attempts to provide these millions with the transforming word of God and all the previous and present liberative witnesses in this direction are under question.

Muslims and Christians

To form a Hindu nation with one culture and one language Christian and Muslim presence is an obstacle. Hence, Hindutva groups concentrate on infiltrating the notion that the forefathers of Muslims were Hindus, that they should return to the Hindu fold as self-respecting persons, that they should give up their aggressive mode of the Moghul days and wake up to the realities of the present century and merge in the national current of life.[29] Hindutva questions the patriotism of Muslims and attacks them for enjoying the benefits of a minority religious community.[30]

Christians are accused of 'keeping themselves aloof from the freedom struggle' and practicing not Christianity but 'churchianity.'[31] Another allegation is that there is no true religion in them they are only trying to further their political ambitions.[32] It is falsely attached that 'the open rebellion' going on in the Naga Hills is all engineered by the Christian missionaries was accepted even by Pandit Nehru.[33]

---

26 M. S. Golwalkar, *Bunch of Thoughts,* 220.

27 M. S. Golwalkar, *Bunch of Thoughts,* 217.

28 M. S. Golwalkar, *Bunch of Thoughts,* 112.

29 M. S. Golwalkar, *Bunch of Thoughts,* 143.

30 M. S. Golwalkar, *Bunch of Thoughts,* 185.

31 M. S. Golwalkar, *Bunch of Thoughts,* 159.

32 M. S. Golwalkar, *Bunch of Thoughts,* 189.

33 M. S. Golwalkar, *Bunch of Thoughts,* 191.

If Christians do not subscribe to the ideology of Hindutva 'they will remain here as hostiles and will have to be treated as such.'[34] In the view of M. S. Golwalkar, "together with the change in their faith, gone is the spirit of love and devotion for the nation."[35]

In a way, these two minority communities are pictured as 'working against the nation', a dangerous charge that can bring about very adverse consequences to these communities. There are many efforts to press Hindutva ideology in to service while the BJP government is at the Centre and to bridle the religious minorities.

Shaking our Foundation

The inherent secular character of Indian Constitution has bestowed freedom to call her children proudly as Indians. However, ever since the inception of RSS in 1925 there have been efforts to undo the secular framework of our constitution and call India a Hindu nation. This has become obvious when the time-tested principle of 'Secular State' is again dragged into controversy by the BJP Government in the centre. In one of the Republic Day advertisements of the Union Government, the facsimile of the Preamble of the Constitution was shown without the words "Socialist" and "Secular." BJP leaders defended it saying that it was the facsimile of the original Constitution which was signed on 26th January, 1950, where the words "Socialist" and "Secular" were not mentioned. It is also a fact that the words "Socialist" and Secular" were added in the year 1976 by virtue of 42nd amendment of the Constitution. Nevertheless the question is whether the original Constitution without the words "Socialist" and "Secular" was chosen because it better suited the ideology of the ruling party or it was an inadvertent omission.[36]

It cannot be an inadvertent omission because even the Union Minister for Information technology, Ravi Shankar Prasad, suggested a debate on this issue. This is also in line with the argument that had been advanced when Vajpayee was the Prime Minister that the Constitution needed a comprehensive review.[37] The 'Justice Venkatachelliah commission he had appointed did not suggest deletion of the words Secular and Social even if they had been adopted by parliament in the years of the State of Emergency.'[38]

The founders of RSS maintained that the very notion of 'secularism' is western and it has no relevance to our country. They also argued that the word 'secular' is nowhere to be found in our Constitution; People are confusing

34 M. S. Golwalkar, *Bunch of Thoughts,* 194.

35 M. S. Golwalkar, *Bunch of Thoughts,* 125.

36 Irfan Engineer, "Preamble, Secularism and Constitution," *NCC Review* Vol. Cxxxv /1 (January-February, 2015), 37.

37 John Dayal, "Raj Dharma in 2015," *Indian Currents* vol. xxvii/5 (02-08 February. 2015), 33.

38 John Dayal, "Raj Dharma in 2015," *Indian Currents* vol. xxvii/5 (02-08 February. 2015), 33.

'secularism' with 'nationalism.'[39] In their effort to subvert the plurality/diversity and bring about a Hindu Nation they say 'let the Constitution be re-examined and re-drafted, so as to establish this unitary form of Government.'[40]

It is a fact "contrary to what many in the BJP seem to think, secularism is not a policy option for a government, but one of the original principles that inform the Constitution."[41] Any efforts to replace a secular state with Hindu state or Hindu nation will have enormous difficulties for the religious minorities in India.

Curtailing Freedom of Religion

Even before the addition of the word 'Secular' in the Preamble to Indian Constitution, Article 25 guaranteed freedom of conscience, and freedom to profess, practice and propagate any religion as one of the fundamental rights. Although, protecting the right of all persons to freedom of religion is the constitutional duty of the government of the day, there is an effort to dilute freedom of religion.

President Mukherjee in his Republic day address said, we have always reposed our trust in 'equality' where every faith is equal before the law and every culture blends into another to create a positive dynamic.[42] Indian civilization has celebrated pluralism, advocated tolerance and promoted goodwill between diverse communities. These values need to be preserved with utmost care and vigilance.[43]

US President, Obama spoke in clear terms to a crowded audience of mostly young people at New Delhi that our nations are strongest when we see that we are all God's children – all equal in His eyes and worthy of His love. Upholding Article 25 of the Indian Constitution is the responsibility of government, but it's also the responsibility of every person.[44]

Obama also said, 'diversity is our strength.' And we have to guard against any efforts to divide ourselves along sectarian lines or any other lines. He, with a sense of concern, forcefully declared, "India will succeed so long as it is not splintered along the lines of religious faith – so long as it's not splintered along any lines- and is unified as one nation.[45]

Freedom of religion is a fundamental right in the Indian Constitution and in the universal human rights. A government that cannot ensure the fundamental

---

39 M. S. Golwalkar, *Bunch of Thoughts,* 162.

40 M. S. Golwalkar, *Bunch of Thoughts,* 227.

41 "Secularism is Not a Policy Option," *The Hindu* (Vijayawada), 19 February 2015, 8.

42 John Dayal, "Raj Dharma in 2015," *Indian Currents* vol. xxvii/5 (02-08 February. 2015), 32.

43 John Dayal, "Raj Dharma in 2015," *Indian Currents* vol. xxvii/5 (02-08 February. 2015), 32.

44 Kay Abey, "Obama's Parting Shot," *Indian Currents* vol. xxvii/5 (02-08 February. 2015), 28.

45 Kay Abey, "Obama's Parting Shot," *Indian Currents* vol. xxvii/5 (02-08 February. 2015), 29.

rights guaranteed by the Constitution equally to all its citizens will quickly lose its political legitimacy and representative character.[46]

It is a paradox that a few states in India have legislated anti-conversion laws. It is more disturbing that the BJP government is creating disturbing situations to bring in debate on freedom of religion and enact an anti-conversion law thereby depriving the religious minorities their right to profess, practice and propagate their own religion.

Religious Tinge to Democracy

Democracy helps religious minorities to express their concerns and grievances in a peaceful, acceptable and parliamentary way. Indian President said, "the Indian Constitution is the holy book of democracy."[47] It is also brought to the fore that "indeed, freedom of religion is integral to any democratic society, and India, by definition, cannot remain a democracy without allowing its citizens the freedom to practice a religion of their choice."[48]

Undermining the significance of Indian democracy M. S. Golwalkar said, "the spirit of democracy at its best, which confers the right of freedom of speech, thought and action on the individual, is nowhere more fully recognized and practiced than in the age-old Hindu tradition."[49] Comparing democracy with Hinduism is risky.

Another false Hindutva understanding of democracy is that "in a democracy the opinion of the majority has to hold sway in the day-to-day life of the people. As such it will be but proper to consider the practical conduct of the life of majority as the actual life of the national entity. From this point of view also, efforts to uplift the life of Hindus is national and not communal."[50]

It is the sacred principles of Democracy that helped the (numerically insignificant) opposition in the parliament to prevent the government of the day from going ahead with a debate leading to anti-conversion law. We should actively involve ourselves in the democratic processes and exercise our democratic rights and privileges. It is not a call for forming a religious political party but to be vigilant and to learn to work with secular political parties and ideological groups democratically to safeguard our constitutional privileges.

Growing Intolerance to Reforms

The shooting in Kolhapur, Maharashtra, of respected Communist leader and activist Govind Pansare and his wife, on February 16th, 2015 and his consequent death five days later drew the attention of many. Pansare, spearheaded anti-road

46 "Secularism is not a policy option," *The Hindu* (Vijayawada), 19 February 2015, 8.

47 John Dayal, "Raj Dharma in 2015," *Indian Currents* vol. xxvii/5 (02-08 February. 2015), 32.

48 "Secularism is Not a Policy Option," *The Hindu* (Vijayawada), 19 February 2015, 8.

49 M. S. Golwalkar, *Bunch of Thoughts,* 337.

50 M. S. Golwalkar, *Bunch of Thoughts,* 165.

toll agitation, he ruffled the feathers of right-wing groups when he published his best-selling pamphlet in Marathi, "Shivaji kon hota," (Who was Shivaji?), emphasizing the Muslim contribution in Shivaji's Maharashtra. He was a tireless spokesman against eulogizing of Godse and was forever cautioning against the Godse-cult taking root among impressionable minds.[51]

Secular progressives believe that there is an infiltration and dominance of right wing groups in Maharashtra's educational institutions. They also fear that all eminent higher educational institutions in Pune, to an extent, veered towards the ideology of the RSS.

Perumal Murugan's novel "'Madhorubhagan' (One Half Woman) is based on a ritual that was prevalent during Pre-Independence era on the occasion of annual car festival of Sri Arthanareeshwarar Temple in Tiruchengode, the abode of Siva in the form of half-woman, half-man. It is the sacred temple to which childless couples flock to this day hoping to extend their lineage.

As per the ritual, in and around the temple, childless women could go with any man on the night of the festival. Any consenting man and woman could have sex. A child born out of such a relation was treated as a gift of God. Classical Hindu tradition refers to this practice as *niyoga* or *niyoga dharma*. It enjoyed the sanction of the society and religion.

The book Madhorubhagan was first published in 2010 and now it is into fourth edition. Protests seem to have been triggered only after the English translation 'One part woman' was published by Penguin in 2014. 'Why only now? Is the question hanging on everybody's mind? The protest is suspected to be a result out of an unholy alliance of caste group and (Hindutva) religion which is dangerous.[52]

The Gospel has been instrumental of transformation In India, be it Sati, child marriage, human sacrifice, social discrimination, etc. We are called upon to continue the service. As Hindutva ideology is inherently intolerant of social and religious reforms, there is a possibility of our transforming efforts being challenged.

Revival of An Old Argument

A popular charge against Muslims in India has been that each man has four wives, and the family ends up with 25 children, as opposed to the average Hindu with two or three children. They will first outnumber and then totally overwhelm the Hindu population, converting India into an Islamic state much as Pakistan and Saudi Arabia.[53]

The same allegation is leveled against Christians as well. M. S. Golwalkar wrote, "everybody knows that only a handful of Muslims came here as enemies

51 "Death for dissent and disbelief," *The Hindu* (Vijayawada), 23 February 2015, 9.

52 G. John, "The Writer is Dead," *Indian Currents* vol. xxvii/4 (26 Jan.-01 Feb. 2015), 15.

53 John Dayal, "Saffronising the Womb," *Indian Currents* vol. xxvii/4 (26 Jan.-01 Feb. 2015), 28.

and invaders. So also, only a few foreign Christian missionaries came here. Now the Muslim and Christians have enormously grown in number. They did not grow just by multiplication as in the case of fishes. They converted the local population."[54] According to BJP MP Yogi Adityanath, due to the "mistakes of the past" the population of the Muslims in the country "rose from 3 percent to 15 percent" and that of Christians "from.01 percent to 3 percent.[55] This notion continues to influence the thoughts of many BJP leaders too.

Every census operation in India is followed by slogans calling for the "return" or Ghar wapsi of people converted to Islam and Christianity, the limiting of population of these two groups by compulsory family planning laws, a demand for Common Civil Code that would outlaw polygamy.[56]

BJP MP, Sakshi Maharaj, at a function in Meerut in Uttar Pradesh, said the time has come when a Hindu woman must bear at least four children in order to protect Hindu religion. While Hindu families are opting for one or two child norm the Muslims are having seven to eight children. He suggested that of these four children the Hindus should send one of them to army and give another to Sant Samaj for propagation of Hindu religion. The third should be sent to join RSS and the fourth sibling should serve his parents.[57] Shankaracharya of Badrikashram, Vasudevanand Saraswati, said Hindus should have ten children.[58] Many Indian women had become victims of child rape in the guise of traditional marriage, and now is presented as a political womb for the service of a fundamentalist ideology and its aversion towards other communities.

This is purely a communal propaganda towards attaining Hindu Majority political platform. It is also aimed at developing communal hatred among people of different faiths in order to gain political mileage. The increase in the number of Christians and Muslims is interpreted as 'a political strategy' under the garb of religious propagation.'[59] The RSS notion of Hindu majority politically controlling the Muslim and Christian minorities is an unsafe thought from the point of communalism, women's liberation, Christian witness, etc.

Home Coming/Ghar Vapsi/Reconversion

On the grounds of unfounded fears of losing majority status the RSS has programs (Suddhi/Home coming/Ghar Vapsi) to reconvert people to Hinduism from the religions where the dalits, discriminated and neglected of this country found liberation, respect and acceptance. For the RSS, 'it is their duty to call

54 M. S. Golwalkar, *Bunch of Thoughts,* 127.

55 "Jihadi Politics, Not Poverty, the Problem: Adityanath," *The Hindu* (Vijayawada), 25 February 2015, 7.

56 John Dayal, "Saffronising the Womb," *Indian Currents* vol. xxvii/4 (26 Jan.-01 Feb. 2015), 28.

57 John Dayal, "Saffronising the Womb," *Indian Currents* vol. xxvii/4 (26 Jan.-01 Feb. 2015), 30.

58 John Dayal, "Saffronising the Womb," *Indian Currents* vol. xxvii/4 (26 Jan.-01 Feb. 2015), 30.

59 M. S. Golwalkar, *Bunch of Thoughts,* 128.

these our forlorn brothers, suffering under religious slavery for centuries, back to their ancestral home.' It is 'a call for all those brothers to take their original place in our national life.' It is also said "this is only a call and request to them to understand things properly and come back and identify themselves with their ancestral Hindu way of life in dress, customs, performing marriage ceremonies and funeral rites and such other things."[60] Here, religious conversion is mixed up with nationalism and culture.

Security concerns is also attributed saying "conversion of Hindus into other religions is nothing but making them succumb to divided loyalty in place of having undivided and absolute loyalty to the nation. It is dangerous to the security of the nation and the country. It is therefore necessary to put a stop to it."[61] Jawaharlal Nehru refuted this false allegation and said, 'Indian converts never ceased to be Indians on account of a change of their faith.'[62]

Nevertheless, starting from Swami Dayananda Saraswati's Suddhi program, reconversion has been a program of Hindutva. Mr. Togadia said the VHP would focus on the movement against conversion of religious minorities.[63] This is true in the case of Delhi where, churches are burned; people going for prayer are stopped and beaten up; forcefully Muslims are made to accept Hinduism in the name of Ghar Vapsi.[64] In a context such as this our witness need to be vigilant and diligent to overcome unfounded communal designs.

Communalizing History and Education

Hindutva brigades are bent on developing a religious history particularly Hindu religious history rather than Indian history, wherein Hindu heroes will be interpreted as saviors of this nation.[65]

It is claimed that 'Hindus are the only people who have succeeded in preserving their history which began from the Vedas.'[66] The process of communalizing history is obvious in the method of the functioning of the BJP government. For instance, the Indian Council of Historical Research (ICHR) was entirely reconstituted with 18 fresh appointees including office-bearers of the RSS-backed Akhil Bharatiya Itihas Sankalan Yojana (ABISY). In reconstituting the council, the Union Human Resource Development Ministry set aside the

60 M. S. Golwalkar, *Bunch of Thoughts,* 129.

61 M. S. Golwalkar, *Bunch of Thoughts,* 170.

62 Jawaharlal Nehru, *The Discovery of India*, 62.

63 "Development without Hindu Rashtra is of No Use: Togadia," *The Hindu* (Vijayawada), 27 January 2015, 10.

64 Lima VM, "Letter to the Editor," *Indian Currents* vol. xxvii/5 (02-08 February. 2015), 7.

65 Vinayak Damodar Savarkar, *Hindutva: Who is a Hindu?*, 45.

66 Vinayak Damodar Savarkar, *Hindutva: Who is a Hindu?*, 93.

long-standing convention of reappointing members who had completed just a single term.[67]

Another dimension of communalizing is felt in educational institutions. For example "the BJP Government in Gujarat, MP, Rajasthan and Haryana are introducing Hindu religious texts in schools and making Saraswati Vandana and surya namaskar Hindu rituals compulsory on schools even though they are contrary to Art. 28 and 29 of Constitution."[68]

A Hindu history in place of Indian history is a calculated effort to obliterate the real historical process and to perpetuate communal unrest in the future. Making education as a source of infiltrating Hindu view-pints is another perilous attempt. A country like India needs a factual history and freedom to receive the desired education and knowledge.

A Note of Caution

While challenging situations are around, the minorities should not add to further conflicts. The benefits of secular state, freedom of religion and democracy should not be misused for interests that contravene the law of the land. In a case challenging the jurisdiction of Indian Criminal law over Canon Law, the Supreme Court underlined the need to "stamp out" religion from civil laws and the Supreme Court expressed anxiety over the challenges faced by secularism in the country. During the hearing, the court referred to honor killing as an example of the dangers that may ensue if religious or self-styled socio-political institutions were given legal backing.[69]

In a case illustrative of this, Khursheed Ahmad Khan filed a petition against the Uttar Pradesh government's decision to remove him from service as Irrigation Supervisor for contracting a second marriage when his first marriage was still in existence. Khan challenged that it violated his right to freely practice his religion. Confirming the sacking of his service for bigamy, the Supreme Court ruled that the fundamental right to religion did not include practices which ran counter to public order, health and morality. It was also pointed that 'a practice did not acquire sanction of religion simply because it was permitted.' Further "What was protected under Article 25 was the religious faith and not a practice which may run counter to public order, health or morality. Polygamy was not integral part of religion and monogamy was a reform within the power of the State under Article 25," The court further noted that "Sharp distinction must be made between religious faith and belief and religious practices. What the State protects is religious faith and belief. If religious practices run counter to public order, morality or

67 "Saffron hue in revamped ICHR," *The Hindu* (Vijayawada), 2 March 2015, 1.

68 Irfan Engineer, "Preamble, Secularism and Constitution," *NCC Review* Vol. Cxxxv /1 (January-February, 2015), 37.

69 "Stamp Out Religion from Civil Laws, Observes SC," *The Hindu* (Vijayawada), 10 February 2015, 10.

health or a policy of social welfare upon which the State has embarked, then the religious practices must give way before the good of the people of the State as a whole."[70]

It is a call for the minorities to be sensitive towards the constitutional provisions. Efforts to thwart reforms under minority banner are counterproductive to our witnessing.

Challenges

The very communal idea of Hindutva, Hindu and Hinduism threatens the possibilities of other religions being considered equal. It further intensifies intolerance towards plurality/unity in diversity. Replacing secular state with Hindu state, framing anti-conversion laws against freedom of religion and democracy being compared with Hindu religious point of view are real challenges to our witnessing. In order to protect our constitutional rights we need to learn to work with secular political parties and ideologies.

Religious freedom has an important role in unifying a country. Peace depends on human freedom, and religious liberty is perhaps the most precious of such freedom. Full religious liberty includes not only freedom from outside coercion and suppression but also from the suppression or restriction of human rights within each particular religious or belief community. The defense of religious liberty is integral to the mission of the church and the affirmation of religious liberty is inseparable from Christian witness.[71]

We may use our communication and educational channels to raise awareness about the importance of religious freedom which is especially essential for peace in our country and in the world. Minority religious community needs to make clear distinction between faith, belief and social practice within the framework of the Constitution for healthy witnessing. The strength of Christian witness includes courageous initiatives towards reforms-social, religious, etc. Unless these transforming witnesses go undisturbed there is an obstacle to Christian witness and the salvation of God's creation. The reforms brought about by early missionaries and secular ideologies like DK was quite impacting. We need to incorporate these aspects along with other forms of Christian witness.

The perception that religious minorities are a threat to the nation requires deliberate correction/adjustment from us to instill trust in our programs. We also need conscious paradigm to present untainted Christian image free from political interference. Also, there needs to be alertness to democratically dissent any efforts to Hinduvise Indian history and education.

From the point of theology, we need an ecumenical theological vision. No theology is absolute. We need to honor the possibility of multiple interpretation

---

70 "Right to Religion Not Above Public Morality: SC," *The Hindu* (Vijayawada), 10 February 2015, 10.

71 Ninan Koshy, *Religious Freedom in a Changing World* (Geneva: WCC Publications, 1992), 115.

and perspectives for positive witnessing. A united Christian persuasion along with other minorities, political parties and ideologies can even change the 1950 Presidential order depriving Christian dalits of their government privileges.

Dialogical living and witnessing is essential for a plural society like ours. For example, ISKCON is taking initiatives to have dialogue with Christians in spite of both being mission oriented traditions. While asking whether developmental promises have unevenly induced young Indians to overlook communalism, we need to resolutely live the 'life of Jesus Christ.'

13

Role of the Youth in Developing Religious Harmony

Introduction

This chapter attempts to graphically highlight a few challenges that affect religious harmony in India and to suggest seemingly possible space for youth to engage themselves in working towards religious harmony. In this process I have sketchily mentioned some salient characteristics of youth and why Christian youth should involve themselves in bringing about religious harmony.

Youth

It is not easy to exactly categories 'youth.' However the UN defines 'youth,' as those persons between the ages of 15 and 24 years. It is a period where persons move from childhood (dependence) to adulthood (Independence) and realize the necessity of interdependence. Identity-seeking, choosing a peer-group, developing a passion for social acceptance, confrontations with parents and other authority figures, and decisions of right and wrong, 'are often the pressures' which 'draw youth to religion'or keep them away from religion.[1] Nevertheless the fact remains that the "youth as individuals vary greatly in their ideological interests."[2] As youth are vibrant, the church and the society look for their creative and constructive role in shaping the future and the future of their very lives. We, therefore, discuss the 'Role of Youth in Developing Religious Harmony.'

1 Paul B. Irwin, *The Care and Counseling of Youth in the Church* (USA: Fortress Press, 1975), 59.

2 Paul B. Irwin, *The Care and Counseling of Youth in the Church* (USA: Fortress Press, 1975), 61.

Why We

Religious harmony is a constitutional duty bestowed upon every citizen of India. Hence, the starting point for discussion on religious harmony can be the Indian Constitution.[3] The Preamble envisages fraternity, secularism and guarantees religious neutrality of the state; the principle of democracy provides space for our views; fundamental rights guarantee religious freedom subject to public order, health and morality; directive principles prevent inequality; and fundamental duties call for religious harmony. Religious harmony can be pursued on the basis of Human Rights and common humanness as well.

We are concerned with it because our faith mandates. Psalm, 133:1 reads "Behold, how good and pleasant it is when brothers dwell in unity!" It is written in Ephesians 2:14 "For he himself is our peace, who has made us both one and has broken down in his flesh the dividing wall of hostility." Jesus prayed "that they may all be one, just as you, Father, are in me, and I in you, that they also may be in us, so that the world may believe that you have sent me." (John 17:21)

I. Challenges for Religious Harmony

I shall now discuss a few sketchy factors, although not exhaustive, that affect religious/communal harmony in India. The list is short of grass roots issues, but these are the issues that at higher/intellectual levels trigger disharmony which spread ripples to every corner of the nation.

1. Constitution

The framers of the Indian Constitution have allowed necessary space in the Constitution to promote harmony among (religious) communities. The disturbing fact is that there is a call occasionally for a debate on the Constitution to deal with religious/communal issues. It is an intentionally worked out strategy of the RSS towards imagining a Hindu Nation while downgrading religious minorities. They say 'let the Constitution be re-examined and re-drafted, so as to establish this unitary form of Government.'[4]

This happens in spite of the provision in the Preamble of the Constitution, among other things (justice, liberty and equality), for fraternity. Even after incorporating the word Secular in the Preamble of the Constitution, it is often hard to find 'religious neutrality' in the functioning of governments. The point that religion should not be used for political ends is becoming a rarity. Even the principle of democracy is misinterpreted as "in a democracy the opinion of the majority has to hold the sway in the day-to-day life of the people. As such it will

---

3 Rudolf C. Heredia, "Mission as Text in Context: Religious Conversions in Contemporary India," *Vidyajyoti Journal of Theological Reflection* 73/7 (July, 2009), 6.

4 M. S. Golwalkar, *Bunch of Thoughts,* 3rd ed., Reprint (Bangalore: Sahitya Sindhu Prakashan, 2000), 227.

be but proper to consider the practical conduct of the life of majority as the actual life of the national entity."[5]

'In stark contrast B. R. Ambedkar, could say, Hinduism is a menace to liberty, equality and fraternity and it is incompatible with democracy. In any given national context, the more politically dominant a religion, the greater its capacity to undermine democratic values.'[6]

These in fact, contravene the spirit of the directive principles of the Constitution which envisage a spirit of equality and justice to everyone. Call for a national debate on article 25 is a well calculated plot to paralyze freedom of religion in India. This in turn contributes to disturbance among different communities. Replacing secular state with Hindu state, framing anti-conversion laws against freedom of religion and democracy being compared with Hindu majority point of view are real challenges to religious harmony.

2. Rejection of Plurality

Rejection of the existence of many/different religions is a major threat to religious harmony in India. One of the RSS ideologues maintained that "we are Hindus even before we emerge from the womb of our mother. We are therefore born as Hindus. About the others, they are born to this world as simple unnamed human beings and later on, either circumcised or baptized, they become Muslims or Christians."[7] Superiority claims, arguing/debating for higher status on grounds of religion and provoking minority religions perpetuate religious disharmony. In the words of Ravi Tiwari, "the fact of plurality of religion, in which Hinduism is merely one among many, has been very uncomfortable to the propounders of neo-Hindu ideologues."[8]

3. Nationalisms

Territorial/geographical nationalism versus religious nationalism is another contentious debate that causes religious disharmony in India. It distinguishes between independence struggle and real nationalism. The advocates of such a debate say anti-British activities are different from real nationalism (Hindu nation). People who adhere to other faith traditions are discarded from this communal nationalism. Establishing a Hindu nation is called as World Mission of RSS.[9]

5 M. S. Golwalkar, *Bunch of Thoughts,* 165.

6 "The Missing Conservative Intellectuals," *The Hindu* (Vijayawada), 25 July 2015, 10.

7 M. S. Golwalkar, *Bunch of Thoughts,* 117.

8 Ravi Tiwari, *Reflections and Studies in Religion* (Delhi: ISPCK, 2008), 138.

9 M. S. Golwalkar, *Bunch of Thoughts,* 9.

Using religious symbols or images for nationalism is a real challenge for religious harmony because this does not provide space for other religious communities to identify with. Even their contributions towards nation-building and transformations are undermined, belittled or misinterpreted.

India's nationhood was intimately tied to a religious, and specifically Hindu, imaginary. 'As independent India's first Prime Minister, Jawaharlal Nehru, summed up in his *Discovery of India*, "That mixture of religion and philosophy, history and tradition, custom and social structure, which in its wide fold included almost every aspect of the life of India, and which might be called Brahminism or (to use a later word) Hinduism, became the symbol of nationalism.'[10] 'Clearly, this Hindu conservatism, whose nationalism is a curious amalgam of revivalism, xenophobia and triumphalism, can never attain respectability except in a self-contained discursive ghetto. Indeed, it is an ideology which consigns a few hundred million non-Hindus to second-class citizenship.'[11] That is why, "religious nationalism" is a genuine fear among the country's minorities.'[12]

Suchitra Vijayan writes, "In a secular democracy, citizenship is the civic religion. Religious nationalism is the antithesis of this principle and excludes the notion of a secular state, and denies equal participation of those who do not identify with the dominant religion."[13] Further, 'the disastrous marriage between religion and nationalism will ultimately subvert the values that have held this nation together.'[14]

4. Mono Culture

The beauty of Indian culture is plurality (of cultures). Religion is an integral part of any culture. Talk of monoculture, rather majority culture, in place of multi-culture is another source of discrimination that leads to disharmony. We are faced with the claim that the Hindu Rashtra 'stands for cultural and religious unity.'[15] This is further expanded as our concept of Hindu Nation is 'essentially cultural.'[16]

It implies that only a particular set of teachings, morals, standards and practices are final and similar other resources do not have relevance. The followers of such resources compel the minority, and they have to adhere to the values of the majority otherwise they do not find place in India.

Jawaharlal Nehru however refuted such a notion and wrote "a Buddhist or Jain in India is a hundred per cent product of Indian thought and culture, yet neither is a Hindu by faith. It, is, therefore, entirely misleading to refer to

10 "The missing conservative intellectuals," *The Hindu* (Vijayawada), 25 July 2015, 10.

11 "The missing conservative intellectuals," *The Hindu* (Vijayawada), 25 July 2015, 10.

12 "Rewriting the nation state," *The Hindu* (Vijayawada), 17 March 2015, 9.

13 "Rewriting the nation state," *The Hindu* (Vijayawada), 17 March 2015, 9.

14 "Rewriting the nation state," *The Hindu* (Vijayawada), 17 March 2015, 9.

15 M. S. Golwalkar, *Bunch of Thoughts,* 129.

16 M. S. Golwalkar, *Bunch of Thoughts,* 34.

Indian culture as Hindu culture. In later ages this culture was greatly influenced by the impact of Islam, and yet it remained basically and distinctively Indian."[17] Further, 'it is, therefore, incorrect and undesirable, to use 'Hindu' or 'Hinduism' for Indian culture.'[18] The monoculture advocates are thus unaware of the reality that in some parts of India their so called "Hindu Culture" is strange, not-known and irrelevant.

5. Sanskrit

Language is the vehicle that carries the rich resources of different religious traditions. Any effort to promote one language and undermine the value of other languages is another form of religious discrimination. The value of Urdu for Muslims cannot be substituted. It applies to the scriptures of all the other religions also. There is a need in India even to credit the religious resources that mainly depend upon oral traditions. Unmindful of these stark realities it is often argued that "Sanskrit is to this day one of the greatest cementing factors of our national life."[19] And it shall become the 'lingua franca,' in India.[20]

The spirit of absorption particular to Hinduism is vivid in the declaration that 'the theme present in the *Tirukkural* is the same old Hindu concept of *catuvidha-purushartha*'[21] It is a fact that in some parts of India people are unaware of Sanskrit and there is no necessity for them. Sanctifying and promoting a particular language and ignoring other can lead to dissension and disharmony.

6. History and Education

We are faced with the aspiration of rewriting Indian history and Hinduvising of educational system. The notion behind such aspiration is that the existing histories are based on different periods (Hindu, Mughal, British, etc) and the education system in vogue is not based on Indian (Hindu) values. The new history is expected to be in line with the heroes (mainly religious) of India and the education system is to be framed after Hindu literature. The idea behind the new history project is that, 'Hindus are the only people who have succeeded in preserving their history which began from the Vedas.'[22] Similarly, "the raising of Godse's statue is not an isolated act by fringe elements. It is a political maneuver, aimed at rewriting the history of the Indian polity, and its principles of secular,

---

17 Jawaharlal Nehru, *The Discovery of India*, Centenary Edition (Delhi: Oxford University Press, 1989), 75.

18 Jawaharlal Nehru, *The Discovery of India*, Centenary Edition (Delhi: Oxford University Press, 1989), 75.

19 M. S. Golwalkar, *Bunch of Thoughts*, 112.

20 M. S. Golwalkar, *Bunch of Thoughts*, 112.

21 M. S. Golwalkar, *Bunch of Thoughts*, 112.

22 Vinayak Damodar Savarkar, *Hindutva: Who is a Hindu?*, 6th ed. (New Delhi: Bharti Sahitya Sadan, 1989), 93.

pluralistic statehood."[23] That is why it is said, "India's future lies in pluralism, parity, reasonable and principled cosmopolitanism and not with settling scores in history."[24]

There is an observation that "It is no secret that the Bharatiya Janata Party-led National Democratic Alliance (NDA) government has been struggling to find intellectuals to head various academic and cultural institutions."[25] RSS had even set up an informal committee to come up with saffron-friendly candidates for some 680 positions. But it could come up with only 160 names. None of these names has inspired much confidence in the constituencies these bodies serve. Many have charged the NDA with not just saffronising but also degrading the country's premier institutions by appointing under qualified candidates to the post.'[26] This is also called "the closing of the Indian mind," and viewed that "the present government despises writers, scholars, artists and film-makers."[27]

There is a fundamental distinction 'between intellectuals and ideologues. Intellectuals contribute to the growth of knowledge, whereas ideologues are "more interested in promoting their political or religious beliefs." Most of the so-called intellectuals, including RSS sympathizers on the Narendra Modi team, would automatically fall into the category of ideologues.'[28] An ideology which relegates a few hundred million non-Hindus to second-class citizenship can ever form the basis of serious scholarship.'[29]

It is true that 'the BJP Government in Gujarat, MP, Rajasthan and Haryana are introducing Hindu religious texts in schools and making Saraswati Vandana and Surya Namaskar Hindu rituals compulsory in schools.'[30] The entire exercise is aimed at imposing a particular point of view without space for other views. This then leads to discrimination and disharmony.

7. Muslims and Christians

Often the patriotism of Muslims is suspected and they are accused of enjoying the benefits of a minority religious community.[31] Another allegation is that there is no true religion in them as they are only trying to further their political ambitions.[32]

23 "Rewriting the nation state," *The Hindu* (Vijayawada), 17 March 2015, 9.

24 "Rewriting the nation state," *The Hindu* (Vijayawada), 17 March 2015, 9.

25 "The missing conservative intellectuals," *The Hindu* (Vijayawada), 25 July 2015, 10.

26 "The missing conservative intellectuals," *The Hindu* (Vijayawada), 25 July 2015,10.

27 "The missing conservative intellectuals," *The Hindu* (Vijayawada), 25 July 2015, 10.

28 "The missing conservative intellectuals," *The Hindu* (Vijayawada), 25 July 2015, 10.

29 "The missing conservative intellectuals," *The Hindu* (Vijayawada), 25 July 2015, 10.

30 Irfan Engineer, "Preamble, Secularism and Constitution," *NCC Review* Vol. Cxxxv/1 (January-February, 2015), 37.

31 M. S. Golwalkar, *Bunch of Thoughts,* 185.

32 M. S. Golwalkar, *Bunch of Thoughts,* 189.

Christians in India are also subjected to criticism like, "together with the change in their faith, gone is the spirit of love and devotion for the nation."[33] They are also warned that, if the Christians do not subscribe to the ideology of Hindutva 'they will remain here as hostiles and will have to be treated as such.'[34] In a way, these two minority communities are pictured as 'working against the nation,' a dangerous charge that can bring about hatred among religious communities.

A sense of insecurity is another cause for disharmony. The majority community fears that, the increase in the number of Christians and Muslims is 'a political strategy' under the garb of religious propagation.'[35] Hence 'it (Hinduism) feels threatened.'[36]

Savarkar 'defines the Hindu identity based on inclusion and exclusion. He includes Jains, Buddhists and Sikhs as inheritors and partakers in the legacy of Hinduism, but he clearly excludes Islam and Christianity as foreign ideologies brought from outside.'[37]

Disharmony, hatred and disturbances are often manufactured 'through riots, destruction of religious sites such as churches, organizing religious conversion camps, beef bans, rewriting textbooks, censoring works of history, literature and fiction that challenge the 'Hindu' version of history, appropriating political icons, and raising monuments.'[38]

8. Reconversion

The effort of converting people back to Hinduism is differently called as Home coming/Ghar Vapsi/Reconversion/Suddhi, a process that began with Dayananda Saraswathi continues even to this day. This is to reconvert people to Hinduism from the religions where the dalits, discriminated and neglected of this country found liberation, respect and acceptance. For the RSS, 'this is only a call and request to them to understand things properly and come back and identify themselves with their ancestral Hindu way of life.'[39]

Security concerns is often attributed to other forms of religious mobility, saying "conversion of Hindus into other religions is nothing but making them succumb to divided loyalty in place of having undivided and absolute loyalty to the nation. It is dangerous to the security of the nation and the country."[40] Jawaharlal Nehru refuted this false allegation and said 'Indian converts never

---

33 M. S. Golwalkar, *Bunch of Thoughts,* 125.

34 M. S. Golwalkar, *Bunch of Thoughts,* 194.

35 M. S. Golwalkar, *Bunch of Thoughts,* 128.

36 Ravi Tiwari, *Reflections and Studies in Religion* (Delhi: ISPCK, 2008), 129.

37 "Rewriting the nation state," *The Hindu* (Vijayawada), 17 March 2015, 9.

38 "Rewriting the nation state," *The Hindu* (Vijayawada), 17 March 2015, 9.

39 M. S. Golwalkar, *Bunch of Thoughts,* 129.

40 M. S. Golwalkar, *Bunch of Thoughts,* 170.

ceased to be Indians on account of a change of their faith.'[41] Attempt to clothe re-conversion with nationalism is another dangerous threat to religious harmony.

9. Politicization of Religion

The serious threat to religious harmony comes from political parties that use religious sentiments to polarize the society. It is now a reality that election manifestos of some political parties include highly inflammable and sensitive and controversial religious issues. It is also becoming a reality that just before elections communal riots are instigated. It was seen in Uttar Pradesh before the general elections. Gujarat became a strong BJP stronghold, presumably, after an ugly communal clash. Earlier, even a few political leaders became popular after demolishing a mosque. Another new trend that has developed is the ones who make incriminatory and provocative communal attack on minority communities are given attractive positions in the government.

'Mobilizing the masses using religion and religious symbols for political ends started along with independence movement (Bharat Matha).' And "almost fifty years later, the Ayodhya Ram Janmabhoomi campaign employed similar strategies to mobilize popular support for its vision of Hindu nationhood."[42] These mobilizations are aimed at constructing the Hindu nation.[43] Such acts ruthlessly undermine the existence and rights of religious minorities to the point of extreme hatred and mistrust.

10. Suppression of Voices

The process of politicization of religion targets people who help the victims of communal hatred. 'In an interview to the Hindu Teesta Setalvad said, that under the Modi regime the future is dark for activists.'[44] She was 'the face of the fight for justice for the victims of the Gujarat riots in 2002. She has tirelessly fought scores of cases, provided legal aid to the survivors through her non-governmental organizations and played a role in securing conviction of 120 perpetrators. But today, she is accused of forgery and criminal breach of trust, facing multiple inquiries and six FIRs. Her organizational and personal accounts were frozen in early 2014, and a travel ban was imposed recently.'[45]

This is a sign of growing intolerance towards others and intolerance towards transformation-social, religious. People who voice their opinions for the cause of justice are treated with contempt. Without justice, there cannot be peace or harmony.

---

41 Jawaharlal Nehru, *The Discovery of India*, 62.

42 "Rewriting the nation state," *The Hindu* (Vijayawada), 17 March 2015, 9.

43 "Rewriting the nation state," *The Hindu* (Vijayawada), 17 March 2015, 9.

44 "I have been a hate target, says Teesta," *The Hindu* (Vijayawada), 25 July 2015, 13.

45 "I have been a hate target, says Teesta," *The Hindu* (Vijayawada), 25 July 2015, 13.

II. Role of Youth

In the context of these issues, we can look at some measures that the youth of the country who have a love for the nation, desire to serve, passion for righteous life and leading purpose driven life may engage in promoting religious harmony. One way of doing it is by "opinion building." This can be done among the peer group, in working places, worship places and in all the places.

1. Protecting Constitutional Provisions

Youth can mobilize towards protection of constitutional provisions that guide religious harmony in India. All efforts to do away with secularism should be handled diligently. If there is no religious neutrality the minority religious communities may have to live at the mercy of the majority. Such a state will lead to more tensions and suspicions. Religious harmony will be almost impossible then similarly, we cannot lose our democratic provisions which help representing our views. It is said, "one of the important values that religions will have to promote is democracy or a reverential attitude for others."[46]

Not to ignore the values of equality and justice the guiding principles that are enshrined in the directive principles are to be upheld. With all the democratic tools alone we will be able to realize the vision of fraternity that is enshrined in the Preamble of the Indian Constitution.

As opinion builders youth can be pro-active in exploring various possibilities to uphold the sanctity of the Constitution as it is the only firm foundation for the establishment of religious harmony. In order to protect our constitutional rights we need to learn to work with secular political parties and ideologies as well.

2. Fulfilling Fundamental Duties

One of the fundamental duties of every Indian citizen is to promote (religious) harmony: [Part IV, Article 51-A(e) "to promote harmony and the spirit of common brotherhood amongst all the people of India transcending religious, linguistic and regional or sectional diversities; to renounce practices derogatory to the dignity of women;"] There cannot be any blame or insult when we fulfill our constitutional responsibilities. The avenue of fundamental duties can be more authentic for youth to pursue religious harmony because it is free from religious stigma. The majority community cannot accuse us of desperate attempt to promote religious harmony. Youth can discuss and involve their peer-group so actively if the concern for harmony emerges from fundamental duties as found in the Indian Constitution.

---

46 Varghese Manimala, *Toward Mutual Fecundation and Fulfilment of Religions* (Delhi: Media House and ISPCK), 2009, 506.

3. Right Perspective on Freedom of Religion

Youth should develop a right and clear perspective on freedom of religion. Article 25 provides for freedom of conscience, freedom to profess, practice and propagate any religion. It is often mistakenly claimed that, the article allows conversion of others. In fact what is guaranteed is freedom of religion and not freedom to convert others.

Everyone has freedom to convert him/herself to any religion of his/her choice. Nobody has the right to convert others. But, every Indian citizen has freedom to choose his/her choice of religion. A right understanding will eliminate unnecessary controversies with neighbors of other faiths and help promote religious harmony.

What is at stake is the freedom to choose any religion. This freedom is hindered through freedom of religion bills. The present government's effort to have a national debate on conversion is to ban freedom of religion as a whole. A blanket ban on conversion will be the final death blow to freedom of religion in India which will generate so much of unrest among communities. Youth of our country should rise to the occasion and should not fall prey to such deceptive political schemes.

One more aspect that needs our careful attention is that freedom of religion is not absolute freedom but subject to public order, morality and health. This implies that the state is in its right to control freedom of religion when it feels necessary. It applies to both majority and minority religions. When there is suspicion over state actions, it is appropriate to seek legal remedies. Youth should be educated in this process. This can promote religious harmony and avoid hatred towards each other.

The Supreme Court has often stressed the need to 'stamp out' religion from civil laws.[47] The court has said what was protected under Article 25 was the religious faith and not a practice which may run counter to public order, health or morality. What the State protects is religious faith and belief. 'If religious practices run counter to public order, morality or health or a policy of social welfare upon which the State has embarked, then the religious practices must give way before the good of the people of the State as a whole.'[48]

According to Pope Francis, "One does not have the right to offend and ridicule the fiath of others in the name of freedom of religion."[49] Shallow understanding of crucial facts can lead to fundamentalist attitude and hatred. This can be overcome if we place ourselves within the ambit of the Constitution.

---

47 "Stamp out religion from civil laws, observes SC, "*The Hindu* (Vijayawada),10 February 2015, 10.

48 "Right to religion not above public morality: SC," *The Hindu* (Vijayawada), 10 February 2015, 10.

49 "Reclaiming a space for the Church,' The Hindu (Vijayawada), 29 July 2015, 11.

No reasonable human being can oppose religious harmony if pursued within the framework of the Constitution.

4. Legal Remedies

Religious freedom has an important role in unifying a country. Unless religious freedom is complete there cannot be any effort for religious harmony. When everyone is equal before the law, those equals can come together to utilize their potentials for religious harmony resulting in public good.

In the contexts of religious conflicts 'without justice and fairness' we cannot strive for reconciliation and harmony. Swami Agnivesh points, "Peace without justice will be simply a euphemism for reinforcing the social and economic status quo."[50]

We live in a country where worship places are razed to the ground by a mammoth mob under the leadership of communal political leaders, in the full view of cameras and security forces. No one is punished. Thousands of people belonging to a particular religious community are killed as genocide under the banner of communal conflicts and the responsibility could not be exactly fixed. An increasing number of elected members of the parliament makes provocative and communally sensitive statements and goes unpunished.

It is true "Justice is a necessary precondition for the existence of unity and harmony at every level of society."[51] Youth of the country who are committed for religious harmony have to explore the possibilities of bringing about fairness in justice delivery system. All issues that affect harmony need to be legally resolved. Justice can promote harmony.

5. Legislative Process

Another option opened before the youth to establish religious harmony through legislative system. The drawback to this process is that there is less number of legislative members from minority communities compared to the larger number from the majority community. Court rulings that are to be set right for healthy and harmonious future can be done only through legislative process.

For example, the Supreme Court has ruled that freedom of religion bills legislated by different states do not infringe the freedom of religion. In reality these bills have made the choice for Freedom of Religion more difficult and complicated. As human beings are becoming more civilized and global, the possibility to change religion should become simple and individual's affair without

50 Swami Agnivesh., "Promotion of Peace through Social Justice," in *Towards a Culture of Harmony and Peace,* edited by T. D. Singh (New Delhi & Kolkata: Delhi Peace Summit & Bhaktivedanta Institute, 2005), 185.

51 Zena Sorabjee, "Interfaith Education," in *Towards a Culture of Harmony and Peace,* edited by T. D. Singh (New Delhi & Kolkata: Delhi Peace Summit & Bhaktivedanta Institute, 2005), 126.

government interference as long as it does not violate the Constitution of India. This can now be achieved only through reasonable legislations.

Another pretentious effort to curb freedom of religion and to endanger peaceful coexistence is the effort to initiate a national discussion on conversion. This is a willful attempt to completely seal freedom of religion and promote hatred and disharmony in the place of unity and harmony. Youth need to build opinions in the political arena to nullify those efforts.

The Supreme Court has earlier declared Special status to Sanskrit as the ancient Indian literatures are in Sanskrit. This shows the subjective consideration of issues and the unpalatable nature of the verdict in our context. It requires a legislative process to set right matters. Similarly the presidential order disallowing government privileges to Scheduled Caste Hindus converted to Christianity needs a bold legislative correction. A united Christian persuasion along with other minorities, political parties and ideologies can be of help to achieve this end.

While respecting the Courts it is worthwhile to look for better environments for harmonious living. Youth must be empowered to take up these challenges by providing necessary resources so that religious harmony can become a reality.

6. Human Rights

Religious harmony cannot be devoid of human rights; it is the respect for human rights that will curb religious disharmony. Youth can explore this possibility as well. There are many young and old who have chosen this process to work for harmony. The point of caution is that in the UN's declaration of human rights "religious freedom (has) now emphasized the right to change or maintain one's faith, not the right to convert or proselytize other."[52]

Felix Wilfred writes: 'no social harmony is possible without recognition of the dignity and rights of people.' 'By defending human rights Christianity will effectively champion the cause of peace in the Asian societies.'[53]

As per UN declaration, freedom of religion is a fundamental human right. When it is recognized as inalienable it automatically implies that irrespective of different religious affiliations people need to live in harmony because no individual is wrong as he or she adheres to the faith tradition to which he or she is affiliated. Human rights channel can bring together youth from any number of religious traditions for the sake of promoting religious harmony.

7. Humanness

One way of youth working towards religious harmony is to recognize the common humanity behind the many religious followers. What is common is humanness not religion. Religion is a choice. A. P. J. Abdul Kalam writes "in whatever field

52 Rudolf C. Heredia, "Mission as Text in Context: Religious Conversions in Contemporary India," *Vidyajyoti Journal of Theological Reflection* 73/7 (July, 2009), 6.

53 Felix Wilfred, *Religion and Culture for social Amity* (Bangalore: ECC, 2006), 16.

we work, be it science, technology, medicine, politics, policing, theology, religion or the judiciary, we have to remain in the service of the common man whose well-being is central to all human knowledge and endeavor."[54]

According to Raimon Panikkar, "What religion needs to do is to make the human beings realize their common humanity and strengthen the bonds of friendship and affection."[55] Plurality of religions should be celebrated but should not become obstacle to harmony. Harmony is not possible without differences for a specific oneness. In promoting religious harmony "some of the principles that are to be looked onto are the fundamental principles of the oneness of humankind, not just in the form of an intellectual acceptance but also observing it in practice in one's day-to-day life."[56] Realization of a common humanity behind the multiplicity of religions can inspire young minds to build teams to bring about religious harmony among people of different faith orientations.

Poverty is a mass killer of humanity in spite of following different religions. Felix Wilfred remarks, "the pervasive threat to peace is caused by poverty."[57] As poverty is a common human concern youth can rally around towards eradication of poverty. This will bring them together as harmonious lot.

8. Change

Paul F. Knitter affirms, "Study, prayer, interreligious dialogue, and action to promote justice, peace, liberation, and the integrity of creation have changed me."[58] He also maintains "A new way of understanding other religions implies a new way of understanding Christianity."[59] It is true that "we must all remember, very often we tend to forget that religion is an accident of birth except perhaps for that minuscule minority which might adopt it by choice. It is, therefore, essential that we realize that the purpose and objective of every religion is to foster peace, harmony, brotherhood, and not to quarrel needlessly."[60]

---

54 A. P. J. Abdul Kalam, "The Joy of Human Life," in *Towards a Culture of Harmony and Peace,* edited by T. D. Singh (New Delhi & Kolkata: Delhi Peace Summit & Bhaktivedanta Institute, 2005), 13-14.

55 Raimon Panikkar, "Introduction," in *Toward Mutual Fecundation and Fulfilment of Religions,* Varghese Manimala (Delhi: Media House and ISPCK), 2009, 18.

56 Zena Sorabjee, "Interfaith Education," in *Towards a Culture of Harmony and Peace,* edited by T. D. Singh (New Delhi & Kolkata: Delhi Peace Summit & Bhaktivedanta Institute, 2005), 120.

57 Felix Wilfred, *Religion and Culture for Social Amity* (Bangalore: ECC, 2006), 15.

58 Paul F. Knitter, *Introducing Theologies of Religions* (Maryknoll, New York: Orbis Books, 2002), 4.

59 Paul F. Knitter, *Introducing Theologies of Religions* (Maryknoll, New York: Orbis Books, 2002), 13.

60 A. M. Ahmadi., "Towards a Global Society," in *Towards a Culture of Harmony and Peace,* edited by T. D. Singh (New Delhi & Kolkata:Delhi Peace Summit & Bhaktivedanta Institute, 2005), 18.

The perception that religious minorities are a threat to the nation requires conscious correction/adjustment from us to instill trust in our programs. We also need a conscious paradigm to present untainted Christian image free from political interference.

From the point of theology, we need an ecumenical theological vision. No theology is absolute. We need to honor the possibility of multiple interpretation and perspectives for positive harmony. Our priority should be the 'Life sustaining vision of Jesus.' His life and work was to make life meaningful and not to make religion rigid. His ministry was extended not just for Christians alone. We are to transcend our imaginary dogmatic barriers to bring about "a new heaven and a new earth." We cannot be passive as we are the 'salt, light and city on the hill.'

Elisha granted permission to Naaman to go into the house of Rimmon with the king, even after declaring that there is no god in all the earth but in Israel. Jesus appreciated the faith of the Roman centurion who constructed temples for the Jews. Thus a change of theological viewpoints and mutual openness and respect shall contribute to religious harmony.

9. Dialogue

We have the habit of organizing prayers for our own groups in work places, offices, etc. We need extra effort to form dialogue groups/ friendship groups with friends/ colleagues belonging to different faith traditions. This has to be done with utmost sincerity. In the words of Ravi Tiwari, "no experience of dialogue is worthy if it is conducted, or engaged in, without sincerity and integrity of purpose."[61] Further, "the purpose of interfaith dialogue is not to argue and win but to listen and understand the true teachings of other religions."[62]

Dialogical living and witnessing is essential for a plural society like ours. For example ISKCON is taking initiatives to have dialogue with Christians in spite of both being mission oriented traditions. It is a unique experience.

A youth leader 'Builds healthy relationships,' has 'Passion for harmony,' is 'A team player' and 'A mobilizer of young people.' Hence he/she should play a pro-active role in maintaining communal and social harmony.

There is a definite need for dialogue for the sake of peace and harmony among religions. Communal harmony should become the passion for youth.

Godwin R. Singh writes, "Communal violence reveals the stark fact that there is communication gap among individuals and among communities. One possible way of bridging this gap is through dialogue which enables peoples

61 Ravi Tiwari, *Reflections and Studies in Religion* (Delhi: ISPCK, 2008), 186.

62 P. K. Shamsuddin, "Religion and Harmony," in *Towards a Culture of Harmony and Peace,* edited by T. D. Singh (New Delhi & Kolkata:Delhi Peace Summit & Bhaktivedanta Institute, 2005), 113.

of various communities to come together and to think out for themselves the implication for the life which they live as communities in a pluralistic context."[63]

Pope Francis: "While there will necessarily be a variety of religious convictions, honest and transparent expression of the same would bring out what unites and divides the believers,"[64]

10. Creating Awareness

We may use our communication and educational channels to raise awareness about the importance of religious harmony. Wise, meaningful and innovative use of social/media is essential to create awareness about religious harmony. "The search for communal harmony will be futile if the approach is not geared along with participation of the people in realizing their objective. Particular attention has to be given to the growth of awareness of the people; and to help them to translate their awakened consciousness into action at grassroots level."[65]

Awareness programs should be used for opinion building. Youth must rise above fear, jealousy and hate on opinion building towards respecting plurality and diversity. "No expert or social scientist, not even a religious leader or a prophet will be able to solve the communal problem unless the masses join hands to accomplish it. Peoples' participation is the crucial element in this search."[66] That is why we read statements like: "I think that in all our educational institutions, it is necessary to form interreligious fora so that our children, the growing generation, who have to mould the destiny of our country, know the essential teachings of different religions."[67] Awareness about politicization of religion has to take place as well. This is evident from the role of communal programs behind electoral success in UP, Gujarat, Karnataka.

Creating awareness to continue with works of social transformation can be another effective way of dealing with religious harmony. The reforms brought about by early missionaries and secular ideologies like Dravidian Movement was quite impacting. We need to incorporate these aspects along with other forms of Christian witness.

---

63 Godwin R. Singh, *In Search of Communal Harmony* (Delhi: ISPCK, 1985), 63.

64 "Reclaiming a space for the Church,' The Hindu (Vijayawada), 29 July 2015, 11.

65 Godwin R. Singh, *In Search of Communal Harmony* (Delhi: ISPCK, 1985), p. 62.

66 Godwin R. Singh, *In Search of Communal Harmony* (Delhi: ISPCK, 1985), p. 62.

67 P. K. Shamsuddin, "Religion and Harmony," in *Towards a Culture of Harmony and Peace*, edited by T. D. Singh (New Delhi & Kolkata: Delhi Peace Summit & Bhaktivedanta Institute, 2005), 114.

11. Conclusion

There may be numerous other challenges to religious harmony than the ones discussed. Similarly there may be many more methods for youth to engage in religious harmony. Though the possibilities discussed are very essential for working towards religious harmony, an actual encounter with different situation will help understand the other causes of disharmony and solutions for harmony. It is an ongoing process. Hence, continuous study/research, engagement and explorations are necessary for a fruitful search for harmony.

14

Recollection of Insights for Diligent Christian Witness in India A Study on the Freedom of Religion based on Article 25 of the Indian Constitution

Introduction

This chapter attempts to recollect insights from the various Supreme Court interpretations of Article 25 of the Indian Constitution to understand the nuance of the freedom of religion to bear diligent Christian witness. Detailed study of each case is an interesting research, but owing to our purpose I have restricted myself to the verdict of cases as interpreted by eminent jurists. Anyone interested in detail may use the foot notes to trace the cases.

Articles 25-28 of the Indian Constitution provides for secularism and "freedom of religion" and article 25 is often read with article 26. I, however, have decided to dwell only on the Article 25 to make it converse with us in some details, though for the purpose of clarity there may be references to article 26. The emphasis in Article 25 is on 'the practice of religious freedom for individuals'[1] and "Article 26 deals with the right of a religious denomination or a section of a religious denomination."[2]

Article 25 comes under part III of the Indian Constitution under the heading "fundamental rights." However, "the rights conferred by part III of the

1 P. M. Bakshi, *The Constitution of India*, 6th ed. (Delhi: Universal Law Publishing Co., 2005), 64.

2 Chaudhari & Chaturvedi, *Law of Fundamental Rights*, 4th ed. (Delhi: Delhi Law House, 2002), 800.

Constitution are not absolute. They are relative and subject to certain limitations which were considered necessary for the safety and security of the State."[3] In other words 'the right to freedom of religion is not an unqualified right.'[4] The freedom of religion is 'not only for Indian citizens but for all persons in India and to religious groups.'[5]

As all discussions on the freedom of religion, particularly based on Article 25 of the Indian Constitution, begin with a note on secularism, I too have done the same, though it was not my sole concern. My efforts to describe the salient aspects of Article 25, can facilitate a clear understanding for diligent witness in India.

I, to derive at this objective, have discussed the essential aspects of a secular state and the definition of religion as found in the Supreme Court judgments. Graphic but useful insights are highlighted to understand freedom of conscience, freedom to profess, practice and propagate religion. The expression 'religious practice' has gone through many lengthy legal considerations to determine the integral, essential, and non-secular aspect of religion. A recollection of these distinctions is helpful to us.

'Propagation' is another important word that witnessed huge discussion to decide whether this expression provides for conversion. Moderate endeavor is taken to understand the expressions public order, morality and health to which the entire freedom of religion is subjected to. Freedom of religion can be regulated through legislations by States in matters of economic, financial, political and secular activities associated with religious practices is another area touched upon to help Christians aware of these insights. Another paramount insight helpful for diligent witness considered is that religious practices should give way to providing for social welfare and reforms.

In the light of these considerations suggestions are made for diligent Christian witness in the Indian context. This study is helpful for 'diligent witness' in a way prophetic, to help avoid confrontation and waste of resources on indefensible matters. It is a call for Christians in India to be good law abiding citizens to bear witness to Christ.

Secularism

The word secular is not defined in the Constitution but the prevailing definitions that are in vogue are based upon the Supreme Court judgments on various matters related to freedom of religion. The concept of secularism and freedom of religion

---

3 D. C. Ahir, *Dr. Ambedkar and Indian Constitution,* 2nd ed. (Delhi: Low Price Publications, 1997), 90.

4 T. K. Tope, *Constitutional Law of India*, 2nd ed. (Lucknow: Eastern Book Company, 1992), 225.

5 M. P. Jain, *Indian Constitutional Law*, 3rd ed. (Bombay: N.M. Tripathi Private LTD, 1983), 526.

is implicit in the Preamble and other provisions of the Constitution, even before the word 'secular' was inserted in the Preamble by the 42nd Amendment Act in 1976. The amendment is intended merely to spell out clearly the principle of 'secularism' in the Constitution.'[6] Also 'to make sure what India seeks to achieve as a secular State.'[7]

Secularism in India means respect for all religions and it does not mean irreligion.[8] It 'is not indifference to religion' and 'does not behave hatred on any religion.' 'Secularism conceptualizes peaceful co-existence of different faiths' and considers each individual citizen as a free normal person in his/her own right.'[9] The essence of secularism is non-discrimination on the basis of religious differences.

'Secularism can be practiced by adopting a complete neutral approach towards religions or positively making one section of religious people to understand and respect religion of another.' The Supreme Court has held that the 'study of religions in school education is not against the secular philosophy of the Constitution.' It can help avoid 'mutual distrust and intolerance.' This approach is called positive secularism.'[10] It is 'positive in its meaning in as much as it is an active instrument to prevent followers of different religions from perpetrating violent acts and atrocities against each other.'[11] These principles are to be practiced by a secular State (India).

Secular State

India under the Constitution is a Secular State which means, the State observes an attitude of neutrality and impartiality towards all religions. There shall be no "State religion." The State will neither establish a religion of its own nor confer any special patronage upon any particular religion. 'Every person is guaranteed the freedom of conscience and the freedom to profess, practice and propagate his/her own religion.[12] However, 'the religion of the individual or denomination has nothing to do in the matter of socio-economic change.'[13]

Further, under secular constitution, 'the State will protect all religions but interferes with none, and no person is to be discriminated against on the ground

6 J. N. Pandey, *The Constitutional Law of India*, 47th ed. (Allahabad: Central Law Agency, 2010), 323.

7 P. K. Majumdar & R. P. Kataria, *Commentary on the Constitution of India*, 11th ed. 9 (New Delhi: Orient Publishing company, 2014), 494.

8 M. P. Jain, *Indian Constitutional Law*, 526.

9 Charles Prabakar and Paul Mohan Raj, ed., *Rights & Responsibilities of the Minorities* (Bangalore: Theological Book Trust, 1999), 55-58.

10 J. N. Pandey, *The Constitutional Law of India*, 323-24. [AIR 1994 SC 1918].

11 Charles Prabakar and Paul Mohan Raj, 55.

12 Durga Das Basu, *Introduction to the Constitution of India*, 19th ed. (Nagpur: Wadhwa and Company, 2003),114-15.

13 P. K. Majumdar & R. P. Kataria, *Commentary on the Constitution of India*, 481.

of religion. And it treats all religions equally.'[14] It is not an 'atheistic State' but it is 'neutral' in matters of religion.[15] In a secular stat "the state does not identify itself with any religion."[16] It is opposed to intolerance[17] but it regulates the secular activities connected with religion 'by enacting law'[18] without interfering with 'things which are essentially religious.' It can interfere if a particular religious practice offends public order, morality, health and contravenes any law of social, economic or political regulation.'[19] No doubt, many questions arise in our minds but let us wait a while for more clarity.

Religion

Like the word "secular," the term "religion" is also not defined in the Constitution,[20] and therefore one has to rely upon some of the definitions given in the Supreme Court Judgments. It is also true that the term 'religion' is beyond any form of convincing definition.

The Supreme Court has held that religion is a matter of faith with individuals or communities and it is not necessarily theistic. A religion may only lay down a code of ethical rules for its followers to accept, it might prescribe rituals and observances, ceremonies and modes of worship which are regarded as an integral part of religion, and those forms and observances might extend even to maters of food and dress.[21] Further "religion is not merely an opinion, doctrine or belief; it has its outward expression in acts as well. Hence, religious practices or performances of acts in pursuance of religious belief are as much part of religion as faith or belief in particular doctrines."[22]

The courts have made a distinction that "religion in its doctrinal and ritual aspect is a private purpose while the administration of property dedicated to the public for religious purposes is a public purpose."[23] Also, the court is competent to decide whether 'doctrines and practices' of each religion are essential or nonessential.'[24] These wider definitions of religion help understand 'freedom to practice religion' in the context of many religions and even ideologies.

14 V. D. Mahajan, *Constitutional Law of India*, 7th ed. (Lucknow: Eastern Book Company, 1991), 274.

15 J. N. Pandey, *The Constitutional Law of India*, 323.

16 M. P. Jain, *Indian Constitutional Law*, 526.

17 Charles Prabakar and Paul Mohan Raj, 57.

18 J. N. Pandey, *The Constitutional Law of India*, 323. [AIR 1994 SC 1918].

19 Durga Das Basu, *Introduction to the Constitution of India*, 116.

20 T. K. Tope, *Constitutional Law of India*, 225.

21 J. N. Pandey, *The Constitutional Law of India*) 325.

22 The Madras Law Journal Office, *The Constitution of India* (Madras: The Madras Law Journal Office, 1970), 259.

23 The Madras Law Journal Office, *The Constitution of India*, 260.

24 P. M. Bakshi, *The Constitution of India*, 63.

Before entering into detailed aspects of religious freedom in India it is worthwhile to recollect some of the limitations. They are: (1)it is subject to public order, morality and health, (2) subject to the other provisions of Part III of the Constitution, (3) subject to any existing law regulating or restricting an economic, financial, political, or other secular activity which may be associated with religious practice, (4) subject to law providing for social welfare and reform, and (5) subject to any law that may be made by the State and regulating or restricting the activities aforesaid or providing for social welfare and reform.[25]

Freedom of Conscience

To begin with, "freedom of religion under the Indian Constitution means freedom to have any religion, freedom to convert to any religion and freedom to have no religion."[26] The first step towards right to freedom of religion is freedom of conscience. Although Art. 25 (1) provides for freedom of conscience[27] to every person, whether citizen or non-citizen,[28] the Constitution has not defined the expression 'freedom of conscience.'[29] Thus here too for definition one has to rely on the judgments of the Supreme Court.

Accordingly, the term 'freedom of conscience' connotes the right of a person to entertain beliefs and doctrines concerning matters which are regarded by him to be conducive to his spiritual well-being. The freedom of conscience is the inner freedom of the citizen to mould his own relation with God in any way he likes.'[30]

Article 25 guarantees "freedom of conscience" to every citizen, and not merely to the followers of one particular religion. Hence, if a person purposely undertakes conversion of another person to his religion, as distinguished from his effort to transmit or spread the tenets of his religion that would impinge on the "freedom of conscience," guaranteed to all the citizens of the country alike.'[31]

One can, of course, voluntarily adopt another religion, but 'force, fraud, inducement or allurement' takes away the free consent (freedom of conscience) from the individual.'[32] The Constitution gives full freedom to individuals 'to develop inner life in their own way and in accordance with the dictates of their conscience.'[33]

Freedom of religion begins at 'internal' or conscience (psychological) level. And hence the decision to accept or change over to a religion is personal in the

25 The Madras Law Journal Office, *The Constitution of India*, 259.

26 P. K. Majumdar & R. P. Kataria, *Commentary on the Constitution of India*, 493.

27 J. N. Pandey, *The Constitutional Law of India*, 325.

28 The Madras Law Journal Office, *The Constitution of India*, 259.

29 T. K. Tope, *Constitutional Law of India*, 225.

30 V. D. Mahajan, *Constitutional Law of India*, 274-75. [AIR 1954 SC 388: 1954 SCR 1055].

31 J. N. Pandey, *The Constitutional Law of India*, 323-26.

32 Durga Das Basu, *Introduction to the Constitution of India*, 117.

33 Charles Prabakar and Paul Mohan Raj, 55.

first place. Does India really provide for 'freedom of conscience' in the present situation?

Profess

When freedom of conscience becomes articulate and expressed in outward form it is 'to profess, practice and propagate religion. Art. 25 (1) guarantees freedom to profess religion.[34] It means 'to state publicly one's creed or faith.'[35] It also means 'to declare freely and openly one's faith and belief.'[36] Further it means, 'to avow publicly and to make an open declaration of one's belief. A declaration of one's belief means, it would be known to those whom it may interest.[37]

The constitution has envisaged that the first level of freedom of religion is personal, internal or at the conscience level and the second stage of the freedom of religion is public declaration of a person's belief and faith. Every person who has decided in his/her conscious to follow a particular religion has the freedom to publicly declare his/her beliefs and faith.

Practice/Religious Practice

The third stage of the freedom of religion guaranteed in the Indian Constitution is 'to practice' one's religion. It is an outward expression of one's inner conviction and public profession. The expression 'practice religion' is complicated and has been subjected to rigorous legal scrutiny. Here comes the issue of essential and nonessential of religions; and religious and secular aspects of practices.

Art. 25 (1) guarantees a person freedom to 'practice' religion.[38] It means 'the freedom to perform certain acts in pursuance of the faith,'[39] 'religion, religious belief,[40] and 'practical expression in any manner.' In simple terms, 'practice of religion' 'is concerned primarily with religious worship, ritual and observations.'[41]

These acts are prescribed by religious order in which one believes and they are 'as much a part of religion as faith or belief in any particular doctrine.'[42] These practices are subject to 'State regulation imposed to secure order, public health and morals of the people.'

The first criterion to consider whether a religious practice is integral to or essential part of a religion, that practice 'must be regarded by the said religion as its essential and integral part.' Secondly, whether the 'community following

34 J. N. Pandey, *The Constitutional Law of India*, 325.

35 T. K. Tope, *Constitutional Law of India*, 225.

36 J. N. Pandey, *The Constitutional Law of India*, 325.

37 The Madras Law Journal Office, *The Constitution of India,* 260.

38 J. N. Pandey, *The Constitutional Law of India*, 325.

39 T. K. Tope, *Constitutional Law of India*, 225.

40 The Madras Law Journal Office, *The Constitution of India,* 260.

41 P. M. Bakshi, *The Constitution of India*, 64.

42 V. D. Mahajan, *Constitutional Law of India*, 275.

the religion' accepts such acts.[43] Thirdly and mainly it has to be decided by the courts.[44]

In conflicting situations, 'the Court may have to enquire whether the practice in question is religious in character and if it is whether it can be regarded as an integral or essential part of the religion.'[45] These are not to clearly distinguish between religion and religious practice, but only to resolve conflicts.

Integral

In a case related to a temple in UP the Supreme Court said 'Right to manage temple is not an integral part of religion. It can be regulated by law.'[46]

In Jammu and Kashmir, in a case related to a Hindu temple, "the Court made distinction between 'religious service' and the person who performs service.' The performance of the religious service according to the tenets, customs and usages prevalent in a place of worship is an integral part of the religion's faith and belief and it cannot be regulated by the State. But, the State has powers to regulate the appointment of the priest and can fix his emoluments. The Government can also abolish his customary share in the offerings to the deity."[47]

Another significant judgment was 'a disposition towards making gift for charitable or religious purpose may be a pious act of a person but the same cannot be said to be an integral part of any religion.'[48]

'Khursheed Ahmad Khan filed a petition against the Uttar Pradesh government's decision to remove him from service as Irrigation Supervisor for contracting a second marriage when his first marriage was still in existence. Khan challenged that it violated his right to freely practice his religion. The Court held that 'what was protected under Article 25 was the religious faith and not a practice which may run counter to public order, health or morality. Polygamy was not integral part of religion and monogamy was a reform within the power of the State under Article 25.'[49]

43 The Madras Law Journal Office, *The Constitution of India*, 261.

44 V. N. Shukla, The Constitution of India, 8th ed. (Lucknow: Eastern Book Company, 1990), 162.

45 The Madras Law Journal Office, *The Constitution of India*, 261.

46 P. M. Bakshi, *The Constitution of India*, 65.

47 J. N. Pandey, *The Constitutional Law of India*, 330. [*Bhuri v. State of J.& K.*, AIR 1997 SC 1711].

48 P. M. Bakshi, *The Constitution of India*, 62. [*John Vallamattom v. Union of India*, AIR 2003 SC2902: (2003) 6 SCC 611: (2003) 3 KLT 66].

49 "Right to Religion not Above Public Morality: SC," *The Hindu* (Vijayawada), 10 February 2015, 10.

Essential

In a significant case the Supreme Court held that, 'State can in exercise of its sovereign power acquire places of worship like mosques, churches, temples etc., 'if it is necessary for maintenance of law and order.' 'While offer of prayer or worship is a religious practice its offering at every location where such prayers can be offered would not be an essential religious practice, unless the right to worship at a particular place is itself an integral part of that right.' A mosque is not an essential part of the practice of the religion of Islam and Namaz (prayer) by Muslims may be offered anywhere, even in open.'[50]

"After the Babari Mosque was demolished on December 6, 1992 at Ayodhya, the Union Government acquired the whole property surrounding the mosque. This was challenged by the petitioners on the ground that it was violative of Arts. 25 and 26 of the Constitution as they were deprived of their right to worship in the mosque but Hindus were allowed to worship therein. The Court held the Act valid as it does not interfere with the essential element of religion."[51]

The Commissioner of Police in Calcutta refused permission to the use of a loud-speaker five times a day for calling the Azan (call for prayer) as several residents of the locality complained against the practice.'[52] The Calcutta High Court said, restrictions imposed by the State on the use of microphones and loudspeakers at the time of Azan is not violative of right under Art. 25. Azan is certainly an essential and integral part of Islam, but use of microphone and loudspeakers are not an essential and integral part. Traditionally and according to the religious order, Azen has to be given by the Imam or the person in charge of the mosques through their own voice and this is sanctioned under the religious order.[53]

In the Church of God (Full Gospel) in India v. K.K.R.M.C. Welfare Association, in KKR Nagar, Madhavaram 'the Supreme Court has held that in the exercise of the right to religious freedom under Arts. 25 and 26, no person can be allowed to create noise pollution or disturb the peace of the others.' The custom of religious prayer through the use of loudspeaker is not an essential element of any religion.[54] It was also said, "no religion prescribes that prayers should be performed by disturbing the peace of others nor does it preach that they should be through voice-amplifiers or beating of drums.[55]

---

50 J. N. Pandey, *The Constitutional Law of India*, 328.[(1994) 6 SCC 360].

51 J. N. Pandey, *The Constitutional Law of India*, 328.[(1994) 6 SCC 360].

52 The Madras Law Journal Office, *The Constitution of India,* 261.

53 J. N. Pandey, *The Constitutional Law of India*, 329. [AIR 1999 Cal 15].

54 J. N. Pandey, *The Constitutional Law of India*, 329-30.

55 P. M. Bakshi, *The Constitution of India*, 64. [*Church of God (Full Gospel) in India v. K.K.R. Majestic Colony Welfare Association*, AIR 2000 SC 2773: (2000) 7 SCC 282: 2000 SCC (cri) 1350].

"One of the prescriptions of religious rites introduced from the year 1966 for daily performance by an Ananda Margi is Tandava dance of Lord Siva. This dance is to be performed with a human skull, a small symbolic knife, a Trishul, a Lathi and a Damroo."[56] The commissioner of police prohibited such practice in public. The Court, after going into the religious books and practices of the Ananda Margis, held that tandava dance in public is not an essential part of Ananda Marga.'[57]

In a case related to Bihar, the Supreme Court held that the sacrifice of cow on the *Bakrid* day was not an essential part of Mohammedan religion and hence could be prohibited by State under clause (2) (a) of Article 25 though the practice was enjoined by the Koran. Art. 25 exempts only the essential religious practices from State regulation.[58]

Secular/Non-Secular

In the case of national leaders, when calamity or tragedy overtakes them the State is obligated to arrange for their funeral in a manner befitting their status and in accordance with the pursuits of the particular religion to which the departed personality belonged. The performance of such duty by the State can, by no stretch of imagination, be characterized as non-secular activity.[59]

In a judgment of far reaching importance in the *National Anthem* case, where three Jehova's Witnesses children were expelled from a school for refusing to sing the National Anthem, 'the Supreme Court has held that no person can be compelled to sing the National Anthem "if he has genuine, conscientious religious objection."'[60] The court upheld the prohibition of the religious order that prevented the children to sing the National Anthem.[61] Having delved deep into 'religious practice' let us move to another interesting aspect of freedom of religion.

Propagate

The third level of religious freedom guaranteed by the Constitution under Article 25 is to propagate a religion. The original expression used by Ambedkar was 'right to preach and to convert.'[62] Propagation is transmitting one's religious conviction and practices (tenets) to others[63] for edification. It only means persuasion and

56 V. D. Mahajan, *Constitutional Law of India*, 276.

57 V. N. Shukla, The Constitution of India, 162. [(1984) 4 SCC 522].

58 J. N. Pandey, *The Constitutional Law of India*, 335- 36. [AIR 1958 SC 731].

59 Chaudhari & Chaturvedi, *Law of Fundamental Rights*, 787.

60 J. N. Pandey, *The Constitutional Law of India*, 326. [Bajoe Emmanual v. State of Kerala, (1984) JSCC 615], [three children].

61 Charles Prabakar and Paul Mohan Raj, 59.

62 D. C. Ahir, *Dr. Ambedkar and Indian Constitution*, 83.

63 T. K. Tope, *Constitutional Law of India*, 225.

exposition of one's religion without an element of coercion. The propaganda may be done by a person in his individual capacity or on behalf of some church or institution.'[64]

The right to propagate religion does not include the right to 'insult the religion of other persons.' Anyone who propagates the benefits of his religion is likely to extol his own and, to some extent, dispute the truth and efficiency of another religion. Propagation of religion cannot otherwise be carried on and within limits, regard being had to the law of blasphemy, profanity, etc.[65] Only 'the aggravated form of insult to religion is penalized' under IPC but 'insult to religion offered unwittingly or carelessly or without any deliberate or malicious intention to outrage the religious feeling of that class are covered under the freedom of expression.'[66]

Propagation does not include 'a right to forcible conversion.'[67] Plainly, there is no fundamental right to convert any person to one's own religion. Hence legislation prohibiting conversion by force, inducement and fraud to one's own religion is not violative of Article 25 (1). In Rev. Stainislaus v. state of M.P., the Court laid down that Article 25 (1) grants only the right to convert another person to one's own religion by an exposition of its tenets.[68] The appellant argued that right to 'propagate' one's religion meant the right to convert person to one's own religion and was a fundamental right under Art. 25 (1) of the Constitution. Secondly, he argued Parliament alone had the power to make the law and not the State Legislature. Rejecting the contentions of the appellant the Supreme Court held that impugned Acts were meant to avoid disturbances to the public order by prohibiting conversion from one's religion to another in a manner reprehensible to the conscience of the community.[69]

Public Order, Morality and Health

These expressions have wide connotations as they are not exactly defined in the article. Our freedom of conscience, freedom to profess, practice and propagate religion can no way disturb public order, morality and health. 'Our history is witness to this.'[70] For example, slaughter of cattle or indecent exposure of one's person in a public place cannot be justified on plea of practice of religious rites. Of course, "Morality in this context, has reference to that morality which the law

64 V. D. Mahajan, *Constitutional Law of India*, 275.

65 The Madras Law Journal Office, *The Constitution of India*, 262.

66 P. K. Majumdar & R. P. Kataria, *Commentary on the Constitution of India*, 482.

67 P. M. Bakshi, *The Constitution of India*, 64.

68 T. K. Tope, *Constitutional Law of India*, 225.[*Stainislaus v. State of Madhya Pradesh*, AIR 1977 SC 908: (1977) 1 SCC 677:1977 Cri LJ 551].

69 J. N. Pandey, *The Constitutional Law of India*, 333. [AIR 1977 SC 908].

70 P. K. Majumdar & R. P. Kataria, *Commentary on the Constitution of India*, 479.

has concerned itself to maintain."[71] Likewise, in the name of religious practice, 'untouchability or traffic in human beings' *e.g.*, system of *Devadasis* (as prevalent in South India) cannot be tolerated. The freedom to practice religion cannot affect the exercise of the other freedoms under this part.[72]

Conversion by prohibited means can lead to breach of public order.[73] Prohibition of Tandava dance is done with the same spirit. On the one hand, 'the right to take out religious processions through its public streets subject to such directions as a magistrate may lawfully give is guarantee by Art. 25, on the other, the right to take a profession along the highway is not a fundamental right and the Magistrate can impose restrictions if he apprehends a breach of the peace.[74] This is done to protect public order, morality and health.

In Bombay, under the Provincial Municipal Corporation Act, 1949, the Municipal Corporation had ordered the demolition of some parts of the two mosques situated on the main road of Surat district of the State of Gujarat to widen the road. The Court held that the acquisition of a religious place or a part thereof is not prohibited by the Constitution and therefore can be acquired in the public interest for widening the road. However, the court categorically suggested that before such acquisition or demolition all other options are to be thoroughly examined.[75]

Graves in unauthorized and illegal places can be shifted.[76] In U.P. Varanasi, two graves belonging to Sunnis were in the vicinity of Shias. The Supreme Court upheld that the shifting of two Sunni graves to avoid clashes between two religious communities or sects does not affect religious rights being in the interest of public order, though the Shariat Law is against shifting of graves. Again "the ecclesiastical edict or right not to disturb an interred corpse is not absolute as will be clear from Sec. 176 (3) of the criminal Procedure Code which permits its exhumation for the purpose of crime detection."[77]

Having elaborately analyzed the aspects of freedom of conscience, freedom to profess, practice and propagate religion subject to public order, health, morality and the other provisions of this part, let me take you through the areas in which States can legislate laws and regulate religious practices.

---

71 Chaudhari & Chaturvedi, *Law of Fundamental Rights*, 791.

72 J. N. Pandey, *The Constitutional Law of India*, 333.

73 V. D. Mahajan, *Constitutional Law of India*, 276.

74 The Madras Law Journal Office, *The Constitution of India,* 261.

75 J. N. Pandey, *The Constitutional Law of India*, 329. [AIR 1998 Guj. 234.]

76 Chaudhari & Chaturvedi, *Law of Fundamental Rights*, 799.

77 J. N. Pandey, *The Constitutional Law of India*, 334-35.

Economic, Financial, Political and Secular Activities Associated with Religious Practices – Clause (2) (a)

Freedom to 'practice religion' extends only to those activities which are essential to religion. It does not cover secular activities connected with religion. 'The legislation contemplated under Article 25 (2) (a) can modify even the personal law.'[78]

Article 25, clause 2 (a) saves the power of the State to regulate or restrict secular activities associated with religious practice. What is the dividing line between religious and secular activities is difficult to decide and it is for the court to determine. But subject to that, the religious denomination is entitled to lay down its rites and ceremonies.'[79] In the case of determining whether a matter is religious or secular, 'each case must be judged by its own facts and circumstances.'[80] For example, "Service of a priest is a secular activity and can be regulated by the State under article 25 (2)."[81]

Religious missions have freedom to spend their money as they deem necessary. The Government is concerned, (i) to inquire how much foreign money has come in aid to a foreign mission.; (ii) to see whether money is being used in a way which may promote breach of public order, morality and health; (iii) to see whether there has been any attempt forcibly or fraudulently to convert a person from his own belief to another.

The Government also may initiate, (i) an enquiry into the political activity associated with religion; (ii) inquiry into the attitude of foreign missions towards Indians; (iii) inquiry into social relations between Christians and non-Christians, (iv) inquiry into the operations of foreign missions, particularly to see whether such operations extend to areas largely populated by Scheduled Castes and the aborigines; and (v) inquiry into whether the *pracharakas* of any mission adopt methods offending public order, health or morality.[82]

Providing for Social Welfare and Reform

Under clause (2) (b) of Art 25, the State is empowered to make laws for social welfare and social reform. The State can also eradicate social practices and dogmas which stand in the path of the country's onward progress. Where there is a conflict between the need of social welfare and reform on the one hand and religious practice on the other, religion must yield.[83] Therefore, a law enacted for

78 Chaudhari & Chaturvedi, *Law of Fundamental Rights*, 795.

79 P. M. Bakshi, *The Constitution of India*, 62-63.

80 J. N. Pandey, *The Constitutional Law of India*, 335.

81 P. M. Bakshi, *The Constitution of India*, 62. (*Bhuri Nath v. Stae of jammu& Kashmir*, AIR 1997 SC 1711: (1997 2 SCC 745).

82 Chaudhari & Chaturvedi, *Law of Fundamental Rights*, 792.

83 J. N. Pandey, *The Constitutional Law of India*, 337. [AIR 1953 Bom 84].

introducing social reform cannot be challenged as violating the right freely to profess, practice and propagate religion.[84]

For example, 'polygamy is not an essential part of the Hindu religion, therefore, it can be regulated by law.'[85] A prohibition of the same by law does not contravene the freedom of religion because providing for compulsory monogamy and prohibiting bigamy is valid as a measure of social reform.[86] Further, 'marriage is a social institution.'[87]

Haryana Panchayati Raj Act, 1994 disqualifies persons having more than two children from contesting election for the post of Sarpanch and Panch in panchyat does not violate Article 25 of the Constitution. The court held 'the Muslim law permits marrying four women but does not anywhere mandates it as a duty to perform four marriages. Such practices which encourage bigamy or polygamy can be regulated by making law.'[88]

Under this sub-clause the State is empowered to throw open all Hindu religious institutions of a public character, to all classes and sections of Hindus.' But the State cannot regulate the manner in which the worship of the deity is performed by the authorized *pujaris* of the temple or the hours and days on which the temple is to be kept open for *darshan* or *puja* for devotees. Similarly 'the right of Sikhs to carry *Kirpans* is recognized as a religious practice in Explanation 1 of article 25. 'This does not mean that he can keep any number of *Kirpans.*'[89] Therefore, legislation in the area of personal laws cannot be challenged on the ground that it interferes with religious freedom.[90]

Recollection of insights from Article 25 through an almost thorough discussion has helped one to obtain a broader, but not a complete, understanding of freedom of religion in India within the frame work of the Indian Constitution. Now, it is possible to consider 'diligent Christian witness.'

Diligent Christian Witness

The word 'diligent' broadly means industrious, meticulous, conscientious, attentive, careful, etc. It has been deliberately chosen to convey that there is a need in India for Christians (Church) to labor hard with much prudence in the light of the freedom of religion guaranteed under fundamental rights.

It is so because we are faced with the challenge of our secular principles of non-discrimination on religious grounds and religious neutrality of the State are

84 The Madras Law Journal Office, *The Constitution of India,* 262.

85 J. N. Pandey, *The Constitutional Law of India*, 337.[AIR 1953 Bom 84].

86 The Madras Law Journal Office, *The Constitution of India,* 260-63.

87 P. K. Majumdar & R. P. Kataria, *Commentary on the Constitution of India*, 474.

88 J. N. Pandey, *The Constitutional Law of India*, 335. [AIR 2003 SC 3057].

89 J. N. Pandey, *The Constitutional Law of India*, 337-38. [*VenkataramanuDevaru v. State of Mysore*, AIR 1958 SC 255.,*Vaguapurushcdji v. Muldas*, AIR 1966 SC 1119].

90 T. K. Tope, *Constitutional Law of India*, 226.

under constant threat and pressure from communal ideologies that are lurking behind political organizations. There is a possible and legitimate apprehension that efforts are on to replace non discrimination and neutrality of the State with religious discrimination and partiality. Noted writer Nayantara Sahgal said, 'people were being killed for not agreeing with the ruling ideology' and 'in this rising tide of hatred, India is being unmade, being destroyed.'[91] Our witness can become part of rebuilding and remaking India.

The secular State of ours cannot fail to providingthe same constitutional protection to all the religions in India. She is expected to fight 'religious intolerance' among different religions. She is beautiful and fascinating as long as not wedded to 'identify with one religion.' However, the concern for our witness is that the government might consciously protect one religion, identify with one religion and become intolerant of other religions. That is why 'Nayantara Sahgal has returned the prestigious Sahitya Akademi Award in protest against what she called "vanishing space" for diversity.'[92] Can Christian witness ignore these concerns?

It is too early but often we are overwhelmed, because of the new developments around us, to question the sincerity of the government to maintain the credibility of the principles of secularism. President Pranab Mukherjee said, 'India's core civilisational values of diversity, tolerance, and plurality have kept it united for centuries and that cannot be wasted.'[93] These principles are the bedrock of our witness at all times and at all situations. To continue this blessed privilege we should be vigilantly diligent and our witness too should be relevant. It is said, "rarely do foundational threats to Constitutions come as sudden events, they often build up as liberties and freedoms are incrementally compromised."[94] We have to raise a contextual voice that can synchronise with other similar voices.

The identification of 'positive secularism' within the frame work of Indian Constitution is encouraging. It implies a conscious attempt to coexist with each other (religions). It is hard to find any such effort from the power centers. Rather, what we see is a clear effort to exclude the other irrespective of their potentials and contributions towards nation building and transformation. These naïve signs call for continuous struggle and prudent witnessing. Our sustained engagement in dialogue is a fruitful consideration.

Although, the Supreme Court has time and again attempted a broader and inclusive definition of religion we are to be conscious of the jurisdiction of

91 Smriti Kak Ramachandran & Anuradha Raman, "Nayantara Sahgal Protests Dadri Lynching, Returns Akademi Award," *The Hindu* (Vijayawada), 7 October 2015, 1.

92 SmritiKak Ramachandran & Anuradha Raman, 1.

93 Smita Gupta, Pranab Warns against Letting Go of India's core Values," *The Hindu* (Vijayawada), 8 October 2015, 1.

94 Anup Surendranath, Beefed-up Curbs, Feeble Resistance," *The Hindu* (Vijayawada), 10 October 2015, 10.

courts in deciding essential, integral and non-secular aspects of religion. The only worrying concern is whether the same yard stick and speed is applied for all the religious practices in India. Referring to the many recent killings (rationalists, etc.,) it is said, "in all these cases, justice drags its feet. The Prime Minister remains silent on this reign of terror."[95] What is law to one religion should become law to all the religions, including Christian.

Freedom of conscience is expected to be free from influence. The reality however is that psychological threats are created. It prevents from freely deciding for oneself without coercion. Often terrorizing and fake circumstances are engineered to influence people's conscience. There is a tendency to dictate what an Indian should say, respect, and practice. Failure to do so is threatened with dare consequence of exclusion. Ensuring our careful attention to such developments can be part of our witness.

Subjects that are considered non-essential, non-integral and secular aspects of religion have to be carefully handled to eliminate artificial doubts about our commitment and contributions to the Constitution and Nation.

It is healthy that courts can interfere in 'freedom of religion' and regulate matters when abuse is apprehended. If partisan consideration is perceived, we have a responsibility, as a part of our witness, to make available such data to the public.

The States' power to legitimately acquire or alter religious structures for the purpose of public order and social welfare has to be complied with. The advice that such acts should be the final consideration is appreciable. Doubt is whether property, structures and practices of numerically powerful experience similar situation. Why could not an idol illegally placed in a mosque removed and the situation is allowed to spiral up leading to constant tension while even Muslim and Christian tombs can be exhumed or shifted. We may need to show our solidarity, as a part of our witnessing, towards acceptable solutions.

It is true that "the exercise of our rights should not infringe the rights of others."[96] But a seeming presumption is that Muslim's Azan (five times a day) and Christian prayers with loud music are restricted while the noise pollution and public nuisance caused all through the year are not regulated by the States. The increasing number of bans on certain practices and the newer presentation of Hinduism in contrast to British, Nehru and Indian intellectuals are worrying. It is unheard in the recent past that communal programs and social evils of numerically powerful are banned in India. Our plans of witness can include some lawful awareness programs.

Leave alone the apprehensions and make clear that fixing a grave or religious structure in disputed places is not the alternative to law abiding. Being law abiding

95 Smriti Kak Ramachandran & Anuradha Raman, 1.

96 V. K. Kuriakose, "Religious Pollution," *Indian Currents* XXVII/38 (21-27 September, 2015), 39.

citizens and avoiding unreasonable conflicts can be a form of witness. Hence, it is said, "if we seek justice from the State and the law, we have a moral obligation to act with justice within our churches, communities and families."[97]

The State honor accorded to public personalities in accordance with their particular religious rites cannot uncharitably be accused as non-secular. Even the court had respected the religious sentiments of people who did not participate in the singing of the national anthem. It is to be respected that although force, fraud and allurement or inducement is not accepted in the process of propagation (religious mobility), exposition of one's religious tenets and disputing one's faith with others without causing insult is accepted. In spite of freedom of religion Acts being legislated, we may work out our diligent witness keeping these opportunities in mind.

Even when our personal laws are intervened, our witness can be focused and supportive to the health of the society (social welfare) at large with the responsibility that state can regulate our financial, political and secular activities.

Conclusion

To conclude, "hatred begets hatred. In the modern world, there is no place for chauvinism. How could anyone forget the noble contribution of the Christian Missionaries as pioneers in the field of education and Medicare extending to the remote interiors of tribal areas? The role of the Christian in presenting the image of a united and integrated India cannot be lost of."[98]

No religion seems to be non-missionary. Love your enemy has no parallel nor 'do unto others what you would expect them to do for you' found any alternative. Render to Caesar the things that are Caesar's, to God the things that are God's, for diligent witness.

97 Sarasu Esther Thomas, *Law for Christians in Contemporary India* (Bangalore: BTESSC, 2014), 150.

98 Charles Prabakar and Paul Mohan Raj, 61.

15

Narratives of an Ideology and Sustainable Capability Enhancement

Introduction

This chapter is an attempt to study 'a belligerent ideological narrative' that challenges to obliterate the thus-far prevalent constructs in various realms and to prepare ourselves for improving the capabilities of the deprived sections through a sustainable interpretation of the word of God in the background of 500th year of the dawning of the Reformation.

The word ideology, in essence, has an aggressive nature and political underpinning that are occasionally explicit and more often implicit in some of its narratives. The narratives are ideological goals that wish to replace broader perspectives. The expression 'Sustainable capability enhancement' is used to highlight the dynamic role of 'interpreting scripture' to derive substantial resources to empower people who are otherwise disadvantaged of basic facilities and privileges to improve themselves. It is also to reflect that any interpretation of scripture should preserve its classic nature. While allowing critical musings, it should do justice to all the previous interpretations and explore relevant contextual interpretations to allow the inherent potency of the word of God to enhance the capabilities of the ones who are in need. More aptly and precisely 'sustainable' refers to the principle of interpretation or hermeneutics and 'capability enhancement' to mission, implying that both interpretation and mission should be 'sustainable.'

It is not unusual to be aggressive for any ideology that enjoys 'state patronage' as the Church might have been in the pre-reformation era. What is striking in the present context is that we are amidst the new narrative and reforming ourselves to continue in a sustainable capability enhancement.

Prevalence of the Ideology

The Hindutva (loosely translated as Hinduness) ideology that was once on an experimental mode has switched over to implementation [mode] of its ideologies in conjunction with the policies of the government. As a result, the 'modern, secular and democratic' and 'inclusive' India is in for change.[1] This change brings in political gains to Bharatiya Janata Party (BJP), the off shoot of Rashtriya Swayamsevak Sangh (RSS) which advocates Hindutva. The Hindutva affiliates, as an essential step forward, work 'to create a pan-Hindu identity.'[2] The ideology has used 'democratic processes like elections' and 'majority minority polarity' to gain political power.[3] Further consolidation of the narrative is glaringly obvious in the appointment of ideologically inclined persons to important constitutional positions of the country.[4] It is an irony that this move has been financially supported by thousands of educated and well-to-do Hindu NRIs who migrated to Europe and USA to enjoy the freedom and wealth under democracy.[5]

The main objective of the narratives seems to bring in 'singularity' in the place of 'plurality,' 'majoritarian state in the place of secular,' 'prohibition in the place of freedom,' 'terrorizing instead of confidence building,' 'polarizing in the place of harmony,' 'hatred in the place of understanding,' 'intolerance in the place of tolerance' mob lawlessness in the place of constitutional justice and myth in the place of science, reason and history. Sitaram Yechury in his farewell speech in the Rajya Sabha lucidly cognized the risk underlying the new narratives as "if you try to impose a uniformity, whether it is religious uniformity or linguistic uniformity or cultural uniformity, on our diversity, then this country can never remain together."[6] The combination of an aggressive ideology and the emergence of BJP in the context of identity politics of India, together aid the new narratives.

Ideology and Identity Politics

The BJP's contemporary political articulations and policy formulations are a paradigm shift driven by powerful ideological forces. It's an altogether new brand of politics[7] that had its inception in the 'development of identity politics', in 1980s and 90s. The identity politics of BJP utilizes 'community and caste prejudice' to polarize the people.[8] It is apprehended that the new paradigm [narrative] can cause

1 Lancy Lobo, "De-Humanization through Caste and Religion: Two Shining Human Rights Activists of Gujarat, India," *Third Millennium XX*/2 (April-June, 2017), 17.

2 Vikhar Ahmed Sayeed, "Communal Cauldron," *Frontline* (September 30, 2016), 52.

3 Lancy Lobo, 17.

4 Lancy Lobo, 17.

5 Lancy Lobo, 17.

6 Special Correspondent, "Yechury thanks BJP, Cong. leaders," *The Hindu* (Vijayawada), 11 August 2017, 11.

7 Happymon Jacob, "When the paradigm shifts," *The Hindu* (Vijayawada), 10 August 2017, 8.

8 Madhu Prasad, "Learning in a saffron-tinted market," *Frontline* (September1, 2017), 60.

'ideological struggles, street battles, regional divisions, and attempts at revisiting the fundamentals of the Indian Union, among others.'[9] If the paradigm shift does not consider the 'pluralistic accommodation, religious sensitivity, regional differences and civil rights then there may be 'civil war-like situations, mounting dissent and violence.'[10]

The outcome of the combination of ideology and identity politics seems to be startling. According to Mohammad Hamid Ansari, former Vice President, in recent times there were "enhanced apprehensions of insecurity amongst segments of our citizen body, particularly Dalits, Muslims and Christians."[11] In connivance with this combination, governments remain silent as mobs have taken law in their hands 'to terrorize Dalits and religious minorities'[12] in pursuit of the new narrative.

Risks of the Present Narrative

Amartya Sen analyses the danger of promoting singular identities like-civilization, religion, nationalities, class, etc., and calls this as a "solitarist" approach to human identity. And he writes, "a solitarist approach can be a good way of misunderstanding nearly everyone in the world."[13] He, without mincing words, says "our shared humanity gets savagely challenged when the manifold divisions in the world are unified into one allegedly dominant system of classification."[14]

Sen points out that 'indeed, many of the conflicts and barbarities in the world are sustained through the illusion of a unique and choiceless identity.' It is relevant in the context of the new narrative to note that "in fact, a major source of potential conflict in the contemporary world is the presumption that people can be uniquely categorized based on religion or culture."[15] He also said a solitarist approach 'makes the world much more flammable'[16] and 'contribute to social tension and violence.'[17] According to him, in the context of many identities 'reasoning and scrutiny can play a major role both in the specification of identities and in thinking through the relative strengths of their respective claims.'[18]

---

9 Happymon Jacob, 8.

10 Happymon Jacob, 8.

11 Venkitesh Ramakrishnan, "Creed above country: Rise of the Right," *Frontline* (September 1, 2017), 15-16.

12 Prabhat Patnaik, "From Revolution to Counter-revolution," *Frontline* (September1, 2017), 7-8.

13 Amartya Sen, *Identity and Violence: The Illusion of Destiny*, (London: Penguin Books, 2006), xii.

14 Amartya Sen, *Identity and Violence: The Illusion of Destiny*, xiii.

15 Amartya Sen, *Identity and Violence: The Illusion of Destiny*, xv.

16 Amartya Sen, *Identity and Violence: The Illusion of Destiny*, 16.

17 Amartya Sen, *Identity and Violence: The Illusion of Destiny*, 21.

18 Amartya Sen, *Identity and Violence: The Illusion of Destiny*, 29.

Unfortunately the present narrative is opposed to 'reasoning and scrutiny' of its claims.

Brand Nationalism

'Brand nationalism' is a part of the project of the current narrative. It conveniently distinguishes between political nationalism and geographical nationalism and suggests that people who fought for Independence upheld political nationalism and people who did not involve in freedom struggle uphold geographical nationalism. The root of the scheme is setting one against the other.

Mohammad Hamid Ansari said 'the version of nationalism that places cultural commitments at its core is usually perceived as the most conservative and illiberal form of nationalism' and that 'it promotes intolerance and arrogant patriotism.'[19] Eric J. Lott writes, "nowhere, probably, have communal roots been as defining of a person as in traditional India."[20]

Some call the present state of affairs as a counter-revolution where rapid strides are being made towards a corporate-backed Hindu Rashtra.[21] In spite of the unreasonableness of the 'singular' narrative, "the combination of communalism and collaboration from Big Business imparts to the present regime a seeming invincibility."[22]

Suffocating Other Voices

The new narrative subverts the architects of democracy and democratic principles. For example, suspecting the intents of Ram Nath Kovind, the President of India, it is appealed that "though the government under Prime Minister Narendra Modi has gone to extraordinary lengths to eliminate references to the architect of democratic India, we expect the head of state to stand above partisan party politics."[23]

Democracy must have space for variety without leaning towards an identity or ideology. Sen writes, "Political and civil rights, especially those related to the guaranteeing of open discussion, debate, criticism, and dissent, are central to the processes of generating informed and reflected choices."[24] He goes on to say, "this is essential for the survival and prosperity of a country as remarkably varied

19 Venkitesh Ramakrishnan, "Creed above country: Rise of the Right," *Frontline* (September 1, 2017), 15-16.

20 Eric J. Lott, "Issues in Shaping an *Indian*-Christian Identity," in *We, the Church: Studies in Mission & Evangelization*, edited by Smitha P. Coffey & Donna Tracy Paul (New Delhi: Christian World Imprints, 2017), 39.

21 Prabhat Patnaik, "From Revolution to Counter-revolution," *Frontline* (September 1, 2017), 6.

22 Irfan Habib, "Inventing history to Inculcate Hatred," *Frontline* (September1, 2017), 36.

23 Neera Chandhoke, "Why Nehru Matters More Than Ever," *The Hindu* (Vijayawada), 8 August 2017, 8.

24 Amartya Sen, *Development as Freedom*, (US: Alfred A. Knopf, Inc., 1999), 153.

as India, which may have a Hindu majority, but which is also the third largest Muslim country in the world, in which millions of Christians, along with most of world's Sikhs, Parsees, and Jains, live."[25] Mohammad Hamid Ansari quoting S. Radhakrishnan, said "a democracy is distinguished by the protection it gives to minorities" and that it was "likely to degenerate into tyranny if it does not allow the opposition groups to criticize fairly, freely and frankly the policies of the government."[26] Many of the current 'terrorizing' incidents move in this direction.

Amartya Sen argues that "developing and strengthening a democratic system is an essential component of the process of development."[27] He also warns that mere democratic freedoms are of no avail. Sen illustrates from Sundarban that 'while the tigers are protected, nothing protects the miserable human beings [honey gatherers] who try to make a living by working in those woods.'[28] He deplores further 'if poverty drives human beings to take such terrible risks and perhaps to die terrible deaths' 'it might well be odd to concentrate on their liberty and political freedoms.'[29] His concerns fit fairly well into our context. It is a paradox that human lives being valued lesser than animals and killing an animal for a living is treated as more serious crime than killing a human being. We are in a situation where murderers roam free and the family and community of murdered are ostracized and booked.

Majority Psyche

A part of the new narrative is to obliterate the 'secular' character of the Indian Constitution and to instil a majority opinion. Hence, the Constitution is presented as "anti-Hindu"[30] and therefore to replace it with *Manusmriti* (Codes of Manu).[31] In reality, "it is not the Constitution which has failed the nation. It is the leaders who betrayed the trust which the framers of the Constitution reposed in them."[32] BJP's choices for top government positions poignantly are in this direction.

Ambedkar had apprehended this concern and said on November 4, 1948, that the Constitution 'is workable, it is flexible and it is strong enough to hold the country together both in peace time and in war time.' He also noted 'if things go wrong under the new Constitution, the reason will not be that we had a bad

---

25 Amartya Sen, *Development as Freedom*, 157.

26 Venkitesh Ramakrishnan, "Creed Above Country: Rise of the Right," *Frontline* (September 1, 2017), 15-16.

27 Amartya Sen, *Development as Freedom*, 157.

28 Amartya Sen, *Development as Freedom*, 146. [Sundarban is the place where the royal Bengal tigers are protected and it is also known for its honey hives which attract the poor to risk their lives for a living].

29 Amartya Sen, *Development as Freedom*, 146.

30 M. P. Raju, "Composite Culture and its Discontents," *Frontline* (September 1, 2017), 28.

31 M. P. Raju, "Composite Culture and its Discontents," *Frontline* (September 1, 2017), 28.

32 A. G. Noorani, "Enemies within the System," *Frontline* (September 1, 2017), 26.

Constitution. What we will have to say is that Man was Vile.'[33] He further added on November 25, 1949, "however good a Constitution may be, it is sure to turn out bad because those who are called to work it happen to be a bad lot."[34]

The Indian Constitution celebrates 'plurality' in contrast to the narrative of devastating 'cultural nationalism or chauvinism.'[35] In our times attempts to 'keeping traditions pure and unpolluted is hard to sustain.'[36] Hence, it is also argued that "the future of the world lies in finding a way in which different cultures can contribute their share to an integral development of humanity."[37]

Thus, Huntington's characterization of India as a "Hindu Civilization" is politically combustible[38] and 'confrontational in form and implication.'[39] This leads to the exploding of a 'majority psyche' in the form of 'mob constitution.'

Terrorizing: A New Paradigm

In the present context, "maligning intellectual and socio-politically sensitive critical inquiry as "extremist," "anti-national" and a seditious threat to state security have become today's common sense and are used as justification for current policy."[40] Assassination of Gauri Lankesh, a journalist, on 5th September 2017 signals a 'new and significant moment in the growing environment of intolerance in the country'[41] and 'has brought to focus again the discussion on ideological intolerance and a new brand of terrorism' 'to further a particular political ideology.'[42]

The US state department noted in its latest report that "there was an increase in violent incidents by cow protection groups against mostly Muslim victims, including killings, mob violence, assaults, and intimidation."[43] It added that 'India did not act against cow vigilantes' and 'the authorities have routinely refused to

33 A. G. Noorani, "Enemies within the System," 26.

34 A. G. Noorani, "Enemies within the System," 26.

35 Amartya Sen, *Development as Freedom*, (US: Alfred A. Knopf, Inc., 1999), 242.

36 Amartya Sen, *Development as Freedom*, 243.

37 S. M. Michael SVD, *Christianity and Cultures: Anthropological Insights for Christian Mission in India* (Delhi & Pune: ISPCK and Ishvani Kendra, 2015, 108.

38 Amartya Sen, *Identity and Violence: The Illusion of Destiny*, (London: Penguin Books, 2006), 48.

39 Amartya Sen, *Identity and Violence: The Illusion of Destiny*, 45.

40 Madhu Prasad, "Learning in a saffron-tinted market," *Frontline* (September 1, 2017), 58-9.

41 Parvathi Menon, "A dissenter silenced," *Frontline* (September 29, 2017), 5.

42 Jacob Peenikaparambil, "New Brand of Terrorism," *Indian Currents XXIX 38* (18-24 September, 2017), 22.

43 Varghese K. George, "India did not act against cow vigilantes, says U.S.," *The Hindu* (Vijayawada), 16 August 2017, 10.

take action against' them.[44] Sober minds consider the sentiments about cow as 'a campaign of terror that has made a mockery of the rule of law in the country.'[45]

The disturbing dynamic of the new narrative is that its programs find governmental assistance. For instance on May 23, 2017 the government introduced the Prevention of Cruelty to Animals (Regulation of Livestock Market) Rules 2017 in addition to the already existing 'Prevention of Cruelty to Animals Act of 1960.' The new rule 'require a person coming to the market to give a written undertaking that he will not sell his cattle for slaughter.'[46] The Supreme Court questioned this and asked the government "how can you [the Centre] insist that a person should give a written undertaking that he(sic) is not bringing cattle to the market for sale for slaughter?"[47] The court further pointed that "this is an interference of his (sic) fundamental right to carry on trade, protected under the Prevention of Cruelty Act."[48]

In fact the 1960 Act allowed slaughter of animals for food and religious sacrifices.[49] The Constitution makes no mention of religious sentiments. Still less does it seek to impose dietary preferences of a section of the population on other communities or individuals.[50] Some see that the rule is intended to 'harassing people involved in the meat trade.'[51] For others, 'there are serious economic interests behind the political backing' because the 'Central government has allowed 100 per cent foreign direct investment in March 2017 through automated route in e-commerce for food production and food-processing.'[52]

In the context of this narrative the Supreme Court 'stated that right to privacy is a fundamental right as it is an intrinsic part of the right to life and personal liberty guaranteed under the Constitution.'[53] On August 24, 2017, the court said, 'the right to privacy enjoyed state protection under Article 21 of the Constitution.'[54]

Government's involvement to protect the so called 'religious interest' of a particular community is against the principle of a secular India. It is also dishonoring other religious traditions and sentiments.

---

44 Varghese K. George, 10.

45 Madhu Prasad, "Learning in a saffron-tinted market," *Frontline* (September1, 2017), 59.

46 Krishnadas Rajagopal, "Law itself allows cattle slaughter, SC tells govt.," *The Hindu* (Vijayawada), 12 August 2017, 11.

47 Krishnadas Rajagopal, 11.

48 Krishnadas Rajagopal, 11.

49 Krishnadas Rajagopal, 11.

50 Madhu Prasad, "Learning in a saffron-tinted market," *Frontline* (September1, 2017), 60.

51 T.K. Rajalakshmi, "In the Name of Cattle Protection," *Frontline* (June 23, 2017), 35.

52 Madhu Prasad, "Learning in a saffron-tinted market," 59.

53 Suresh Mathew, "Strictly Private," *Indian Currents XXIX 2* (04-10 September, 2017), 5.

54 V. Venkatesan, "A Historic Moment," *Frontline* (September 15, 2017), 4.

The following comparison illustrates the paradigm of the new narrative: "Modern Gau Mata and Bharat Mata are contemporaries: the former has given the growth of communalism a boost and the latter has sought to strengthen the Hindutva brand of nationalism."[55]

Back to Myths

After the arrival of 'scientific education' in India the government had taken education under its administration. But, the paradigm of the new narrative is to encourage corporate interests in decision-making in the name of "efficiency" and "professional management."[56] Privatization of education has made quality 'education beyond the reach of the socially and economically oppressed.'[57]

The activism of 'Akhil Bharatiya Vidyarthi Parishad'[58] and the government's interference in the universities 'to curb the intellectual and physical space available for students and faculty to question, dissent from and disturb existing power structures'[59] are serious concerns. Attempting to imbibe 'nationalism' and 'military discipline' like Sainik Schools[60] have disturbed the fabric of education at all levels. It is feared that 'selective appointment' to top academic and administrative positions can threaten the 'credibility of research in the natural and social sciences and the future content and quality of investigative studies.'[61]

Claiming an organic unity between the Vedic world view and modern science has been an agenda of the Hindu nationalists. It is argued that in the end, Vedas-as-the mother-of-science is a "magnificent dead end."[62] Further the 'project of turning modern science into a *smriti* is a massive, and repeated, distortion of the history of science.'[63] Attaching the knowledge of plastic surgery to the story of lord Ganesha and knowledge of genetic engineering to the theory of *kama* are other examples of the new narrative. It is deplored that 'to the shame of this country not a single eminent scientist in India' took to task such claims, 'which may now well enter our textbooks in Central schools and the schools in most States.'[64]

It looks, gone are the days reason and science challenged crude myths. The new paradigm suggests a preference for myths in the place of reason, research,

---

55 D. N. Jha, "Never Kill a Cow in Kaliyuga," *Frontline* (November 25, 2016), 103.

56 Madhu Prasad, "Learning in a saffron-tinted market," *Frontline* (September1, 2017), 58.

57 Prabhat Patnaik, "From revolution to counter-revolution," *Frontline* (September1, 2017), 11.

58 Madhu Prasad, "Learning in a saffron-tinted market," *Frontline* (September1, 2017), 59.

59 Madhu Prasad, "Learning in a saffron-tinted market," 60.

60 Madhu Prasad, "Learning in a saffron-tinted market," 60.

61 Madhu Prasad, "Learning in a saffron-tinted market," 58-9.

62 Meera Nanda, "Hindutva's Science Envy," *Frontline* (September 16, 2016), 46.

63 Meera Nanda, "Hindutva's Science Envy," 47.

64 Irfan Habib, "Inventing History to Inculcate Hatred," *Frontline* (September1, 2017), 36.

history and science. A serious task awaits everyone, including us, who thinks of inclusive India and scientific enquiry (education) for a better future.

Ideology Driven Religious Narrative

The new paradigm is committed to contentious religious narratives like a temple was demolished to construct a mosque, one of the world's wonders was built in the place of a Siva temple symbolizing India as Bharat Matha. These narratives have satisfactorily encompassed the three major strands of Hinduism to facilitate pan Hinduism. The consequence of the new narrative is that 'India has recorded a spike in violence related to religious intolerance in 2016.'[65] In the words of Amartya Sen "violence is fomented by the imposition of singular and belligerent identities on gullible people, championed by proficient artisans of terror."[66]

It is a warning that 'a simplistic characterization of India along an artificially singular religious line remains politically explosive.'[67] It is also against the religious neutrality of the constitutional provision. The religious partitioning of the world/ nation 'has the effect of magnifying one particular distinction between one person and another to the exclusion of all other important concerns.'[68] Singular perception can undermine mines of riches. For example, 'while Akbar was free to pursue his liberal policies without ceasing to be a Muslim' there were others who considered different views.[69] Forcing 'religious identity' alone devastates all other possibilities of appreciation and coexistence.

Madrasas in Uttar Pradesh have criticized the government order to video-graph Independence Day celebrations this year, as 'an attempt to test the patriotism of Muslims.'[70] Prominent citizens who voiced concern over such schemes are questioned about their nationalism. It is also true that more and more number of minorities is convicted in different cases. Heinous crimes against minorities are not fairly investigated for logical conclusions. Many are the 'restrictions imposed' on Christian NGOs.[71] It is unbelievable that the new narrative, unimaginably, claims victimhood.

---

65 Varghese K. George, "India did not act against cow vigilantes, says U.S.," *The Hindu* (Vijayawada), 16 August 2017, 10.

66 Amartya Sen, *Identity and Violence: The Illusion of Destiny*, (London: Penguin Books, 2006), 2.

67 Amartya Sen, *Identity and Violence: The Illusion of Destiny*, 48-9.

68 Amartya Sen, *Identity and Violence: The Illusion of Destiny*, 76.

69 Amartya Sen, *Identity and Violence: The Illusion of Destiny*, 16.

70 Omar Rashid, "I-Day: Madrasas Asked to Videograph Celebrations," *The Hindu* (Vijayawada), 12 August 2017, 7.

71 Varghese K. George, "India did not act against cow vigilantes, says U.S.," *The Hindu* (Vijayawada), 16 August 2017, 10.

Singular narrative is unhealthy. For the harmony of the world/nation there needs to be 'a clearer understanding of the pluralities of human identity.'[72] These identities coexist, interact and cannot be singularized. Even 'the prospects of peace in the contemporary world may well lie in the recognition of the plurality of our affiliations.'[73] At this context of the new narrative we remember, with hope and confidence, the reformation that challenged a particular paradigm.

Remembering Reformation

The 'Narrative of a belligerent ideology is our context,' as we remember the 'event of Reformation' after 500 years. Re-forming the Church, re-reminding the Church and re-affirming faith in Jesus Christ the head of the Church in obedience to the word of God are symbols of gratitude to Jesus and the Reformation. It is gratitude to Jesus because we remain continuously committed to him and to reformation because Reformation was a historical reminder to the Church not to forget her head and the calling.

The Reformation reminded us that God, scripture, faith, grace and salvation, among many more theological contributions, are irrefutably fundamental to Christian life and witness and it is God's justice that has brought equal standing with him (priesthood of all believers).

Catholic thinkers have gracefully accepted that there is a 'need to return to our primordial source: God alone.'[74] They have agreed that the reformation 'gave a fillip to the reading and study of the Word of God in the Catholic Church.'[75] There is a positive acceptance that 'the Catholic charismatic movement' was 'inspired by the Protestant model of prayer.'[76] It is also admitted that 'in different dimensions of church life,' 'interestingly Protestant sections had already gone forward.'[77]

It is also penitently said that the Reformation 'provides the Catholic Church a chance and grace to rethink about her methods of interpreting the Word of God.' Further, 'instead of condemning Martin Luther' we 'confess our wrong approach to it '[Bible], 'and give a re-orientation to the biblical interpretation.'[78] It is more fitting to affirm that Luther's translation of the Bible into the vernacular

72 Amartya Sen, *Identity and Violence: The Illusion of Destiny*, (London: Penguin Books, 2006), xiv.

73 Amartya Sen, *Identity and Violence: The Illusion of Destiny*, xvii.

74 Subhash Anand, "The Reformation as a Return to God: The Indian Significance of Martin Luther," *Third Millennium XX*/2 (April-June, 2017), 20.

75 Jacob Marangattu, CMI, "500 Years of the Great Western Schism: *Another Holy Wound?*," *Third Millennium XX*/2 (April-June, 2017), 4.

76 Jacob Marangattu, 5.

77 Jacob Marangattu, 6.

78 Paul Kullaveettil, CMI,, "Biblical Hermeneutics in the Light of Luther's Challenge," *Third Millennium XX*/2 (April-June, 2017), 59.

made a tremendous impact on both the Church and society.[79] Although denominationalism is attributed to Reformation, the availability of Bible in local languages helped spreading the Gospel in multifaceted ways. Different interpretations and understanding have facilitated innovative mission. We are called upon to continue its impact on our own contexts.

Veiling the Ray of Hope

Contrary to the new narrative that Christianity is a foreign religion, Roger E. Hedlund firmly states that "Christianity is one of the ancient religions of India."[80] He further said, "the Thomas Christians are purely indigenous, born and brought up on Indian soil, nurtured in Indian culture and traditions, their customs Indian and indigenous."[81]

While the new narrative attempts to obliterate other viewpoints and contributions the fact remains that the Bible has from its start inspired millions to commit for an inclusive and sustainable capability enhancement based on Jesus' approach- 'the primacy of human need.[82]

The printing press of the missionaries and the educational institutions set up by them for both men and women are the initial impetus of transformations in India. They opposed child marriage, widow burning and many other inhuman practices.[83] Their publication of newspapers brought 'mass enlightenment.'[84] The Serampore missionaries developed Indian languages 'aimed at the economic and socio-cultural renaissance of India.'[85] Tokenism was never in consideration. Their works were based on 'sustainable capability enhancement' through education, printing press, hospitals, medical education etc. This cannot be stopped even when the new narratives prevail. It is hard to understand the reason for preventing such works and naming them differently. Why cannot Christianity be credited for its sustainable capability enhancement resulting in transformations in India in the past and now?

Like never before, there are challenges to continue the mission. However, the fact remains that "invariably, there are many different ways of being an 'Indian-

79 Paul Kullaveettil, 60.

80 Roger E. Hedlund, "Indigenous People of South Asia," in *We, the Church: Studies in Mission & Evangelization*, edited by Smitha P. Coffey & Donna Tracy Paul (New Delhi: Christian world Imprints, 2017), 34.

81 Roger E. Hedlund, 34.

82 Jose Maliekal, *Standstill Utopias?: Dalits Encountering Christianity*, (Delhi: ISPCK, 2017), 278.

83 Babu K. Verghese, *Let there be India!: Impact of the Bible on Nation Building*, Summary ed. (Chennai: WOC Publishing & Mumbai: Media Concerns, 2016), 165.

84 Babu K. Verghese, 137.

85 Babu K. Verghese, 166.

Christian', just as there are many ways of being 'Indian.'"[86] A reformation in our understanding of hermeneutics and mission is necessary to affirm such faith and conviction.

Hermeneutics of Sustainable Capability Enhancement

The same triune God, faith, Bible, grace and salvation that inspired millions to accept the symbol of the cross for sustainable capability enhancement of the deprived all through the centuries have not lost 'empowering and enhancing potency' until today. Explicating and actualizing this reality solely rests on the Church in her multifaceted engagement with the entire creation. The Bible has not lost its irreplaceable appeal for sustainable capability enhancement leading towards justice and peace.

It may be helpful, in the process, to be reminded that 'transmitting and interpreting'[87] the message/Word of God/Bible is a continuous process. In order to be successful in this exploration it may be cautioned that 'no hermeneute can succeed transcending the boundaries of the original text of the "Revelation." It is also essential that unless the interpreter has 'empathy with the feelings, emotions, imaginations, expectations as well as frustrations, tragedies and comedies of the life of the common people'[88] interpretations may fail.

In our context of interpretation, no doubt, there is a 'need to consider the country's cultural background.'[89] 'Plurality' is the essence of Indian setting. The challenges emerging from the narratives of a belligerent ideology in the process of sustainable capability enhancement call for a "concrete theology of the cross" in contrast to the 'theology of glory' or triumphalism. The hermeneutical principle of 'sustainable capability enhancement' can relevantly address Indian plurality.

Sustainability refers to the nature of interpretation that seriously takes in to account the irreducibility of the Word of God, the life and mission of the Church, various contextual interpretations of the Bible, plurality of the Indian context, the narratives of the belligerent ideology and derive resources for capability enhancement. Our mission of capability enhancement has to be developed from the resources generated from a sustainable interpretation.

---

86 Eric J. Lott, "Issues in Shaping an *Indian*-Christian Identity," in *We, the Church: Studies in Mission & Evangelization*, edited by Smitha P. Coffey & Donna Tracy Paul (New Delhi: Christian world Imprints, 2017), 47.

87 Henry A. Virkler, *Hermeneutics: Principles and Processes of Biblical Interpretation*, Indian ed. (Secunderabad: OM Books, 2005), 15.

88 Thomas Manickam, "Biblical Hermeneutics: An Indian Approach", *Indian Interpretation of the Bible,* ed. By Augustine Thottakara, cmi, (Bangalore: Dharmaram Publications, 2000), 123.

89 Joseph Pandiappallil, "The Encounter of the Semitic/Jewish Culture with the Indian Culture", *Indian Interpretation of the Bible,* edited by Augustine Thottakara, cmi, (Bangalore: Dharmaram Publications, 2000), 132.

Mission as Sustainable Capability Enhancement

Inspite of aggressive ideological narratives in consonance with identity politics, existential context of India remains difficult to change. Poverty, poor health care, child mortality, exclusion, deprivation of basic capabilities, exploitation of all kinds, degradation of human rights, dignity of human beings and accessibility to basic resources are still serious concerns. These 'are rampant in the countryside of the nation.'[90]

Amartya Sen interprets 'poverty as a deprivation of basic capabilities' rather than merely as low income and says 'deprivation of elementary capabilities can be reflected in premature mortality, significant undernourishment (especially of children), persistent morbidity, widespread illiteracy and other failures.'[91] Therefore it is argued that, one of the mission challenges is to work on a fast track 'to eradicate illiteracy; enable the poor access resources for higher and professional education; enhance their bargaining capacity; uncover the poverty hidden behind their cell phones and the televisions; promote mainstreaming of women and the weaker sections through participation in governance and decision making bodies/ levels.'[92]

The present narrative has the capability to project the unreal as real. Nevertheless, our commitment to mission is initiated by God (Missio Dei).[93] Christianity always opted for capability enhancement of deprived sections through, education, health care, fighting social evils, industrial training etc. In spite of the labels like 'foreign religion,' 'attempting to convert;' and banning organizations and blocking financial resources to sustainable capability enhancement we need to move forward with the help of interpretation of the Word of God relevant to different contexts.

Conclusion

The new narratives of Hindutva are really a challenge for Christian mission. The Church has never relaxed even in more adverse contexts than ours. Nor the Word of God failed to speak to any situation. The Reformation event reaffirms that we need to re-form our commitment, re-remind ourselves of our responsibility in varying contexts and recall Christ the head of the Church to inspire us to diligently serve him. The hermeneutical principle of "sustainable capability enhancement" can be explored to relevantly interpret the Word of God in order to derive

90 Jetti A. Oliver, "Mission in a Globalized World: Opportunities and Challenges," in *We, the Church: Studies in Mission & Evangelization*, edited by Smitha P. Coffey & Donna Tracy Paul (New Delhi: Christian world Imprints, 2017), 68.

91 Amartya Sen, *Development as Freedom*, (US: Alfred A. Knopf, Inc., 1999), 20.

92 Jetti A. Oliver, 68.

93 Harold Dalton, "The Mission of God ," in *We, the Church: Studies in Mission & Evangelization*, edited by Smitha P. Coffey & Donna Tracy Paul (New Delhi: Christian World Imprints, 2017), 51.

resources for capability enhancement. It was because of the "sustainable capability enhancement," the mission of the Church all through the centuries continued as 'hope dawned in hopelessness.' Our mission today is 'dispelling various forms of deprivations' and enabling the deprived to see hope and enjoy justice and peace. Our strength is the cross and the crucified Jesus. And our capacity is being able to repent if anything was pursued unjustly and insincerely. The biblical dictum that what you have done to the least you have done to me and what you have not done to the least you have not done to me has not lost its freshness. Reformation, hermeneutics and mission are the continuous rejuvenation of our commitment.

16

Christian Identity and Witness in the Context of Present Day Hindutva Nationalism

Introduction

This chapter attempts to explain Hidutva Nationalism and tentatively think along the possibilities of Christian identity and witness in this context. As Hindutva nationalism is an identity politics and our concern is Christian identity and witness, I shall start with a cursory discussion on identity and move on. In the second place, I will discuss the development of secular nationalism and the growth of Hindutva nationalism which is a derivative of Hindu nationalism. Finally, I will try to sneak through Christian identity and witness for analysis before conclusion.

Inner Self and Identity

Our identities evolve from our inner self's interactions with the outer world/ society. Therefore, 'the self is, both individual and social in character'[1] implying that there is a reciprocal influence between the self and the society. Eric Lot says, "no self emerges wholly free from its historical grounding and biological configuring."[2] Francis Fukuyama argues that 'the inner self is the basis of human dignity' and human dignity 'seeks recognition' and public acknowledgment by others.' Much of our economic/political motivation actually reflects this. Today, 'it is not the inner self that has to be made to conform to society's rules, but society

1 Jan E. Stets and Peter J. Burke, "A Sociological Approach to Self and Identity," in *Handbook of Self and Identity*, edited by Mark Leary and June Tangney (Washington: Guilford Press), 1-4.

2 Eric Lot, *Religious Faith, Human Identity: Dangerous Dynamics in Global & Indian Life* (Bangalore: ATC/UTC, 2005), 379.

itself that needs to change.'[3] This is obvious in moving towards recognizing every section of society.

Since the 'self is organized into multiple parts' (identities),[4] the answer to the question what constitutes 'identity' varies. In the words of Fukuyama, 'identity grows out of a distinction between one's true inner self and an outer world of social rules and norms that does not adequately recognize that inner self's worth or dignity.'[5] Although 'identity' refers most basically to who we are and where we belong, 'late-modernity increasingly assumes that all our identities are *invented* and, if necessary, *re-invented*,'[6] Often we may not know how others identify us. However, it is true that identity is plural and we have multiple identities.

Amartiya Sen makes the point that, we simultaneously belong to 'a great variety of categories'[7] and 'none of them can be taken to be the person's only identity.'[8] It is wrong to see people only through any one single identity. Therefore, Sen, appeals to resist the view that 'we must have a single – or at least a principal and dominant identity. It is dangerous to 'discover' our identity, with no room for any choice.' Reason should decide on the choice and importance of identity.[9] Recognition of this reality is essential for the Indian context.

The fact that all of us, in one or another way, belong to communities does not bar from interaction among them. Nevertheless, our tendency is to identify with whom we are grouped together and to judge members of our own group as superior, no matter how arbitrary or even silly the group boundaries may be. This is called 'othering.'[10] We make 'apparent and real differences among different individuals and groups' 'to stoke anxiety, resentment, and fear of the other.'[11] That is why 'identity can be a source of pride, joy, strength, confidence, richness and warmth.' At the same time it can also be the source of 'violence and terror' and even killing[12] in large numbers. In the process of 'othering' religious myths and symbols play their active role.

---

3 Francis Fukuyama, *Identity: Contemporary Identity Politics and the Struggle for Recognition* (London: Profile Books, 2018), 10-15.

4 Jan E. Stets and Peter J. Burke, 8.

5 Francis Fukuyama, 9-10.

6 Eric Lot, 37.

7 Amartya Sen, *Identity and Violence: The Illusion of Destiny* (London: Allen Lane, 2006), 19.

8 Amartya Sen, *Identity and Violence*, 5.

9 Amartya Sen, *The Argumentative Indian: Writings on Indian Culture, History and Identity* (London: Penguin Books, 2005), 350-352.

10 Eric Lot, 34-35.

11 Jose Nandhikkara, "Identities Matter: Personally and Socially," *Journal of Dharma* 43/2 (April-June, 2018), 115-117.

12 Amartya Sen, *Identity and Violence*, 1-4.

Indian Identity

Plurality of choice is immensely relevant to the understanding and analysis of the idea of Indian Identity. The notion that 'Indian identity has to be in some way derived from a Hindu identity' on the basis that 'Hindus constitute a large majority of people' and 'historically, Hinduism has been the mainstay of the Indian civilization' 'do not in any way indicate that the Indian identity has to be basically derivative from the Hindu identity, or that the Indian identity must privilege the Hindu identity over others.'[13]

The choice and tension between plural and singular identity is so vivid in the formation of the idea of Nation in India particularly during and after the freedom struggles. One is the secular and democratic consideration of India and the other is religious or majority nationalism. We shall begin with the first.

Secular and Democratic India

Amartya Sen traces the tradition of secularism in India back to the tolerant and pluralist thinking in the writings of Amir Khusrau in the fourteenth century and to the non-sectarian devotional poetry of Kabir, Nanak, Chaitanya and others. And this 'tradition got its firmest official backing from Emperor Akbar.' While being a good Muslim all through, his defense of a 'tolerant multiculturalism[14] was based on reasoning.

The Indian Independence movement used the word 'secular' 'merely to refer to a form of democratic government in which no particular religion or religious community was given a dominant role.'[15] Many leaders 'of the Indian Independence movement, especially in the Congress Party, did not want religion to be granted any special privileges in the independent Indian state.'[16] For Sen, identity has 'to be chosen with reasoning' as it 'is the basis of secularism in India.'[17] For them, 'it was possible to have multiple identities' while celebrating 'their roots, their culture and a sense of belonging to the idea of India' and at the same time 'it was equally essential to reach out to others in order to understand, assimilate and even love them.'[18]

Secular leaders of the Indian national movement realized that for the development of India its diversity has to be accepted. Their 'economic' vision was 'deeply humanist and fully committed to social justice' with 'a pro-poor

---

13 Amartya Sen, *The Argumentative Indian,* 352-353.

14 Amartya Sen, *The Argumentative Indian,* 287-288.

15 Eric Lot, 191.

16 Pradeep K. Chhibber and Rahul Verma, *Ideology and Identity: The Changing Party Systems of India* (India: Oxford University Press, 2018), 25.

17 Amartya Sen, *The Argumentative Indian,* 353.

18 Jyotirmaya Sharma, *Hindutva: Exploring the Idea of Hindu Nationalism* (India: Harper Collins Publishers, 2015), 17-18.

orientation.'[19] This broader base enabled 'different streams and forces' and 'various groups and peoples[20] to be part of it. In other words, it had a place for different identities.

The leaders were against communalism, because it was against national interest or was anti-national. They believed only a strong secular nationalism can protect the minorities[21] in India, just the opposite of our present context.

After Independence, India emerged as 'a powerful constitutional-legal authority,' which made 'deep interventions into India's social and political order.'[22] This was not in the interest of some who, from the beginning, had a different idea of India.

Secular nationalism accepted democracy to provide space for those not in the majority. Like modern liberal democracies, Indian democracy enshrined the 'principles of freedom and equality.' That is, 'an equal negative freedom from abusive government power and equal positive freedom to participate in self-government and economic exchange.'[23] This is inevitable in our nation with multiple differences.

The secular and democratic nationalism 'was challenged from within as well as outside the Congress party.' For example, 'Patel's social conservatism' and 'decisive use of political power'[24] was different from the Congress.

The other challenge was that the Hindus 'have found themselves alienated at various levels of national life and its ideology' and for some this was a 'lack of an integrated Hindu identity.'[25] They found post partition Hindu Muslim divides[26] a master narrative to construct clearly defined more nationally integrated self-identity. Therefore, parallel to the vision of hope-filled secularist democratic nation there developed a Hindu Nationalism leading up to today's Hindutva nationalism.

Hindu Nationalism and identity

Both Hindu Nationalism and its later development the Hindutva nationalism claim to stand for the cause of Hinduism inspite of the argument that Hinduism and Hindutva are not the same.

---

19 Bipan Chandra, *Essays on Contemporary India*, 2nd ed. (New Delhi: Har-Anand Publications PVT LTD, 1999), 94-96.

20 Felix Wilfred , "Christians Between Identity-Politics and Nationalism," in *Hindutva an Indian Christian Response*, edited by J. Mattam, S. J. & P. Arockiadoss, S. J. (Bangalore: Dharma publications, 2002), 262-263.

21 Pradeep K. Chhibber and Rahul Verma, 25.

22 Pradeep K. Chhibber and Rahul Verma, 29.

23 Francis Fukuyama, 40-48.

24 Pradeep K. Chhibber and Rahul Verma, 265.

25 Eric Lot, 196.

26 Pradeep K. Chhibber and Rahul Verma, 27.

Hindu Nationalism started with constructing a unified Hinduism. Jyotirmaya Sharma argues, 'Hinduism was invented as a consequence of the encounter between Muslims and the Hindus where identity is, reduced to 'a staged encounter between the 'Self' and its threatening 'Other." For him, 'Hindutva is the dominant expression of Hinduism'[27] in our times.

The formation of Hinduism (political) has incorporated and absorbed wide-ranging indigenous cults, rituals and practices and 'rivalry and even violence between major Hindu sects.' The 19th century Hindu reforming spirit attributed 'a kind of super-identity,' to Hinduism, transcending the particularities of divergent histories.[28] This process has ignored even external religious influences,[29] particularly Sufism on Hinduism. In, fact this was the beginning of Hindu identity and nation.

Political pressures were behind 'the creating of this more clearly defined Hindu identity.'[30] The leaders of Hindu Mahasabha were the most vocal proponents of Hindu Nationalism during the Constituent Assembly debates. As a consequence many Hindu traditionalists drifted 'away from the Congress umbrella'[31] and identified with the others.

Hindu traditionalists, within Congress, 'looked toward Vallabhbai Patel for leadership.'[32] Patel and others sympathetic to the Hindu traditionalist position argued 'the structures and processes of the state should reflect the natural Hindu majority, such that the treatment of minorities, within the dictates of legal equality and fairness, derived from a Hindu position.'

Hindu Nationalists, on the other hand, are 'more in favor of spending money on building an atom bomb, increasing defense spending, and going to war with Pakistan.' They favor building a Ram temple at the site of the Babri Mosque, passing a law to ban religious conversion, and eliminating caste-based reservations and special provisions for Muslims.'[33] They argue that 'definitions of nationalism and identity in India are inextricably linked with the recognition of Hinduism as the defining and deciding factor.' For them national identity is 'Hindu identity'[34] and Christians are 'outsiders.'

Hindu Nationalist Identity was not constructed primarily on the basis of political and economic subjugation but mainly on the religious plank–insult to religion, idol, practices, cultures and symbols. Therefore Golwalkar writes "our

27 Jyotirmaya Sharma, 5-8.

28 Eric Lot, 161.

29 Amartya Sen, *The Argumentative Indian,* 315.

30 Eric Lot, 162.

31 Pradeep K. Chhibber and Rahul Verma, 214.

32 Pradeep K. Chhibber and Rahul Verma, 242.

33 Pradeep K. Chhibber and Rahul Verma, 213-215.

34 Jyotirmaya Sharma, 4.

one supreme goal is to bring to life the all-round glory and greatness of our Hindu Rashtra."[35] Harping on a glorious past, in fact, destroys the present and the future prospects.

Non-violent religious traditions (both Hindus and Jains) transmitted, mostly, 'by some of modern India's wealthiest and most influential communities' have acquired a privileged position in the social and political structures of contemporary India. It is a paradox that 'although Hindu nationalists have sometimes sought to realize their goals violently, the type of Hinduism that they seek to place at the centre of India's nationhood is a version that has a strong affinity with anti-violence issues[36] such as cow protection.'

In the words of Fukuyama, 'Prime Minister Modi's Bharatiya Janata Party is explicitly based on a Hindu understanding of Indian national identity.'[37] It gives priority to Hinduism. Mahatma Gandhi was not assassinated for not being a good Hindu but for being very 'soft' on the Muslims in political matters, and did not give adequate priority to Hindu interests.[38] What else can be a better standard to evaluate Hindu Nationalism and identity?

Hindu nationalism is also communal nationalism because it believes that 'those who follow a religion also acquire because of that fact common economic, political and social interests.'[39] They, to avoid being labeled communal, claim to be protectors of Indian culture and civilization called Hindutva. In other words the conceptualization of Hindu Nationalism culminates in Hindutva Nationalism.

Hidutva Nationalism and Identity Politics

Hindutva Nationalism is again an identity politics based on Hindu values but under the veils of culture, civilization and nation, besides religion. Savarkar says Hindutva cannot be analyzed, it is a history in progress for forty centuries, if not more and Hinduism is only part of it. Hindutva is based on 'the foundation of a great and enduring civilization' of Aryans. Unlike others, Aryans had definitely cut themselves aloof from their cognate and neighboring people especially the Persians' and 'developed a sense of nationality.' Their founding a nation reached its geographical limit when the valorous Prince of Ayodhya made a triumphant entry in Ceylon.[40] The fact is that the logic applied to Aryans is not applied to others and it outrightly denies the culture and civilization of others.

35 M. S. Golwalkar, *Bunch of Thoughts*, 3rd ed. (Bangalore: Sahitya Sindhu Prakashana, 2000), 43.

36 Lawrence A. Babb, *Alchemies of Violence: Myths of Identity and the Life of Traders in Western India* (New Delhi/Thousand Oaks/London: Sage Publications, 2004), 22.

37 Francis Fukuyama, 74 .

38 Amartya Sen, *The Argumentative Indian,* 307.

39 Bipan Chandra, 125-126.

40 Vinayak Damodar Savarkar, *Hindutva*, 2018th ed. (New Delhi: Hindi Sahitya Sadan, 2018), 19-26.

Sudhir Kakar explains the Hindutva process of 'othering' as 'the gods and heroes are offered up as ego ideals, to be shared by members of the community in order to bring about and maintain group cohesion. Identity implies definition rather than blurring, solidity rather than flux or fluidity, and therefore the question of boundaries of a group become paramount.' Then 'the overarching Hindu community is sought to be further enlarged by including the followers of other religions whose birth place is India.'[41] This is in contrast to the reality of multiple identities.

Hindutva Nationalism 'has led to violence between Hindus and Muslims, between Hindus and Christians.' It also brings into question the validity of secular democracy in contrast to culture, traditional values and an imagined past.[42] While the Hindu nationalists wanted Hindu influence everywhere, Hindutva Nationalists exclude everything not in their definition of nation.

For Sudhir Kakar, countering of the Hindu identity constructed by Hindutva 'involves the offer of a different Hindutva with other images, symbols, and myths of the Hindu ethos rather than any abstract concept of secularism, which for most Hindus is empty of all psychological meaning.'[43] The viability of this suggestion is debatable.

There is nothing wrong with identity politics as such; it is a natural and inevitable response to injustice. It becomes problematic only when identity is interpreted or asserted in certain specific ways[44] without considering others. The Hindutva Nationalism has mainly rested on religion, civilization and culture.

Critique of the Fundamentals of Hindu Nationalism

Behind the idea of 'a greater uniformity of Hindu self-identity' and hard Hindutva Nationalism are the leaders of 'socio-religious reform movements in the nineteenth century'[45] of whom some were 'radical, extreme and militant'[46] in their articulations.

Dayananda Saraswati said, instead of worshipping stones, 'Indians should have worshipped heroes and brave men in order to save themselves from the Muslim invasion.' Sri Aurobindo called for the 'revival of kshatriyahood' and believed 'in the Indian cosmology Brahmin is the masculine principle and Kashatriya stood for the feminine principle.[47] Vivekananda preferred Krishna

41 Sudhir Kakar, *Indian Identity* (India: Penguin Books, 2007), 332.

42 Jyotirmaya Sharma, 4.

43 Sudhir Kakar, *Indian Identity* (India: Penguin Books,2007), 328-329.

44 Francis Fukuyama, 115.

45 Pradeep K. Chhibber and Rahul Verma, 235.

46 Jyotirmaya Sharma, 13.

47 Jyotirmaya Sharma, 62-72.

roaring the Gita to Krishna in Vrindavan and appealed for 'muscles of iron and nerves of steel.'[48]

Bal Gangadhar Tilak promoted 'a warrior-morality and a warrior-religion' and said Hindus should use force otherwise 'expect to be impotent witness of the gradual downfall of their ancient institutions.' He promoted the ideal of Shivaji, Ganapathi festival and used Anti-Cow Killing Society' and 'stood for the establishment of a Hindu *rashtra* in India.'[49] His disciple Savarkar claimed that 'the Hindus were a martial race' and 'India must be a Hindu land, reserved for them,[50] because 'Muslims and Christians are foreigners.' Golwalkar writes "today, more than anything else, Mother needs such men – young, intelligent, dedicated and more than all virile and masculine."[51] This radicalization was obvious when people offered 'arrows, maces, swords, tridents and *kripans*'[52] to L. K. Advani during his *yatra*. Our appreciation of and approach to these interpreters requires a fresh look.

Religious identity 'is inextricably intertwined with physical, professional, ethnic, political and national identities.'[53] Therefore, it is not possible to claim that 'Indians must 'go through' their religious identity first, before asserting their Indianness.' India has been a multi-religious country for a very long time. Jews, Christians, Parsees and Muslim traders settled in India over the first millennium. Buddhism, Jainism and Sikhism originated in the country. As this history is not comfortable, 'there has been such a flurry of attempts by political fanatics to rewrite Indian history,'[54] a worrying exercise.

The other protective cover of the Hindutva politics is civilizational identity. It sees 'people primarily as belonging to one civilization or another.' It leads to 'misunderstanding nearly everyone in the world.' Unfortunately 'Huntington's characterization of India as a "Hindu civilization" is 'frequently quoted by many leaders of the politically active "Hindutva" movement[55] in India. In the words of Felix Wilfred[56] 'it is the spirit of pluralism, which has sustained and nourished the Indian civilization.'

Cultural identity was another pretention used by Golwalkar to say Hindu nation is 'essentially cultural.'[57] It reduces the political entitlements and rights

48 Jyotirmaya Sharma, 84-119.

49 J. Kuruvachira, 73-90.

50 Jyotirmaya Sharma, 199.

51 M. S. Golwalkar, 448.

52 J. Kuruvachira, *Hindu Nationalists of Modern India: A Critical Study of the Intellectual Genealogy of Hindutva* (Jaipur: Rawat Publications, 2006), 101.

53 Jose Nandhikkara, 368-369.

54 Amartya Sen, *The Argumentative Indian*, 57.

55 Amartya Sen, *Identity and Violence*, 41- 48.

56 Felix Wilfred, 269.

57 M. S. Golwalkar, 34.

of others and helps 'remove their rights as equal citizens.' It also ignores and destroys the cultural inheritance from Hindu Muslim combines - literature, music, painting, architecture and many other fields including art, food, theater,[58] etc., that have nothing much to do with religious thinking at all. They enrich our lives. Cultures evolve. There can be great variations even within the same general cultural milieu. People are free to decide that their cultural identity is less important than, their political convictions, literary persuasions, and professional commitments.[59] It is a choice for them to make.

Risks of Singular Identity

Militant, religious, civilizational and cultural identities are integral to Hindu and Hindutva Nationalism. Therefore, they appeal for choiceless singular human identity to the point of our shared humanity getting savagely challenged. The 'solitarist belittling of human identity' is an 'illusion used to divide people into hardened categories.'[60] In contrast, reasoning and choice are integral to plurality of identities.

Gurcharan Das poignantly illustrates the futility of Hindutva Nationalism based on Identity politics quoting Tony Joseph's *Early Indians*, in his article "Who are we Indians?" that 'we are all migrants and we are all mixed,' and 'pure Indians never really existed.' The 'vigorous mixing of people came to an end around 100 AD in India' because 'the caste system became rigid.' 'We are all mixed and we are all descended from a single woman in Africa.' 'It is futile to obsess over purity and pollution because we are a product of what Rushdie called 'chutnification' through waves of migrations and mingling in prehistory.' 'But the unity of the human race is bad news for the politics of identity and difference.'[61] It may not be possible to express the anguish of reasoning Indian citizens any further than this.

This takes us to the scanning of Christian identity of both positive and negative and identity crisis and to postulate together what lies ahead for us.

Christian Identity and Witness

The followers of Jesus got the identity 'Christians' from the Greek city of Antioch. Jawaharlal Nehru said in the Lok Sabha in 1955 'that Christianity was as old in India as the religion itself.' Former President Pranab Mukherjee affirmed that 'Christianity is an Indian religion.'[62] To understand Christian identity it may be helpful to recall different identities given to us by others.

58 Amartya Sen, *The Argumentative Indian*, 315-316.

59 Amartya Sen, *The Argumentative Indian*, 356.

60 Amartya Sen, *Identity and Violence*, 16-17.

61 Gurcharan Das, "Who are we Indians?," *The Times of India*, 23 February 2019, 8.

62 Molly Abraham, "Deconstructing the 'Self' and Empowering the 'Other': Visionaries in Colonial South India," *Journal of Dharma* 43/2 (April-June, 2018), 191-192.

Ram Nath Kovind, the President of India said Christianity has contributed so much to our shared culture. Missionary institutions 'have become symbols of scholarship, dedicated teaching and academic excellence.'[63] In the same line Pranab Mukherjee said, Christianity in India is remembered for its enduring contributions to renaissance, reformation, educational institutions, hospitals, discipline and dedication.' For him, 'Mother Teresa tending to the last person on the margin of society personifies the Church in India.'[64] Empowering the other from the margins of the society is 'an unambiguous and explicit phenomenon' associated with Christian witness in India.[65] All of us remember the contributions of missionaries like William Carey in India.

Besides, these positive identities there are many negative identities given to us. Hindutva nationalists accuse Christians that they 'kept themselves aloof from the freedom struggle'[66] during the war of independence in 1857. They say, in the North East India 'a Christian based identity' is 'inevitably alienated from an Indian national identity.'[67] There is a fear that 'the Christians are well on the way to achieve their independent 'Nagaland.'[68] These, of course, are claims that require more substantial justifications.

We are called 'alien' and 'less confident' of being 'integral part of Indian life.'[69] More harshly, 'Christians residing in India are out to demolish the religious and social fabric of our life' and to 'establish political domination in various pockets and if possible all over the land.'[70] Added to this is the perception that 'now the Christians have enormously grown in number,' not by propagation of religion, but a political strategy under its garb. Golwalkar writes, 'together with the change in their faith, gone is the spirit of love and devotion for the nation.'[71] The unfound phobia that once again Hindus will come under the rule of other community is the cause for many such distortions.

Our earnest effort to identify locally is interpreted as 'stealing' their cultural symbols, or of blatantly pretending to be Hindus.[72] When people move from one religion to other at will in the developed countries, in India it is seen as causing religious conflict and dangerous to the security of the nation. Our commitment

---

63 Molly Abraham, 202.

64 "Christianity as Indian as Indic Religions: Pranab Mukherjee," *Indian Currents* xxx/51 (December 17-23, 2018), 30.

65 Molly Abraham,: 192.

66 M. S. Golwalkar, 141.

67 Eric Lot, 248.

68 M. S. Golwalkar, 107.

69 Eric Lot, 301.

70 M. S. Golwalkar, 193.

71 M. S. Golwalkar, 125-128.

72 Eric Lot, 301.

to the poor and the vulnerable is interpreted as 'exploitation of poverty, illiteracy, ignorance, inducements and deceptive tactics'[73] even though unfounded.

Another challenge (identity crisis) to our identity comes from the Post-modern claims that there is no single framework within which the whole of human experience can be understood. It adds to the paradox that there is the divergence between our account of ourselves and the way in which we embody that narrative.

Christian Identity and Witness in Context

In the midst of the given identities both positive and negative and identity crisis our witness can be a constant engagement in what Jesus did and the telling of that story (witness) relevant to the signs of times.

Although, our identity (sameness, oneness) is primarily rooted with the identity of Jesus, a genuine relationship with other communities (religious) 'can positively shape our identity'[74] though not instantly. Eric Lot writes, "we dare not ignore any push to a more inclusive human identity."[75] At the same time we need to remember that there is no one particular and assured way of relating with the other. We should also be willing to cooperate with earnest religious and secular agencies to present the gospel in its manifold forms. The expectation that Christians will fight together on issues that affect them has come under serious question in the wake of recent political alignments in places where significant Christian presence is obvious.

The notion that 'our Christian identity must be deeply rooted in Indian culture', needs a different consideration as the word 'culture' is used to othering the minorities in our context and there is no one Indian culture. We need a spirit of tolerance to respect the pious and just religious practices of others to avoid unnecessarily developing dislike for everything from the others. As identity is not singular, we should 'support any political, legal or social measures in favour of battered identities.'[76] While a temple priest can occupy important constitutional position, churches need not discourage members to play an active role in political engagement to strengthen 'nationalism' with commitment to secularism, democracy and justice. In a context like ours we do not do unjust acts 'to sustain as justification' for all our actions.

We should move towards accepting the law of the land and not Hindu law, or others as the guiding and determining principle. A demand from the international community (UN) is that nations should be law abiding. It has much

73 M. S. Golwalkar, 170.

74 Robert Hunt, Christian Identity in a Pluralistic World," *Missiology: An International Review*, 37/2 (April, 2009), 181-185.

75 Eric Lot, 18.

76 Felix Wilfred, 281.

bearing on our identity and witness. If our house is in order we can courageously raise our legitimate, clear, and loud voices against any form of injustice.

Once the Church was known for her reputed healing services, educational institutions, discipline, transparency, service, etc., which were and are our real identity marks. Are they not some serious areas where our identity can continue to be luminous? If those spaces are no longer feasible, we must become beacons in new concerns - ecology, women, Dalit, disabled, strangers, etc.

Jesus' priority to life over Sabbath (religion), Kurban (ritual), confession and his list of members in the Kingdom of God remind us to be plural in our witness, as there is no single unique witnessing, to accommodate the historically, socially and economically suppressed and neglected identities.

Conclusion

As a part of our witness we have to outrightly thank God for the secular, democratic and constitutional nationalism that has withstood all kinds of challenges and take active part in promoting those values.

Since, Identity politics has become the order of the day, we can actively involve in social and political mobilization through all modern and available means to struggle for our legitimate space. It applies to our theological formulations as well. Our encouragement, in a complex situation is that, Jesus did not serve Christians (alone) but anyone came to him. Even he did not allow all the beneficiaries of his love to be his disciples. Identity is sameness but it (body of Christ) can be lived recognizing other identities (oneness).

Often our identities, freedoms, privileges and protections are diluted or denied in the name of a particular nationalism, safety of nation, national interest and patriotism. Our different viewpoints and genuine grievances are frequently interpreted as supporting other country. Christianity never sailed through smooth passages. It has always overcome temporary hurdles. Let us strive to protect our constitution and repose our faith in it as law abiding citizens of this country.

We accept the existence of multiple identities while not denying the importance of religious identity and freedom of religious identity to everyone. Freedom of religion is a universal human right. Free religious mobility is the sign of times and the opposite is non-freedom.

Religiously our fundamentals are hope, love and faith. The possibility of reasoning is a strong source of hope and confidence in a world darkened by horrible deeds. 'We can reason about the right way of perceiving and treating other people, other cultures, other claims, and examine different grounds for respect and tolerance.' 'We can also reason about our own mistakes and try to learn not to repeat them.'[77] In the words of Sudhir Kakar, 'I can only hope that the violence is short-lived and that it will hasten the creation of a common, tolerant public realm. When hope is destroyed, great grief follows, which is almost equal

77 Amartya Sen, *The Argumentative Indian*, 276.

to death itself.' The movement towards multiculturalism rather than a 'composite culture' is encouraging. Studies show that younger citizens of India 'have little sympathy for majoritarian'[78] politics.

Love is the hallmark of Christian identity and witness. Love has changed many societies for the better. Love withstood all persecutions and hatreds. Therefore, we cannot cease from our acts of love as Jesus. Love is found among others as well. Love makes us genuinely human. It transforms us and our understanding. It is love that 'defines and decides our identities – self and others.'[79] Love alone inspires us to see around (innumerable concerns) and act.

Even when acts of love find hard passage, for us the final hold is faith, unshakable faith. It is our faith history which makes us never-give up. The idea that I am native you are alien is criminal, lawlessness and evil-intended. The tiny powerful cross will continue to be vividly visible even under heavy and large saffron veil (invitation card) if we do not forget our identity, Jesus.

78 Pradeep K. Chhibber and Rahul Verma, 260.

79 Jose Nandhikkara, 257.

17

Equality in Hinduism

Introduction

I always distill appreciable Hindu constructs as a part of my commitment to interreligious relations. It continued in my article (subsequently part of a book) on 'Hindu Spirituality' wherein I profusely appreciated certain Hindu values. My doctoral research was to draw insights for theology of religions from the *Bhakti* tradition of Vaishnava Alvars. However the communal violence that consumes so many lives, constant anti-minority polemic and the murderous lynching that honored animals more than human beings and brutally killed many poor, weak, aged, vulnerable people who eked a living on animals, changed my perceptions. Added to these are my reading on Dr. Ambedkar, Manu Smriti and Bhavagavad Gita and my own analysis of 'Christian identity and witness in India in the context of Hindutva politics.'

However, with due respect to my topic I shall attempt, in the first place, a graphic overview of some of the Hindu concepts, of course not complete, on which equality, although difficult, is claimed in Hinduism. I shall also, in the second place, highlight the inequality or hierarchy prevalent in Hinduism. This of course is an outsider's understanding of Hinduism and hence subject to the necessary limitations.

1. Equality

The possibility of equality in Hinduism can be interpreted, not without ambiguity, from the following formulations. They are: reality, creation, human life, self, salvation, different ways, Sanskritic Hinduism, *Bhakti* and popular Hinduism.

1.1. Reality

Hinduism, in contrast to the general perception, affirms that 'the Reality is one.' Even the manifold forms of rituals and worship (spirituality) are explained as a varied means of adoration to that One Reality. This is reasonably justified in the context of geographical, cultural, linguistic, climatic, and even economic variations.

There is also unanimity that God has attributes. It is expressive even in Sankara's view that only at the higher level of spiritual realization, God can be realized as formless. Another commonality is the acceptance that God is both transcendent and immanent. In the words of Radhakrishna, "God is neither completely transcendent not completely immanent."[1] It is further explained as "an intelligent Hindu thinks of god as residing within himself, controlling all his actions as the 'inner controller' and at the same time god is outside him, manifest in innumerable ways, known and unknown."[2]

These considerations are at a higher level and give the impression that Hindus are one and they are equal in accepting one God, the attributes of God and God's transcendental and immanent natures.

1.2. Creation

Starting from *Purusa sukta*, there are different creation narratives in Hinduism, each claiming that creation is from God-created, emanated, evolved, illusion. Even Manu says, "He, desiring to produce beings of many kinds from his own body, first with a thought created the waters, and placed his seed in them."[3]

Hinduism holds that the world is a 'spiritual entity.'[4] The theory that five elements[5] constitute creation is also in the same line. Often earth is called the mother. Therefore, it can be assumed that everyone is equal in being part of this creation. The Indian Hindu scholars are unanimous in their commitment to represent Hinduism as world-affirming in contrast to the Christian notion that Hinduism is world negating.

1.3. Human Life

Hinduism 'postulates no absolute distinction between divine and human beings.'[6] Human beings are divine and God lives in them. The concept of *rta* in the Vedas,

---

1 S. Radhakrishna, *An Idealist View of Life*, Fourth impression, 2nd edition (London: George Allen & Unwin Ltd., 1951), 106.

2 Jitendra Nath Banerjee, "The Hindu Concept of God", *The Religion of Hindus*, ed. by Kenneth Morgan, Reprint (Delhi: Motilal Banarsidas, 1986), 48.

3 *Manu Smriti* 1:9. N. C. Panda, ed., *Manu Smriti* (Delhi: Bharatiya Kala Prakashan, 2014).

4 A. K. Banerjee, *Discourses on Hindu Spiritual Culture* (New Delhi: S. Chand & Co.1967), 133.

5 *Manu Smriti* 1:27.

6 C. J. Fuller, *The Camphor Flame: Popular Hinduism and Society In India*, Revised and expanded edition (Princeton and Oxford: Princeton University Press, 2004), 3.

in addition, explains that humanity is not only divine, but also is in harmony with nature.[7]

1.4. Self (Soul)/Karma Samsara/Karma Janmantra

The idea about soul that it is 'immortal and eternal' is another expression of equality in Hinduism.[8] It is further strengthened by the doctrine of Karma Samsara that all souls will be subjected to *janmantra* until the final *Moksha*. The theory of *karma* answers the questions of differences and reiterates that each one inevitably undergoes its effect.

1.5. Salvation/Goal

The chief goal of Hinduism is attaining salvation/liberation/*moksha* of the soul from the world (*samsara chakara*). In the process, peace (*santhi*) is guaranteed. It is for everyone and it is attainable in this world itself (*Jivan Mukti* and *Jivan Mukta*). It is said "the *Jivan-Mukti* or liberation-in-life 'ideal' has been customarily enshrined as the highest vision of life in the Indian Tradition."[9] It is also expected that a liberated person leads others to salvation. *Moksha* also is one of the four goals of life (*purusarthas*), which is equally expected of all.

1.6. Different Ways

Hinduism cares for everyone equally can be illustrated from the principles of *adhikāra*[10] and *ishta-devata*.[11] The first one is called the doctrine of the spiritual competence and the second is the doctrine of chosen deity. Hinduism proposes that a seeker of religious truth should choose a means of realization according to his/her ability. If anyone follows a path which is beyond his/her capacity, he/she will meet spiritual death. Similarly a devotee can choose any deity of his/her own choice.

1.7. Sanskritic Hinduism

M. N. Srinivas, in his book, *Religion and Society among the Coorgs of South India* suggests that the 'Sanskritic Hinduism' presents certain common characteristics of higher Hinduism which seem to be equal to all. They are, 'worship of great deities like Vishnu and Shiva, the pan-Hindu sacredness of rivers, the importance of major pilgrimage centers, the currency of the two classical epics (the *Ramayana*

7 Rajendra P. Pandeya, "The Vision of the Vedic Seer", *Hindu Spirituality; Vedas through Vedanta*, First Indian Edition (Delhi: Motilal Banarsidass, 1995), 21.

8 S. Balakrishnan, *Introduction to Hinduism* (Great Britain, Cambridge: Cambridge University Press, 1996), 25.

9 J. G. Arapura, *Hermeneutical Essays on Vedantic Topics* (Delhi: Motilal Banarsidass, 1986), 124.

10 D. S. Sarma, "The Nature and History of Hinduism", in *Religion of the Hindus*, edited by Kenneth Morgan (Delhi: Motilal Banarsidass, 1996), 5.

11 Giorgio Bonazzoli, "Puranic Spirituality", in *Hindu Spirituality, Post Classical and Modern* edited by K. R. Sundararajan and Bithika Mukerji (London: SCM Press, 1997), 166.

and the *Mahabharata*), the sanctity of the cow, belief in the concepts of *karma* and *dharma,* and the preeminent role of Brahmans.'[12]

1.8. Bhakti/Devotionalism

Bhagavad Gita, emphasises on the 'grace'[13] of God and 'devotion of God.'[14] These have become foundations of *bhakti marga* which centers on the doctrine of grace. Devotionalism, seems to be revolutionary, and it insists that 'true Brahmanhood is achieved by devotion to God, not given by birth.'[15] In a way everyone can equally be recipient of God's grace.

To avoid possible limitations (caste hierarchy and strict religious observances) in practicing *bhakti* because of its requirements, *Alvars* in the south propounded *prapatti,* which people of all class and grade could practice. They constantly maintained that, the ultimate reality is one and that is Tirumāl, used Tamil and Tamil poetical skills to convey the content of Sanskrit religious texts. The presence of a woman and people from different caste groups in the band of Alvars are radical reformations. They have also revealed the inherent riches and divinity of nature in their poems.

1.9. Popular Hinduism

Popular Hinduism, like in every religion, is a social and cultural construction.[16] There are innumerable religious developments like Ayavazi, Aathi parasakthi, Narayana Guru, Lingayats, Dalit religion, etc., to enforce equality in Hinduism. I am not in a position to assess their success.

Having presented, as much as possible, the seeming sources for equality claims in Hinduism, let us proceed to the second part of the paper.

2. Inequality

You would have already realized my struggle with the first part of the paper and I am sure that it can be overcome in the second part. My quest for equality in Hinduism helped me to consider the opposite of it as well. Let us start with religion.

2.1. Religion - Hinduism/Dharma

The word Dharma is used in most cases as religious ordinances or rites. Hindu *dharma*/religion is 'really Law or at best legalized class-ethics.' It is 'misrepresented

---

12 C. J. Fuller, 28.

13 S. N. Dasgupta, "Classical Forms of Devotional Mysticism", *Hindu Mysticism,* Republished (New York: Frederick Ungar Publishing Co,1959), 119.

14 A. L. Basham, *The Origins and Development of Classical Hinduism,* ed. and annotated by Kenneth G. Zysk (Delhi: Oxford University Press, 1992), 91.

15 C. J. Fuller, 157.

16 C. J. Fuller, 7.

to the people as religion.'[17] "By "Dharma" the Hindus mean 'right, duty, law' and also 'religious custom and usage.'[18] It is true that "customs have been recognized from the very beginning as a source of the Hindu Dharma."[19]

Ambedkar writes that in Hinduism 'religion, in the sense of spiritual principles, truly universal, applicable to all races, to all countries, to all times, is not to be found' and 'I have, therefore, no hesitation in saying that such a religion must be destroyed.' He goes on to say that "You will succeed in saving Hinduism if you will kill Brahmans."[20] His anger germinated from the view that all the inequalities in Hinduism and society are the product of one group and there is no equality in Hinduism.

2.2. Sanskritic Hinduism

The Sanskritic Hinduism, opposed to its claim of equality, is 'the religion of the high castes' derives universality from its roots in the Sanskrit scriptural tradition mainly perpetuated throughout the country by the Brahman literati.'[21] The reality of this is true in the division of Hinduism as 'higher Sanskritic and lower non-Sanskritic strata' or great and little traditions. The hierarchy and inequality is right through Hinduism.

For example, 'the temples of great deities like Vishnu and Shiva, tend to attract more high-caste worshippers, and they are mainly served by Brahman priests, who make only vegetarian offerings and use Sanskrit as the ritual language.' On the other hand 'the temples of many other deities tend to be patronized by the low castes, and they generally have non-Brahman priests, who make both vegetarian and non-vegetarian offerings and use vernacular languages in ritual.' The bitter fact is that 'the separation is reinforced by the higher-status groups.'[22]

2.3. Bhakti

The so-called *bhakti* tradition, contrary to expectations, has resorted 'to institutionalized inequality.'[23] Often the devotees greet the gurus 'by prostrating at his feet.' In other words 'hierarchical inequality is embedded within the structure of all devotionalist orders, which can never be fully egalitarian.'[24] The entry of *Ācāryas* once again brought Sanskrit and Brahmanic control into prominence.

---

17 B. R. Ambedkar, *Annihilation of Caste*, 2nd ed. (New Delhi: Samyak Prakashan, 2018), 75.

18 Rajbali Pandey, *Hindu Samskaras: Socio-Religious Study of the Hindu Sacraments,* 11th Reprint (Delhi: Motilal Banarsidass Publishers Private Limited, 2018), 7.

19 Rajbali Pandey, 11.

20 B. R. Ambedkar, *Annihilation of Caste*, 75-78.

21 C. J. Fuller, 25.

22 C. J. Fuller, 28.

23 C. J. Fuller, 158.

24 C. J. Fuller, 164.

2.4. Samskaras

Samskaras are Hindu sacraments (of purification). Many social and cultural elements have entered into the religious ceremonies to mold the Samskaras.[25] Most of them are domestic rites and ceremonies based more on precedence and popular traditional usages than on any definite written code.[26] In other words "really speaking, customs were the only source of the Samskaras before they were codified in the Girhya manuals."[27] Yet they were binding on the Hindu householder. Samskaras mark the transition from the Vedic to Smarta (smriti) and Pauranika Hinduism where 'greater restrictions are placed on social sides of the Samskaras.'[28] There is greater amount of inequality in terms of age, duration, rites and ceremonies according to caste. For example "the corpse in its hands, should have a piece of gold if it is of a Brahman, a bow if of a Kshttriya, a jewel if of a Vaisya."[29]

Even different forms of marriages are suggested for different castes. All the once-born and women are not entitled for Samskaras.

2.5. Caste Constrains and Influences

Inequality is pervasive in Hindu literatures. Ambedkar writes that "the literature of the Hindus is full of caste genealogies in which an attempt is made to give a noble origin to one caste and an ignoble origin to other castes."[30]

It is traditionally claimed, as opposed to the current trend, that Hinduism is not missionary in nature. The reason given is that "caste is inconsistent with conversion."[31]

Since Hindu Society is 'a collection of castes and each caste being a close corporation there is no place for a convert.' Therefore so long as caste remains '*shudhi* will be both folly and a futility.'[32] This we see in many contentious discussions related to religious mobility.

Another main reason for this divide and inequality is that Hinduism 'postulates no absolute distinction between divine and human beings.' Often 'human beings are seen as actually divine in one way or another,' and the same 'gesture is made to deities as well as people,' 'so that human superiority is justified by god-like attributes.' Or 'the gesture tends to disguise behind a religious veil

25 Rajbali Pandey, *Hindu Samskaras: Socio-Religious Study of the Hindu Sacraments,* vii.

26 Rajbali Pandey, *Hindu Samskaras: Socio-Religious Study of the Hindu Sacraments,* 1.

27 Rajbali Pandey, *Hindu Samskaras: Socio-Religious Study of the Hindu Sacraments,* 11.

28 Rajbali Pandey, *Hindu Samskaras: Socio-Religious Study of the Hindu Sacraments,* 8.

29 Rajbali Pandey, *Hindu Samskaras: Socio-Religious Study of the Hindu Sacraments,* 251.

30 B. R. Ambedkar, *Annihilation of Caste,* 43.

31 B. R. Ambedkar, *Annihilation of Caste,* 46.

32 B. R. Ambedkar, *Annihilation of Caste,* 47.

the objective bases of social inequality that lie,' 'in unequal control over politico-economic resources.'[33]

2.6. Hindu Society

Ambedkar says that the 'Hindu Society is a myth.' The name Hindu is itself a foreign name given by the Mohammedans to the natives for the purpose of distinguishing themselves. It does not occur in any Sanskrit work 'prior to the Mohammedan invasion.'[34] Hindus did not feel the necessity of a common name because 'Hindu society as such does not exist.' 'It is only a collection of castes.' Similarly 'one of the most fundamental principles in Indian society is hierarchical inequality.'[35] Therefore, it is in place to look for the reasons behind these inequalities and hierarchies.

2.7. The Varna and Caste Hierarchies

The 'hierarchical inequality' in Indian society is most distinctively expressed 'by the concepts of *varna* and caste.' It begins with the *Purusha sukta*.[36] For Ambedkar, Caste is a 'human institution'[37] and it is different from *varna*. *Varna* is necessary because it 'is an ideal model for the caste system despite the latter's more complex structure.'

The word 'caste' is translation of *jati* in all the main Indian languages. It 'literally means "kind" or "species," so that the social unit that we describe as a 'caste' is but one of these kinds.' It is not an abstract, but 'a visible dimension of everyday life.'[38]

Vivekanand Jha defines caste 'as a system of social stratification characterized by hierarchy, heredity, pursuit of one or a few particular occupations, inequality, endogamy, restrictions as to taking food and drink from the outsiders, and the notion of purity and pollution associated with hierarchy.'[39] While dealing with the caste inequality it is a huge surprise to read that 'due to the distribution of the people into castes that India did not lapse into a state of barbarism.'[40]

33 C. J. Fuller, 3-7.

34 B. R. Ambedkar, *Annihilation of Caste*, 41.

35 C. J. Fuller, 12.

36 C. J. Fuller, 12.

37 B. R. Ambedkar, *Castes in India: Their Mechanism, Genesis and Development* (New Delhi: Samyak Prakashan [1917], n. d), 9.

38 C. J. Fuller, 13.

39 Vivekanand Jha, *Candala: Untouchability and Caste in Early India* (New Delhi: Primus Books, 2018), 105.

40 Abbe J. A. Dubois, *Hindu Manners and Customs and Ceremonies*, Reprinted (Delhi: Low Price Publications, 1999), 28.

2.8. Chaturvarnya and Guna

Chaturvarnya is the division of society into four classes instead of the four thousand castes that we have in India.' It is claimed that varna 'is based not on birth but on *guna* (worth).'[41] This has support in Manu,[42] Gita,[43] philosophy and all the Hindu religious literatures. The theory of *guna* is nothing but presenting inequality in creation.

Ambedkar writes 'my whole being rebels against it'[44] because the *varna* is closer to class where caste is by birth. The *varna* and *guna* forms of explanation reinforces inequality.

2.9. Brahmin –Twice Born

As caste is based on birth, linequality is infused into the creation itself that "man is stated to be purer above the navel (than below); hence the Self-existence (*Svayambhu*) has declared the purest (part) of him (to be) his mouth."[45] This is a vivid systematic effort to present the Brahmins superior and unequal to others.

Brahmins' status is portrayed as superior to even kings. For example, "know that a Brahmana of ten years and Ksatriya of a hundred years stand to each other in the relation of father and son; but between those two the Brahmana is the father."[46]

Their food habits, although similar to others, is presented as distinct: "A Brahmana must never eat (the flesh of) animals unhallowed by Mantras; but, obedient to the primeval law, he may eat it, consecrated with Vedic texts."[47]

The religious rights for the Brahmans are performed earlier than others: "In the eighth year after conception, one should perform the initiation (upanayana) of a Brahmana, in the eleventh after conception (that) of a Ksatriya, but in the twelfth that of a Vaisya."[48] The list goes on.

2.10. Sudra-Fourth Varna

The Sudras are treated much unequally from the other three *varnas*. According to Manu, "One occupation only the lord prescribed to the Sudra, to serve meekly even these (other) three castes."[49] Serving the Brahmanas 'is the highest duty of

---

41 B. R. Ambedkar, *Annihilation of Caste*, 53.

42 *Manu Smriti* 12:24.

43 *Bagavad-gita* 4:13.

44 B. R. Ambedkar, *Annihilation of Caste*, 53.

45 *Manu Smriti* 1:92.

46 *Manu Smriti* 2:135.

47 *Manu Smriti* 5:36.

48 *Manu Smriti* 2:36.

49 *Manu Smriti* 1:91.

a Sudra, which leads to beatitude.'[50] The first part of the name of a Sudra should express something 'contemptible'[51] and the second part 'denoting service.'[52] Sudra is treated as a slave and hence, "No collection of wealth must be made by a Sudra even though he be able (to do it); for a Sudra who has acquired wealth, gives pain to Brahmanas."[53]

2.11. Dasyus and Chandalas

Those who are not part of *varna* are called Dasyus.[54] They have to live "near well-known trees and burial-grounds, on mountains and in groves, let these (tribes) dwell, known (by certain marks), and subsisting by their peculiar occupation."[55]

Candalas should live outside the village, 'they must be made Apapatras, and their wealth (shall be) dogs and donkeys.'[56] 'A Chandala, a village pig, a cock, a dog, a menstruating woman and a eunuch' are at the same level.[57] The directions for their life is that "their dress (shall be) the garments of the dead, (they shall eat) their food from broken dishes, black iron (shall be) their ornaments, and they must always wander from place to place."[58] They were prohibited from walking in villages and towns during night.

2.12. Untouchables

A worrying form of inequality in Hinduism is untouchability. Ambedkar argues that 'there is no racial difference between the Hindus and the Untouchables.' Before the arrival of untouchability there was a 'distinction between Tribesmen and Broken Men from alien Tribes.' It is the Broken Men who subsequently came to be treated as Untouchables.

Untouchability has no occupational basis too. It sprung from 'contempt and hatred of the Broken Men' and 'continuation of beef-eating.' The Untouchables are distinct from the Impure. According to Ambedkar "while the impure as a class came into existence at the time of Dharma Sutras the Untouchables came into being much later than 400 A.D."[59]

The hereditary form of Untouchability 'has no parallel in the history of the world.' A polluted person can become pure by purification ceremonies, 'but there

50 *Manu Smriti* 9:334.

51 *Manu Smriti* 2:31.

52 *Manu Smriti* 2:32.

53 *Manu Smriti* 10:129.

54 *Manu Smriti* 10:45.

55 *Manu Smriti* 10:50.

56 *Manu Smriti* 10:51.

57 *Manu Smriti* 3:239.

58 *Manu Smriti* 10:52.

59 B. R. Ambedkar, *The Untouchables: Who were They and Why They Became Untouchables,* Reprint (Delhi: Kalpaz Publications, 2017), v.

is nothing which can make the Untouchables pure. They are born impure, they are impure while they live, they die the death of the impure, and they give birth to children who are born with the stigma of Untouchability affixed to them, it is a case of permanent, hereditary stain which nothing can cleanse.' It is lamented that "there has never been a case of a people treating a section of their own people as permanently and hereditarily impure." Untouchability among Hindus is unknown to humanity in other parts of the world.[60]

2.13. The Position of Women

According to Manu, 'a woman must never be independent.'[61] 'Nothing must be done by her independently, even in her own house.'[62] If her suitor is handsome and same caste she should be married even before age.[63] Early marriage was to avoid mixing caste with the notion that women are more polluting.[64] Even, "though destitute of virtue, or seeking pleasure (elsewhere), or devoid of good qualities, (yet) a husband must be constantly worshipped as a god by a faithful wife."[65] In this, women should not care about beauty, age and look.[66]

Men can be away from home and the woman should wait for him. It is said, "if the husband went abroad for some sacred duty, (she) must wait for him eight years, if (he went) to (acquire) learning or fame six (years), if (he went) for pleasure three years."[67]

Whereas men of the first three *varnas* undergo an initiation rite in early adulthood, women do not and, like all Shudras, women remain disprivileged in religious and legal terms.[68] They are not entitled for rites with sacred texts.[69]

They are considered as seducers of men. Therefore "one should not sit in a lonely place with one's mother, sister or daughter; for the senses are powerful, and master even a learned man."[70]

A wife is an auspicious, perfect Hindu woman only while her husband is alive. Whereas, a widow is inauspiciousness personified and epitomizes every negative quality. 'Widows cannot attend auspicious rituals, such as weddings.'[71]

---

60 B. R. Ambedkar, *The Untouchables: Who were They and Why They Became Untouchables,* 21-22.

61 *Manu Smriti* 5:148.

62 *Manu Smriti* 5:147.

63 *Manu Smriti* 9:88.

64 C. J. Fuller, 22.

65 *Manu Smriti* 5:154.

66 *Manu Smriti* 9:14.

67 *Manu Smriti* 9. 76.

68 C. J. Fuller, 20.

69 *Manu Smriti* 9:18.

70 *Manu Smriti* 2:215.

71 C. J. Fuller, 22.

2.14. King and Justice

Inequality has not spared the king and the justice system too. According to Manu, "the king has been created (to be) the protector of the castes (*varna*) and orders, who, all according to their rank, discharge their several duties."[72] Even the Gita says "it is far better to discharge one's prescribed duties, even though faultily, than another's duties perfectly. Destruction in the course of performing one's own duties is better than engaging in another's duties, for to follow another's path is dangerous."[73]

The king has to 'worship Brahmins'[74] and honor them with gifts.[75] Still further, "when a learned Brahmana has found treasure, deposited in former (times), he may take even the whole (of it); for he is master of everything,"[76] but "when the king finds treasure of old concealed in the ground, let him give one half to Brahmanas and place the (other) half in his treasury."[77]

No great crime is known on earth than slaying a Brahmana.[78] Hence, no Brahmin should be given capital punishment irrespective of the crime: "Let him never slay a Brahmana, though he have committed all (possible) crimes; let him banish such an (offender), leaving all his property (to him) and (his body) unhurt."[79]

In contrast, if a Sudra insults a twice born man with gross invective, 'he shall have his tongue cut out.'[80] And "if he mentions the name and castes (*jati*) of the (twice-born) with contumely, an iron nail, ten fingers long shall be thrust red-hot into his mouth."[81] More severe is that "if he arrogantly teaches Brahmanas their duty, the king shall cause hot oil to be poured into his mouth and into his ears."[82] If 'a low-caste man tries to place himself on the same seat with a man of a high caste, he shall be branched on his hip and be banished, or (the king) shall cause his buttock to be gashed.'[83]

Having reasonably presented the inequality in Hinduism, now we have to conclude whether Hinduism represents equality or inequality.

---

72 *Manu Smriti* 7:35.

73 *Bagavad-gita* 3:35., A. C. Bhaktivedanta Swami Prabhupada, *Bagavad-gita*, 40th Printing (Mumbai: The bhaktivedanta Book Trust, 2014).

74 *Manu Smriti* 7:37.

75 *Manu Smriti* 7:82.

76 *Manu Smriti* 8:37.

77 *Manu Smriti* 8:38.

78 *Manu Smriti* 8:381.

79 *Manu Smriti* 8:380.

80 *Manu Smriti* 8:270.

81 *Manu Smriti* 8:271.

82 *Manu Smriti* 8:272.

83 *Manu Smriti* 8:281.

3. Concluding Lines

The concluding lines are inconsonant with the suggestions of Ambedkar. Innumerable castes and embodiment of inequality are realities. India 'presents more survivals of primitive times than'[84] any other civilized society.

It is also held that 'India forms a homogeneous whole' and 'possess cultural unity,' therefore caste (inequality) thrives. In my view, Hindu culture cannot be Indian culture therefore I am unable to identify the homogeneity and cultural unity. Since endogamy is caste, (can be differed), 'the real remedy for breaking caste is inter-marriage.' 'The real enemy to fight with is the *Shrutis* and the *Smritis* which have inculcated the notion of caste.'[85] It is hard to believe that inequality has taken the place of equality in Hinduism in the name of castes. It is harder that Hinduism has hated and pushed the least in the society to the most unimaginable position without even suggesting any measure to improve their plight. It is so painful that, in Hinduism, there is no 'consciousness of kind' except castes.[86] There is no appreciation of merits in a person unless a fellow caste.[87]

The notion that birth determines one's status is nowhere in the world and this is behind the discussions on freedom of religion in India. As the Constitution of India envisages, equality is our responsibility and it is squarely before us.

84 B. R. Ambedkar, *Castes in India: Their Mechanism, Genesis and Development*, 14.

85 B. R. Ambedkar, *Annihilation of Caste*, 64-67.

86 B. R. Ambedkar, *Annihilation of Caste*, 41.

87 B. R. Ambedkar, *Annihilation of Caste*, 50.

18

Periyar E. V. Ramasami's[1] Critique of Priestly Hinduism[2] and Its Implications for Social Reforms

1. Introduction

Protests against superstitious beliefs and practices associated with religion and the caste system are exceedingly old in India.

The indigenous, ascetic and pre-Aryan religious movement called the *Sramanas* was the first to oppose priestly rituals, superstitions and caste system. Its two offshoots, Jainism and Buddhism laid great emphasis on reason and disapproved irrational practices and inequalities in the society. The materialist *carvaka* system insisted that there is no necessity for faith in religion, rites, priests and Vedas. The Upanishads point to the earnest quest for truth beyond externals of religions. Bhakthi movement in Hinduism, to some extent, disfavored mechanical rites and the caste system. *Siddhars* in the South and *Sants* in the North India advocated simple life and negated ritualism. Ramalinga Swami, in Tamil Nadu condemned caste and superstitious beliefs. Sikkism was still another attempt in this direction. With the influence of the British, people like Ram Mohan Roy, Keshub Chander Sen and Ranade initiated many social reforms. Mahatma Jotirao Phooley and Ambedkar radically criticized priestly exploitations.

It is in this context that Periyar E. V. Ramasami is significant. He was of the opinion that, all the inequalities and oppressions found in the society were created by priestly/Brahmanic religion. Rather than opting for a new religion, Periyar

1 Periyar E. V. Ramasami, is the founder of a Dravidian Movement in Tamilnadu, called 'Dravida Kazhagam'(DK) in 1944. He is dearly called Periyar. He advocated social reforms prior to political.

2 The expression 'priestly Hinduism' is used as synonym to 'Brahmanic Hinduism.'

thought, religions should be rationally evaluated from the perspective of human life. Any religion or religious practice that obstructs human dignity should be abandoned. He stood for self-respect (individual freedom and dignity).

2. Reasons for Critiquing Priestly Hinduism

Periyar can be understood only from the point of the environment in which he grew up.[3] His personal encounters with evils of religion and caste had directly contributed to his rationalist thinking. He was born on September 17, 1879 in Erode (Tamil Nadu).[4] He belonged to the Naicker caste the upper stratum of the *Sudras.*[5] *His father was a well-to-do businessman.*

At the age of six his father admitted him in a school.[6] His interest toward education was insignificant. Yet the dehumanizing experience that he underwent in the school motivated Periyar to be stoutly critical about the social system and religious practices around him.

During the school days, his parents instructed him that he should drink water only from his teacher's house. When he went to the teacher's house, he came across a very unpleasant and unforgettable experience. Periyar writes:

> The teacher was a strict vegetarian. He belonged to a caste called 'Oduvar.' I went to his house once or twice to drink water. In that house a small girl used to place a brass tumbler on the ground, and pour water in to it. I was instructed to lift the vessel and drink without sipping it. After that she would pour water on the vessel, lift it and wash inside and then take it into the house. Because I am accustomed to sip water from the vessel, a part of the water would fall on my body. Only a little water would go in to the mouth. Some times water would enter my nose and cause trouble. I had to spit out the water instantly. Sometimes the girl would get angry on seeing this.[7]

Paulraj describes another, almost similar experience of younger Periyar and remarks that "the boy made a pledge to himself that he should eradicate

---

3 E. Sa. Visswanathan, *The Political career of E. V. Ramasami Naicker,* Ravi & Vasanth Publishers, Madras, 1983, p. 17.

4 Cf, John Kumar, S. J., "A Secular Response: Periyar E. V. Ramasamy Naicker", *Emerging Dalit Theology,* ed. By Xavier Irudayaraj, S. J., Jesuit Theological Secretariat, Madras, 1990, p. 70.

5 Anita Diehl, *Periyar E. V. Ramasami: A Study of the Influence of a Personality in Contemporary South India,* B. J. Publications, 54. Janpath, New Delhi, 1978, p. 19.

6 M. D. Gopalakrishnan, *Periyar Father of Tamil Race,* Emerald Publishers, Annasalai, Madras, 1991, p. 1.

7 *Collected works of Periyar EVR.*, 2nd revised ed., Vol. 1, The Periyar Self-Respect propaganda Institution, "Periyar Thidal", 50, EVK Sampath Salai, Madras, pp. 2-3. Hence forth this book will be cited as collected works, Vol. 1.

this demeaning and dehumanizing caste discrimination."[8] In the words of C. J. Anantha Krishnan, "this incident first sowed the seeds of revulsion against casteism in the impressionable mind of young Ramansami."[9] Contrary to Periyar his parents were very pious and religious people. Because of his irreligious behavior and their orthodoxy 'he was treated as untouchable at home.'[10]

On the basis of these harsh experiences Periyar declared that caste is a social issue but enjoys religious sanction; hence religion should be rationally evaluated. Visswanathan writes "… his early experience of the rigidity of the caste system and the practice that went along with it created in him a feeling of revulsion against those who strove to uphold it as the core of the Hindu way of life."[11] In the words of Johnkumar, "in spite of the enviable position enjoyed by this family, Periyar as a young man had encountered humiliating experiences of the caste discrimination. This was the main impetus that made him anti Brahministic…"[12]

His hatred to caste system was gaining ground. Rajagopalan writes, "from his boyhood he was questioning why his parents prohibited him from drinking water in some houses, why he was prevented from joining Muslim boys and play, why lot of Brahmins are fed by his father when lot of poor non-Brahmins are starving..."[13] Periyar's continued reflection convinced him that the priests/ Brahmins used religion and god to impose caste system upon people. In other words, Periyar was convinced that the caste discriminations were the result of misuse of religion by a group of people.

He was sympathetic to the victims of caste degradations. It is explained as "the question of the baleful custom of condemning a certain section of the society as unworthy of equality of the status and freedom of movement was perhaps the one that was uppermost in his mind."[14] Still further, "their state of penury and squalor on the one hand and on the other the disabling social handicap so deeply moved the tender heart of the young boy."[15]

At the age of twelve Periyar was introduced to his father's business. During his leisure he discussed religious matters with the pundits who visited his home.

---

8 R. Paulraj, *Salvation and Secular Humanists in India,* The Christian Literature Society, Post Box – 501, Park Town, Madras – 3, 1988, p. 111.

9 C. J. Anantha Krishnan, "The early years of Periyar", *The Rationalist,* Vol. XVIII, No. 9, (September 1992), p. 24.

10 Cf. A. Arivoli, *Periyar Sethathum Seiya Thavariyathum,* Anbarasi Veliyeetaham, North Street Porulvai, Sikkal, 1979, p. 13.

11 E. Sa. Visswanathan, *op. cit.*, p. 17.

12 JohnKumar, S.J., *op. cit.*, p. 71.

13 E. M. Rajagopalan, *My Memories About thanthai Periyar Prior to 1930,* "Periyarism", G-6, Lloyds Estate, Madras – 14, 1985, p. 28.

14 An Admirer, *Periyar E. V. Ramasami: A Pen Portrait,* 3rd Revised ed., The Periyar Self-Respect Propaganda Institution, 50. E. V. K. Sampath Salai, Madras, 1992, p. 1.

15 *Ibid.*

This helped him to know more about Ramayana, Mahabharata Puranas etc. Visswanathan says, "through their religious discourses and discussions the young Ramasami learnt the rudiments of the philosophical significance of Hindu Mythology and Theology."[16] Sometimes, the pundits had no answer to Periyar's demanding questions. Even if they answered "different pundits gave different answer."[17] This made him to conclude that Brahmins and Sastras were lies.[18] In the words of Gopalakrishnan, "even from his boyhood Periyar had been feeling that the public discourses of *Ramayana, Mahabharata* and the *Puranas* were employed by the pundits and other religious men only as a means of livelihood for themselves and not in order to make people really pious."[19]

When only nineteen, Ramasami married thirteen-year-old Nagammai, his cousin. After six years of family life he took to *Sanyasi* life and traveled all over India as a religious mendicant. Charles Ryerson writes, "at twenty five he became a wandering *Sanyasi,* traveling with two Brahmins and performing Kalakshepams."[20] It is commonly accepted that Periyar's quarrel or disagreement with his father on certain matter resulted in *sanyasin* life. On reaching Benares, the two Brahmin friends left Periyar, because they got free food and did not need any help from Periyar.[21] This made him to think that the Brahmins were unreliable and untrustworthy.

Periyar was left alone in a helpless situation. Friendless and foodless he wandered the streets of Benaras[22] because all the inns were open only for the Brahmins. He was not allowed to enter an inn where Brahmin *Sanyasis* were fed. Once Periyar was pushed out of an inn because he was not a Brahmin.[23] According to P. Vanangamudi, "without food he starved for days and one day, he even ate the left overs (sic) thrown out on a leaf."[24] Rajagopalan says, "on one occasion he had to eat the food thrown in dust bin along with dogs."[25] Having realized that his long hair and mustache prevented others to accept him as a Sannyasi, Periyar

16 E. Sa. Visswanathan, *op. cit.*, p. 20.

17 *Collected works,* Vol. 1, p. 5.

18 Cf. Arivoli, *op. cit.*, p. 16.

19 M. D. Gopalakrishnan, *op. cit.*, p. 43.

20 Charles Ryerson, *Regionalism and Religion: The Tamil Renaissance and Popular Hinduism,* The Christian Literature Society, Post Box-501, Park Town, Madras – 3, 1988, p. 86.

21 Cf. Sami Chitambaranar, *Tamil Talivar Periyar E.V.K. Valkkai Varalaru,* 7th ed. Periyar Self-Respect Propaganda Institution Publication, Trichy, 1975, p. 44.

22 Cf. K. M. Balasubramaniam, *Periyar E. V. Ramasami,* Periyar Self-Respect Propaganda Institution Publications, Trichy-17, 1973, p. 17.

23 Cf. Sami Chitambaranar, *op. cit.*, p. 44.

24 P. Vanangamudi, *Periyar E.V. Ramasamy's Approach to Modernization,* Thesis submitted in partial fulfilment of the Requirements for the Degree of Doctor of Philosophy in History, Department of History, Annamalai University, Annamalai Nagar, 1986, p. 67.

25 E. M. Rajagopalan, *op. cit.*, p. 28.

shaved them off[26] and looked for a job. According to Charles Ryerson, "finally he found himself in Benares working for a math by collecting leaves for puja."[27] When his real identity was betrayed by his life style, he became jobless.

The situation in Benares was contrary to his expectations. Anita Diehl says, "... he was disappointed with his experience in the Holy city."[28] Among Sannyasis, Brahmins were honored.[29] There was uncontrolled immorality and prostitution.[30] About Periyar's Sannyasi experience Nambi Aroonan says, "he obtained an intimate knowledge of the evils widely prevalent in Hinduism, particularly in pilgrim centers like Benares."[31] Paulraj writes, "during these visits to pilgrim centers he came to know of the evils of popular Hinduism and found out that the Brahmin priest used his priestly role to exploit the masses."[32]

Periyar realized that, it was not human value but caste had given priority in Benares. Religious centers were places of all kinds of hooliganism. This experience accelerated Periyar's anti-Brahminic attitude. About this process Visswanathan states, "Ramasami Naicker's opposition to Hindu Orthodoxy and the caste system became more and more out-spoken in his later life for many incidents and his own personal experience as a Sadhu in the holy centers of India contributed to the hardening of this attitude."[33]

After returning from the *sannyasi* tour, Periyar continued his business. His interest for social works, including protesting against social evils motivated him to join the Congress in 1920.[34] To his surprise he found that, in the name of nationalism Congress was upholding caste system and Brahmins dominated it.

Periyar, as the Congress president of Tamil Nadu participated in the Vaikom Satya Graha, which taught him the gravity of untouchability. Gurukulam affair was another one of this kind. Periyar got involved in the Gurukulam affairs in 1925.[35] Gurukulam was a school in the Brahmin village of Kallidaikurichi, Tirnelveli district, supported by the Congress for the training of national heroes. Here the non-Brahmin students were served food separately and only after the Brahmin students had taken their meals.[36] Rajagopalan states that the non-

---

26 Cf. Sami Chitambaranar, *op. cit.*, p. 45.

27 Charles Ryerson, *op. cit.*, p. 45.

28 Anita Diehl, *op. cit.*, p. 8.

29 Cf. E. M. Rajagopalan, *op. cit.*, p. 28.

30 Cf. Sami Chitambaranar, *op. cit.*, p. 46.

31 K. Nambi Aroonan, *Tamil Renaissance and Dravidian Nationalism 1905 – 1944,* Koodal Publishers, Madurai – 625001, 1980, p. 153.

32 R. Paulraj, *op. cit.*, p. 91.

33 E. Sa. Visswanathan, *op. cit.*, p. 7.

34 Cf. M. D. Gopalakrishnan, *op. cit.*, p. 7.

35 Cf. Charles Ryerson, *op. cit.*, p. 87.

36 Choudhary Brahm Perkash, 'Periyar's Relevance Today', *The Modern Rationalist,* Vol. XVII, No. 10 (September 1991), p. 4.

Brahmin students "... were served food outside the dining hall of the Gurukulam, whereas Brahmin boys were served food neatly inside the hall."[37] Periyar being the treasurer of Tamil Nadu Congress stopped Congress' contribution to Gurukulam. This incident further aggravated his opinion against orthodox Brahmins.[38] He also felt that communal representation could help non-Brahmins. It included reservation of seats to the non-Brahmin communities in the legislature and in the services. Since Brahmins dominated the Congress, the proposal was rejected.

Mangala Murugesan quotes an incident from Kudi Arasu, 12th July 1931, to show the Brahmin arrogance. Once when E. V. R. went with Srinivasa Iyengar to a Brahmin's house for dining, he was supplied food in a separate place, leaves used for serving morning tiffin were not removed during lunch and the leaves in which he ate both in the morning and afternoon were there till a night meal was served.[39]

The social, religious political and economic degradations imposed in the name of gods and religion, through the "structure" called Hinduism, by the Brahmins, gradually contributed to the anti-religious and anti-Brahminical attitude of Periyar.

3. Periyar's Critique of Priestly Hinduism

Periyar's acquaintance with Priestly/Brahminic Hinduism convinced him that, religion was responsible for all the evils, particularly caste system, in the society. Thus he began to scorn religion in general and priestly Hinduism in particular.

3.1. Periyar and Religion

For Periyar, two major aspects of religion were social and spiritual. The social dimension of religion accepts religion as a way of life at the exclusion of any divine or supernatural elements. The spiritual dimension of religion consists of beliefs and practices. He treated the former as essential and the latter as non-essential.

Periyar traced the origin of religion to the uncivilized age. According to him, "when human beings were savages without the ability to think deeply about anything, the ideas that were propagated by some for the benefit of society came to be known as religion."[40] It is a set of rules and ideas framed for the life and conduct of man and help him to achieve his ideal.[41] It is obvious that, the very purpose of religion is the welfare of humanity. He states "... any religion however great it may be was founded by one who had at heart the good of public and not

37 E. M. Rajagopalan, *op. cit.*, p. 30.

38 M. K. Mangala Murugesan, *Self-Respect Movement in Tamil Nadu 1920 – 1940,* Koodal Publishers, 121. West Masi Street, Madurai – 625001, p. 38. (year of publication is not given).

39 M. K. Mangala Murugesan, *op. cit.*, p. 53.

40 Periyar, *Man and Religion,* trans. By R. Sundaraju, Rationalist publication, Madras, 1993, p. 3. Hence forth this book will be cited as Man and Religion.

41 *Ibid.*

by one who had the grace of God or quality of God."[42] This social value of religion is further explained as "a religion should be for fostering love. It should induce one to be helpful to others. It should make everyone respect truth."[43]

Periyar considered religion as a way of life. He was against attributing supernatural/spiritual elements to religion. He says, "it is money and propaganda that gives life to religions. There is no divinity or super qualities that keep the torch or religion bright and burning."[44] In the words of Anita Diehl "the religion that Periyar repudiates is the religion which according to him, upholds and gives sanction to religious, social and economic injustice."[45]

Unfortunately the spiritual dimension of religion finds more expressions than the social. As all religious activities were devised to hoodwink the mass, there was no chance for the molding of human character.[46] It also became the place of idleness.[47] This was the situation that called the attention of Periyar. He said religious activities are generally contrary to nature.[48] And religion makes people stupid.[49]

In short it may be said that (1) Periyar accepted religion as a way of life in this world. It was founded for the well-being of humanity in this world. (2) There is no divine or supernatural element in religion. (3) The spiritual dimension of religion is the work of human mind and (4) there is no divine element (particle) in humanity. With these presuppositions he critiqued Hinduism and Priestly Hinduism in particular.

3.2. Hinduism

Periyar says, "the worst untruth that is in circulation is the claim that there is a religion called Hinduism."[50] The term Hindu originally means Indians, and not a religion.[51] He said, "it is a religion forced on the people with the primary intention of hood-winking the people."[52] M. M. Thomas remarks "for him

---

42 Periyar E. V. R., *Philosophy,* trans. By A. Sundaramurthy, Karnataka Dravidian Association Publications, Bangalore, 1959, p. 7.

43 *Collected works* Vol. 1, p. 332.

44 *Ibid.,* p. 328.

45 Anita Diehl, *op. cit.*, p. 49.

46 Cf. *Periyar Kalangiyam,* Vol. 3, complied by K. Veeramani, Periyar Self-Respect Propaganda Institution, Madras. 1979, p. 76.

47 Cf. Thanthai Periyar *Materialism or Prakritivatham,* 5th ed. Periyar Self-Respect Propaganda Institution, Madras, 1984, p. 18.

48 Periyar, *Man and Religion, op. cit.,* p. 4.

49 *Ibid.,* p. 8.

50 *Ibid.,* p. 17.

51 Cf. Periyar Kalangiyam, Vol. 3, p. 39.

52 *Collected works* Vol. 1, p. 13.

(Periyar), Hinduism is founded by Brahmins for their own power interests; they are built on ignorance, illiteracy and poverty of the people, and exploited them."[53]

Periyar attributes the degraded situation of the non-Brahmins in India wholly to their accepting Hinduism. It considered them as slaves.[54] In the view of S. Manickam, slavery in India, which is closely related to caste and untouchability, is primarily based on religion, i.e., Hinduism.[55]

Periyar went to the extent of saying that, *sati*, child marriage, polygamy, superstitions, rituals and ceremonies, the obscenity in Sanskrit literature and on temple walls and towers, the *devadasi* system, women's slavery are the products of the Hindu religion which is stated to be God-given.[56]

3.3. Priestly Hinduism

Priestly Hinduism or Brahmanical Hinduism is the expression used here to denote Hinduism as practiced by the Brahmin priests. Swami Dharma Theertha defines Brahaminical Hinduism as "it may be defined as a system of socio-religious domination and exploitation of the Hindus based on caste, priest-craft and false philosophy, - caste representing the scheme of domination, priest-craft the means of exploitation, and false philosophy a justification of both caste and priest-craft."[57] P. D. Devanandan remarks that Periyar used the word Brahminism to describe the strategy, which Brahmins had used from the early days of the Aryan expansion in India in order to bring the entire religious and social life of Hindu India under their domination.[58] Brahminic Hinduism specifically implies the ways in which Brahmins used and interpreted Hindu scriptures, religious practices and caste system to accomplish their own ends. This is the religion that Periyar critiqued.

Since certain Hindu scriptures aided the interpretations of the Brahmin priests, Periyar starkly criticized their authenticity and validity. He outrightly condemned Manu Dharma Shastra for it upholds Brahmin supremacy on the one hand and social injustice to the non-Brahmins on the other.[59] Another reason is that it obstructs the self-respect of people. He disapproved of Mahabharata

53 M. M. Thomas, *The Secular Ideologies of India and the Secular Meanings of Christ,* C.L.S., Madras, 1976, p. 128.

54 Cf. *Periyar Kalangiyam,* Vol. 3, p. 4.

55 S. Manickam, *Slavery In the Tamil Country A Historical Over-view,* 2nd enlarged and revised ed. C.L.S., Madras, 1993, p. 3.

56 Cf. K. Veeramani "Builder of Astheism in Tamil Nadu: Periyar E. V. Ramasami", *Periyar An Anthology,* Periyar Self-Respect Propaganda Institute, Madras, 1992. pp. 117-118.

57 Swami Dharma Theertha, *History of Hindu Imperialism,* 5th ed. Babasaheb Ambedkar Foundation, Kerala, 1992, pp. 6-7.

58 P. D. Devanandan, *The Dravida Kazhagam A Revolt Against Brahminism,* CISRS, Bangalore, 1959, pp. 6-7.

59 *Collected works* Vol. 1, p. 43.

for it preserves the caste system.[60] He obnoxiously caricatured the characters of Ramayana and interpreted it as the war between Dravidians and Aryans. Paulraj says, "Naicker openly ridiculed the Puranas (popular Hindu religious literature) and called them imaginary, irrational and grossly immoral fairy tales."[61]

Periyar often said that these scriptures should be burnt because "they are not helpful to us in any manner."[62] He also stressed, "it is because of these Puranas and Ithihasas that we are slaves to the Aryans."[63] According to Periyar, Ramayana and Mahabharata were written in view of subduing the non-Brahmin kings who opposed the Brahmins.[64] Nambi Arooran says that they are the result of Brahminical scheming and they do not recognize the equality of all people.[65] From the moral point of view, he said "indiscipline, prostitution and things devoid of self respect galore in this epics."[66] Anaimuthu remarks, "after long years of deep study and constant thought he said emphatically that those smritis and epics contained neither moral maxims nor political ideas."[67] Periyar says that Brahmin writers had no regard for women and therefore they have written such things.[68]

The credibility of Periyar's critique of popular Hindu scriptures can be questioned. Periyar had attempted to render literal interpretation of these scriptures. He had failed to highlight the moral, ethical, social and religious contents of these scriptures. At the same time, his claim can be justified because, firstly, his main aim was to curb Brahminism. Secondly, this was the way in which Brahmins presented and interpreted the scriptures. Thirdly, his intention was not to probe into these scriptures and find out the truth, but just to make the people to disrespect and disregard them. It is very important to note that, Periyar has emphatically stressed the human authorship of scriptures. This is very much relevant to a religiously pluralistic society. It helps people to be critical of their own religious scriptures.

For Periyar, there is no meaning in religious rituals, practices and festivals. He found them all as the crafty work of Brahmins to maintain their standard of life at the cost of non-Brahmins. All rituals are designed in such a way that, all material benefits would go to the priests. To obtain the benefits periodically,

60 Cf. Periyar E.V. Ramasami, *Rationalist Thinking, op. cit.*, p. 17.

61 Paulraj, *op. cit.*, p. 92.

62 *Collected works* Vol. 1, p. 84.

63 *Ibid.*, p. 91.

64 Cf. Thanthai Periyar, Purattu – *Imalaya Purattu,* 4th ed. Periyar Self-Respect Propaganda Institution, Madras. 1983, p. 57.

65 Cf. Nambi Arooran, *op. cit.*, p. 164.

66 *Ibid.*, p. 85.

67 V. Anaimuthu, *Contribution of Periyar E. V.R. To the Progress of Atheism,* Periyar Nul Veliyittakam, Madras, 1980, p. 6.

68 Cf. Periyar E. V. Ramasami, *Declaration of war on Brahminism,* trans. By A. S. Venu, The Dravidar Kazhagam Publication, Madras, 1987, p. 27.

they have framed rituals that are to be celebrated from the cradle to the grave. As different rituals are prescribed to different castes, rituals also in a way ignite the caste system. Periyar held the view that all religious ceremonies are the result of superstitious beliefs. "The astrologer, the magician and the temple priest have always been the prime and the best exploiters of the people's greed and superstition. The trade of these three parasites are interconnected and of mutual benefit."[69] Periyar went to the extent of ignoring all religious ceremonies and suggested priestless ceremonies.

He held that, festivals are nothing, but the mere construct of priest-craft. The Brahmins have given religious flavor to some incidents that happened in some one's life. They are good young boys and girls and prostitutes.[70] During festivals lot of money is simply wasted while millions of people died without food and other basic materials. Festivals are seasons for spreading cholera because devotees from different places come together, bathe together, and live unhygenically. He failed to consider the social dimension of the festivals. It is important because festivals help people to come together, share their joy, exchange gifts etc. They can facilitate cordial relations among people of varied faith and cultural affirmations.

Johnkumar maintains that, according to Periyar, caste system is reinforced by Hindu religion.[71] Anita Diehl says, "Periyar... became convinced that casteism and Hinduism were one and the same."[72] Periyar said, "truly my endeavor is primarily intended to abolish caste. But this matter of abolishing castes has made me speak about the abolition of God, religion, shastras and Brahmins as far as this country is concerned. Castes will go only after these four disappeared."[73] Periyar had rightly discerned that, since religion is the source of caste it should be liquidated. When individuals begin to evaluate their own religions in the light of reason, many elements of exploitations and disharmony can be averted from the society and peace can be established. Ambedkar was of the view that, unless it is realized that, caste has religious sanction, it cannot be eradicated.[74] The same point is dramatically expressed by Periyar that, "when we meet a Brahmin we must greet him 'come on you Bastard!' If he asks you why you say so, ask him why he used the term Shudra in the Sastras and Statute books."[75]

Periyar's protest was vehement. During 1927-28, he campaigned, for burning Manu Dharma Sastra and in 1942 for burning Ramayana and Periya

69 *Collected works* Vol. 1, p. 231.

70 Cf. Periyar E. V. Ramasami, *Rationalist Thinking, op. cit.,* pp. 42-43.

71 Cf. Johnkumar, S.J., *op. cit.*, p. 72.

72 Anita Diehl, *op. cit.*, p. 13.

73 An Admirer, *op. cit.*, p. 103.

74 Cf. A. M. Raja Sekhariah, *B.R. Ambedkar, The Quest for Social Justice,* Uppal Publishing House, New Delhi, 1989, p. 240.

75 Periyar E. V. Ramasami, *Declaration of war on Bhraminism, op. cit.,* p. 30.

Puranam.[76] In 1953, he broke the images of Vinayaka (Ganesha).[77] Periyar and his followers burned parts of the Indian Constitution in 1957 because it encourages caste system.[78] The same year there was a great attempt to remove the title "Brahmin" from the hotel name boards. In 1960 Periyar burned pictures of Rama. In 1971 Periyar organized a superstition eradication conference in Salem. In this conference Rama's image was taken in procession and was beaten by sandals. Hindu deities were obscenely portrayed.[79] The effigy of Rama was burned publicly. Posters revealing the lust of and birth of Hindu deities were found everywhere. "A Salem poster portrayed Brahmin priests standing around Siva, looking as though, they were masturbating him while Parvathi, Siva's wife, held her hand out."[80] Many other photos depicted naked idols and erotic scenes from mythology.

He arranged remarriage to his niece when her husband died at an early age. Periyar also organized self-respect marriages, which were free from any Brahmin involvement. Without the aid of Brahmins, Periyar gave names to children. He even tried to cut the tuft from Brahmin's heads. He also effectively protested against Temple prostitution. To propagate his ideas Periyar started journals. His aim was to show that, human dignity and welfare are more important than gods and religious affairs.

3.4. Religious Concepts

Periyar was of the opinion that, the concepts of God, Soul, Sin, Heaven and Hell are unreal. These are fashioned after the interests of human beings. In his view, "it is nothing but the existence of desires and unfulfilled wants that is responsible for the faith in God."[81] Man created God.[82] He argued against the existence of God. For instance, "if it is true, God cannot be seen or touched, is there any meaning in offering food for him and that too six times a day."[83] Why do people kill each other if God creates them all? His famous anti-God slogan is:

> There is no god, no god at all
> He who invented god was fool
> He who propagated god was a scoundrel
> He who worships god is a barbarian.[84]

---

76 Cf. Nambi Arooran, *op. cit.*, p. 165.

77 Cf. Charles Reyerson, *op. cit.*, p. 89.

78 Cf. *Periyar An Anthology, op. cit.*, p. 119.

79 Cf. Charles Reyerson, *op. cit.*, p. 91.

80 *Ibid.*, p. 178.

81 *Collected works,* Vol. 1, p. 11.

82 Periyar E. V. Ramasami, *Kataul,* Kudi Arasu Pathipakkam Erode, 1960, pp. 4-5.

83 Periyar E. V. Ramasami, *Rationalist Thinking, op. cit.*, p. 25.

84 An Admirer, *op. cit.*, p. 70.

In fact Periyar's main aim was to reform the religion of its caste elements. Thus he said, "if the idol would get polluted by touch of the people, such a god is not required and the idol has to be broken to pieces and used for constructing good roads. Otherwise it may be put near the river banks to be used for washing clothes."[85] Such gods are used to encourage discrimination in the society.[86]

Periyar said, "I can say that soul is a piece of protective false imagination to protect another false imaginary religion."[87] The idea of soul is developed to maintain the doctrine of rebirth. The idea of rebirth is the best means to preserve caste. Periyar asked, if the same souls are born again, how is it possible that the population increases. If some souls are saved, the population should dwindle. The idea that god will forgive sins persuades man to continue sinning. Heaven and Hell are imaginary worlds of Brahmins to swindle money.

4. Implications for Social Reform

Following Periyar's rationalist interpretation of priestly religion it can be said that he did not reject religion as such. He accepted religion as a way of life. He was fully against superstitious elements and supernatural dimension of religion. He felt that, religion is the cause of all evils, particularly caste, in the society and source of exploitation. He stressed that doctrines and dogmas are mere human constructs. On the basis of these views, certain implications for social reform can be drawn.

The first implication is **self-respect.** It includes human dignity and freedom. Periyar maintained that religions should contribute to the self-respect of humanity. Religions and practices that ransom self-respect of humanity should be discarded. Once Periyar said any religion that operates against human dignity or ill-treats human beings should be destroyed.[88] He emphatically said, "even if I were to lead to life in hell, I would deem it better than the earthly one, if I were regarded there as a human being."[89] Another lucid expression is that "even if I were to live in a place where I would have to experience much worse sufferings than those of a hellish life, I would consider it a pleasanter life than this mean, caste-ridden existence, if only I were respected as a man there."[90] He was concerned with all that affected any human effort or human progress.[91] He puts his mission, as "my work is the emancipation of the society. I am for the eradication of the high and the low. I want to restore dignity and respect for all men. I want equal justice and equal treatment and equal opportunities

85 *Collected Works,* Vol. 1, p. 65.

86 Cf. Viduthali 9-1-50.

87 Periyar E.V.R., Philosophy, *op. cit.*, p. 24.

88 Cf. *Kudi Arasu,* 18-12-27.

89 *The Revolutionary Sayings of Periyar, op. cit.*, p. 4.

90 *Ibid.*

91 Cf. *Periyar Kalagiyam,* Vol. 3, p. 152.

of all. Redemption of self-respect and restoration of dignity to mankind is the dedicated task of mine."[92] Since priestly Hinduism perpetuated exploitation of human beings and caste discrimination he condemned it to the extent, nobody had ever dared. He would accept religions if they are subject to reason and committed to human liberation from any oppressive structure, mainly caste.

The second implication is **right perception** of religion and issues. Periyar said "the two things that render people irrational are god and religion."[93] He also maintained "God and religion are confusing the society."[94] Current Indian situation particularly political, religious and social warrants right perception about religion and the issues that are rocking the fundamental fabric of Indian society. People should know, how and when politics, religions and social issues are mixed together to confuse people and ascend into power. In the words of Periyar "Human knowledge alone can remove the pain caused by human ignorance."[95]

The third implication is **serving humanity.** According to Periyar, service is not in the hands of god, but in the hands of people. He says, "belief in God is not in any way useful to help others."[96] Further, "if we are to share the food and work equally there is no necessity for god."[97] He also said, "complete in doing service to others and thus seek your glory and joy."[98] Although, religions can inspire serving others, they can also become stumbling block to broader concept of service. Periyar suggests that service should transcend all religious differences because human welfare takes precedence over religious periphery.

The fourth implication is **accepting religion as a way of life**. Periyar said that, he had no problem with people who accepted religion as a way of life in this world.[99] His understanding of the way of life is distinct:

> People cannot live without religion. I do not mean relationship between man and god or salvation, fate, pardon, reward in the heaven. What I mean is that there must be regard between man and man through love, devotion, peace, brotherhood, honesty and unity. To say the same in understandable language, I would say religion is a way of life, a human movement. If you want to call it religion I have no

92 *Collected Works,* Vol. 1., p. 161.

93 *Collected Works,* Vol. 1., p. 100.

94 *Ibid.*, p. 18.

95 *The Revolutionary Sayings of Periyar,* trans. By Dr. R. Ganapathy, A Periyar Cenetenary Publication, Department of Information and Public Relations, Government of Tamil Nadu, 1985, p. 111.

96 *Collected Works,* Vol. 1., p. 111.

97 *Ibid.*, p. 102.

98 *The Revolutionary Sayings of Periyar, op. cit.*, p. 108.

99 Cf. Kudi Arasu, 1-7-28.

objection: without even a religion of this type it would be difficult for man to live in this earth.[100]

Periyar's interpretation of religion as a way of life is based upon the present requirements of human life here on the earth. It is enlightening and appropriate to the Indian context where religions are turning out to be weapons of large-scale violence and avaricious power politics.

The fifth implication is **human progress**. Periyar's concern was not limited to the individual alone but to the society as a whole. According to him, real progress of a society can take place only when the leaders of the society stop infusing blind faith in fate, destiny, religion and god in the minds of people.[101] He also said, "my only goal is the welfare of the people."[102] Periyar did not reject faith as such but blind faith or superstitious beliefs. He knew that under the disastrous caste hierarchy, non-Brahmins couldn't find hope of development. The harsh caste rules barred them from all progressive efforts. His expectation was that religions would contribute to the development of entire society but not to a group of people. This attitude is essential in a multi religious context.

The sixth implication is **high regard for morality**. Since Periyar has accepted religion as a way of life, he demands morality in religious exercises. For him, morality is more important because it is concerned with this world and life in this world. He says, "religious devotion is for the individual. Character is for all. There is no loss if there is no devotion. Everything is lost if there is no character."[103] Again "God religion, salvation, etc., are an individual's and not a society's concern. Character and honesty are social in the sense that they involve a man's relationship with others."[104] It is also crucial to recognize that Periyar realized the need of sound morality for societal life.

The seventh implication is **harmonious life**. Periyar was eager to accept religion if it offered morality and harmony of life. He says, "I want a religion in which there is true brotherhood, unity and discipline."[105] He was of the opinion that the first obstacle for harmonious life in this world is religion.[106] Periyar's expectation has come as a prophetic realization in the present Indian context. Religions have been used to divide communities in an immoral way. He also suggested "people all over the world should untie. They should have an existence that does no harm to other beings. Means must be found for a peaceful life, free

100 Periyar E. V. Ramasami, *The Salvation to Shudra Slavery,* Dalit Sahitya Akademy, Bangalore, 1986, p. 23.

101 Periyar, *Man and Religion, op. cit.,* p. 2.

102 *The Revolutionary Sayings of Periyar, op. cit.,* p. 7.

103 *The Revolutionary Sayings of Periyar, op. cit.,* p. 107.

104 Periyar, *Man and Religion, op. cit.,* p. 9.

105 Periyar E. V. Ramasami, *The Salvation to Shudra Slavery, op. cit.,* p. 24.

106 Cf. *Periyar Kalagiyam,* Vol. 3, p. 133.

from envy, care, deceit, hatred and sorrow."[107] Further "we should not think that life is only for the sake of the individual. It is also for the welfare of others."[108] People should aim for a life, which is joyful, helpful to others and not causing difficulty to others.[109] Periyar's expectations look simple but that is what the whole world is longing for. Corrupt and communalized power centers, looking for progress, can find appealing corrective measures from the harmonious vision of Periyar.

5. Conclusion

Periyar used "rationalist interpretation" as a hermeneutical principle to critique priestly Hinduism. His supreme aim was to eradicate caste discrimination from the society, which he suffered from his school days. Since religion was the cementing force behind the evil of caste, which is a social issue, he critiqued it from the point of life here in society. His entire contention was that religion as such is not abominable but the way in which it is interpreted to manipulate, subjugate, and enslave sections of the society. He was pained to witness the influence of caste even in the so-called national political party.

Since Brahmanic Hinduism perpetuated caste system with the aid of Hindu religious scriptures, he condemned them and caricatured the scriptural characters to ventilate his unquenchable revulsion against the gruesome religious practices. His portrayal of religious doctrines further vindicates his utter unfaith and disappointment over the validity and utility of religions.

Periyar was unacceptable to many because his stark critique of priestly Hinduism did not acknowledge the positive aspects of religions. Acceptance of the social dimension of religions alone does not suffice to the fuller realization of the positive potentials of religions.

Nevertheless, the implications from the critique of priestly Hinduism for social reforms stand still. Periyar's persistent demand for self-respect for the people, earnest appeal for a right perception of religions and social issues, incessant plea for serving others, unremitting persuasion to the consideration of religion as a way of life, relentless urging for human progress, unwavering appreciation for morality and profuse summon for harmonious life are essential for any society aspiring for reforms. Although his approach was quite rugged, his contributions will always remain as a beacon to many reforms.

---

107 *The Revolutionary Savings of Periyar, op. cit.*, p. 5.

108 *The Revolutionary Savings of Periyar, op. cit.*, p. 107.

109 Cf. *Kudi Arasu* 15-4-28.

19

At the Lord's Disposal

Introduction

Although the traits of prophet, priest, preceptor or a reformer can be discerned from the life of William Carey I do not know whether he was one among them in the strict sense but am sure, like them, he too was 'at the Lord's disposal.' The following description is to illustrate his life so that we may learn a few characteristics of people who are at the Lord's disposal. It is also fitting that the Serampore College (William Carey established) celebrated this year (2018) as its bicentenary.

Early Life

William Carey was born on August 17, 1761 in a little village called Paulerspury, in Northamptonshire of England. His father became a parish clerk in James Anglican church when his traditional weaving gave way. Consequently he had the additional duty as a schoolmaster of the parish school. The family moved to the school house in 1767.

William was the eldest among five children. He started schooling at six in the parish school, worked as an altar boy and attended the choir in the Church. While still in school, he read every book he could find. He also developed interests in birds, insects, plants, seeds, etc., and did things with a never-give-up spirit.[1]

1 Ralph Woodworth, *Father of Modern Missions*, (Hyderabad: Authentic Books, 2012), 8.

Gardener

In 1773, at the age of 12, William finished school and began working as a gardener. Soon he had to stop this work as he became sick due to heat. His father however, found him another job.

Shoe Maker Cobbler at Piddington (1775-1785)

William began his apprentice work as a shoemaker (under Clarke Nichols) in Piddington, seven miles from Paulerspury. There, he met John Warr (3 years older to him) of Potterspury who was also working under the same master. They became friends.

ln 1776, during the Christmas season William replaced a counterfeit shilling with his master's. When the matter came to light William was afraid but his master allowed him to continue his work. This made William draw closer to God and began to pray for Clarke Nichols (married in October 1777).

William was an Anglican but John Warr, led him to become a Baptist and won the seventeen year-old William to Christ.[2]

The prayer of William and John Warr drew Nichols closer to God before his untimely death in September 1779. Soon after his death, the widow's cousin, Thomas Old of Hackleton told him that he will take over the shop and we must do everything possible to ease the widow's grief.

Marriage

Thomas Old's wife Elizabeth, introduced her sister Dorothy Plackett to William. William and Dorothy were married on June 10, 1781. They began a simple life, even friends collected money to help them. William's mother seemed frailer each year. Polly, one of his sisters now fourteen, suffered a nerve disease, as parts of her body became numb. Her elder sister Ann now seventeen said 'the tender mercies of the Lord can be cruel.'[3] William continued to be active in the Hackleton Meeting House which became a church in May 19, 1778.

Carey and Dorothy dwelt in their cottage for six years. Their first child was born in the summer of 1782. She (child) fell sick and died in 1784. William was sick for a long time to the extent he lost his hair on the head. Dorothy feared for William's life. But he told her, it shows you don't trust the Lord.

Thomas Old died unexpectedly in 1783 when not even forty. Carey had to shoulder the responsibility of taking care of his wife's widowed sister and her four orphans as well as the business.

On October 20, 1785, a second child was born to William and Dorothy, named him Felix which means "happiness."

---

2 L. Prabhudass, William Carey (Madras: Glad Tidings Distributors,1993), 8.

3 Sam Wellman, *William Carey: Father of Modern Missions*, Indian ed. (Secunderabad: OM Books, 2004), 38.

Skills and Vision

William was a gifted linguist. At twelve, he memorized a Latin vocabulary book. After coming across a Greek New Testament in Nichols' shoe shop, immediately, he bought a Greek Dictionary and a Grammar book and began to learn Greek. Thomas Gotch a shoe dealer financially helped William to concentrate on language study and ministry in the church.

After the marriage of John Warr in April of 1780, William was often in the shop alone and even he began to attend the Church of England again. Once he listened to Thomas Scott, an Anglican and was shocked to learn Scott had mastered Latin, Greek, and Hebrew! William began to learn Hebrew too with Scott's help and books.

William made a large map drawn by hand on several pieces of paper/leather stuck together and marked on it information about each country as he had found them in his reading.

Anglican to Baptist

On 10th February, 1779 William Carey joined the Protestant church much to the disappointment of his parents.[4] He was baptized on 5th October, 1783. Just a few weeks later his sisters also were baptized.

Teacher at Moulton (1785-1789)

William struggled to keep food on the table all through 1784. On March 25, 1785, he moved to Moulton and started a school there. The church at Moulton invited him to be the pastor. He also continued his business of shoe making. The strength as well as income of the school declined when a previous school teacher returned and restarted his school. William continued to learn different languages.

William was ordained on August 1, 1787 in the Baptist Church of Moulton, Just weeks after his mother's funeral. His coat for the occasion was bought by collection made among friends.

Pastor Carey

When twenty and married, the Church at Hackleton asked the apprentice shoemaker, William, to preach.

The congregation of Baptists at Earls Barton, east of Northampton, even persuaded him to preach there every other week. Even there was a request to preach once a month at Paulerspury.

William Carey was now twenty-two, preacher, shoemaker and bald headed. To others it seemed he had a thousand problems. To himself he was enraptured by faith. His faith was blossoming, he was sure. He was now being tested by sickness, mourning, and poverty, but no longer doubt.

4 L. Prabhudass, William Carey (Madras: Glad Tidings Distributors, 1993), 9-10.

William recovered his health again. At the Hackleton Meeting House he joined discussions. Once a month now they discussed the churchman's [sic] obligation to evangelize, not just within his parish but the entire world. William found himself drawn more and more to the idea that the "Great Commission"[5] did indeed require churchmen to spread Christ to the entire world.

He also served the Baptist Church at Olney and the Harvey Lane Church in Leicester.

Missionary Urge

The birth (1790) and death of a daughter, Lucy, made the ordeal even worse. Lucy's tender innocence reminded William he could fail too.[6]

From his early days William was intensely interested in the people of other lands. His conviction grew that it was the duty of the Church to take seriously Christ's command to go 'into the entire world and preach the gospel,' and he began to press for the formation of a society to further this aim.[7]

He was careful about bringing up the subject in association meetings. In 1788 while raising money in Birmingham for the church building in Moulton he met Thomas Potts, a businessman who supported (offering £10 towards the cost of printing) William to publish his book: *An Enquiry into the Obligations to Use Means for the conversion of the Heathens [sic], in Which the Religious State of the Different Nations of the World, the Success of Former Undertakings, and the Practicability of Further Undertakings are Considered.* It was published on May 12, 1792.[8]

In this book, he rebutted all ideas against mission/great commission, discussed history of mission from apostle to the present, countries and their religious statistics including cruel practices, practicality of undertaking mission, responsibility of Christians and ended with a future hope.

Once in a ministers' meeting William asked them to discuss "if the command to the disciples to teach all nations did not mean all ministers to the end of the world." To that, Ryland, as chairman of the meeting, answered: "Young man, sit down. When God pleases to save the people of other lands, He will do it without asking you or me."[9]

---

5 Mark 16:15 "Go into all the world and proclaim the gospel to the whole creation."

6 Sam Wellman, *William Carey: Father of Modern Missions*, Indian ed. (Secunderabad: OM Books, 2004), 56.

7 E. L. Wenger, "The Serampore Mission and its Founders," in *The Story of Serampore and its College*, 4th ed. (Serampore: The Council of Serampore College, 2005), 1.

8 Ralph Woodworth, *Father of Modern Missions*, (Hyderabad: Authentic Books, 2012), 22.

9 Ralph Woodworth, *Father of Modern Missions*, (Hyderabad: Authentic Books, 2012), 21.

Baptist Mission Society

In a meeting held in May 30-31, 1792 William preached a sermon (Isaiah 54: 2-3) and ended with the famous saying:

Expect great things from God
Attempt great things for God.

The same year the Baptist Mission Society was established in England. William's father feared that he would offer himself to go as a missionary. William replied that **he was at the Lord's disposal** but had little expectation of actually going to a foreign country himself. Dr. John Thomas, volunteered to be the first missionary to India. William could not contain himself any longer and offered himself as Dr. Thomas's assistant!

To India

The Baptist Missionary Society had agreed to send William and Thomas as missionaries to Bengal as its first field. Dorothy blindly rejected and she did not want to go. East India Company was not giving permission to missionaries to travel. But Thomas out of his previous experience suggested not getting licences was not a problem. The ship in those days was small and uncomfortable. But Carey was not afraid of facing such hardships.

Captain White of the *Earl of Oxford* agreed to take them to India without licence. Soon a team of seven was aboard the *Earl of Oxford.* Finally, one day in early May the captain summoned Dr. Thomas to come immediately. It seemed someone had warned the captain that the authorities in Calcutta have been put on notice that there is one passenger aboard without a licence. William, his son and Thomas were de-boarded from the ship.

Next Ship

William took it that it happened for good. They went home and waited until they came to know that a Danish ship *Krön Princess Maria* was going to Bengal. Meanwhile, Thomas persuaded Dorothy to join William. Dorothy insisted that her sister Kitty should go with her. Kitty, after prayer, agreed. With that Dorothy finally agreed to go to India. Money was collected for their tickets. The ship had arrived. Two hours later they were on the ship. Soon it was sailing. They were on their way to India at last. And best of all, Carey had his whole family with him, including Jabez, less than two months old. Since he now had his family with him, William never expected to return to England.

During the voyage Carey was dangerously ill. God healed him. Then he faced a storm and the tidal waves almost sank the ship. In the mornings and evenings and Sundays William led a worship service in their large cabin for their own eight and a fairly constant dozen others.

A black woman and her infant were not so fortunate. They died before the *Kron Princessa Maria* could reach Cape Town. The entire ship offered up their prayers as their bodies were claimed by the deep.

A few days later a ship's carpenter died. A third body was claimed by the sea. William prayed it was their last sacrifice to the sea. And at long last the ship entered the Hooghly river. The voyage took nearly five months; eventually William Carey with family and companions arrived in Calcutta, India on 11th November, 1793.

Carey used the time (in ship) by having Thomas teach him the Bengali language. Thomas had translated the Gospels of Mark and Matthew into that language. Now he and Carey worked together to translate Genesis.

In India

Advised by the friendly Captain Christmas of the Danish vessel Maria, Carey landed at the mouth of the river Hooghly and, to avoid opposition of the British officials, reached Calcutta in a native fishing boat!

The missionaries had gone ashore at a very large market. Thomas had already made various arrangements. He had sent a messenger to the house where his wife and the three others were staying. They were to meet the new arrivals north of Calcutta in a Portuguese settlement called **Bandel.**

In Bandel, Thomas introduced Ram Ram Basu (interpreter) to William. They traveled by boat and by foot to the small villages around.

But at Bandel, Felix, then Dorothy, became very sick with what was called the "bloody flux." It was a form of diarrhea so severe it was accompanied by blood. It was the bane of foreigners in India.

Manicktullo

From Bandel the family moved to Monicktullo and stayed in a rented house. His wife grew unhappy. William visited some Englishmen in Calcutta during the day, only to be treated with contempt. Even a prominent clergyman to whom he had an introduction written by John Newton had refused to see him. Dorothy and her sister became more and more discontented.

Departed to Sundarbans

With the help of a money lender William found free land in Debhatta. On the evening of February 3, 1794, Carey, now thirty-two years old, Dorothy, who had just turned thirty-eight, and Kitty, thirty, stepped into a boat with the boys: Felix, eight, Willy, five, and Peter, four. Dorathy carried nine-month-old Jabez. Ramram Basu also went.

William and Felix walked to their land each day and cleared it. The two laid out a garden, then William paced off the dimensions for a house. The house, built on stilts high off the ground, would be framed and floored with bamboo, then walled and roofed with mats. Until they completed the work they lived in the bungalow of Charles Short.

One day Charles Short got a letter for William from Dr. Thomas. George Udny was now an important East India Company official there, one entrusted with encouraging business enterprises. Would Dr. Thomas be interested in running an indigo processing plant near Malda? he had asked. The salary was fixed and quite substantial. The plant manager would have a nice house, even servants. Thomas agreed to run the indigo plant at Mahipaldighi.

Would William be interested in running a similar plant near Mudnabati? The generous salary would be the same! And William too would have a nice house and servants. Udny believed he could even pull strings to get the two men licenses, so at least they would be free from the threat of being arrested. If William was interested, he must write to Thomas at once. Then Thomas would send him the money to make the three-hundred-mile trip north.

William abandoned his bamboo house. He spent all his time learning Bengali.

And what could be more ambitious, festering in a muddy forest with a distraught wife, then to begin translating the Bible into Bengali? But that was exactly what he began to do with Ram Ram Basu's help.

At last the money came from Thomas. It was nearly the last week in May, the traditional start of the monsoons. William hurriedly loaded a large, canopied boat he had hired in advance. Kitty decided to marry Charles Short.

Malda

On the dawn of May 23, 1794, without Kitty, the Careys headed north. They were welcomed warmly by the George Udnys. The house pleased Dorothy. William developed a garden. As steward of God's gift, he also intended to raise ducks, chickens, cattle and sheep. Soon he hoped to even have the luxury of a horse!

William continued to labor on his translation of the Bible into Bengali. This was very important. Its by-product was to be a mastery of Bengali sufficient to actually preach to the natives. He started a school, church and a clinic to help the people.

William and his five year old son Peter fell sick – due to Jungle fever. On October 11 Peter died. The death and the events following death shattered Dolly. She began losing control of her mind.

Indigo Plantation Further North

Due to heavy flood the indigo business suffered. Udnys wanted to shut the plant. Thus William decided to move further north to establish another plant. And make provisions for accommodating new missionaries. But the new missionaries went to Serampore. They invited William to Serampore.

Moving to Serampore

By January 1, 1800, William with all his goods headed to Serampore. There with the help of other missionaries set up a printing press. He became professor of Bengali, Sanskrit and Marathi at Fort William College in Calcutta. During the free hours he concentrated on translation, preaching etc.

He translated the Bible into Bengali, Sanskrit, Oriya. Marathi. There are reports that during his time the Bible was translated into more than 30 languages in full or in part. From there missionaries were sent to China, Burma. During their fast moving printing activity their printing press met with a huge fire accident. William was also involved in social concerns.

Although the Serampore missionaries enormously contributed to education, journalism, etc, in 1818 the Serampore College was established, a vision William waited for so long. Subsequently the King of Denmark granted a Royal charter authorizing the college to confer degrees. [1918, Bengal Government by an act authorized the establishment of the Senate of Serampore College].

Successful End

William was the one who said: Attempt great things for God
and expect great thinks from God

The emblem of the Serampore College has in it a Bible, the cross and a pelican feeding the young ones from her own blood.

One day William used his meager remaining energy to admonish a visitor who had repeated praise too often, "Dr. Carey this, Dr. Carey that! Cried William, "Please, sir, after I am gone, praise nothing about Dr. Carey. Praise only Dr. Carey's Savior!"

William instructed that the following words be written on his tomb:

A wretched, poor, and helpless worm,
On Thy kind arms I fall.

William Carey died at sunrise on June 9, 1834. Funeral was attended by Hindus, Muslims, Christians...

Conclusion

A few insights can be underlined from the life of William Carey who was 'at the Lord's disposal.' The life and journey of God's servants go through multifaceted experiences, uncertainties and even very rugged path. God's choice of his servants is not based on family and status but perseverance and full dedication. God's servants attribute overcoming of failures to the grace of God. Being in God's service does not mean being free from sorrow and pain but having strength to withstand and be focused. All loses and heavy burdens in the process of God's service are not to abandon service but move forward in the midst of them. For servants of God poverty and hardship are not obstacles. They always look for opportunities to dedicatedly serve without being discouraged bust steadily moving forward.

Bibliography for Further Study

Beck, James R. *Dorothy Carey: The Tragic and Untold Story of Mrs. William Carey*. Grand Rapids: Baker, 1992.

Carey, Eustace. *Memoir of William Carey D. D.* Hartford: Canfield and Robins, 1837; microfiche, Louisville: Lost Cause Press, 1996.

Carey, S. Pearce. *William Carey, D. D., Fellow of the Linnean Society*. London: Hodder & Stoughton, 1923. Reprint, London: Wakeman Trust, 1993.

Carey, William. *An Enquiry into the Obligations to Use Means for the Conversion of the Heathens*. Leicester: Ann Ireland, 1792, new facsimile ed. With intro by Ernest A. Payne. London: Carey Kingsgate Press, 1961.

Drewery, Mary. *William Carey: A Biography*. Grand Rapids: Zondervan, 1979.

Finnie, Kellsye, *William Carey: By Trade a Cobbler*. London: Kingsway Publications, 1986.

Gardner, Brian. *The East India Company*. New York: McCall, 1971.

George, Timothy. *Faithful Witness: Life and Mission of William Carey*. Birmingham, Ala: New Hope, 1991.

Marshman, John Clark. The Life and Times of Carey, Marshman and Ward, 2 vols., London: Longman, Brown, Green, Longman, and Roberts, 1859; microfiche.

Potts, E. Daniel. *British Baptist Missionaries in India, 1793-1837: History of Serampore and Its Missions*. Cambridge: U Press, 1967.

Prabhudass, P. L. *William Carey*. Madras: Glad Tidings Distributors, 1993.

Smith, George. *The Life of William Carey*. 2nd ed. London: John Murray, 1885; microfiche.

The Council of Serampore College. *The Story of Serampore and its College*, 4th ed. Serampore: The Council of Serampore College, 2005.

Wellman, Sam. *William Carey: Father of Modern Missions*. Indian ed. Secunderabad: OM Books, 2004.

Woodworth, Ralph. *Father of Modern Missions: William Carey D. D.* Hyderabad: Authentic Books, 2012.

Conclusion

In sum, one notices the intent of offering these reflections and suggestions, to help coordinate the courses on Religion in the Senate M.Th. and BD syllabus. The key to religious harmony has been principled on living with the people of other faiths in dialogue. Life sustaining existence is thus based on understanding the other as one journeying in the path of faith and knowing the problems and challenges of the same on that journey. The following pointers convey these issues and challenges and the way to address them.

1. While evaluating the new curriculum one has to bear that different strands of thoughts will continue to exist side by side with the favored and the newly emerging ones. Therefore emphasizing one aspect does not mean other aspects are ignored. What is important is to prioritize the relevant concerns. Every branch of M.Th. study needs to include a course on pedagogy even before the commencement of evaluation of M.Th. curriculum as M.Th. being the basic degree for teaching. In order to avoid the notion of 'too ambitious' clear demarcation between BD and M.Th. courses, standards are necessary to be set. It helps limit the scope of different courses and make it manageable. It can be helpful in managing stipulated time frame for different courses. The emerging view points out that many courses that are lengthier needs serious consideration. In this regard the senate fraternity should courageously be satisfied with courses in consonance with time limit permissible to a BD degree course. It will also be immensely credible if the Senate can workout course numbers that are the same in the syllabus and examination registration form. Of course the one inalienable factor that has to motivate the religion pedagogy is to ensure that God's Mission is carried out at all circumstances in collaboration even with other religions and ideologies. Finally to sum up, the pedagogy of religions needs to help religions to be viewed as a vital ingredient in the varied story of humankind's various experiments in living, to help grasp the meanings and values of the plural cultures of today's world, to help see the great ideas and practices of various important cultures and civilization, to help judge people, help animate community relations in plural contexts, help

analyze the importance of religions in human life, help interaction between religion and ideologies, help religious communities to participate in the struggle for an inclusive human community, help understand and appreciate the religious experience of people of other faiths, help gain new insights for the Christian faith-experience, help encourage intra and inter-faith dialogue, help avoid fear of Hinduism, help promoting democratic living, help avoiding reduction of religion to mere ethics, help overcome traditional religious education based on scriptures, help recognizing common humanness, help cooperation between religion and ideologies, help interaction between religion and theology, help see causes for renewal of religious traditions, help recognize plurality of religions, help promote dialogical approach, help sincere study of tribal and dalit religions and help adequate space for other significant developments.

2. Various factors and persons have contributed to the establishment of the 'Science of Religion.' While science of religion has benevolent objectives, there are objections to it as well. If religions are to be studied as the founding parents envisaged, the end result would be harmony and fellowship among religions. Although, the scientific study of religions is now well developed than originally intended, it needs to be pursued with due respect to the plurality of faith traditions and to the underlying principle of religious harmony among adherents of diverse faith orientations.

3. Max Muller founded the "Science of Religion." Its main task is to study religion scientifically. The scientific study of religion concentrated on the origin of religion. For this the comparative and historical perspectives were applied. The early anthropological theories saw the origin of religion in animism, animatism, manism, supreme beings, magic etc. The anthropologists of religion used rigorous empirical method to study this. The sociologists of religion interpreted religion as a social phenomena. The phenomenological perspective found the essence of religion in some 'sacred focus.' And the psychological perspective located religion in human psyche.The science of religion therefore had to tackle some crucial issues. One of them was whether religion should be defined at all. Whether the insider or the outsider should study religion is another issue. The ever-growing quantity of data raises serious concern to the scholars of religion. The study of living religions faces new issues, which were never a problem to the scholars of primal religions. To avoid all seeming hardships in the study of religion, a multi-methodic approach is convincing. The scientific study of religion offers valuable insights, which are relevant to the specific Indian context. A challenging Indian perspective for the scientific study of religion can be formulated on the basis of these insights. Any relevant perspective for the scientific study of religion should take "Life" as the hermeneutical principle.The growing communal conflicts in India can be lessened, if religions are studied scientifically and their findings

are made known to their adherents. It will be promising to implement the 'Science of religion' in the regular college curriculum. The Indian pluralistic context demands that every citizen is aware of the findings of the "Science of Religion."

4. Our context is overshadowed with forceful advocacy of a singular ideology. It demands prudent understanding and interpretation of other traditions and concepts. Dialogically orienting our researches can be one way of providing a loving response to this context. This can help our continuous commitment to a sustainable capability enhancement to the multifariously deprived ones.
5. In the face of the active communal tensions triggered by terrorizing activities, for one or other purpose, as a theological community we have a responsible role to play as we learn from others and educate others for the challenging tasks ahead for a harmonious living in a pluralistic context like India.

The specific call for such a responsible role is emerging from the reality of many faith-traditions that are some time conflicting but at the same time dynamic and willing to relate with the other and work with the other towards an all inclusive sustainable goal.In this process we need to constantly strive to discern the really religious concerns from the other accidental or incidental accumulations for the sake of cooperation and working together towards life sustaining vision and mission. This will be further strengthened if we can recognize the unity of real purpose that underlies all the religions in spite of the obvious differences. Once this recognition is achieved we can move forward in establishing mutual sharing or substantial relationship with other faith-traditions for the sake of committing ourselves to struggle for a sustainable existence. As we progress in this direction, we need to humble ourselves about our own faith affirmations which are ultimate and absolute to us, while accepting the possibility of ultimate and absolute faith affirmations that may be in different forms than ours, in other faith-traditions as well. This bold challenge is indispensable to avoid the destructive utility of the power of religions. This is looking beyond the set proposals to approach other faith-traditions in order to address the currently emerging threats to establishing a sustainable existence.

One of the basic signs of embarking on this hard terrain in accordance with our faith commitment to God which, we inherited from the faith in the life and work of Jesus Christ is to instill these acknowledged challenges in our theological formulations which, of course is the interpretation of our faith relevant to the contextual realities. It is not mere Indian Christian theology, but theology resulting from the realistic existence of many faith-traditions. The culmination principle of this process, at least in our times, is the confluence of religious resources towards hammering a paradigm to address the struggles of life in order to seek and establish a sustainable existence.

Creating and involving (in) such a paradigm has become the trend emerging in the present missiological considerations. Although this consideration is not free from challenges, an open approach free from traditional ones to include the other as well, in our study and application, can lead us further. Positively, considering the other and cooperating with the other and working together with the other towards sustainable existence is not only a religious affair, it is not only the missiological consideration of Christians. It is also the inherent and implicit expectation of secularism, at least from the point of the Indian Constitution in India, which cannot be ignored at any level as we work together towards a sustainable existence. It is not at all surprising that all the afore maintained appeals are the reality of the life and work of Jesus, which inspire and embolden all of us to advance further in our commitment to serve God purposefully in the given context. In the end, in our approach to other faith-traditions we should not fail to recognize the basic principles that all are committed to the ultimate through diverse channels and life that needs to be strengthened towards sustainable existence. Above all, faith in Jesus is the key to our theological agenda, as we open ourselves to the truth that there are other faith-traditions as well. The relevant method to approach other faith-traditions, in our context, is "Life Sustaining" based on the "Struggles for Life," which helps crossing the boundaries with purpose and at the same time necessitate safe return and relaxation in one's own faith-tradition. Therefore the kinds of struggle and contents of sustainable life are kept open-ended so as to be always open to the newer possibilities.

6. The 'life sustaining dialogue' demands that every individual or community must be rooted and filled with the Sakti or spirit of their particular religion or ideology while being open to learning from each other and working with each other even with differences. It is a long, laborious and sacrificial process comparable to the notion of "Jivan Mukta" in the Indian setting that considers the world as one, i.e., Vasudevakudumbam, where concern for the lives of others is the sign of spiritual maturity attained in and through interreligious and inter ideological dialogues. This process takes spiritual inspiration for dialogue seriously because the person who is rooted in the spiritual foundation can be the upholder of *dharma* towards people, creatures, and the cosmos as a whole. This realization dawns on to the Christian because of his/her intensive commitment to the principles of Jesus.

   A close observation of life of the people of different traditions can teach us that every human being is striving to live. A better life is what every one aspires for. No one wants to enslave himself/herself to poverty or suffering of any kind. In this stark-naked struggle for life, rather better life, no individual is comfortably placed because of his/her religious identity. Interreligious/ideological dialogue is an unavoidable tool to realize the multifaceted potentials of humanity to establish 'life sustaining vision.' Our endeavor in working for the friendliness of religions is to strengthen life. Life sustaining vision of dialogue is the tangible solution for religious harmony, peace and prosperity.

The church has the responsible mission of facilitating cooperation between religions and ideologies through a selfless dialogue which is symbolized in the death of Jesus on the cross with the firm hope of glory. One has to be strong in his/her faith and conviction for an effective and a fruitful dialogue.

Jesus came to enrich life, to obliterate all the religious systems and practices which worked against 'life.' To give life to the needy, Jesus broke away many traditional laws. He was always of the view that religion is for life and life is not for religion. Hence, 'life sustaining vision of dialogue' can help religions and ideologies to explore their best for a sustainable life.

7. The current global situation requires that religions need to be united without losing their individuality and differences for the sake of presenting a better life. A viable paradigm for such an undertaking is the life sustaining pluralist perspective. It does justice to the many forms of religion on the one hand and struggles of humanity on the other. This is also in consonance with the life and mission of Jesus Christ, which the church is expected to bear witness.

8. In the traditional societies the sway of religion on the politics was an accepted principle. The modernity discourses have brought in secularization and secular polity mainly through colonialization. Yet the fact remains in India that secularization and communalization of politics exists simultaneously. Religion is used by politicians to galvanize support for them, as it facilitates mass mobilization.

   Although the Congress was a secular party in its early phase, in its later stage, it became a mix of secular as well as communal politics. Thus the purely secular commitment of the Congress came under the attack of the religious radicalssoon.

   Consequently the religious fanatics formed political parties to implement religious programs. The dangers of the failures of the process of secularization and secularism became thus really a matter of concern.

   In order to fight the communal political affiliates, without disturbing the genuinely religious sentiments of the committed people a consideration of Gandhian model seemed beneficial against communal politics, in accordance with the Constitution in terms of the beauty of plurality in India as Nehru conceived.

9. One of the prerequisites for any form of peace building efforts is freedom of religion which is often challenged by majority-minority conflicts and its resulting gross injustice and inequality. Prevalence of injustice and inequality

causes hostilities. At this juncture nonreligious bodies using religious sentiments for other than religious reasons add fuel to fire.

Our commitment to the Indian Constitution however to establish justice and equality which are basic to peace and peaceful coexistence often comes under the attack of misrepresentation and misinterpretation generating willful disturbances.

It is important that we need to follow the constitutional commitment to establish communal harmony and fraternity which help peace building. It is also our basic duty to contribute towards facilitating a conducive atmosphere for the principles of the Constitution to function.

Poverty which is the net product of injustice and inequality of all sorts is the main challenge for the peace initiatives. It needs to oppose plans of any form of dominance allowing healing to take place.

As freedom of religion is a constitutional and ahuman rights guarantee, it is a basic requirement for peace building, as religions and their adherents need to learn to live together by accepting and respecting each other. This is possible if we approach the ultimate as a mystery and consider our knowledge of it as partial. Once the source of superiority claims is properly understood, dialogical activities among varying faith-traditions towards peace initiatives become meaningful.

In order to make peace initiatives relevant and positive, our dialogical endeavors need to rest on human rights concern based upon the common humanness behind all the apparent differences and undertakings in a sustainable way.

10. I have highlighted, not the entire, but a few challenges that are at hand for the minorities to be vigilant and active in our commitment to the church and society. The programs suggested both broad and active are not the whole range of solutions. May God enlarge our wisdom to stand up to the occasion.

11. Aleaz's definition/meaning of religion would be substantial had it emphasized the need for religions to focus upon life sustaining issues. Further, the life sustaining implications present in the methodology should become explicit. Aleaz's definition of theology of religions is focused on the pursuit of relational convergence of religions. Yet it needs to have space for religions and ideologies which believe in the nonexistence of God, yet committed to the life sustaining relational convergence of religions.

    Although a proponent of pluralistic inclusivism, Aleaz is sympathetic with the school of pluralism. His evaluation of pluralism can also include the necessity of considering the ideologies and atheistic religions that contribute to common causes. In the light of the relativist school, Aleaz's view that Hinduism stands for religious pluralism needs reconsideration. His expectation of the return of the pre-Diamper Christianity cannot ignore the growing exclusivistic tendencies of the churches. Other related questions are how does pluralistic inclusivism and universal Jesus go together.

Considering the entire religious resource of the universe as a common property of all may well fit within the parameters of freedom of religion/ human rights rather than pluralistic inclusivism. Relational convergence of religions in the frame work of pluralistic inclusivism is not the solution to all issues, but it is the life sustaining vision that leads to relevant solution. Promoting one particular thought pattern alone, for strengthening religious relations may lead to another form of exclusivism.

Over emphasis of the connection between religion and culture may shelter communal ideologies and fundamentalist thinking. Pursuing a composite culture, in the place of multi culture, may lead to a mono-culture which is not Indian at all. Likewise, promoting the assumption that there is a connection between culture and politics in India can also bring about adverse consequences in the line of Sangh Parivar's ideology. Hence, there is a great need to reiterate the fact of many religions and many cultures in India. Accepting Hindu culture as Indian culture is incorrect.

Aleaz's uncritical acceptance and application of Indian philosophical *pramanas* for the construction of Indian Christian philosophy is not in consonance with the spirit of the present theological developments. His respect for Advaita on the basis of its world-god-life relation cannot draw the conclusion that Advaita is the only way to relational convergence of religions. Aleaz's overemphasis on Advaita, is not in conjunction with his idea that 'even within the same school of religious experience (Swami Ram Tirtha and Sister Nivedita) there is the possibility of divergent expressions.'

In the definition, sources and the main thrust of Indian Christian theology, the Advaitic elements flow profusely. It also needs to be noted that many Christians in India connect Advaita with the symbol of oppression.

Aleaz's presentation of Eastern Christian thought of God and creation, supposed to be from Advaita point of view, swings among, Advaita, Visistadvaita and Eastern mystery. His invitation to Advaita to assist Eastern Christian thought is the outcome of the concerns that Aleaz is addressing.

In Aleaz's presentation of the Fall and restoration, the proposal for descent and ascent is comprehensive as they have space for the entire cosmos but there is no role for Advaita because the church, sacrament and liturgy are quite conclusive in their role to the members of the church.

Whether salvation as deification comprehends the Advaitic god-human-nature composition is a legitimate question. Aleaz's anticipation for the pre Diamper days, i.e., pluralism, does not synthesise his constant appeal for pluralistic inclusivism. Parallel to this is the position of Aleaz that Advaita best suits Dalit theology, in the context of Dali theologians' protest against Advaita.

Most advanced and comprehensive form of thought is found in Aleaz's proposal for Indian Christian spirituality where he ventures in to the life sustaining model of Jesus or Christo-centric model. Here he comes explicitly and declares that other religions can contribute to Indian Christian spirituality.

Having concluded that the Christian understanding of 'Son' does not explain the meaning of Jesus, Aleaz is of the view that Hindu categories, particularly Advaita, can explain Jesus well. He does not accept the Pauline presentation of Jesus as providing the atonement on the cross. For Aleaz, the mission of Jesus is to present Brahman as the whole.

Aleaz's original and radical insights in relation to religious harmony or relational convergence of religions from the perspective of pluralistic inclusivism shines as he declares that our proclamation is not atonement theories, but the truth in other religions. For him, proclamation of the truth in other religions is not enough but also we need to ask for forgiveness from other religious communities for the damages we have done to them. This is what he calls as Mission of reconception or conversion. Apart from the other pleas, Aleaz also feels that Christ-centerd humanism is relevant and any good understanding of religion must have place for the liberation of women.

One may be tempted to say that Aleaz has concentrated on Advaita and applied this paradigm to all his ideas, rather than aspiring for a systematic and gradual development of theological thinking. It may be also alleged that rather than promoting Kingdom values Aleaz has worked for the promotion of other religious values limiting himself to a select few concerns.

Besides the above observations there are many constructive insights in the theological contributions of Aleaz. To start with, his consideration that religions have to be defined on the basis of their fruits is constructive from the point of Indian realities. Added to this is the appeal to develop positive consideration about the positive aspects of other religions. Aleaz's broader perspective is clear as he states that all religions are authentic in their own context and plurality of religions is natural. More comprehensive is the view that expressions of the same religious experience can vary according to the context.

The major shift in Aleaz's definition of religion is from content to applicability of a religion to the texture. The underlying expectation in his integral method to study religion is religious harmony or relational convergence of religions. Correspondingly, in his definition of theology of religions, the focus has moved from the other to one's own faith tradition.

The magnitude of pluralistic inclusivism is that all religions become pluralistically inclusive and inclusivistically pluralist.

One of the radical thoughts of Aleaz is that Christian faith receives insights from other religions. His openness to dialogical approach while upholding pluralistic inclusivism conveys that in the ultimate analysis all are seeking for religious harmony.

Other new thoughts are that all the religious resources of the universe is the common property of all and others will be viewed as superior to us, in pluralistic inclusivism. In the relational convergence of religions, there is a mutual conversion and the context will decide the content of the gospel of God in Jesus for India.

Aleaz's uncritical acceptance of other religious insights is the revelation of his urge for religious harmony and respect for other religious traditions. He asserts that no one else has attempted an Indian Christian philosophy based on *pramans,* Advaita and very specially Sabda-dvani method, which is relevant for biblical interpretation.

An unselfish struggle for religious harmony is vivid in his invitation and request to Advaita to assist Eastern Christian thought. His hope for the pre-Diamper approach to people of other faiths shows his commitment to the church to come forward with openness in relation to other religions.

Aleaz's Indian Christian spirituality based on inclusion of resources from Indian religions, his interpretation that Jesus is the reflection of Brahman, and his view that the gospel has to emerge from the religio-cultural context of India are courageous proposals. His ultimate dedication for religious harmony is fully embedded in his view of proclamation and mission.

12. The very communal idea of Hindutva, Hindu and Hinduism threatens the possibilities of other religions being considered equal. It further intensifies intolerance towards plurality/unity in diversity. Replacing secular state with Hindu state, framing anti-conversion laws against freedom of religion and democracy being compared with Hindu religious point of view are real challenges to our witnessing.

    In order to protect our constitutional rights we need to learn to work with secular political parties and ideologies.

    Religious freedom has an important role in unifying a country. Peace depends on human freedoms, and religious liberty is perhaps the most precious of such freedom. Full religious liberty includes not only freedom from outside coercion and suppression but also from the suppression or restriction of human rights within each particular religious or belief community. The defense of religious liberty is integral to the mission of the church and the affirmation of religious liberty is inseparable from Christian witness.[1]

We may use our communication and educational channels to raise awareness about the importance of religious freedom which is especially essential for peace in our country and in the world. Minority religious community needs to make clear distinction between faith, belief and social practice within the framework of the Constitution for healthy witnessing

The strength of Christian witness includes courageous initiatives towards reforms-social, religious, etc. Unless these transforming witnesses go undisturbed there is an obstacle to Christian witness and the salvation of God's creation. The reforms brought about by early missionaries and secular ideologies like Dravida Kazaham are quite impacting. We need to incorporate these aspects along with other forms of Christian witness.

The perception that religious minorities are a threat to the nation requires deliberate correction/adjustment from us to instill trust in our programs. We also need a conscious paradigm, to present an untainted Christian image free from political hues. Also, there need to be alertness to democratically dissent any efforts to Hinduvise Indian history and education.

From the point of theology, we need an ecumenical theological vision. No theology is absolute. We need to honor the possibility of multiple interpretations and perspectives for positive witnessing. A united Christian persuasion along with other minorities, political parties and ideologies can even change the 1950 Presidential order depriving Christian dalits of their government privileges.

Dialogical living and witnessing is essential for a plural society like ours. For example, ISKCON is taking initiatives to have a dialogue with Christians in spite of both being mission oriented traditions. While asking whether developmental promises have unevenly induced young Indians to overlook communalism, we need to resolutely live the 'life of Jesus Christ.'

13. There may be numerous other challenges to religious harmony than the ones discussed here. Similarly there may be many more methods for youth to engage in religious harmony. Though the possibilities discussed are very essential for working towards religious harmony, an actual encounter with different situation will help understand the other causes of disharmony and solutions for enabling harmony. It is an ongoing process. Hence, continuous study/research, engagement and explorations are necessary for a fruitful search for harmony.

14. To conclude, "hatred begets hatred. In the modern world, there is no place for chauvinism. How could anyone forget the noble contribution of the

---

1 Ninan Koshy, *Religious Freedom in a Changing World* (Geneva: WCC Publications, 1992), 115.

Christian Missionaries as pioneers in the field of education and Medicare extending to the remote interiors of tribal areas? The role of the Christian in presenting the image of a united and integrated India cannot be lost of."[2]

All religions seem to be 'mission' oriented. 'Love your enemy' has no parallel, nor 'do unto others what you would expect them to do for you,' has found any alternative. "Render to Caesar the things that are Caesar's, to God the things that are God's," is relevant for diligent witness.

15. The new narratives of Hindutva pose real challenges to Christian mission. The church has never relaxed even in more adverse contexts than ours. Nor the word of God has failed to speak to any situation. The Reformation event reaffirms that we need to re-form our commitment, re-remind ourselves of our responsibility in varying contexts and recall Christ the head of the church to inspire us to diligently serve him. The hermeneutical principle of "sustainable capability enhancement" can be explored to relevantly interpret the word of God in order to derive resources for capability enhancement. It was because of the "sustainable capability enhancement," the mission of the church all through the centuries provided 'hope in hopelessness.' Our mission today is 'dispelling various forms of deprivations' and enabling the deprived to see hope and enjoy justice and peace. Our strength is the cross and the crucified Jesus. And our capacity is being able to repent if anything was pursued unjustly and insincerely. The biblical dictum that 'what you have done to the least you have done to me and what you have not done to the least you have not done to me,' has not lost its freshness. Reformation, hermeneutics and mission are the continuous rejuvenation of our commitment.

16. As a part of our witness, we have to out rightly thank God for the secular, democratic and constitutional nationalism that has withstood all kinds of challenges and the active space it provides to take part in promoting those values.

Since, Identity politics has become the order of the day, we can actively involve in social and political mobilization through all modern and available means to struggle for our legitimate space. It applies to our theological formulations as well.

Our encouragement, in a complex situation is that, Jesus did not serve Christians (alone) but anyone who came to him. Even he did not allow all the beneficiaries of his love to be his disciples. Identity is thus sameness but it (body of Christ) can be lived out recognizing other identities (oneness).

Often our identities, freedoms, privileges and protections are diluted or denied in the name of a particular nationalism, safety of the nation, national interest and patriotism. Our different viewpoints and genuine grievances are

2 Charles Prabhakar and Paul Mohan Raj, 61.

frequently interpreted as supporting other countries. Christianity never sailed through smooth passages. It has always overcome temporary hurdles. Let us strive to protect our Constitution and repose our faith in it as law abiding citizens of this country.

We accept the existence of multiple identities while not denying the importance of religious identity and freedom of religious identity to everyone. Freedom of religion is a universal human right. Free religious mobility is the signs of the times and the opposite is non-freedom.

Religiously our fundamentals are hope, love and faith. The possibility of reasoning is a strong source of hope and confidence in a world darkened by horrible deeds. 'We can reason about the right way of perceiving and treating other people, other cultures, other claims, and examine different grounds for respect and tolerance.' 'We can also reason about our own mistakes and try to learn not to repeat them.'[3] In the words of Sudhir Kakar, 'I can only hope that the violence is short-lived and that it will hasten the creation of a common, tolerant public realm. When hope is destroyed, great grief follows, which is almost equal to death itself.' The movement towards multiculturalism rather than a 'composite culture' is encouraging. Studies show that younger citizens of India 'have little sympathy for majoritarian[4] politics.

Love is the hallmark of Christian identity and witness. Love has changed many societies for the better. Love has withstood all persecutions and hatred. Therefore, we cannot cease from our acts of love as Jesus. Love is found among others as well. Love makes us genuinely human. It transforms us and our understanding. It is love that 'defines and decides out identities – self and others.'[5] Love alone inspires us to see around (innumerable concerns) and act.

Even when acts of love find hard passage, for us the final hold is faith, unshakable faith. It is our faith history which makes us never to give up. The idea that I am native you are alien is criminal, lawlessness and evil-intended. The tiny powerful cross will continue to be vividly visible even under heavy and large saffron veil (invitation card) if we do not forget our identity, with Jesus.

17. The concluding lines are inconsonant with the suggestions of Ambedkar. Innumerable castes and embodiment of inequality are realities. India 'presents more survivals of primitive times than'[6] any other civilized society.

It is also held that 'India forms a homogeneous whole' and 'possesses cultural unity'; therefore caste (inequality) thrives. In my view, Hindu culture cannot

3 Amartya Sen, *The Argumentative Indian*, 276.

4 Pradeep K. Chhibber and Rahul Verma, 260.

5 Jose Nandhikkara, 257.

6 B. R. Ambedkar, *Castes in India: Their Mechanism, Genesis and Development*, 14.

be Indian culture therefore I am unable to identify homogeneity and cultural unity.

Since endogamy is caste, (can be differed), 'the real remedy for breaking caste is inter-marriage.' The real enemy to fight with is the *Shrutis* and the *Smritis* which have inculcated the notion of caste.'[7]

It is hard to believe that inequality has taken the place of equality in Hinduism in the name of castes. It is harder that Hinduism has hated and pushed the least in the society to the most unimaginable position without even suggesting any measure to improve their plight. It is so painful that, in Hinduism, there is no 'consciousness of kind' except castes.[8] There is no appreciation of merits in a person unless he is a fellow caste.[9]

The notion that birth determines one's status is nowhere in the world and this is behind the discussions on freedom of religion in India. As the Constitution of India envisages equality our responsibility is squarely before us.

18. Periyar used "rationalist interpretation" as a hermeneutical principle to critique priestly Hinduism. His supreme aim was to eradicate caste discrimination from the society, which he suffered from his school days. Since religion was the cementing force behind the evil of caste, which is a social issue, he critiqued it from the point of life here in society. His entire contention was that religion as such is not abominable but the way in which it is interpreted to manipulate, subjugate, and enslave sections of the society. He was pained to witness the influence of caste even in the so-called national political party of his day.

Since Brahmanic Hinduism perpetuated the caste system with the aid of Hindu religious scriptures, he condemned them and caricatured the scriptural characters to ventilate his unquenchable revulsion against the gruesome religious practices. His portrayal of religious doctrines further vindicates his utter unfaith and disappointment over the validity and utility of religions.

Periyar was unacceptable to many because his stark critique of priestly Hinduism unacknowledged the positive aspects of religions. Acceptance of the social dimension of religions alone does not suffice to the fuller realization of the positive potentials of religions.

Nevertheless, the implications from the critique of priestly Hinduism for social reforms stand stall. Periyar's persistent demand for self-respect for the people, earnest appeal for a right perception of religions and social issues, incessant plea for serving others, unremitting persuasion to the consideration of religion as a way of life, relentless urging for human progress, unwavering

7 B. R. Ambedkar, *Annihilation of Caste*, 64-67.

8 B. R. Ambedkar, *Annihilation of Caste*, 41.

9 B. R. Ambedkar, *Annihilation of Caste*, 50.

appreciation for morality and profuse summons for harmonious life are essential for any society aspiring for reforms. Although, his approach was quite rugged, his contributions will always remain as a beacon to many reforms.

19. A few insights can be underlined from the life of William Carey who was 'at the Lord's disposal.' The life and journey of God's servants go through multifaceted experiences, uncertainties and even very rugged path. God's choice of his servants is not based on family and status but perseverance and full dedication. God's servants attribute overcoming of failures to the grace of God. Being in God's service does not mean being free from sorrow and pain but having strength to withstand and be focused. All losses and heavy burdens in the process of God's service do not let any one to abandon service but encourages to move forward in the midst of them. For the servants of God, poverty and hardship are not obstacles. They always look for opportunities to dedicatedly serve without being discouraged steadily moving forward.